Is Christianity True?

Is Christianity True?

by
JONATHAN MENN
foreword by
R. FOWLER WHITE

RESOURCE *Publications* · Eugene, Oregon

IS CHRISTIANITY TRUE?

Copyright © 2024 Jonathan Menn. All rights reserved. Except for brief quotations in critical publications or reviews, no part of this book may be reproduced in any manner without prior written permission from the publisher. Write: Permissions, Wipf and Stock Publishers, 199 W. 8th Ave., Suite 3, Eugene, OR 97401.

Resource Publications
An Imprint of Wipf and Stock Publishers
199 W. 8th Ave., Suite 3
Eugene, OR 97401

www.wipfandstock.com

PAPERBACK ISBN: 979-8-3852-2958-1
HARDCOVER ISBN: 979-8-3852-2959-8
EBOOK ISBN: 979-8-3852-2960-4

10/25/24

Unless otherwise indicated, all Scripture quotations are taken from the New American Standard Bible®, Copyright © 1960, 1962, 1963, 1968, 1971, 1972, 1973, 1975, 1977, 1995 by The Lockman Foundation. Used by permission. (www.Lockman.org)

Scripture quotations marked NIV are taken from the THE HOLY BIBLE, NEW INTERNATIONAL VERSION®, NIV® Copyright © 1973, 1978, 1984, 2011 by Biblica, Inc.™ Used by permission. All rights reserved worldwide.

Scripture quotations marked NKJV are taken from the New King James Version®. Copyright © 1982 by Thomas Nelson, Inc. Used by permission. All rights reserved.

To those of my family and friends who have either rejected, or otherwise do not yet believe in, the lordship of Jesus Christ. May this book help you to check out who he really is.

Contents

List of Tables | ix

Foreword by R. Fowler White, PhD | xi

Preface | xvii

Introduction | xxi

Part 1 The Bible and Jesus Christ

1   The Bible is Trustworthy | 3

2   Jesus Christ Demonstrates that God Exists and Who He Is | 31

3   Jesus' Fulfillment of Prophecy | 53

4   The Crucifixion and Resurrection of Jesus: Introduction | 61

5   The Crucifixion of Jesus Christ Is a Historical Fact | 63

6   The Resurrection of Jesus Christ Is a Historical Fact | 74

Part 2 The Impossibility of the Alternative

7   Christianity and Science | 103

8   Naturalism: Introduction | 107

9   Naturalism Is Self-Referentially Incoherent (i.e., Self-Refuting) | 110

10   Naturalistic Evolution Is Contrary to the Facts of Nature | 124

11   Naturalism Cannot Account for Existence as It Is | 167

Part 3 The Problem of Evil

12 The Problem of Evil: God's Sovereignty, Humanity's Responsibility, and the Existence of Sin and Evil | 223

Appendix 1: The Gospel | 269

Appendix 2: Biblical Examples of the Doctrine of Concurrence | 278

Appendix 3: Who Created God? | 282

Bibliography | 289

Subject and Name Index | 325

Scripture Index | 345

List of Tables

Geologic ages | 133n.50

Names/Titles/Attributes applied to God and Jesus | 47

Prophecies re. Jesus as Messiah | 54

Prophecies re. Jesus' death and burial | 55

Biblical Examples of the Doctrine of Concurrence | 278

Foreword
by R. Fowler White, PhD

THE BEST AUTHORS AND teachers we ever have in our lives dedicate themselves to challenging our minds, to nurturing our souls, and to equipping us to engage the world. I would ask you to keep those words in mind as you read this outstanding book by Jonathan Menn. As you read and turn the pages that follow, you will notice, if you experience nothing else, that he challenges your mind, nurtures your soul, and engages the world. But, before you dive into this book, let me offer a justification for you to take it up and embrace what Menn is doing in it. In sum, the justification is this: Menn brings some things that sound strange to many ears in our world, but if we are intentional as we read, we may realize that the trustworthiness of the Bible and the truth of Christianity are, as Menn argues, the fundamental prerequisites necessary to have the possibility of reason, meaning, and coherence, including a coherent basis for any view of morality, good and evil. Let me expand on what I mean when I say that Menn brings some things that sound strange to many ears in our world. What I say may come off as negative or even harsh, but bear with me.

We have entered a brave new world in the midst of what some social engineers are calling the Great Reset. The moral vision that used to unite most of Western society had gradually faded away. What I mean is this: you know from your own experience and study of history that our culture, on the whole, was once guided by the truth that we live in a moral universe, ruled by a just and merciful Creator and Judge who has revealed His eternal power and Godness in nature and made known His gospel of forgiveness for sinners in Scripture. Sure, we would acknowledge that that consensus was, in too many cases, a mile wide and an inch deep. But my point is that that moral vision has pretty much vanished. It is now viewed as painfully cringeworthy, quaint, and outdated, even bigoted.

In our brave new world, we are desperately eager to seek and find community in the idea that nature, reason, and pleasure are supreme and have no relationship whatsoever to a transcendent divine Creator and Judge. We have come to rest our hope for a better world in humanity, not in deity. The chief and highest end that binds our society together now is pleasure (painlessness) with no fear of God in our eyes. As a result, our hope for a better world rests on a humanity who "lives for the weekend" and "follows the science"—except when we do not want to and when it does not suit our self-interest.

No longer can we take for granted that neighbors will share a common worldview or a common morality. Though we have no shared morality, we do still have those in our society who see themselves as our moral superiors and whose job it is to be the enforcers of the moral conventions that society has fabricated. Their assignment is to instruct and control the rest of us when it comes to the thoughts we have, the words we use (yes, even our pronouns), and the deeds we prescribe or forbid. We have seen enough already to know that the enforcers of this Great Reset in our brave new world tell us that we really should not talk about what we read in Jonathan Menn's book in polite society. We really should not talk about universal truths anymore, but only about individual truths. Individual substitutions for universal truths abound. We cannot focus on the content of our character or the elements of our biology, but on the category of our personality and self-identification. We will affirm our individual "self," while we will deny "the image of God" in us. Substitutions like these have confused and divided the morality of our world, at least wherever consciences have not been fatally seared or defiled.

Meanwhile, many of those in our political class no longer use their rhetorical skills to inspire us to civic virtue, but to manipulate our trust, anger, and fear. Elitist influencers use their bully pulpits to convince their fellow citizens to share their beliefs about the future of humanity, but it is a future they define in terms of power and wealth for themselves and for the favorites they choose to support. Meanwhile, society's enforcers come in alongside these influencers to impose double standards on others to squeeze them into the proper mold of membership in society. They push and pull those they label as "undesirables" and "extremists" to the margins and shadows of public life. To get their fellow citizens to conform, they offer protections and pleasures that are tempting even to Christians. But those terms of societal membership—which require Christians to cut corners or to compromise on the tenets of Christian confession—are more and more at odds with the historic terms of membership in Christ's church.

So, welcome to the Great Reset. Welcome to our brave new world. You had no idea that the book you are about to read was so counter-cultural, did you? So, what is required of us who would take Jonathan Menn's book and read it? Here are some suggestions.

Foreword

First, let this book challenge your mind. Soak up the knowledge he offers, learn from the broad base of facts he presents, and grow in understanding by applying and integrating what you learn herein. Yes, take time to work, to worship, and to rest. Keep in mind, however, that our brave new world is no place for zoning out. Society now intends to hold you accountable, to keep you looking over your shoulder. So keep your mind in gear. Do not let social media, entertainment, or wealth take over your mind. Do not "let life just happen" to you. None of us gets to coast to the finish line. Live intentionally. Never let it be said of you that today was the day you finished seeking knowledge. As the Apostle Paul puts it in his letter to the church at Rome, "be transformed"—indeed, keep being transformed—"by the renewing of your mind" (Rom 12:2). Then you will be able to test and approve what God's will is—His good, pleasing, and perfect will.

Second, in that it sets forth the Bible's trustworthiness and Christianity's truth, let this book nurture your soul. Our tendency is to neglect the nourishment of our souls. So we have to push ourselves to make sure that our souls get a good diet and exercise. Once again, Paul sums it up well: "train yourself for godliness." Why? Because, says the Apostle, godliness "holds promise for the present life and also for the life to come" (1 Tim 1:7b–8). As you read this book, take note of how its content pushes you to take seriously the proposition that God, your Creator and Judge, your Redeemer and Sustainer, has not been and is not silent—nor does He stutter. So, listen to all that God says in His written Word. He teaches no error in Scripture (2 Tim 3:16). So, do not trifle with His promises and His warnings. Take them seriously. He tells us what to avoid. He tells us what to pursue. How can He do this? Because He alone knows the future. So, keep growing in your knowledge of God and His Word. Mature in faith, hope, and love. As J. I. Packer wrote, "Make it your supreme desire … to know and enjoy God as He makes Himself known to us sinners in the Written Word and in the Living Word." As Menn puts it, the Bible is trustworthy; Christianity is true. So, nurture your soul accordingly.

Third, follow the example set in this book: keep engaging the world. Anti-Christian voices are building a brave new world that is indifferent and even hostile to Christ and His church. But, as Jonathan Menn labors so ably to show us, this is still our Father's world. He rules and overrules the brave new world. So, there is reason not to be afraid; there is reason to take courage. As Paul told the church at Ephesus, stand your ground with your Lord Christ against the forces that oppose Him and His church (Eph 6:10–18). Yes, some of the people we know—perhaps some of our neighbors—will seek, sadly, to live life on their own terms and to persuade us to adjust, perhaps by force. But we, grounded in the gospel of Christ and

His commandment to love, know how to live life on better terms, on God's terms. So, while you engage with the brave new world, outdo your neighbors in zeal, zeal for the fame of Christ's name, for the good of His church, even for the good of your hostile neighbors. You know that the one true God is good, just, and merciful, and that He far surpasses any achievement or pleasure this world, brave and new or not, has to offer.

All things considered, take a moment and remember that ideas, true and false, have consequences, including the communities and civilizations built on those ideas. The world in which we live is very confused and very divided. The Great Reset is underway. The terms of membership in our brave new world, with the protections and pleasures it offers, are more and more at odds with the historic terms of membership in Christ's church.

So, do not underestimate the importance of what you do with your mind, with your soul, and with your engagement with the world. We are experiencing the corrosive effect of unbelief and vice in classrooms, in government offices, and in the workplace. Anti-Christian opposition and even bigotry is becoming the norm in society at large. Some in the church may even try to persuade us to shrug off the historic Christian faith and moral vision and to embrace the priorities of this world. We may even watch as church leaders give up and give in to the pressures of the majority culture. They will make the choice that the church at Thyatira did (Rev 2:18–29): to secure "a place at the table" of the world and, with it, the survival of their congregations, they will blur the boundary between the world and Christ's church. Squeezed into the mold of this brave new world, they will compromise or even give up the defining Christian confession.

With this book, Menn exhorts us: do not let life just happen to you. The ideas of the world in which we live and move have borne to us a culture and civilization that denies any common reality—except for the reality of the narcissistic and nihilistic swamp in which we all paddle around in a vain hope of landing on some common ground. Confused and divided as our world is, we should not be afraid to ask, "How's that working for us?" Failure pervades our culture at virtually every turn, yet we persist in our disdain for any notion of transcendent reality, preferring to deify each individual self and thus to reimagine a polytheistic world of competing moralities in which there is no universal morality possible. This is insanity by another name.

Into such an environment comes Jonathan Menn, with others like him, shining a light on the pathway to the truth that we live in a moral universe preserved by the self-revealing holy, just, and merciful God. It is high time for the thought leaders and their followers in this world to be honest: their alternative is proving the impossibility of the contrary. As Menn boldly contends: the Bible is trustworthy, Christianity is true, and the views that are posited in their place are impossible.

R. Fowler White, PhD\
Teaching Elder (Honorably Retired)\
Presbyterian Church in America

Preface

It has been said that "you can't argue anyone into the kingdom of God." In one sense, that is true. You can't argue, or force, or preach, or pray, or even love anyone into the kingdom. The reason is that why anyone comes to faith in Christ ultimately is not dependent on us, but is the work of God himself (John 1:13; Acts 13:48; Eph 2:8–9; Heb 12:2). As a friend of mine, to whom I gave a draft of this book, said in response to what I had written, "How successful have apologetics through the centuries been in converting people to the way of Christ? If you're a 'fruits' person, you would look at the feelings, thoughts, and actions of people who claim to be Christian and judge them on the basis of the way Jesus called us to live." There is also some truth in that. The hypocritical lives of certain professing Christians have acted as impediments to many people's checking out the truth of Christianity, who Jesus is, and what he has done. On the other hand, when Richard Wurmbrand was in prison in Romania following WWII, he told of a pastor who talked with other prisoners about Jesus, and who also gave away everything he had (food, medicine, his coat) to others, even though he needed those things himself. One day, a fellow-prisoner asked him what Jesus is like, because he had never met anyone so good and loving and truthful. The pastor said, "Jesus is like me." The prisoner replied, "If Christ was like you, then I love him."[1]

God uses means—human means—in his bringing people to faith. Those means include arguments, reason, facts, evidence, rational discourse, and all that the term "apologetics" encompasses. The Bible talks quite a bit about this. Paul *"reasoned"* with people, *"explaining and giving evidence,"* with the result that *"some of them were persuaded"* (Acts 17:2-4). Jesus said he is *"the truth"* (John 14:6) and said we are to love God *"with all of your mind"* (Matt 22:37). President Richard Nixon's "hatchet man," Chuck Colson, came to faith in just this way. A friend had given him a copy of C. S. Lewis's book *Mere Christianity*. Colson was struck by Jesus' claim to be

---

1. Wurmbrand, *In God's Underground*, 126.

God himself, come to earth as a man. He took a legal pad and spent a week thinking about the facts, arguments, issues, and their significance, writing down the *pros* and *cons,* and being confronted by "an intellect so disciplined, so lucid, so relentlessly logical that I could only be grateful that I had never faced him in a court of law."[2] In the end, he accepted without reservation Jesus Christ as the Lord of his life, and his life was transformed.

One may say that, since I am a former lawyer as was Colson, people like us are naturally drawn to facts, reason, logic, and argumentation. Again, there may be some truth in that. On the other hand, the claims of Christ are universal. Jesus, Paul, and the other apostles occasionally interacted with lawyers, but the vast bulk of their interactions were with "regular" people—men, women, and children—from all walks of life. Their preaching, teaching, and reasoning, from the Bible and from life, resonated with the people, who were persuaded—contrary to everything they had previously been taught and believed—that Jesus Christ was, indeed, the prophesied Messiah, God himself come to earth as a man. That message continues to resonate with people today, from all walks of life, all over the world. Christians should have a resource to know *why* their faith is well-grounded; and non-Christians should have a resource that exposes them to philosophical, scientific, and historical data with which they previously may not have been familiar. Since, according to Jesus and the Bible, the issues are so momentous, people should have the facts and issues clearly presented so as to be able to make an informed choice. That is why this book has been written.

The subject of this book has long been an interest of mine. I have always been a "reader." Particularly since I became a Christian in 1982, I have read extensively on issues pertaining to the Bible and Jesus Christ. My writing for Equipping Church Leaders East Africa (www.eclea.net) includes some of the material regarding Jesus as the divine Son of God, his crucifixion, and his resurrection, that are included in this book. Although I do not have a science background, for a long time I have been fascinated by paleontology and developed a fairly extensive personal library concerning the creation-evolution issue. In short, this book is the culmination of interests, research, and work I have been doing for well over forty years.

No book of this nature can be done only by one person. I am grateful to my wife, Nancy, who makes it possible for me to travel to East Africa five times per year and who also enjoys our "library weekends" at Rolfing Library at Trinity Evangelical Divinity School, where I pursued my formal theological education. I particularly want to thank the people who have contributed a foreword to and endorsements of this book: Dr. R. Fowler

---

2. Colson, *Born Again,* 121.

White, pastor, professor, and seminary administrator, who was very helpful with respect to certain matters regarding the second edition of my book *Biblical Eschatology*, who critiqued a paper I have written, and who made an excellent suggestion concerning a portion of the introduction to this book; Dr. Ingrid Faro, Affiliate Professor of Old Testament at Northern Seminary, whom I met as a fellow-student at Trinity; Josh McDowell, through whose book *Evidence That Demands A Verdict* my wife came to faith in Christ; and Michael Newnham, the "Phoenix Preacher," whose posts at his online community of faith (www.phoenixpreacher.com) have been very insightful concerning Christianity as it should be lived out (and often how it is not), and whose review of my first book was very kind and helpful.

In this book, I have endeavored to deal, clearly and comprehensively (without being exhausting), with what I see as the three central issues concerning the truth of Christianity: (1) the reliability of the Bible and the identity of Jesus Christ; (2) the impossibility of the biggest alternative to Christianity, namely, "naturalism," which, I endeavor to show, cannot explain existence as it is; and (3) the biggest objection to Christianity, namely, the so-called "problem of evil," i.e., if God is all-powerful, all-knowing, and all-good, then why is there so much evil in the world. In appendices, I set forth what I think is a clear statement of the gospel, multiple examples of the biblical doctrine of "concurrence" (i.e., the same event is attributable both to God and to secondary agents), since this has relevance to the "problem of evil," and answer the question raised by Richard Dawkins and other atheists, "If God created the world, then who created God?"

I hope this book will show Christians that their faith is based on a solid foundation; I also hope it will raise issues and present evidence that non-Christians may not have considered before and, God willing, will help them to check out for themselves the truth of Christianity and who Jesus is. To that end, in the bibliography I have included the web addresses for all the sources I have cited that are online.

Introduction

EVERYONE ASKS THE "BIG questions" of life: Why is there something rather than nothing? Is there a God and, if so, how can I know it/him/her or, on the other hand, are we, and all of existence, just cosmic accidents? What is the meaning of life, or is there none? Is there a right and wrong? If there is a God who is all good and all powerful, why is there so much evil in the world? And how can I know any of these things for sure?

Truth is that which corresponds to reality and is undeniable.[1] Any worldview must be able to account for all of the facts in an internally consistent way.[2] There are many religions and worldviews, including monotheistic religions such as Judaism, Christianity, and Islam, pantheistic, monistic philosophies such as those of Parmenides, Plotinus, Hegel, and Spinoza, pantheistic, monistic religions such as Hinduism and Buddhism, and atheistic worldviews, i.e., naturalism (scientific materialism).[3] Many people do not adhere to any established religion or worldview but, in effect, "pick-and-choose" aspects from different worldviews. Each religion or worldview has its own answers to questions such as the above.

My contention is that Christianity is true. In saying that Christianity is true, I am not arguing for any particular denominational position or discussing specific Christian doctrines (e.g., eschatology). I am not attempting to justify the Crusades, the Inquisition, other acts that have been committed in the name of Christianity, or various political positions espoused by various Christian leaders or churches. Rather, I am considering only what C. S. Lewis called "mere Christianity" or John Stott called "basic Christianity." Specifically, I am contending that God exists and we can know him; we are not cosmic accidents but have been created by God. The God who is revealed in the Bible and who manifested himself in the person of Jesus Christ

---

1. See Geisler, *Christian Apologetics,* 143–45.

2. See Geisler, *Christian Apologetics,* 143–45.

3. A good, basic introduction to the major different worldviews is James Sire, *The Universe Next Door,* 4th ed. (Downers Grove, IL: InterVarsity, 2004).

provides the answers to the above questions. In short, the gospel, which is the essence of Christianity (see Appendix 1) is true.

The position of the Bible is that God has given humanity sufficient natural revelation to everyone not only that he exists but who he is. Rom 1:19–20 says, *"That which is known about God is evident within them; for God made it evident to them. For since the creation of the world His invisible attributes, His eternal power and divine nature, have been clearly seen, being understood through what has been made, so that they are without excuse."* Thus, those who deny God's existence *"suppress the truth"* of this revelation (Rom 1:18) and, as a result, become *"futile in their speculations"* and *"foolish"* in their reasoning (Rom 1:21–22; see also Ps 14:1; 53:1).

This biblical position is confirmed by both internal and external reasons. These include: (1) The impossibility of the contrary, i.e., God's existence is necessary and is, in fact, presumed by everyone (even by those who deny his existence), because without him it would be impossible to know anything. In other words, only an eternal, omniscient, good God provides the ultimate ground for any and all universal, abstract, absolutes, including the laws of logic, reason, science, morality, truth, etc. No other worldview can account for existence as it is. (2) Although there are many religious books purporting to be divine oracles, the Bible is both unique and reliable. (3) The truth of Christianity and why we can know that the Bible is trustworthy ultimately rest on the person of Jesus Christ. Although Jesus was a real man in space-time history, he claimed to be more than just a man: he claimed to be the eternal, omnipotent, omniscient God come to earth as a man. His identity as such is indicated primarily by two things: (A) his fulfillment of prophecy; and (B) his resurrection from the dead. Fulfilled prophecy reveals the existence and identity of God, because it demonstrates that there is an intelligent being outside of time-space (or not bound by time-space) who can and does tell us in amazing detail things that will happen hundreds of years in advance. The resurrection is the ultimate "bottom line," because Jesus said, in essence, "I am God (become a man), and I will prove it by doing something that is impossible for anyone who is only a man to do, namely, I will be killed and buried and then, in three days, I will bodily rise from the grave, alive again forevermore." His resurrection is not just a matter or "faith"; it is a matter of historical fact, akin to Julius Caesar's crossing the Rubicon—either he did or he did not. If Jesus did not bodily rise from the grave, then Christianity is untrue, as the apostle Paul acknowledges in 1 Cor 15:12–19. However, if Jesus did rise from the dead, that fact validates who he is, what he said, what he did, and what he believed. In short, Christianity is based on a historical claim and a historical fact. As such, in principle Christianity is falsifiable in a way that no other religion, philosophy, or worldview is.

That Christianity is true is not a personal or moral condemnation of anyone who adheres to any other religion or worldview and does not mean that everything in all other religions and worldviews is false. There is much truth in various aspects of all other religions and worldviews. C. S. Lewis set forth many of these commonalities in what he called the *Tao* in his book *The Abolition of Man* (1947). But if Christianity is what it claims to be and if Jesus is who he claims to be, then to the extent that other religions and worldviews differ from and contradict Christianity and Jesus, to that extent and in those particulars they, of necessity, would be false.

The issue here is the truth or falsity of Christianity, nothing more or less. It should be noted that I have discussed the major monotheistic rivals to Christianity elsewhere: I discuss and critique Islam in *Christianity and Islam: The Essentials* (2020). With respect to Judaism, Christianity grew out of and is, in fact, the fulfillment or completion of Judaism, as I discuss in *Biblical Theology* (2021). In this book, Part 2—The Impossibility of the Alternative discusses and critiques the primary alternative to Christianity (and, for that matter, to every other theistic position), namely, the worldview of naturalism (also referred to as scientific naturalism, materialism, and physicalism).[4] In Part 2, I will also briefly discuss other religious views, particularly Islam and pantheistic monism, where pertinent.

As will become clear, with many important issues—e.g., the resurrection of Christ, the existence of abstract, invariant, universals such as the laws of logic, the existence of truth, the existence of morality, and with respect to such issues as the origin of life, the existence of the universe, the ability of the human mind to reason, the significance of the fossil record, and the significance of evil—the primary matter is not so much the facts themselves (which are largely undisputed), but the interpretation of those facts. Different interpretations of facts that are generally agreed upon stem from differences in people's fundamental underlying philosophical or worldview presuppositions. On an evidential level, we are contending that the issues mentioned above and others to be discussed cohere with Christianity but do not and cannot be made to cohere with naturalism or other worldviews.

---

4. I am treating naturalism as synonymous with materialism and physicalism. "On an ontological level [the study of what exists], philosophers often treat naturalism as equivalent to materialism"; according to this view, "nature is best accounted for by reference to material principles. These principles include mass, energy, and other physical and chemical properties accepted by the scientific community. Further, this sense of naturalism holds that spirits, deities, and ghosts are not real and that there is no 'purpose' in nature." "Naturalism," *Wikipedia*, Introduction. This is also known as metaphysical naturalism.

At an even more fundamental level, we will endeavor to demonstrate in Part 2 that, although all people reason, seek meaning and coherence, and have beliefs concerning morality and good and evil, the truth of the Bible and Christianity are the fundamental prerequisites necessary even to have the possibility of reason, meaning, and coherence, including a coherent basis for any view of morality, good and evil.

If, as is asserted and argued for here, Christianity is true, that will have implications for the lives and eternal destinies of those who currently are not Christians and also for those who claim to be Christians but who are not living in conformity with their faith. Those personal implications are not the focus of this book; Appendix 1—The Gospel deals with this significantly, but not exhaustively. Given the profound and everlasting stakes for all people if what Jesus and Christianity claim are true, any reasonable person should at least consider the evidence so as to make an informed choice.

Part 1

The Bible and Jesus Christ

1

The Bible is Trustworthy

WE ARE BEGINNING WITH the uniqueness of the Bible because the Bible provides the basis for understanding God's revealed will and the Christian worldview.[1]

THE BIBLE IS UNIQUE

Although the Bible is usually thought of as one large book, it actually is a small library consisting of 66 "books": 39 in the Old Testament (OT), i.e., the Hebrew Bible, the sacred Scriptures of the Jews; and 27 in the New Testament (NT).[2] The word "Bible" is from the Greek word *biblia* (neuter plural), which means "books." However, over time the Jewish and Christian texts came to be considered as one unit. Consequently, "the same plural term in medieval Latin began to be understood in popular usage as feminine singular, no longer denoting 'The Books' but 'The Book.'"[3]

---

1. Unless otherwise noted, quotations from the Bible will be from the *New American Standard Bible* (1995).

2. The Hebrew Bible consists of 24 books in three divisions, the Torah (Law), the Nevi'im (Prophets), and the Ketuvim (Writings). F. F. Bruce points out that these 24 books "are identical with the thirty-nine of the Protestant Old Testament; the difference in reckoning arises from counting the twelve ('minor') prophets separately and dividing Samuel, Kings, Chronicles and Ezra-Nehemiah into two each." Bruce, *The Canon*, 29, 29n.4. It should be noted that the Roman Catholic Church includes as part of their canon a number of books written after the books that constitute the Hebrew Bible were completed and before the NT books were written; these books were not part of the Hebrew canon of scripture but were included in the Septuagint (the translation of the OT into Greek) and are typically referred to as the Apocrypha or deuterocanonical books.

3. Metzger, "Bible," 79.

The books of the Bible were written by approximately 40 authors over a period of approximately 1500 years (the OT being written from approximately 1450 BC to 430 BC and the NT from approximately AD 50–95). The books which compose the Bible were written in different cultures and circumstances, on three continents (Asia, Africa, and Europe), in three languages (Hebrew, Aramaic, and Greek), and in multiple genres (historical narratives, poetry, proverbs, prophecy and apocalyptic, and others). Given such diversity of time, place, culture, circumstance, authorship, and style, any other book composed in such a manner would be an incoherent mish-mash consisting primarily of ancient superstition that has little or no relevance to us today. However, that is not the case with the Bible. Professor emeritus at the University of Wisconsin-Madison, Keith Schoville, who specializes in ancient languages, points out that the Bible is the oldest surviving body of ancient literature which also possess a unique homogeneity, "permeated by a basic unity about the nature of God and the nature of man."[4]

The Bible tells a coherent story, and Jesus Christ is at the heart of that story.[5] Each book of the Bible contributes something to that story, and the overall story offers a framework within which each book may be best interpreted. The Bible is the story of the creation, history, and destiny of the world and of mankind: God created a beautiful world and human beings to live joyful, fulfilled lives in fellowship with him. Through our sin we lost that fellowship and brought evil and death into the world. However, God did not leave us in our sin and death. By means of a grand plan which involved calling Abraham and the nation of Israel, he prepared the way for his own coming to earth in the person of Jesus Christ to bring forgiveness of sin and to restore fellowship with him. He is coming again to utterly destroy sin and death; consummate our restoration and our relationship with him; and renew the earth and the cosmos to be even more glorious than when it was first created.

The writers of the Scripture testify that the Bible is God's special revelation of himself and of his plan, for humanity.[6] The writers of the Bible equate what the Scripture says with the very words of God himself (see Rom 9:17; Gal 3:8), often using such phrases as *"God says," "God said,"* or *"the Holy*

---

4. Schoville, "The Reliability," 67.

5. Luke 24:25–27, 44–47; John 5:39; Acts 3:18; 10:43; 26:22–23; 1 Pet 1:10–12; see Kaiser, *Old Testament*, 219–21.

6. See, e.g., Exod 17:14; 20:1; 24:4, 7; 34:27; Neh 9:13–14; Jer 1:4, 9; Ezek 2:7; Luke 3:2–4; 1 Cor 2:12–13; 7:10; 11:23; Gal 3:16; 1 Thess 2:2–9, 13; 2 Tim 3:16–17; 2 Pet 1:20–21; 3:14–16.

*Spirit says."*⁷ The absolute and final authority of the Bible is summarized in the often-used phrase, *"It is written."*⁸

In its "Chicago Statement on Biblical Inerrancy" (1978), the International Council on Biblical Inerrancy summarizes the nature of the Bible as follows:

1. God, who is Himself Truth and speaks truth only, has inspired Holy Scripture in order thereby to reveal Himself to lost mankind through Jesus Christ as Creator and Lord, Redeemer and Judge. Holy Scripture is God's witness to Himself. . . .

2. Holy Scripture, being God's own Word, written by men prepared and superintended by His Spirit, is of infallible divine authority in all matters upon which it touches: it is to be believed, as God's instruction, in all that it affirms: obeyed, as God's command, in all that it requires; embraced, as God's pledge, in all that it promises. . . .

4. Being wholly and verbally God-given, Scripture is without error or fault in all its teaching, no less in what it states about God's acts in creation, about the events of world history, and about its own literary origins under God, than in its witness to God's saving grace in individual lives.⁹

Although Christians consider the Bible to be the Word of God, in order to investigate the truthfulness of whether or not an event happened in the ancient past, the Bible can be looked at as one would look at other ancient writings. As Habermas and Licona state in their book concerning the historicity of the resurrection of Jesus Christ, they are regarding the NT only as a volume of ancient literature and are considering only the data that are well-accepted by scholars, including those who are skeptical of Christianity.¹⁰ That also is how Greg Gilbert approached the NT and the four Gospels, i.e., as *historical documents*; yet, he concluded that "at every turn,

---

7. See, e.g., Gen 1:3, 26–29; 3:13–14; 6:13; 17:9; Exod 3:14; Num 22:12; 1 Kgs 3:11; Ps 50:16; Jer 3:1; 42:20; Jonah 4:9; Matt 15:4; Luke 11:49; Acts 2:17; 21:11; 2 Cor 6:16; Heb 3:7.

8. See, e.g., Josh 8:31; 2 Kgs 3:21; 2 Chron 25:4; 31:3; Ezra 3:2–4; Dan 9:13; Matt 4:4–10; 21:13; 26:24, 31; Mark 7:6; 14:21, 27; Luke 2:23; 19:46; 24:46; John 12:14; Acts 1:20; 7:42; Rom 1:17; 2:24; 3:4, 10; 8:37; 11:8; 12:19; 14:11; 15:3, 9, 21; 1 Cor 2:9; 3:19; Gal 3:10, 13; 4:22; Heb 10:7.

9. "Chicago Statement," 3. Van de Weghe, *Prepared*, 265–334 discusses scientific revelations, prophecies, unity, the ability to transform lives, the testimony of Christ, and various structural elements, all of which indicate that the Bible was inspired by God, i.e., is the Word of God, not merely the words of people.

10. Habermas and Licona, *The Case*, 51–52; see also Gilbert, *Why Trust*, 19.

we've also concluded with a high degree of historical confidence that they do in fact seem reliable."[11]

THE DEVELOPMENT OF THE BIBLE

With respect to the Torah (the first five books of the Bible, also known as the Pentateuch), both Jewish and Christian tradition holds that Moses was the Torah's author/compiler.[12] Most conservative scholars date Israel's exodus from Egypt to approximately 1446 BC.[13] Consequently, "the forty-year period of Israel's wanderings in the wilderness, which lasted from about 1446 to about 1406 B.C., would have been the most likely time for Moses to write Genesis."[14] After discussing the history of scholarly assessment about the dating and authorship of the Torah, Kenneth Matthews concludes that "several lines of internal evidence, while unable to prove traditional Mosaic authorship, indicate the concurrence of a second millennium [BC] date."[15] William F. Albright, perhaps the premier biblical archaeologist, who helped to authenticate the Dead Sea Scrolls, points out that, although most critical scholars formerly thought that Genesis 14, which recounts Abraham's defeat of certain Mesopotamian kings in battle, was very late and not historical, this no longer is the case. Some of its allusions

> are exceedingly early, carrying us directly back into the Middle Bronze Age. For instance, the strange word for "retainers", used in verse 14, which occurs nowhere else in the Bible, is now known to be an Egyptian word employed in the Execration Texts of the late nineteenth century B.C. of the retainers of Palestinian chieftains, and used four centuries later in one of the Taanach tablets. Several of the towns mentioned in this chapter are now proved to be very ancient, and the archaic words and poetic expressions with which the chapter abounds are clear indications of an old verse form underlying the present text.[16]

---

11. Gilbert, *Why Trust*, 125–26; see also Blomberg, *Gospels*, 323 ("the Gospels must be subjected to the same type of historical scrutiny given to other writings of antiquity but that they can stand up to such scrutiny admirably").

12. Jesus accepted Moses's authorship. See Matt 8:4; 19:7–8; Mark 1:44; 7:10; 10:3–5; 12:26; Luke 5:14; 16:29–31; 20:37; 24:27, 44; John 3:14; 5:45–46; 6:32; 7:19, 22–23.

13. Payne, *Encyclopedia*, xix; *New American*, 1; see also Kennedy, *Unearthing*, 56–59 for archaeological evidence which indicates that Amenhotep II, whose reign as Pharaoh of Egypt began approximately 1450 BC, was the pharaoh at the time of the exodus.

14. *New American*, 1.

15. Matthews, *Genesis 1—11:26*, 79–80; see also Van de Weghe, *Prepared*, 104–6.

16. Albright, *The Archaeology*, 237.

The ancient date of the early chapters of the OT was corroborated in 2019 when, on Mt. Ebal, Israel, an ancient "curse tablet" was discovered. It is dated between 1400–1250 BC and is "the oldest Hebrew text found within the borders of ancient Israel."[17] The tablet is significant in that "the use of the divine name YHW leaves no doubt that the text is Hebrew and not Canaanite. The recovery of this formulaic curse from an altar on Mt. Ebal synchronizes with Joshua 8, which mentions the construction of an altar (vss. 30–31), writing (vs. 32), and pronouncement of curses (vss. 33–34)."[18] Bruce Waltke adds that the Torah had to have been ancient, since preexilic biblical writers knew of the contents of the Torah; for example, in Psalm 1 David (c.1000 BC) put the story of creation into the form of a psalm.[19] The Ketef Hinnom scrolls (also known as the "silver scrolls") were discovered in 1979. They contain portions of Num 6:24–26, and have been dated to approximately 600 BC.[20] These scrolls are preexilic (i.e., before the destruction of the temple in 586 BC and the deportation of Israel to Babylon). Thus, they too corroborate the ancient dating of the Torah.[21]

The last book of the OT, as set forth in the Christian ordering of the Bible, is Malachi. Explanatory notes in the *New American Standard Bible* state, "The book was probably written around 433–430 B.C."[22] In the Hebrew Bible (i.e., the Jewish ordering of what the Christians consider the OT), the final book is Chronicles.[23] Chronicles was written for the exiles

17. Stripling, et al., "You are Cursed," 22.
18. Stripling, et al., "You are Cursed," 22.
19. See Waltke, *Genesis*, 21–29.
20. "Ketef Hinnom scrolls," *Wikipedia*, Introduction.
21. See Van de Weghe, *Prepared*, 144–45. During the nineteenth century, "historical (or 'higher') criticism" of the Bible and a "documentary hypothesis" were developed, which hold that the Torah was a compilation of from three to seven hypothetical sources, dating between the tenth and sixth or fifth centuries BC, woven together early after the return from the Babylonian exile. See Alter, *Genesis*, xl–xli; Kaiser, *Old Testament*, 53. This approach to the Bible was not based actual documents, but on philosophical ideas which have since been undermined, and is subject to a number of fatal evidentiary and logical flaws. See Kaiser, *Old Testament*, 53–54, 133–38; McDowell, *The Resurrection*, 25–184. Georg Huntemann notes that "it is well known that Kantian or Hegelian philosophy provides the suppositions for historical criticism; that, for example, Hegel's scheme of evolution was applied to the origin of the Old Testament, especially the Pentateuch, and that precisely this scheme of evolution has been rendered extremely questionable by archaeological discoveries, as Samuel Külling has shown in one of his seminal works [*Zur Datierung der "Genesis-P-Stücke"* (1964)]." Huntemann, *The Other*, 135. The significance of the findings of archaeology will be discussed in more detail below.

22. *New American*, 909.
23. "Hebrew Bible," *Wikipedia*, Book order.

who returned to Israel after the Babylonian captivity. "A growing consensus dates Chronicles in the latter half of the fifth century B.C."[24] There is no real dispute about these dates. Consequently, the entire OT was completed over 400 years before Jesus was born and the events of the New Testament took place. Indeed, the Hebrew Bible and some related texts were translated from Hebrew into Greek, a translation known as the Septuagint (LXX), beginning in the third century BC and completed by 132 BC.[25]

No specific group or council decided which books would be included in the OT canon of Scripture.[26] Rather, "The writers themselves evidenced an unusual awareness that what they were writing was not only a divine revelation from God, but that it was part and parcel of an ongoing body of communications from God. The accuracy of such bold claims was scrutinized by their contemporaries. . . . They judged them to be different and separate from other writings or words those same authors expressed on other occasions or even those by other authors."[27] Toward the end of the first century AD, Jewish historian Josephus wrote that "we have not an innumerable multitude of books among us, disagreeing from and contradicting one another [as the Greeks have], but only twenty-two books, which contain the records of all the past times; which are justly believed to be divine."[28] Jesus recognized the OT canon of Scripture.[29]

With respect to the NT, to be included in the NT, books were required to meet a number of criteria: (1) *Apostolic authority*: either apostolic authorship or, if not, some indicia of apostolic authority had to be established.[30] Those whose apostleship was established and recognized were Christ's agents, spoke with his authority, and their interpretation of the OT was held

---

24. *New American*, 378.

25. "Septuagint," *Wikipedia*, History; see also Bruce, *The Canon*, 43. The Torah (the first five books of the OT) were translated from 285–247 BC; the other books were completed later. "Septuagint," *Wikipedia*, Introduction, History.

26. The word "canon" derives from Hebrew and Greek words meaning "measuring rod," "rule" or "standard." Bruce, *The Canon*, 17–18. The canon is the list of books accepted by Christians (and by Jews with respect to the OT) as being authoritative. See Kaiser, *Old Testament*, 29–30; Gilbert, *Why Trust*, 62.

27. Kaiser, *Old Testament*, 38–39.

28. Josephus, *Against Apion*, 1.8. Bruce notes, "When Josephus speaks of twenty-two books, he probably refers to exactly the same documents as the twenty-four of the traditional Jewish reckoning, Ruth being counted as an appendix to Judges and Lamentations to Jeremiah." Bruce, *The Canon*, 33; see also Kaiser, *Old Testament*, 35–36.

29. Matt 23:35; Luke 11:51; see Kaiser, *Old Testament*, 38.

30. Bruce, *The Canon*, 258; see also Carson and Moo, *An Introduction*, 736; Sproul, *Essential Truths*, 23.

to be authoritative.³¹ (2) *Antiquity:* only writings during the apostolic age, i.e., the lifetimes of the recognized apostles, were eligible for inclusion in the NT; writings of a later era, however worthy otherwise, were not included.³² (3) *Orthodoxy:* the writings had to be consistent with "the faith set forth in the undoubted apostolic writings and maintained in the churches which had been founded by apostles."³³ (4) *Catholicity (universality):*³⁴ "Scarcely less important a criterion is a document's widespread and continuous acceptance and usage by churches everywhere."³⁵ Writings which were recognized only locally were not eligible for inclusion.³⁶

John A. T. Robinson has made a strong case that the entire NT was completed before the destruction of the temple in AD 70, which would have meant that the NT was completed only 40 years or less after Jesus' death.³⁷ Richard Bauckham, in an exhaustive study, concludes that, contrary to the assumption of nineteenth and early twentieth century liberal and critical scholars that the Bible was written a hundred years or more after the events based on anonymous oral traditions, the Gospels have the character of *testimony* and "embody the testimony of the eyewitnesses, not of course without editing and interpretation, but in a way that is substantially faithful to how the eyewitnesses themselves told it, since the Evangelists were in more or less direct contact with eyewitnesses, not removed from them by a long process of anonymous transmission of the traditions."³⁸ Even the names of the people mentioned in the Gospels confirm this. The frequency and use of particular names "corresponds well to the relative frequency in the full database of three thousand individual instances of names in the Palestinian Jewish sources of the period . . . and could not possibly have resulted from the addition of names outside Jewish Palestine, since the pattern of Jewish name usage in the Diaspora [i.e., the dispersal of the Jews after AD 70] was

---

31. Bruce, *The Canon*, 119–20.

32. Bruce, *The Canon*, 259.

33. Bruce, *The Canon*, 260; see also Carson and Moo, *An Introduction*, 736.

34. The word "catholic" (Greek = *katholikos*) means universal and stands for the universal church, not the modern Roman Catholic Church. It early-on was used to describe the orthodox, universal church, as opposed to splinter groups, and was so used until the East-West Schism in 1054. Since then and since the Protestant Reformation in the 1500s, the term "catholic" has been used to refer to the Roman Catholic Church.

35. Carson and Moo, *An Introduction*, 737.

36. Bruce, *The Canon*, 261; see also Sproul, *Essential Truths*, 23; Gilbert, *Why Trust*, 69–72.

37. See Robinson, *Redating, passim*; see also Moreland, *Scaling*, 151–57; Williams, *Can We Trust*, 78–81.

38. Bauckham, *Jesus*, 6; see also Lewis, "Modern Theology," 155 (the gospel accounts are "reportage," not "poems, romances, vision-literature, legends, [or] myths").

very different."[39] In other words, it is not plausible to believe that the accounts in the Gospels originated outside of Palestine after AD 70.[40] Timothy Keller adds a corollary to this: if the NT was written long after Jesus' life in order to promote the policies of the early church leaders and consolidate their power (as some people believe), one would expect to see Jesus taking sides in debates that were going on in the early church (e.g., whether Gentiles should be circumcised). However, this does not occur.[41] Jesus' silence concerning such matters is evidence that the NT was written early and not for polemical church-related reasons.

Insofar as the specific books included in the NT is concerned, although the vast majority of books that are now included in the NT clearly functioned with canonical authority from the time they were written, there were a few books whose inclusion in the NT canon was disputed. These included Hebrews, James, 2 Peter, 2 and 3 John, Jude, and Revelation. There were also several books vying for canonical status that were not included. The overwhelming majority of these were spurious works written by second-century Gnostic heretics. These books were never given serious consideration. (This point is missed by critics who ask, "What are the odds that the correct twenty-seven were selected?" out of multiple contenders.)[42] In fact, only about three books that were not included ever had real consideration. These were *1 Clement, The Shepherd of Hermas,* and *The Didache.* These books were not included because they were not written by apostles, and the writers themselves acknowledged that their authority was subordinate to the apostles."[43] Greg Gilbert points out that "the *only* Christian writings that have been confidently dated to the first century are the very ones that finally made up the New Testament."[44]

Barker, Lane, and Michaels observe, "The fact that substantially the whole church came to recognize the same twenty-seven books as canonical is remarkable when it is remembered that the result was not contrived. . . .

---

39. Bauckham, *Jesus,* 84.

40. See Keller, *The Reason,* 265n.8.

41. Keller, *The Reason,* 104–6.

42. That is the type of argument made by Muslim apologist Jerald Dirks. He lists 41 apocryphal gospels and concludes that "only four of over 45 gospels found their way into the *New Testament,* a meager 9% of what was possible." Dirks, *The Cross,* 82–83. Dirks does not mention that his 41 apocryphal "gospels" fail every one of the criteria for authenticity. See text, above; see also Van de Weghe, *Prepared,* 133–42; Gilbert, *Why Trust,* 64.

43. Sproul, *Essential Truths,* 22.

44. Gilbert, *Why Trust,* 64, emph. in orig.; see also Geisler, *Christian Apologetics,* 370–71.

When consideration is given to the diversity in cultural backgrounds and in orientation to the essentials of the Christian faith within the churches, their common agreement about which books belonged to the New Testament serves to suggest that this final decision did not originate solely at the human level."[45] Later, in response to the rise of various issues and heresies, the NT canon "was ratified at the Council of Hippo in 393 CE, the Synod of Carthage in 397 CE, and the Carthaginian Council in 419 CE."[46] "Ratified" is the operative word because, as Sproul notes, "The church recognized, acknowledged, received, and submitted to the canon of Scripture. The term the church used in Council was *recipimus*, 'We receive.'"[47]

We therefore can be confident that the Bible consists of the "right books." All the books in the NT meet the four criteria of apostolic authority, antiquity, orthodoxy, and universality. Hence, no book should *not* be there. On the other hand, and just as important if not more so, "no document has existed in the entire history of the world that belongs in the canon but is not in it. Sure, some books raised eyebrows in the early centuries of the church, but in the end, each and every one of them was judged not to have been ancient, apostolic, orthodox, or widely recognized—or some combination of those."[48]

THE BIBLE IS AN ACCURATE TRANSLATION OF THE ORIGINAL BIBLICAL MANUSCRIPTS

Both the OT and the NT include a number of admonitions not to alter the text as given (see Deut 4:2; 12:32; Prov 30:6; Matt 5:19; Rev 22:18–19). The original documents written by the OT and NT writers no longer exist, but multiple manuscripts attest to the accuracy of the Bible as we now have it and specifically to the fact that it was not altered or corrupted. The Masoretic Text is the authoritative Hebrew text of the Hebrew Bible (OT). "The MT was primarily copied, edited and distributed by a group of Jews known as the Masoretes between the 7th and 10th centuries CE."[49] The Dead Sea Scrolls, discovered in caves near the Dead Sea, date back to the fifth-second centuries before Christ. They include hundreds of manuscripts. "About a quarter of the total manuscripts are of Old Testament books in Hebrew, Greek, and Syriac," and every OT book except Esther is represented by at

---

45. Barker, Lane, and Michaels, *The New Testament*, 29.
46. Dirks, *The Cross*, 43.
47. Sproul, *Essential Truths*, 23.
48. Gilbert, *Why Trust*, 73–74.
49. "Masoretic Text," *Wikipedia*, Introduction.

least one scroll (usually multiple scrolls).[50] Included among them is the Isaiah Scroll, which is "the largest (734 cm) and best preserved of all the biblical scrolls, and the only one that is almost complete. . . . It is also one of the oldest of the Dead Sea Scrolls, some one thousand years older than the oldest manuscripts of the Hebrew Bible known to us before the scrolls' discovery."[51]

The discovery of the Dead Sea Scrolls gave scholars manuscripts a thousand years older than the Masoretic Text manuscripts. This enabled comparative studies of the two sets of manuscripts. The result of comparative studies reveals that "there is a word-for-word identity in more than 95 percent of the cases, and the 5 percent variation consists mostly of slips of the pen and spelling."[52] In fact, in the Isaiah scroll, "only three words exhibiting a different spelling were found for a book that runs about one hundred pages and sixty-six chapters in our English texts."[53] Josh McDowell and Don Stewart state, "The Dead Sea Scrolls demonstrated unequivocally the fact that the Jews were faithful in their transcription of biblical manuscripts."[54]

Robert Wilson did a thorough examination of the OT manuscripts before the Dead Sea Scrolls were discovered. Even without the corroborating evidence provided by the Dead Sea Scrolls, Wilson found that "in the whole Old Testament there are scarcely any variants supported by more than one manuscript out of 200 to 400, in which each book is found, except in the use of the full and defective writing of the vowels. This full, or defective, writing of the vowels has no effect either on the sound or the sense of the words."[55] He concluded that the minute accuracy of the copying and transmittal of these Hebrew manuscripts over a period of thousands of years is "a phenomenon unequalled in the history of literature."[56]

This scribal accuracy stemmed from an almost superstitious reverence for the Bible. According to the Talmud (the central text of Rabbinic Judaism), regulations governed the kind of skins to be used, the size of the columns, the kind of ink to be used, the spacing of words, and prohibited writing anything from memory, and prescribed a religious ritual that had to be performed before writing the name of God. Further, "If a manuscript

---

50. Livingston, *The Pentateuch*, 215–16.
51. "The Great Isaiah Scroll," *The Digital*, n.p.
52. Geisler and Nix, *A General Introduction*, 265.
53. Kaiser, *Old Testament*, 45–46, 164.
54. McDowell and Stewart, *Answers*, 26.
55. Wilson, *A Scientific Investigation*, 69.
56. Wilson, *A Scientific Investigation*, 82.

was found to contain even one mistake, it was discarded and destroyed."[57] As a result, "The thousands of Hebrew manuscripts, with their confirmation by the LXX [i.e., the Septuagint] and the Samaritan Pentateuch, and the numerous other crosschecks from outside and inside the text provide overwhelming support for the reliability of the Old Testament text."[58]

Concerning the NT and the entire Bible, "No other ancient writings from the same era have such a mass of manuscript evidence as that for the Greek New Testament."[59] The NT text is found in approximately "5,366 partial and complete [Greek] manuscript portions that were copied by hand from the second through the fifteenth centuries. By way of contrast, most other books from the ancient world survive in only a few and late manuscript copies."[60] Sam Shamoun observes,

> There are nearly 25,000 whole or fragmentary copies of the individual books of the Bible in our possession. Due to the fact that everything was hand-copied, thousands of variants arose. Yet, textual critics, who are not necessarily Christians, have carefully examined these variants and have concluded that we have 98.33% of the original reading, with the 1.67% still remaining intact within the variants. Hence, we have virtually 100% of the original reading faithfully preserved via the manuscript copies. Further, the critics have also established the fact that none of these variants affect any major doctrine, since most of them are nothing more than misspellings, numerical discrepancies, and scribal notes which were assumed to be part of the text by later scribes.[61]

After discussing the preservation and transmission of the biblical text through the manuscripts and other evidence, Randall Price summarizes, "The science of textual criticism has attained an extremely high degree of accuracy in the Old Testament and in the New Testament. This accuracy is such that textual variants (usually exceptionally minor) occur in only about 40 pages out of some 830 in our modern translations of the Old Testament and in only three pages out of some 200 in the New Testament."[62]

---

57. Geisler and Nix, *A General Introduction,* 263–64.
58. Geisler and Nix, *A General Introduction,* 265.
59. Gilchrist, *Facing,* 19.
60. Geisler and Nix, *A General Introduction,* 267; see also Habermas, "Why I Believe," 148–49; Kitchen, *The Bible,* 131–32.
61. Shamoun, "Quranic Witness," n.p.; see also Habermas and Licona, *The Case,* 85.
62. Price, *Searching,* 252.

In addition to the actual biblical manuscripts, "the works of early Christians like Clement of Rome, Polycarp, Ignatius, and Papias contain nearly every verse of the New Testament."[63] This is important, since all of these men were born in the early-to-mid first century. Thus, the NT "can be traced to the first century easily and corresponds with what we have today."[64]

Not only do thousands of biblical manuscripts exist, but the four Gospels and the book of Acts, dating from the early third century (i.e., early 200s), are found in a single manuscript, Papyrus 45, located in the Chester Beatty Library in Dublin.[65] The entire Bible was compiled into book form between approximately AD 325–440. These copies of the Bible are known as Codex Vaticanus, Codex Sinaiticus, and Codex Alexandrinus; they include the entire or virtually the entire Bible (OT and NT) in Greek.[66] The entire Bible also was translated into Latin in the fourth century (the Latin Vulgate). The thousands of biblical manuscripts, letters of the church fathers quoting the NT, and the complete translations into Greek and Latin are the same as the Bible as it exists today. They prove conclusively that the biblical manuscripts and translations are consistent and that the Bible has not been lost, changed, or corrupted.[67]

CLAIMS THAT THE BIBLE HAS BEEN CORRUPTED

Muslims and others believe that the books of the Bible are not the same as they were originally written. For example, Muslim apologist Jerald Dirks alleges that the existing Torah "is a far cry from the original *Torah*, although traces and elements of the original *Torah* may continue to be found"; likewise, the book of Psalms "is a poor resemblance of the original *Psalms* of David, although occasional chapters or verses in the 'received Psalms' may be part of the original *Psalms*"; and "the original gospel of Jesus can nowhere be found in the corpus of the *Bible*, although various sayings attributed to Jesus in the *Bible* may represent perverted fragments from the original gospel."[68] Muslim scholar Muhammad bin Abdullaah As-Suhaym

---

63. Sundiata, *Look Behind*, 74.

64. Sundiata, *Look Behind*, 75.

65. Williams, *Can We Trust*, 38.

66. These books still exist. Codex Vaticanus is located in the Vatican Library; Codex Sinaiticus and Codex Alexandrinus are located in the British Library in London.

67. A good summary of the manuscript record of the Bible compared to that of other historic books is "Is there Much Evidence for the Bible's Reliability?" *Evidence for God's Unchanging Word*; see also Williams, *Can We Trust*, 111–22; Moreland, *Scaling*, 134–36; Geisler, *Christian Apologetics*, 306–13.

68. Dirks, *The Cross*, 189; see also A'la Mawdudi, *Towards Understanding*, Q. 3:4n.2.

maintains that "the contents of most of these Books have been lost and have become extinct, and interpolation and alterations have entered them."[69]

How, when, where, why, and by whom did this happen? Neither Muslims nor anyone else who claims that the Bible has been corrupted can say. All Muslim apologist Yahiya Emerick can do is liken the situation to "the game in which one person whispers a message to another and we then see how the message comes out with the last person. Now multiply this by centuries of transmission and you will see how legends and new rituals can become part of a faith, although without any authority from the original messenger."[70] Suhaym attributes corruption to ignorance and resorts to name-calling, "As for the Jews and Christians, the Books that were revealed to their Prophets have been lost as a result of their ignorance of what was in their Books; their taking men as gods beside Allah and the long time that had passed between them and their acquaintance with these Books. So their priests wrote some books which they claimed were from Allah while they were not from Allah but only wrong assumptions of liars and distortions of fanatics."[71]

Any contention that the Bible has been corrupted is both unreasonable and contrary to fact. We have already discussed the meticulous accuracy of translation of both the OT and NT and the manuscript evidence which demonstrate that the Bible has not been corrupted. No plausible persons, motives, abilities, or opportunities to corrupt the Bible have ever existed or have ever been claimed. Ancient Jewish historian Josephus articulated the view held by Jews concerning copying the books of the Hebrew Bible, "How firmly we have given credit to those books of our own nation, is evident by what we do; for during so many ages as have already passed, no one has been so bold as either to add anything to them, to take anything from them, or to make any change in them; but it becomes natural to all Jews, immediately and from their very birth, to esteem those books to contain divine doctrines, and to persist in them, and, if occasion be, willing to die for them."[72] Christians view the OT and the NT the same way. During the first three centuries of Christianity, Christians were an often-persecuted minority in the Roman Empire. Abbas Sundiata points out, "They did not have the power to either write or rewrite history. Those tough and loving Christians had a list of books that they held as Scriptures. It is absurd to think that this

---

69. As-Suhaym, *Islam*, 153–54.
70. Emerick, *Understanding*, 88.
71. As-Suhaym, *Islam*, 78.
72. Josephus, *Against Apion*, 1.8.

group of determined survivors would allow anyone to add to or subtract from the texts that helped their survival for centuries."[73]

Both Jews and Christians hold the Hebrew Bible (OT) in common and hold it to be the Word of God. Walter Eric observes, "Muslims must seriously think about this fact – the Old Testament is held to be the Word of God by two very different religions and has been scrupulously maintained by each one independently of the other. There is thus no possibility of a perversion of the text by either of the two faiths, for the very act of alteration by the one would have been immediately exposed by the other."[74] John Gilchrist concludes that one should challenge anyone who claims that the Bible has been corrupted to produce historical evidence to substantiate their allegation. "What was it originally? What, precisely, was changed to make it the book it is today? Who made these changes? When were they made? Once you challenge any Muslim to identify the actual people who are supposed to have corrupted the Bible, at what time in history it took place, and precisely what textual changes were made to original manuscripts, you will find them entirely unable to do so. Such evidences quite simply do not exist."[75]

CLAIMS THAT THE BIBLE IS SUBSTANTIVELY INACCURATE

The above evidence demonstrates that the Bible we have today is accurate in its form or wording and accurately represents the Bible as it originally was written. The other claim concerning the Bible's inaccuracy is that it is inaccurate *substantively*. In other words, the claim is that the Bible is contrary to known scientific or historical facts. Such contentions are themselves inaccurate. Chairman of the Department of Hebrew and Semitic studies at the University of Wisconsin-Madison and president of the Near East Archaeological Society, Keith Schoville, states, "We ought to take the Bible seriously because its essential historicity has been established."[76] One important way in which the historicity of the Bible has been established is through archaeology. Archaeologist Titus Kennedy states that "the degree of historical corroboration between the Bible and the artifacts that have been discovered in the last 150 years is startling, surpassing previous expectations and estimates, and continuing to astound."[77] These archaeological remains have

73. Sundiata, *Look Behind*, 72–73.
74. Eric, *Why Trust*, 9–10.
75. Gilchrist, *Facing*, 20.
76. Schoville, "The Reliability," 68.
77. Kennedy, *Unearthing*, 238–39; see the research reports from Associates for

illuminated and confirmed events, chronologies, practices, terminology, locations, and individuals reported in the Bible that would otherwise have remained mysteries to us.

One caveat to this is the fact that much of the Bible concerns what God, Jesus, and other prominent biblical characters did and said. Unless a specific document is discovered that reiterates the words of the Bible, archaeology cannot demonstrate that the persons actually did or said what is recorded in the Bible. On the other hand, archaeology can demonstrate that the places, customs, historical events, living conditions, coins, buildings, people, and numerous other "stage props" correspond to how the Bible identifies and describes them; such correspondence renders far more plausible the reliability of the Bible's other reports than would be the case if there were no such correspondence.[78] As Craig Blomberg states, when that which can be checked proves accurate, "it is entirely proper to believe that what cannot be checked is probably accurate as well"[79] More will be said of archaeological corroboration of the Bible below.

Several lines of evidence demonstrate the substantive reliability of the Bible. First, over and over again the biblical authors make clear that they believe what they are reporting and want us to believe it also.[80] These explicit or implicit statements of authorial intent are connected to a second and related fact, namely, that in form and style the Bible's accounts of various historical events are not fictional, legendary, or mythical. For example, the prose accounts of the exodus of Israel from Egypt in the Pentateuch are designed as accurate historical narratives in a way that later poetical celebrations of God's faithfulness during the exodus found in the Psalms are not. Kenneth A. Kitchen, professor at the School of Archaeology, Classics, and Egyptology, University of Liverpool, notes that "the close correspondence to Nilotic [i.e., relating to the Nile River] and related conditions demonstrable in the text of Exodus has clear implications. First and foremost, it rules out any attempt to give preference to the poetical retrospects found in Pss. 78 and 105. . . . This illustrates a basic literary phenomenon endemic to the

---

Biblical Research listed on their website by chronological categories. Associates for Biblical Research (https://biblearchaeology.org/) and the Near East Archaeological Society (https://www.neasociety.org/) are two organizations that are doing extensive archaeological work in biblical lands.

78. See Blomberg, *Gospels*, 327.

79. Blomberg, *Gospels*, 320.

80. See, e.g., Deut 30:19; 31:19, 26, 28; 1 Sam 12:3–5; Luke 1:1–4; John 21:24–25; Acts 4:19–20; 1 John 1:1–3; 2 Pet 1:16; see also Gilbert, *Why Trust*, 84; Waltke, *Genesis*, 29 ("From the standpoint of modern historiography, internal evidence within the Pentateuch supports the narrator's inferred claim to represent what really happened").

ancient Near East.... When prose and poetry accounts coexist, *it is prose that is the primary source and poetry that is the secondary celebration.*"[81]

The historical and factual, as opposed to fictional, legendary, or mythical nature of the biblical narratives is particularly true of the gospel accounts of Jesus Christ. C. S. Lewis, who was a Fellow at Oxford for thirty years in Medieval and Renaissance literature and then was awarded the newly founded chair in Medieval and Renaissance Literature at Magdalene College, Cambridge, wrote that if someone "tells me that something in a Gospel is legend or romance . . . I have been reading poems, romances, vision-literature, legends, myths all my life. I know what they are like. I know that not one of them is like this."[82] Richard Bauckham adds that the Gospels exhibit the attitude of the Greco-Roman historians of the time, who valued above all eyewitness reports and the reports of those who had themselves been participants in the events reported."[83] This is reinforced in that many events are reported independently by more than one witness or report; this is significant in that "multiple attestation is an important criterion in determining historical authenticity."[84] The gospels even incorporate, if only to refute them, the perspectives on Jesus of his contemporaries who did *not* believe in him. Those are not the marks of fictitious accounts penned long after the events recorded to advance political or some other personal interests. Indeed, the technique of the realistic novel did not even exist in the first and second centuries and wasn't invented until approximately the nineteenth century.[85] Further, the books of the NT were written only about 20–40 (up to a maximum of about 65) years after the ministry, death, and resurrection of Jesus. Consequently, "There simply was not enough time for a great deal of myth and legend to accrue and distort the historical facts in any significant way."[86] Finally, throughout the Bible, there are too many embarrassing or damaging details pertaining to most of the major characters to make it plausible to suggest that the authors were trying to make themselves look good or get rich. Indeed, most of the NT apostles were martyred for their faith—and people do not die for what they know to be a lie.

Third, the biblical authors regularly refer to specific, verifiable historic events and circumstances. For example, the biblical narratives in Exodus to

---

81. Kitchen, *On the Reliability,* 252, emph. in orig.

82. Lewis, "Modern Theology," 154–55; see also Geisler, *Christian Apologetics,* 320; Blomberg, *Gospels, passim.*

83. Bauckham, *Jesus,* 497.

84. Blomberg, *Gospels,* 199.

85. Lewis, "Modern Theology," 155; see also Lewis, "What are We," 158–59.

86. Moreland, *Scaling,* 156.

Deuteronomy directly reflect earthy reality, not fantasy. "Salt-tolerant reeds, water from rock, habits of quails, *kewirs,* etc. reflect *real* local conditions, requiring local knowledge (not book learning in Babylon or Jerusalem)."[87] Similarly, in in the NT, Luke 3:1–3 alone includes multiple references to historical people, places, circumstances, and events, each of which is or was testable and verifiable, or falsifiable if Luke was wrong. The four Gospels all contain accurately-conveyed descriptions of names, places, local botany, financial practices, peculiarities of local languages, unusual and local customs, all of which required real local knowledge and all of which rendered the Gospels falsifiable.[88]

The gospel of John provides detailed geographical information, often noting that one place is "near" another (see John 3:23; 11:18; 19:20, 42) or providing the Hebrew names for locations, so that they can be identified precisely (see John 5:2; 19:13, 17). John notes that one comes "down" from Cana to Capernaum (John 4:47, 49, 51) and goes "up" from Capernaum to Jerusalem (John 2:13). Typically, in the northern hemisphere people think of going "up" as going north and going "down" as going south. Jerusalem is south of Galilee. However, Capernaum is actually about 700 feet below sea level whereas Jerusalem is about 2500 feet above sea level. Hence, John's statements are in accord with the topography. That is one of the little indications that the biblical writers knew what they were talking about.[89]

Matthew and Mark both refer to a group known as "the Herodians" (Matt 22:16; Mark 3:6; 12:13), Mark and Luke refer to "the insurrection" as a result of which Barabbas was imprisoned (Mark 15:7; Luke 23:19, 25), and John notes that Annas was Caiaphas's father-in-law (John 18:13). Paul Barnett comments, "Such information is not found in Josephus or any other source known to us. Details such as these—and we have only mentioned a few—simply could not be contrived later and elsewhere. The details are intrinsic to the context of the Jesus history as it was remembered by participants and told from the beginning."[90] In short, the biblical narratives all have the indicia of being substantively accurate accounts of people, places, and events reported by witnesses who knew what they were talking about.

Fourth, another aspect of the Bible makes it unique and falsifiable. Specifically, the Bible is "the only volume ever produced by man, or a group

---

87. Kitchen, *On the Reliability,* 311.

88. See Williams, *Can We Trust,* 51–86.

89. See Williams, *Can We Trust,* 51–62 regarding the large amount of sophisticated and accurate geographical knowledge displayed by the writers of the four Gospels ("the Gospels are not merely accurate in their geography when compared with other sources; they are themselves valuable geographical sources").

90. Barnett, *Behind the Scenes,* 81; see also Williams, *Can We Trust,* 51–62.

of men, in which is to be found a large body of prophecies relating to individual nations, to Israel, to all the peoples of the earth, to certain cities, and to the coming of One who was to be the Messiah."[91] Approximately 27% of the Bible contains prophetic or predictive elements.[92] Jesus himself made prophetic statements on multiple occasions (e.g., Matt 24:25; John 13:19; 16:13). Prophecies served, among other things, to demonstrate the presence and active involvement of God in the lives of his people (Josh 3:10; Isa 42:9), to exalt godly leaders in the eyes of the people (Josh 3:7), to provide reassurance and comfort (Gen 28:15–22; Exod 3:11–12; 1 Sam 10:1–7), to demonstrate a person's faith (1 Sam 17:37; Heb 11:22), and to motivate belief and holy living (Nah 1:15; John 14:29; 2 Pet 1:19; Rev 1:3). Wilbur Smith points out, "The ancient world had many different devices for determining the future, known as divination, but not in the entire gamut of Greek and Latin literature [or the Qur'an of Islam and the books of all other religions], even though they use the words of prophet and prophecy, can we find any real specific prophecy of a great historical event to come in the distant future, nor any prophecy of a Savior to arise in the human race."[93]

The organization Reasons to Believe discusses thirteen biblical prophecies that cover mostly separate and independent events. They conclude,

> The probability of chance occurrence for all thirteen is about 1 in 10^{138} (138 equals the sum of all the exponents of 10 in the probability estimates above). For the sake of putting the figure into perspective, this probability can be compared to the statistical chance that the second law of thermodynamics will be reversed in a given situation (for example, that a gasoline engine will refrigerate itself during its combustion cycle or that heat will flow from a cold body to a hot body)—that chance being 1 in 10^{80}. Stating it simply, based on these thirteen prophecies alone, the biblical record may be said to be vastly more reliable than the second law of thermodynamics.[94]

The subject of biblical prophecy will be considered again in chapter 3, Jesus' fulfillment of prophecy.

Fifth, it is simply factually incorrect to contend that the Bible is full of mistakes and contradictions. With respect to the OT, Walter Kaiser notes, "The facts, from whatever source, when fully known have consistently provided uncanny confirmation for the details of Old Testament persons,

91. Smith, *Incomparable*, 9.
92. Payne, *Encyclopedia*, 12–13.
93. Smith, *Incomparable*, 9.
94. Reasons, *Why the Bible*, 4.

people and places by means of the artifactual, stratigraphical and epigraphic remains evidence uncovered."[95] Although, largely "due to the use of papyrus and leather as a common medium for writing," only a few manuscripts from the second millennium and first part of the first millennium BC exist (i.e., the time of the events described in the Pentateuch), "the artifacts recovered by archaeologists have brought together the Patriarchs [i.e., Abraham, Isaac, and Jacob] and the cultural life of the Middle Bronze Age in a remarkable manner."[96] J. A. Thompson adds that the patriarchal towns of Ur, Haran, Nahor, and "many other towns in this [Mesopotamian] area are known from documents, and sometimes the same name is used for a person in the biblical record."[97] In fact, the "Lament for the Destruction of Ur" (a Mesopotamian poem) documents the destruction of Ur during the final year of King Ibbi-Sin of the 3rd Dynasty of Ur around 1950 BC.[98] That corroborates that Abraham had to have left Ur before 1950 BC, which is in accord with the timing of the biblical account in Gen 11:31—12:5. The account of Joseph in Egypt (Genesis 39–50) "must have been written by someone who was well acquainted with the customs of Egypt," and even the titles of the characters in the story are documented by non-biblical sources to be correct.[99]

As one moves forward in time through the history of OT Israel, consistency of the OT accounts with that which is otherwise known of life in the Ancient Near East continues unabated. This includes the account of Moses and the exodus. An Egyptian papyrus translated and published by Egyptologist William C. Hayes in 1972 lists the names of 95 slaves. It corroborates that even such minor points as the name of one of the Egyptian midwives listed in Exod 1:15 ("Shiphrah") is accurate.[100] An inscription dating from 1400 BC on an interior wall of an Egyptian temple refers to "land of the nomads of Yahweh." Kennedy observes, "Since the only ancient people known to have worshipped Yahweh were the Israelites or Hebrews, it

---

95. Kaiser, *Old Testament*, 108; see also Schoville, "The Reliability," 69–74.
96. Livingston, *The Pentateuch*, 205, 261; see Albright, *The Archaeology*, 236.
97. Thompson, "Marginalia," 26.
98. See Kennedy, *Unearthing*, 24–25.
99. Thompson, "Marginalia," 46–47; see also Kaiser, *Old Testament*, 84–96; Kennedy, *Unearthing*, 29 ("The laws, customs, and prices found in the Code of Hammurabi from the 18th century BC in the Middle Bronze Age and the patriarchal narratives from the time of Isaac, Jacob, and Joseph in Genesis suggest that the events occurred in the same period and accurately reflect conditions of that specific time.").
100. Aling, "Joseph," n.p.; Albright, *The Archaeology*, 237; see also Rohl, *Exodus*; Associates, *Evidence*; Windle, "Top Ten," and the documentary film *Patterns of Evidence: The Exodus* (2014) for additional archaeological evidence related to Moses and the exodus.

logically follows that these nomads were the Israelites before they settled in Canaan."[101] The timing of that inscription also corresponds to the timing of the exodus as indicated in the Bible. The route taken by the Israelites in the land of Canaan following the exodus from Egypt as recorded in Num 33:45b–50 has been confirmed by Egyptian maps to be "an official, heavily trafficked Egyptian road through the Transjordan in the late Bronze Age."[102] Substantively, "the law codes and legal documents of the Mesopotamian area show that Mosaic laws were premonarchial [i.e., before Saul became Israel's first king in approximately 1050 BC] and fit the time of Moses well."[103] Similarly, the *form* of the Mosaic covenant and its laws (Exodus–Deuteronomy and Joshua 24) is "a form proper to the general period of the exodus, current in the 14th/13th centuries BC, and *neither earlier nor later* on the total available evidence."[104] Recently, a small piece of red-dyed fabric was discovered, dated approximately 3800 years old, which was found to be colored using dye extracted from oak scale insects, that corresponds to the "scarlet worm" mentioned twenty-five times in the Bible (see, e.g., Exod 26:1; Lev 14:6). This dye was used in the tabernacle and priestly garments. The discovery "provides tangible evidence of a sophisticated textile industry in the ancient world, bridging the gap between written sources and archaeological findings."[105]

The biblical accounts of Israel's conquest of the Transjordan region following the exodus likewise are corroborated by non-biblical archaeological and other data. For example, Professor Emeritus of Ancient Near Eastern Languages and Literature at the University of Michigan, Charles Krahmalkov, points out that the accounts in Judges 4–5 "contain specific historical and geographical information about the Late Bronze Age whose accuracy is dramatically validated by an Egyptian document of that time. There was indeed a king named Jabin. The places mentioned in the Biblical accounts did in fact exist at the time. None of these pieces of information was fabricated."[106] "Israel" is explicitly referred to on the stele (an upright stone slab or pillar bearing an inscription) of Merneptah, who ruled Egypt from 1224–1216 BC, which "shows that by this time there was already a

---

101. Kennedy, *Unearthing*, 61.
102. Krahmalkov, "Exodus Itinerary," 58.
103. Livingston, *The Pentateuch*, 261.
104. Kitchen, *The Bible*, 79, emph. in orig.
105. "Discovery of ancient textile," *Israel Hayom*, n.p.; see Sukenik, et al., "Early evidence," 104673.
106. Krahmalkov, "Exodus Itinerary," 62.

recognizable people of this name in Palestine."¹⁰⁷ After discussing ancient Egyptian maps and other data, Krahmalkov concludes, "In short, the Biblical story of the invasion of the Transjordan that set the stage for the conquest of all Palestine is told against a background that is historically accurate."¹⁰⁸

After Israel became a monarchy, excavations at ancient Dan in 1993 uncovered fragments of a ninth-century BC Aramean victory stele which refers to a "king of Israel" and the "house of David"; it is "now confidently dated by additional fragments to the reign of Joram ('Jehoram') of Judah, who ruled ca. 847–842."¹⁰⁹ This confirms that David was known even outside of Israel as the king of Israel and head of the Davidic dynasty and also confirms the biblical dating of David's reign.¹¹⁰ A tenth-century jasper seal, excavated from the gatehouse or palace in ancient Megiddo in northern Israel, bearing the Hebrew inscription "belonging to Shema, servant of Jeroboam," confirms the dating and reign of King Jeroboam I, first king of the northern kingdom of Israel after its split from Judah.¹¹¹ Kings Ahab, Jehu, Omri, Ahaz, Joash, Pekah, Menahem, Hezekiah, Manasseh, and Queen Jezebel are also attested by various artifacts, as are the prophets Balaam (who had been hired to curse Israel [see Numbers 22–24]), Isaiah, and Jeremiah's scribe Baruch.¹¹² In fact, Baruch's personal seal, bearing his name, has been found.¹¹³ H. G. M. Williamson states, "Every king of Israel or Judah who is mentioned in any source outside the Bible (Moabite, Assyrian, Babylonian, Aramaic, and so on) comes with the right name in the right order and at the expected time."¹¹⁴

Robert Wilson did a comparative analysis of the lists of kings as set forth in the OT and the records of Egypt, Assyria, Babylon, and other Ancient Near East nations. He found that

> the writers of the Old Testament have put the names of the 40 or more that are mentioned in records of two or more of the nations, in their proper absolute and relative order of time and in their proper place. Any expert mathematician will tell you, that do such a thing is practically impossible without a knowledge of

---

107. Thompson, "Marginalia," 64.
108. Krahmalkov, "Exodus Itinerary," 58.
109. Dever, *What Did*, 128.
110. Kennedy, *Unearthing*, 99.
111. Kennedy, *Unearthing*, 108–9.
112. Kaiser, *Old Testament*, 101, 125–28; Kennedy, *Unearthing*, 116–19, 122–23, 130–31, 138–39, 146–47; Kitchen, *The Bible*, 88–89 (regarding Balaam).
113. Dever, *What Did*, 206.
114. Williamson, "Book Review," 115–16.

the facts such as could be drawn from contemporary and reliable records. When we consider that there are nine distinct lines of kings in the countries mentioned, and that there are several hundred kings in all, and that the length of the reigns of the kings could be determined only from the most accurate records, the chance of anyone who did not have access to reliable sources to get a record as exact as that preserved for us in the Hebrew Scriptures would be so small that no mathematician on earth could calculate it.[115]

There is attestation of even seemingly incidental biblical data. For example, a place like Ophir, from which King Solomon received gold (1 Kgs 9:28) and which had been thought to be imaginary, was corroborated in 1956 by the discovery of a small ostracon [potsherd] containing a shipment notice referring to "gold from Ophir" to be a real location and a source of gold.[116] Beersheba, the southern limit of the settled zone in monarchical times, was excavated in 1969–1975. "Among the most spectacular finds were several large, dressed blocks of stone that make up a monumental four-horned altar like those that perhaps stood in the Levitical 'cities of refuge', where one could seek asylum by clinging symbolically to the horns of the altar."[117] The Siloam inscription, dating from the eighth century BC, is the only known inscription from ancient Israel which commemorates a public construction work. That inscription confirms King Hezekiah's construction of a tunnel, water conduit, and pool to aid in the defense of Jerusalem against the Assyrians, as is recorded in 2 Kgs 20:20; 2 Chron 32:2–4.[118] The deportation of the northern kingdom of Israel (2 Kgs 18:9–12) was celebrated in inscriptions of Assyrian king Sargon II and an Assyrian ostracon, dated about 720–700 BC, contains a list of obviously Hebrew names.[119]

---

115. Wilson, *A Scientific Investigation*, 87. In a footnote to that statement, Wilson calculated the odds that the OT could have accurately listed the names and order of the Ancient Near East kings by chance: "If there were 300 names of kings, each reigning 20 years, and 40 to be taken by chance, then, according to the algebraic rule that $n\,(n-1)\,(n-2)\,\ldots\,(n-r+1)$ equals the number of permutations, there would be one chance in about $75 \times 1{,}000{,}000$ to the 16th power of getting the names in the correct order. Even this chance would be made more impossible from the fact that the kings did not all reign an equal and synchronous period, but for periods of from one month to 66 years." Wilson, *A Scientific Investigation*, 87n.94a.

116. Kaiser, *Old Testament*, 105–6.

117. Dever, *What Did*, 180–81; see 1 Kgs 1:50–53.

118. "Siloam inscription," *Wikipedia*; Falde, "Inscription"; Kennedy, *Unearthing*, 134–35.

119. See Kitchen, *The Bible*, 113; see also Kaiser, *Old Testament*, 99–100.

After the fall of Judah to Babylon, Babylonian cuneiform clay tablets detail the rations provided Jehoiachin, who had been Judah's king, and his sons, as had been recorded in 2 Kgs 25:29–30. Daniel 5 identifies Belshazzar as the king of Babylon when the Persians captured the city in 539 BC. However, no sources outside of Daniel identified Belshazzar as king until ancient Babylonian cuneiform texts were discovered in 1854. They confirm the biblical account and also explain why Dan 5:29 says that Daniel was made the "third ruler" in the kingdom.[120] A Hebrew inscription has been recovered, dating from the period of Judah's exile in Babylon, which states, "Yahweh (is) the God of the whole earth; the mountains of Judah belong to him, to the God of Jerusalem. The (Mount of) Moriah Thou has favored, the dwelling of Yah, Yahweh." William Dever observes that "its 'Jerusalem temple theology' is fully consistent with that of the Deuteronomistic history in Kings, with which the inscription is contemporary."[121] In the post-exilic period, Nehemiah's opponents, Sanballat, Tobiah, and Geshem (Neh 2:10, 19) have all been validated by archaeology.[122]

All of this demonstrates that the events recorded in the OT were written and took place when they claim to have been written and to have taken place. After discussing multiple sources of direct and indirect archaeological, literary, cultural, and other historical evidence corroborating the biblical record, Kitchen recaps the overall picture by saying, "We have a consistent level of good, fact-based correlation right through from circa 2000 B.C. (with earlier roots) down to 400 B.C."[123] Albright summarizes that archaeology has "corroborated biblical tradition in no uncertain way"; he concludes "Biblical historical data are accurate to an extent far surpassing the ideas of any modern critical student."[124]

The situation is similar with respect to the NT. Keith Schoville states that the NT texts "are more firmly established as authentically historical than any other ancient documents from the classical world."[125] In fact, William F. Albright stated that the former, critical NT schools that arose primarily in the nineteenth century and which still exist "are pre-archaeological, and are, therefore, since they were built *in der Luft* [in the air], quite antiquated today."[126] Because Jerusalem was destroyed by the Romans in AD 70 and a

---

120. See Kennedy, *Unearthing*, 160–61; see also Kaiser, *Old Testament*, 99–100.
121. Dever, *What Did*, 218.
122. Kaiser, *Old Testament*, 100–101.
123. Kitchen, *On the Reliability*, 500; see also Kennedy, *Unearthing*, 11–173.
124. Albright, *The Archaeology*, 123–24, 229.
125. Schoville, "The Reliability," 69.
126. Albright, "Retrospect," 29.

new pagan city was founded there in AD 135, and because modern Jerusalem is now densely populated, it is difficult to do archaeological digs and identify archaeological sites in Jerusalem referred to in the NT. However, the NT references to those sites that have been excavated invariably have proven to be accurate. Those include the pool of Bethesda and its five porticoes referred to in John 5:1–2[127] and the "Pavement" called "Gabbatha" in Hebrew (Aramaic) referred to in John 19:13. Their excavation confirms John's accounts.[128] The crucifixion of Jesus is documented in writing and even in pictorial form by pagan Romans as early as the late first to early second century.[129] Bruce lists a number of other archaeological confirmations of NT accounts, including even "minor details in the New Testament narrative."[130] Pre-eminent classical scholar Sir Frederic Kenyon concludes, "The interval then between the dates of the original composition and the earliest extant evidence becomes so small as to be in fact negligible, and the last foundation for any doubt that the Scriptures have come down to us substantially as they were written has now been removed. Both the *authenticity* and the general integrity of the books of the New Testament may be regarded as finally established."[131]

In addition to the archaeological, literary, cultural, and other historical corroboration, the Bible is "filled with references to scientific discoveries that wouldn't occur until up to 3,000 years later. These statements in most cases directly contradicted the science of the day in which they were written."[132] These scientific statements include: the number of stars exceeds a billion (Jer 33:22); every star is different (1 Cor 15:41); light is in motion (Job 38:19–20); air has weight (Job 28:25); wind blows in cyclones (Eccl 1:6); blood is a source of life and healing (Lev 17:11).

Multiple books have been written that deal with and correct all manner of false allegations that have been made against the Bible's accuracy.[133]

---

127. See Bruce, *The New Testament*, 94; Wenham, "A Historical View," 8.
128. See Albright, *The Archaeology*, 245.
129. Kennedy, *Unearthing*, 194–97.
130. Bruce, *The New Testament*, 95; see also Kitchen, *On the Reliability*, 132; Kennedy, *Unearthing*, 175–236; Blomberg, *Gospels*, 326–31.
131. Kenyon, *The Bible*, 288–89, emph. in orig.; see also Kitchen, *On the Reliability*, 132.
132. Reasons, *Why the Bible*, 5.
133. A small sample of such books is the following: Randall Price, *Searching for the Original Bible* (Eugene, OR: Harvest House, 2007) (Bible translations, canonization process, reliability); Robert Wilson, *A Scientific Investigation of the Old Testament* (New York: Harper, 1929) (reliability of the OT); Craig Blomberg, *The Historical Reliability of the Gospels*, 2nd ed. (Downers Grove, IL: IVP Academic, 2007) (discussions of literary criticism, miracles, and other indicia of the reliability of the gospels); Craig Blomberg,

Gilbert points out that even though the Bible has been subjected to detailed attacks by critics for more than two hundred years, "every alleged contradiction, inconsistency, and error has been met with at least one plausible resolution and often more."[134] In short, given what the Bible claims about itself, the nature and evident purposes of the biblical writers, the trustworthiness the Bible demonstrates, and the multiple ways in which the biblical accounts have been corroborated by extra-biblical evidence, we can have strong confidence in the reliability of what the Bible reports.[135]

Probably the biggest issue concerning whether or not the Bible is substantively accurate, of course, is the issue of creation, i.e., whether contemporary science, and particularly evolution, has demonstrated that the Bible is scientifically inaccurate. This is dealt with in Part 2 of this work. In this regard, it should be understood that, in endeavoring to rightly understand what the Bible says about creation—including the different biblical genres, and use of literal versus figurative and phenomenological

---

The Historical Reliability of the New Testament (Nashville: B&H Academic, 2016) (discussions of literary criticism, miracles, and other indicia of the reliability of the NT); C. Stephen Evans, *The Historical Christ and the Jesus of Faith: The Incarnational Narrative as History* (New York: Oxford University Press, 1996) (discussion of the philosophical and literary assumptions of contemporary critical biblical scholarship and the historical reliability of the biblical accounts of Jesus); J. Warner Wallace, *Cold-Case Christianity* (Colorado Springs: David Cook, 2013) (reliability of NT from a former atheist and cold-case homicide detective); Richard Bauckham, *Jesus and the Eyewitnesses: The Gospels as Eyewitness Testimony* (Grand Rapids: Eerdmans, 2008) (the gospels are eyewitness testimony); Norman Geisler and Thomas Howe, *The Big Book of Bible Difficulties* (Grand Rapids: Baker, 1992) (concise answers to alleged problems from Genesis to Revelation); Gleason Archer, *Encyclopedia of Bible Difficulties* (Grand Rapids: Zondervan, 1982) (alleged contradictory or problem passages from each book of the Bible); Jason Lisle, *Keeping Faith in an Age of Reason* (Green Forest, AR: Master Books, 2017) (refutes alleged biblical contradictions); John Haley, *Alleged Discrepancies of the Bible* (Grand Rapids: Baker, 1977) (alleged doctrinal, ethical, and historical discrepancies); Titus Kennedy, *Unearthing the Bible* (Eugene, OR: Harvest House, 2020) (archaeological discoveries that confirm biblical accounts); Ray Comfort, *Scientific Facts in the Bible* (Gainesville, FL: Bridge-Logos, 2001) (multiple scientific facts contained in the Bible); Henry Morris, *The Biblical Basis for Modern Science* (Green Forest, AR: Master Books, 2002) (the scientific accuracy of the Bible); Josh McDowell, *Evidence that Demands a Verdict* (San Bernardino, CA: Here's Life, 1979) and *More Evidence that Demands a Verdict*, rev. ed. (San Bernardino, CA: Here's Life, 1981) (historical evidence for the reliability of the Bible and the truths of Christianity); Norman Geisler and Paul Hoffman, eds., *Why I am a Christian: Leading Thinkers Explain Why They Believe* (Grand Rapids: Baker, 2006) (historical and other evidence for the reliability of the Bible and that Jesus Christ is the divine Son of God); N. T. Wright, *The Resurrection of the Son of God* (Minneapolis: Fortress, 2003) (the most comprehensive demonstration of the fact of the resurrection of Jesus Christ).

134. Gilbert, *Why Trust*, 97.

135. See Geisler, *Christian Apologetics*, 314–27.

JESUS CHRIST ACCEPTED THE TRUSTWORTHINESS OF THE BIBLE

Steve Moyise points out, "The four Gospels found in the New Testament present Jesus quoting from nearly 60 different verses of Scripture [i.e., the OT] and making at least twice that number of allusions and more general references."[136] These quotes are from the entire corpus of the OT, including 26 quotations from the law, 16 from the writings, and 15 from the prophets.[137] This is important because Jesus believed that the OT was the Word of God and that its words had not been corrupted (Matt 5:17–19; John 10:33–36). He cited the Bible as authoritative (Matt 4:1–11; 22:23–30; Luke 4:1–13; John 13:18; 17:17). He called the OT *"the word of God"* (Mark 7:13; see also Matt 22:31–32; John 10:34–35), *"the commandment of God"* (Matt 15:3), and *"the truth"* (John 17:17). He said the OT was verbally inspired right down to individual words and tenses of the verbs (Matt 5:17–19; 22:31–32, 43–45; Luke 16:17). He affirmed that God spoke through men (Matt 22:43; 24:15) but, at the same time, he distinguished the Bible from men's traditions (Matt 15:6; John 5:46–47). He said that everything he himself spoke was the word of God (John 8:28–29; 12:44–50). He criticized men's failure to understand the Bible (Matt 22:29; Luke 24:25; John 3:10). He said *"the Scripture cannot be broken"* (John 10:35) and that *"it is easier for heaven and earth to pass away than for one stroke of a letter of the Law to fail"* (Luke 16:17; see also Matt 5:18).

Jesus believed that the events and persons depicted in the OT were real and not fictional, including the biblical accounts of creation, Adam and Eve, and God's institution of marriage (Matt 19:4–6; Mark 10:6; Luke 11:50); Cain and Abel (Matt 23:34–35; Luke 11:51); Noah and the Flood (Matt 24:37–39; Luke 17:26–37); Abraham, Isaac, and Jacob (Matt 22:32; Luke 16:22–31; John 8:56–58); Lot and the destruction of Sodom (Matt 10:15; 11:23–24; Luke 10:12; 17:28–32); Moses and the burning bush (Luke 20:37–38); Moses and the lifting of the serpent in the wilderness (John 3:14); the manna in the wilderness during the exodus (John 6:49); Moses's authorship of the Torah (Matt 8:4; 19:7–8; Mark 1:44; 7:10; 10:3–5; 12:26; Luke 5:14; 16:29–31; 20:37; 24:27, 44; John 3:14; 5:45–47; 6:32; 7:19, 22–23);

---

136. Moyise, *Jesus*, 3–4.
137. Moyise, *Jesus*, 4.

Elijah and Elisha were prophets and did miracles (Luke 4:25-27); Jonah in the great fish (Matt 12:39-40); Jonah and the repentance of Nineveh (Matt 12:41); Daniel was a prophet (Matt 24:15-16); John the Baptist had been prophesied in the OT (Matt 11:10; Mark 1:2; 9:13; Luke 3:4; 7:27); Satan (Matt 25:41; Luke 10:18; 22:31-32; John 8:44); demons and spirits (Matt 8:28-32; 9:32-33; 12:25-28; Mark 1:23-26; 3:11-12; 5:1-13; 7:26-30; Luke 4:33-35; 9:1, 37-42; 10:17-20); angels (Matt 13:41, 49; 16:27; 18:10; 22:30; 24:31, 36; 25:31; 26:53; Mark 8:38; Luke 15:10; 16:22; 20:36; John 1:51; Rev 3:5); life after death, heaven, and hell (Matt 10:28; 22:29-32; 25:31-46; Mark 12:24-27; Luke 16:19-31; 20:34-38; 23:42-43; John 3:16; 5:24-29; 11:25-26; Rev 1:18); and OT miracles (Matt 12:39-40; Luke 4:25-27). Arthur Lindsley concludes, "It seems that he accepted the entire historical fabric of the Old Testament including those stories that are most troublesome to modern minds."[138]

Jesus held that the OT was directly relevant and foundational to who he was and his mission (see Luke 24:13-27). Thus, he taught that OT prophecies were genuinely from God and ultimately pertained to him (Matt 11:7-10; 12:40; 13:14; 26:24, 31; Mark 9:12-13; 14:21, 27; Luke 4:18-21; 7:24-27; 16:31; 18:31-33; 22:37; 24:25-27, 44-45; John 5:39; 13:18; 15:25; 17:12); he said that the Bible must be fulfilled in himself (Matt 5:17; 26:56; Luke 4:21; 22:37). In light of this, Josh McDowell and Don Stewart point out, "The conclusion is simple. If a person believes in Jesus Christ, he should be consistent and believe that the Old Testament and its accounts are correct. Many want to accept Jesus, but also want to reject a large portion of the Old Testament. This option is not available. Either Jesus knew what He was talking about or He did not. The evidence is clear that Jesus saw the Old Testament as being God's Word; His attitude toward it was nothing less than total trust."[139] Jesus also authorized the NT (see John 14:26; 15:26; 16:13-15; 1 Cor 2:10-13; 4:1; 14:37; Gal 1:11-16).[140] The same level of authority accorded the OT attaches to the NT (see John 20:31; Acts 2:42; 1 Cor 4:1; 14:37; 15:1-2; Eph 2:19-20; 2 Thess 2:15; 3:14; Heb 2:1-4; 2 Pet 3:15-16; 1 John 4:6; Rev 1:3; 22:18-19).

As is discussed throughout the rest of Part 1, although Jesus Christ was a man, he claimed to be more than just a man; he claimed to be God come to earth as a man. The issue of who Jesus is intimately bound up with the issue of the accuracy and trustworthiness of the Bible.[141] If Jesus is, in

---

138. Lindsley, "Christ and the Bible," n.p.

139. McDowell and Stewart, *Reasons*, 31; see also Wenham, "Christ's View," 3-36; Carter, "What Did Jesus"; Butt, "Believing."

140. See also Geisler, *Christian Apologetics*, 368-71; Corduan, "Why I Believe," 186-87; Gilbert, *Why Trust*, 134-42; Carter, "What Did Jesus."

141. Norman Geisler observes that Jesus' point in his quotation of Matt 19:4-6

fact, God come to earth as a man, then his identity as such establishes the accuracy and trustworthiness of the Bible in all its particulars, since he accepted the accuracy and trustworthiness of the Bible in all its particulars.[142] In other words, the identity of Jesus establishes an independent basis for the accuracy and trustworthiness of the Bible.

---

regarding marriage and divorce "is void unless the Old Testament quotation about Adam and Eve refers to actual historical persons of flesh and bone. . . . Here the very validity of Jesus' answer to the question about marriage and divorce depends on the reliability of there being a literal creation in the beginning of a male and a female whom God had joined together as 'one flesh.'" Geisler, *Christian Apologetics,* 358–59.

142. See Lindsley, "Christ and the Bible," n.p. ("At stake in the debate on the authority of Scripture is the authority of Christ Himself. Either we have a divine Christ and an infallible Bible, or a fallible Bible and no divine Christ.").

2

Jesus Christ Demonstrates that God Exists and Who He Is

VERY FEW MODERN SCHOLARS posit that Jesus Christ never existed. In addition to the eyewitness biblical accounts of his life, Gary Habermas notes that "at least seventeen non-Christian writings record more than fifty details concerning the life, teachings, death, and resurrection of Jesus, plus details concerning the earliest church."[1] Additionally, archaeological evidence corroborates the historical facts concerning the life of Jesus.[2] The available historical records provide a wealth of detail regarding Jesus' life. The primary sources, of course, are the multiple eyewitness accounts of the NT.

Jesus was a man.[3] But Jesus claimed to be more than just a man; he claimed to be the Messiah prophesied in the OT and, specifically, to be God

---

1. Habermas, "Why I Believe," 150.

2. See Habermas, *Ancient Evidence*, 152.

3. In the Bible we see Jesus had a human body of flesh, blood, and bone (e.g., Luke 22:44; John 1:14; 19:34; Rom 1:3; Phil 2:7; Col 2:9; 1 Tim 3:16; Heb 2:14; 10:5; 1 Pet 2:24; 1 John 1:1–3; 2 John 7); Jesus identified Himself as a "man" (John 8:40) and was recognized as a "man" by others (e.g., Matt 8:27; Mark 2:7; Luke 5:21; John 4:29; Acts 5:28; Rom 5:15; 1 Cor 15:21; Gal 2:20; Eph 5:2; Phil 2:8; 1 Tim 2:5).

Jesus experienced all of the normal human, bodily experiences: He grew (Luke 2:40, 52); he was hungry and thirsty and ate and drank (Matt 4:2; 21:18; 27:48; Mark 11:12; 15:36; Luke 4:2; John 4:6; 19:28–30); he became tired and slept (Matt 8:24; Mark 4:38; Luke 8:24); he experienced weariness and weakness (Matt 4:11; 27:32; Mark 15:21; Luke 23:26; John 4:6); he suffered (e.g., Matt 26:67; 27:26–31; Mark 14:65; 15:16–20; Luke 22:63–64; 23:11; John 19:1–3; Heb 5:8); he died and was buried (Matt 27:50, 57–66; Mark 15:37, 39, 42–47; Luke 23:46, 50–56; John 19:30–42; Acts 25:19; Rom 5:8; 1 Cor 15:3–4; Phil 2:8; Heb 2:14); when He died, out of His side came blood and water (John 19:34).

Jesus had normal human emotions and expressed them: He felt compassion (e.g., Matt 9:36; Mark 1:41; 6:34; 8:2; Luke 7:13); he loved (Mark 10:21; John 11:5, 36; 13:23);

himself come to earth as a man (Matt 12:1–8; John 5:16–18; 10:24–33; Rev 1:8). Beginning in this section, the rest of Part 1 will show that Jesus is exactly who he claimed to be.

JESUS EQUATED HIMSELF WITH GOD AND IDENTIFIED HIMSELF AS GOD

Muslim apologist Alhaj A. D. Ajijola correctly states, "God is comprehended from His attributes. If it is proved and granted that Jesus is Master of Divine attributes, one is justified in taking him for God."[4] Jesus is, indeed, "Master of Divine attributes," as the following words and deeds of Jesus demonstrate:

1. He claimed to be pre-existent (i.e., to have existed before he became a man) (John 8:58; 17:5, 24). He is in fact pre-existent (e.g., John 1:1–2, 14–15, 30; 8:58; Phil 2:6–7; Col 1:15–17; Heb 1:2).

2. He claimed to come from the Father in heaven (e.g., John 3:13; 6:38; 7:33; 8:23, 42; 16:5, 27–28). He in fact did so (e.g., John 3:31; 13:3; 1 Cor 15:47; 1 John 4:9–10, 14).

3. He claimed to be the only one who knows the Father and can reveal the Father (Matt 11:27; John 6:46; 17:25). That is true (John 1:18; Heb 1:1–2; 1 John 5:20).

4. He claimed to do nothing on his own but only what the Father showed him (John 5:19, 30; 6:38; 8:28; 12:49; 14:10). He in fact lived a perfectly holy life and is the perfect manifestation of the Father (e.g., Mark 1:24; Luke 1:35; 23:22, 40–41, 47; John 5:30; 8:29, 46; 2 Cor 5:21; Col 1:15, 19; 2:9; Heb 1:3; 3:2; 4:15; 7:26; 9:14; 1 Pet 1:19; 2:22).

5. The Bible says that God sends the prophets (2 Chron 36:15; Jer 26:5; Luke 11:49–51). To show that he is God come to earth, Jesus said that He was the one who was sending the prophets (Matt 23:34–35).

---

he got angry (Matt 21:12–13; Mark 3:5; 11:15–17; Luke 19:45–46; John 2:13–16); he felt sorrow (Matt 26:38); he marveled (Matt 8:10; Mark 6:6); he rejoiced and experienced joy (Luke 10:21; John 13:11); he was moved and troubled in spirit and experienced grief, agony, and distress (Matt 26:37–38; Mark 3:5; 14:33–34; Luke 22:44; John 11:33, 38; 12:27; 13:21); he wept (Luke 19:41; John 11:35; Heb 5:7); he experienced temptation (Matt 4:1–10; Mark 1:13; Luke 4:1–13; Heb 2:18; 4:15).

4. Ajijola, *The Myth*, 20.

6. He claimed to send and baptize with the Holy Spirit (Luke 24:49; John 15:26; 16:7; 20:22). He in fact does so (Matt 3:11; Mark 1:8; Luke 3:16; John 1:33; Acts 1:8; 2:1–21).

7. He knows and can foretell the future (e.g., Matt 12:40; 16:21; Mark 8:31; John 2:18–22; Acts 1:5, 8).

8. He said and demonstrated that he was the Lord of the Sabbath. The Pharisees claimed that Jesus' disciples were guilty of breaking the Sabbath because they picked heads of grain on the Sabbath. Jesus answered that his disciples were innocent precisely *because* Jesus is the Son of Man and therefore is Lord of the Sabbath (Matt 12:1–8; Mark 2:23–28; Luke 6:1–5). By saying that, Jesus was asserting his "superiority over the Sabbath and, hence, of the authority to abrogate or transform the Sabbath law."[5] This amounts to a claim to being equal to God because the Sabbath was part of the Ten Commandments (the Decalogue), which was the law of God given by God Himself to Moses on Mount Sinai (Exod 20:1–17). In other words, only God could promulgate God's Law, and therefore only God is superior to God's Law and has the authority to change or break His Law. Jesus made a similar claim to have equality with God in John 5:17–18 when he healed a man on the Sabbath and told him to *"pick up your pallet and walk,"* in violation of Sabbath regulations. Thus, Jesus' claim to be "Lord of the Sabbath" relates not only to His own conduct, but also affects the conduct of others (i.e., made it lawful for the man to carry his pallet when that was prohibited). Consequently, Jesus' authority "stands even over the Decalogue."[6] He could do this because "He speaks with the same authority as the One who originally gave the law (cf. Mark 2:28, Luke 6:5)."[7]

9. He claimed the authority to forgive people of their sins (e.g., Matt 9:2–8; Mark 2:3–12; Luke 5:17–26; John 8:1–11). He, in fact, is the savior who alone can save people from their sins (e.g., Matt 1:21; Luke 2:11; John 1:29; 3:17; Acts 3:26; 4:12; Rom 5:1, 6–11; 10:9; 1 Cor 6:11; 2 Cor 5:18–21). C. S. Lewis noted the significance of Jesus' claim to forgive sins—any sins. We all understand that a person has the right and authority to forgive someone who has offended or hurt the forgiver personally; but what right or authority does someone have to forgive a person for treading on other men's toes and stealing

---

5. Moo, "Jesus and the Authority," 17.
6. Moo, "Jesus and the Authority," 29.
7. Ramm, *An Evangelical*, 43.

other men's money? "Yet this is what Jesus did. He told people that their sins were forgiven, and never waited to consult all the other people whom their sins had undoubtedly injured. He unhesitatingly behaved as if He was the party chiefly concerned, the person chiefly offended in all offences. This makes sense only if He really was the God whose laws are broken and whose love is wounded in every sin. In the mouth of any speaker who is not God, these words would imply what I can only regard as silliness and conceit unrivalled by any other character in history."[8]

Indeed, when Jesus told a crippled man in the presence of Jewish leaders, *"Son, your sins are forgiven"* (Mark 2:5; see also Matt 9:2), the Jewish leaders recognized the significance of this and reasoned to themselves, *"Why does this man speak that way? He is blaspheming; who can forgive sins but God alone?"* (Mark 2:7; see also Matt 9:3)

10. He claimed to have the power to give people eternal life (John 3:16; 4:14; 5:25–29, 40; 6:27; 17:1–3; Rev 1:18). He in fact does so (Rom 6:23; 2 Tim 1:10; 1 John 5:11–13, 20).

11. He claimed to be the author of life itself (John 11:25). He in fact is (John 1:4; 5:26; Rev 1:18).

12. He claimed to have all authority (e.g., Matt 11:27; 28:18; Mark 14:62; Luke 10:22; John 17:1–3). He in fact has all authority and rules as King of Kings and Lord of Lords (e.g., Luke 1:32–33; John 3:31; 13:3; Acts 2:30–36; Eph 1:20–22; Phil 2:9–11; Col 2:10; Heb 1:3; 1 Pet 3:22; Rev 1:5; 17:14; 19:11–16).

13. He says He will judge the world (e.g., Matt 7:21–23; 16:27; 25:31–46; John 5:22, 27–29; Rev 22:12). He in fact will do so (e.g., Matt 3:12; Acts 10:42; 17:31; Rom 2:16; 1 Cor 4:4–5; 2 Cor 5:10).

14. Jesus equated and identified himself with God in general (e.g., Mark 9:37; Luke 22:69–70; John 5:17–23; 10:30, 34–38; 14:6–11; 17:21–23). He said that whatever he taught came from God and had absolute and final authority (Matt 5:21–48; 7:24–26; 24:35; John 5:24; 8:26–28; 12:48–50). He said that he does in like manner whatever the Father does (John 5:19); all will honor him even as they honor the Father, and to not honor him is to not honor the Father who sent him (John 5:23); only he has seen the Father (John 6:46); to know him is to know the Father (John 8:19); he and the Father are one (John 10:30); to believe in him is to believe in the one who sent him (John

---

8. Lewis, *Mere Christianity*, 55.

12:44); to see him is to see the Father who sent him (John 12:45; 14:9); and to hate him is to hate the Father (John 15:23).[9]

The magnitude of the claims Jesus made about himself is astounding. The magnitude of Jesus' claim to be God is enhanced by the context: Jesus was not a pantheist who held that that God is all and all is God. He was a first-century Jew who held that God was a being different from and outside the world, who made the world, and that to worship any human being as God was blasphemy. The magnitude of the claims themselves, made in that context, should cause any reasonable person to seriously investigate the truth of who Jesus is. This is particularly the case since, although anyone can claim to be God, and a few people (generally "cranks") have done so, there is nothing of the "crank" about Jesus. He has persuaded billions of people from all walks of life, education, and position, throughout the world, over the last 2000 years, that he is exactly who he claimed to be. Of course, billions of people could all be wrong in their conclusion. But that level of acceptance should at least raise the issue that there are good reasons why so many people, in so many places, and for so long have accepted Jesus' claims. Further, any reasonable person should seriously investigate the truth of who Jesus is because, if he is right, then one's eternal destiny hangs on one's answer to the question of who Jesus is and what that entails for our lives.

In light of Jesus' first-century Jewish context and his conception of the nature of who God is, C. S. Lewis summarizes the significance of the above claims by Jesus,

> A man who was merely a man and said the sort of things Jesus said would not be a great moral teacher. He would either be a lunatic—on a level with the man who says he is a poached egg—or else he would be the Devil of Hell. You must make your choice. Either this man was, and is, the Son of God; or else a madman or something worse. You can shut Him up for a fool, you can spit at Him and kill Him as a demon; or you can fall at His feet and call Him Lord and God. But let us not come with any patronizing

---

9. In addition to all of the above, Jesus demonstrated his deity by performing multiple, public miracles or "signs." He miraculously healed people (e.g., Matt 8:1–17; Mark 2:1–12; Luke 4:38–40; John 4:46–53); raised the dead (Luke 7:11–17; 8:40–56; John 11:1–16); cast out demons (e.g., Matt 8:28–34; Mark 1:23–28, 34, 39; Luke 4:31–36, 41); gave others authority over spirits and diseases (Matt 10:1; Mark 6:7; Luke 9:1; 10:17–19); could read minds (e.g., Matt 9:4; Mark 2:8; Luke 5:22; John 13:10–11); miraculously fed multitudes of people (e.g., Matt 14:13–21; Mark 8:1–9); could walk on water (Matt 14:22–33; Mark 6:45–51; John 6:16–21); caused others to walk on water (Matt 14:28–31); had authority over nature and the weather (e.g., Matt 8:23–27; Mark 4:35–41; Luke 8:22–25); and could turn water into wine (John 2:1–11).

nonsense about His being a great moral teacher. He has not left that open to us. He did not intend to.[10]

JESUS' SINLESS LIFE IS EVIDENCE OF HIS DEITY

John Stott points out, "What Christians call sin is a congenital disease that is endemic throughout the human race. We are all born with its infection in our nature."[11] Sundiata observes an important corollary of this, namely, that even when we do not actively sin, we still have the inclination to do so. "In contrast, God does not have such inclinations. Therefore, if God lived among men as a man, then the one thing that would attract attention to Him and distinguish Him from others would be the perfect life He would live, because God cannot sin."[12]

Of all people who have ever lived, Jesus alone lived a perfect and sinless life.[13] Jesus himself said he was without sin (John 8:46; see also John 8:1–11) and only did what the Father showed him (John 5:19, 30; 6:38; 8:28; 12:49; 14:10). This is best corroborated by the testimony of his enemies

---

10. Lewis, *Mere Christianity*, 55–56; see also Lewis, "What are We," 157–58.

The validity of Lewis's "trilemma" (i.e., Jesus' claim confronts us with only three possibilities: he was either a liar, or insane, or was, indeed, the Son of God) is indicated by the speciousness of Richard Dawkins' positing a fourth possibility, "that Jesus was honestly mistaken." Dawkins, *The God Delusion*, 92. A person cannot be "honestly mistaken" if he believes and announces himself to be God Almighty, creator of heaven and earth! Only severe mental illness would lead a person to say such a thing (assuming he was not consciously lying) unless, of course, he was telling the truth about himself.

11. Stott, *Basic Christianity*, 46.

12. Sundiata, *Look Behind*, 201.

13. This is acknowledged even by the Qur'an and Muslims. Q. 19:19 says an angel announced to Mary that, although she was a virgin, she would be given "*a holy son*" (Ali), "*a faultless son*" (Pickthall), "*a righteous son*" (Hilali-Khan), "*a boy most pure*" (Arberry; see also Sahih, Shakir, Sarwar, Haleem). Abd al-Masih states, "The Muslim scholars al-Tabari, al-Baidawi, and al-Zamakhshari agreed that the expression 'most pure' means blameless, guiltless and sinless. Before Christ was born, divine inspiration declared that the one who was going to be born out of the spirit of God would always live pure, without a single sin. There was no need to purify His heart, for He was holy in Himself. The Son of Mary did not hear the Word of God only; He was it. There was no difference between His actions and His words. He remained blameless and without." Al-Masih, *A Question*, 13. Sayyid Abul A'la Mawdudi concludes, "God endowed Jesus with a pure, impeccable soul. He was therefore an embodiment of truth, veracity, righteousness, and excellence." A'la Mawdudi, *Towards Understanding*, Q. 4:171n.213. The uniqueness of Jesus is highlighted by Muslim professor Mahmoud Ayoub: "Jesus is therefore free from the taint of evil and impurity. . . . This purity, which Adam had till he was touched by Satan's finger and thus lost it, now remains exemplified by Jesus alone." Ayoub, "Towards an Islamic," 93.

(who had no motive to acknowledge his sinlessness, but who had every motive to discover his faults, sins, and errors and denigrate his character) and the testimony of those who knew him best (who were, therefore, in the best position to observe his "real" character that he demonstrated out of the public eye). With respect to his enemies, in John 8 Jesus had a lengthy confrontation with Jewish leaders who opposed him. He asked them, *"Which one of you convicts me of sin?"* (John 8:46) Although they accused him of being a Samaritan and of having a demon, and tried to stone him for making himself out to be God, no one could accuse him of sin. After he betrayed Jesus, Judas returned the money he had been given and told the Jewish leaders, *"I have sinned by betraying innocent blood"* (Matt 27:4). Pontius Pilate twice said, *"I find no guilt in this man"* (Luke 23:4, 14). At his crucifixion, one of those being crucified with him said, *"We are suffering justly, for we are receiving what we deserve for our deeds; but this man has done nothing wrong"* (Luke 23:41). The centurion in charge of the crucifixion concluded, *"Certainly this man was innocent"* (Luke 23:47) and *"Truly this was the Son of God!"* (Matt 27:54).

Those who knew Jesus best, and therefore were in the best position to know the truth, likewise stated that Jesus lived a perfectly holy life and is the perfect manifestation of the Father. Peter called Jesus *"a lamb unblemished and spotless"* (1 Pet 1:19) and added that he *"committed no sin, nor was any deceit found in his mouth"* (1 Pet 2:22). John called him *"Jesus Christ the righteous"* (1 John 2:1, 29; 3:7) and added, *"In Him there is no sin"* (1 John 3:5). The moral difference between Jesus and others was recognized early-on. In Luke 5, Peter and his companions had fished all night without success. Jesus told them to put out into the deep water and let down their nets again. When they did so, they then caught a great quantity of fish. Luke 5:8 reports, *"But when Simon Peter saw that, he fell down at Jesus' feet, saying, 'Go away from me Lord, for I am a sinful man, O Lord!'"* As he was dying, Jesus said of the very people who were killing him, *"Father, forgive them; for they do not know what they are doing"* (Luke 23:34). Jesus was utterly selfless. As John Stott concludes, "Jesus was sinless because he was selfless. Such selflessness is love. And God is love."[14]

JESUS CLAIMED TO HAVE A UNIQUE RELATIONSHIP WITH GOD THE FATHER

In Matt 7:21; 10:32-33; 11:27; 12:50; 16:17; 18:10, 19; 20:23; 25:34; 26:39, 42, 53; Luke 2:49; 10:22; 22:29; 24:49; John 2:16; 5:17, 43; 6:32, 40; 8:19, 38,

---

14. Stott, *Basic Christianity*, 55.

49, 54; 10:18, 25, 29, 37; 14:2, 7, 20, 21, 23; 15:1, 8, 10, 15, 23, 24; 20:17; Rev 2:27; 3:5, 21 Jesus indicated his special relationship with God the Father by calling him *"My Father."* Jesus did not refer to God as *"our Father,"* which He taught His disciples to say when praying to God (Matt 6:9; see also Luke 11:2; Rom 1:7; 1 Cor 1:3; 2 Cor 1:2; Gal 1:3; Eph 1:2; Phil 1:2; Col 1:2; 2 Thess 1:1; Phlm 3). Rather, Jesus addressed the Father directly, using the Aramaic word "Abba," a term of intimate, personal affection (Mark 14:62). Although there are very rare instances of other Jews *describing* God as Abba, "we have no evidence that others before Jesus *addressed* God as Abba."[15] Rom 8:15 and Gal 4:6 indicate that Jesus taught His disciples to use his own distinctive address of God as Abba. That unique form of address shows that "the primitive church was aware that in this form of address to God it had a distinctive privilege which it owed to Jesus. In that case it was Jesus' own relationship to God as Abba which he shared with his disciples: *their sonship derived from his own.*"[16] It was Jesus' calling God *"my Father"* that caused the Jews to try to kill him for blasphemy. They recognized that when Jesus called God *"my Father"* he *"was calling God His own Father, making Himself equal with God"* (John 5:18; see also John 8:38–59).

Similarly, Jesus said, *"I and the Father are one"* (John 10:30). D. A. Carson explains this, "The word for "one" is the neuter *hen,* not the masculine *heis:* Jesus and his Father are not one person, as the masculine would suggest, for then the *distinction* between Jesus and God already introduced in [John] 1:1b would be obliterated, and John could not refer to Jesus praying to his Father, being commissioned by and obedient to his Father, and so on. Rather, Jesus and his Father are perfectly one in action, in what they do: what Jesus does, the Father does, and vice versa."[17] Jesus' statement about his being "one" with the Father followed his statement in John 10:28 that *"I give eternal life to them [his sheep] . . . and no one will snatch them out of My hand."* John Gilchrist notes, "Who but God alone can give not only life but *eternal life?*"[18] Jesus' statement about his oneness with the Father is not qualified or limited but "clearly means 'one in all things' and Jesus would hardly have made such a striking claim without qualifying it if he had not intended to convey the impression that there was an absolute oneness between the Father and the Son and that he therefore possessed deity."[19] That is exactly how the Jews understood Jesus' claim; they wanted to kill him for

---

15. Bauckham, "The Sonship of the Historical Jesus," 249, emph. added.
16. Bauckham, "The Sonship of the Historical Jesus," 248, emph. added.
17. Carson, *The Gospel,* 394.
18. Gilchrist, *Christ in Islam,* 14, emph. in orig.
19. Gilchrist, *Christ in Islam,* 14.

blasphemy, *"because you, being a man, make Yourself out to be God"* (John 10:33). Further, Jesus could not make the claim about no one being able to snatch his sheep out of his hand, which is also said about the Father in John 10:29, unless he possessed the same power to preserve his followers that his Father possessed. In short, Jesus was claiming that he was in the possession of absolute, eternal power.

The intimate union between Christ and the Father was made clear on another occasion. In John 14:6–14 the following interchange took place between Jesus and his disciples Thomas and Philip:

> *⁶ Jesus said to him, "I am the way, and the truth, and the life; no one comes to the Father but through Me. ⁷ If you had known Me, you would have known My Father also; from now on you know Him, and have seen Him." ⁸ Philip said to Him, "Lord, show us the Father, and it is enough for us." ⁹ Jesus said to him, "Have I been so long with you, and yet you have not come to know Me, Philip? He who has seen Me has seen the Father; how can you say, 'Show us the Father'? ¹⁰ Do you not believe that I am in the Father, and the Father is in Me? The words that I say to you I do not speak on My own initiative, but the Father abiding in Me does His works. ¹¹ Believe Me that I am in the Father and the Father is in Me; . . . ¹³ Whatever you ask in My name, that will I do, so that the Father may be glorified in the Son.¹⁴ If you ask Me anything in My name, I will do it."*

Jesus' comments describe the complete unity between himself and the Father; indeed, "it is precisely this degree of unity that ensures Jesus reveals God to us."[20]

JESUS CALLS HIMSELF THE "SON OF GOD" AND ACCEPTS TO BE CALLED THE "SON OF GOD" BY OTHERS

Jesus called himself the "Son" to describe his unique relationship with God the Father. In Matt 11:27 (Luke 10:22) Jesus said, *"All things have been handed over to Me by My Father; and no one knows the Son except the Father; nor does anyone know the Father except the Son, and anyone to whom the Son wills to reveal Him."* What Jesus is saying is that he is the *only one* who truly knows God, and *the only way to know God* is through him! Note that it is the *Son's* will which must be exercised if anyone is to know the Father. That is

---

20. Carson, *The Gospel*, 494.

a stunning claim which must be taken seriously. By making this statement, Jesus is claiming divinity for himself and is placing himself far above anyone else. In telling his disciples to make disciples of all the nations, Jesus told them to baptize believers *"in the name of the Father and the Son and the Holy Spirit"* (Matt 28:19). Again, he is calling himself the "Son" in a unique relationship with the Father. Similarly, in John 3:16–18 Jesus called himself the *"only begotten Son,"* the *"Son,"* and *"the only begotten Son of God."*[21] In connection with the works he did, Jesus called himself the *"Son of God"* in John 5:25; 10:36; 11:4. The context was his doing what only God has the power to do (raise the dead). In the parable of the vineyard (Matt 21:33–46; Mark 12:1–12; Luke 20:9–19), Jesus contrasted himself with all the prophets who had been sent before, predicted his own death, indicated that he was the only way of salvation, and said that the kingdom was not limited to the Jews. In the parable, God the Father sent prophets to Israel who had mistreated them; so at last he decided to send his own Son (Jesus). N. T. Wright correctly concludes, that "once the father has sent the son to the vineyard, he can send nobody else. To reject the son is to reject the last chance."[22]

Second, *God Himself* on more than one occasion called Jesus "His Son" in circumstances that can only be referring to Jesus' divine Sonship. At Jesus' baptism *"a voice out of heaven said, 'This is My beloved Son, in whom I am well-pleased"* (Matt 3:17; Mark 1:11; Luke 3:22). Again, when Jesus was transfigured before three of His disciples, *"a voice out of the cloud said, 'This is My beloved Son, with whom I am well-pleased; listen to Him!'"* (Matt 17:5; Mark 9:7; Luke 9:35).

Third, the *angel Gabriel* called Jesus the *"Son of God."* When announcing to Mary that Jesus was to be born, Gabriel stated, *"He will be great and will be called the Son of the Most High"* (Luke 1:32). When Mary then asked *"How can this be, since I am a virgin?"* (Luke 1:34), Gabriel replied, *"The Holy Spirit will come upon you, and the power of the Most High will overshadow*

---

21. Since ancient texts did not use quotation marks or similar markers, there is dispute as to whether or not John 3:16–21 are Jesus' words (i.e., the end of his answer to Nicodemus that began in v. 10) or are a comment by the writer of the Gospel of John. See Carson, *The Gospel*, 203–4; Burge, "John," 851.

22. Wright, *Jesus and the Victory*, 362, 365. This same point is made in Heb 1:1–2 which states, *"God, after He spoke long ago to the fathers in the prophets in many portions and in many ways, in these last days has spoken to us in His Son, whom He appointed heir of all things, through whom also He made the world."* In the book of Revelation, Jesus again equates himself with God. In Rev 1:8 God says, *"I am the Alpha and the Omega."* In Rev 1:17 Jesus then says, *"I am the first and the last."* In Rev 21:6 God says, *"I am the Alpha and the Omega, the beginning and the end."* In Rev 22:13 Jesus then concludes, *"I am the Alpha and the Omega, the first and the last, the beginning and the end."* All of these statements are modeled on Isa 44:6; 48:12 (*"I am the first, and I am the last"*) which apply to God (which Jesus reapplies to himself).

Jesus Christ Demonstrates that God Exists and Who He Is 41

you; and for that reason the holy Child shall be called the Son of God" (Luke 1:35). In that context, Gabriel's reference to *"the Son of God"* can only be referring to Jesus' divine Sonship.

Fourth, Satan and demons called Jesus the *"Son of God"* in circumstances that can only be referring to Jesus' divine Sonship. In Matt 4:3, 7 (Luke 4:3, 9) Satan, in tempting Jesus, called him the *"Son of God."* Chamblin points out that "the devil, far from questioning Jesus' sonship, capitalizes upon it: '*Since* [a better translation than 'if'] you are the Son of God."[23] Jesus did not dispute being called the "Son of God." Instead, He simply responded to Satan by quoting Scripture. In Matt 8:29 (see also Mark 5:7; Luke 4:41; 8:28) Jesus had cast out demons and they cried out, *"What business do we have with each other, Son of God? Have you come here to torment us before the time?"* Joe Kapolyo states, "The demons had no problems recognizing that Jesus was the king in whom the kingdom of God had come, although not yet in its fullness. So they addressed him as the *Son of God* and as the judge who would put an end to their activities."[24]

Fifth, other people called Jesus the *"Son of God"* in circumstances indicating his divine Sonship. In Matt 14:33, Jesus had just finished walking on water, commanding and empowering Peter to walk on water, and controlling nature; then *"those who were in the boat worshipped Him, saying 'You are certainly God's Son!'"* Blomberg observes that "in demonstrating his mastery over wind and waves, Jesus clearly is exercising prerogatives previously reserved for Yahweh himself (cf. Job 9:8; Ps. 77:19)."[25] Note that being called *"God's Son"* is coupled with the disciples "worshipping" Jesus—and Jesus does not rebuke them either for worshipping him or for calling him God's Son. Instead, he accepts the title and the worship. In John 11:27, Martha confessed her faith that Jesus is *"the Christ, the Son of God, even He who comes into the world."* Carson comments, "Her confession is neither mere repetition, nor the pious but distracted and meandering response of someone who has not followed the argument. Her reply carries the argument forward, for she holds that the one who is 'the resurrection and the life' [Jesus' statement about himself in John 11:25] must be such by virtue of the fact that he is God's promised Messiah."[26]

---

23. Chamblin, "Matthew," 727; see also Kapolyo, "Matthew," 1115.
24. Kapolyo, "Matthew," 1128.
25. Blomberg, *Gospels*, 50.
26. Carson, *The Gospel*, 414.

JESUS' USE OF THE TERM "SON OF MAN" IS A REFERENCE TO HIS DIVINITY

Jesus is called the *"Son of Man"* approximately 80 times in the Gospels; it is his most frequent description of Himself. The *"Son of Man"* is both human and divine, just as Jesus is both human and divine. The phrase *"Son of Man"* alludes to Dan 7:13–14 (*"I kept looking in the night visions, and behold, with the clouds of heaven One like a Son of Man was coming, and He came up to the Ancient of Days and was presented before Him. And to Him was given dominion, glory and a kingdom, that all the peoples, nations and men of every language might serve Him. His dominion is an everlasting dominion which will not pass away; and His kingdom is one which will not be destroyed."*). In Rev 1:13–14 John received a revelation from Jesus, who is described as *"one like a son of man . . . [whose] head and His hair were white like wool, like snow."* Those images are taken from Daniel's vision in Dan 7:9, 13. However, in Daniel's vision (Dan 7:9) it was *"the Ancient of Days"* whose *"vesture was like white snow and the hair of His head like pure wool."* Given this context, "John sees 'one like a son of man' who is distinguished from and identified with the Ancient of Days—a mysterious combination but consistent with the fact that he lays claim to the title 'the first and the last' ([Rev] 1:17), by which God proclaimed his divine eternity (Isa. 41:4; 44:6; 48:12). The Son of Man is God, infinite in wisdom and holiness."[27]

Whenever Jesus used the term *"Son of Man"* he was making an assertion that he was, in fact, God come to earth *as a man*. In John 3:13 he explicitly said, *"No one has ascended into heaven, but He who descended from heaven: the Son of Man."* Similarly, in John 6:62 Jesus said, *"What then if you see the Son of Man ascending to where He was before?"* Thus, Jesus both came from heaven and returned to heaven, and his reference to *"where He was before"* affirms his pre-existence.[28] In short, he was no mere man.

We see Jesus claiming to be deity in his other references to the *"Son of Man."* For example, Jesus' claim that *"the Son of Man has authority on earth to forgive sins"* (Matt 9:6; Mark 2:10; Luke 5:24) is a claim to be God *come to earth as a man*, because only God has the authority to forgive sins; yet here Jesus is claiming to forgive sins on his own authority.[29] In Matt 12:8; Mark 2:28; Luke 6:5 Jesus said, *"The Son of Man is Lord of the Sabbath."* As was discussed above, by saying that, Jesus was claiming to be God Himself. In Luke 9:58 Jesus said, *"The Son of Man did not come to destroy men's lives, but*

---

27. Johnson, *Triumph*, 59.
28. See Carson, *The Gospel*, 301.
29. See the quote from C. S. Lewis, *Mere Christianity*, 55 above.

to save them" (see also Luke 19:9–10). The granting of salvation to anyone is something that only God can do. In Matt 13:41–42 Jesus said, *"The Son of Man will send forth His angels, and they will gather out of His kingdom all stumbling blocks, and those who commit lawlessness, and will throw them into the furnace of fire; in that place there will be weeping and gnashing of teeth."* This refers to the final judgment. Similarly, in Matt 16:27 Jesus says that *"the Son of Man is going to come in the glory of His Father with His angels, and will then repay every man according to his deeds."* J. Knox Chamblin points out that "as in Daniel 7:13–14, the Son of man is revealed as divine (the angels are *his*, not just the Father's, v. 27)."[30] Sending the angels and rendering eternal judgment are the acts of God. That is the same context in which Jesus calls himself the *"Son of Man"* in Matt 24:30–31; 24:42–44; 25:31–46; Mark 8:38; 13:26; Luke 9:22–26; 12:8–9; John 9:35–39.

In Matt 16:13–17, John 1:49–51, and John 5:19–29 the *"Son of Man"* is equated with the *"Son of God."* In Matt 24:42–44 the *"Son of Man"* is specifically equated with the "Lord." In Matt 25:31–46 the *"Son of Man"* is equated with the "King" who *"will sit on His glorious throne"* and judge all the people of the earth, sending some to hell and others to eternal life. That, of course, can only refer to God. Thus, again, when Jesus calls himself the *"Son of Man"* he is equating himself with God Almighty. In Matt 19:27–28 Jesus says that, *"in the regeneration [or, renewal of all things] when the Son of Man will sit on his glorious throne, you also shall sit upon twelve thrones, judging the twelve tribes of Israel"* (see also Luke 22:29–30). The "throne" can only be the throne of God. In John 6:27 Jesus says that people should work for *"the food which endures to eternal life, which the Son of Man will give to you."* Again, eternal life is something that only God can give, and here Jesus is saying that he will give it (see also John 6:40, 53–54).

Finally, at his trial before the high priest in Matt 26:63–65 (Mark 14:61–63; Luke 22:66–71), the following interchange took place: *"The high priest said to Him, 'I adjure You by the living God, that You tell us whether You are the Christ, the Son of God.' Jesus said to him, 'You have said it yourself; nevertheless I tell you, hereafter you will see the Son of Man sitting at the right hand of Power and coming on the clouds of heaven.' Then the high priest tore his robes and said, 'He has blasphemed! What further need do we have of witnesses? Behold, you have now heard the blasphemy.'"* Craig Blomberg discusses why Jesus' claim to be the *"Son of Man"* in this context is so significant:

> This "Son of Man" saying, rather than the claim that he was some kind of messiah, is what would have led the high priest

---

30. Chamblin, "Matthew," 743.

to tear his garments and proclaim that Jesus had blasphemed (26:65). Alleging messiahship was no capital offense; otherwise, the Jews could never have received a messiah! But claiming to be the exalted, heavenly Son of Man, one who was Lord and next to the Father himself in heaven, transgressed the boundaries of what most of the Jewish leaders deemed permissible for mere mortals.[31]

JESUS' OPPONENTS RECOGNIZED THAT HE WAS CLAIMING TO BE GOD AND SOUGHT TO KILL HIM FOR BLASPHEMY BECAUSE OF HIS CLAIM TO BE GOD'S UNIQUE SON

In Matt 9:2–3; 26:63–66; Mark 2:6–7; 14:61–64; Luke 5:20–21; 22:66–71; John 5:17–18; 8:53, 59; 10:30–33, 39; 19:7 Jesus' opponents recognized that Jesus was claiming to be God's unique Son and sought to kill him because of that claim. The law of Moses prescribed the death penalty for blasphemy (Lev 24:14, 16, 23; see John 19:7). John 5:18 says that the Jews were seeking to kill Jesus *"because He not only was breaking the Sabbath [by healing a man on the Sabbath], but also was calling God His own Father, making Himself equal with God."* Muslim commentator and translator of the Qur'an Yusuf Ali admits that "Jesus was charged by the Jews with blasphemy as claiming to be God or the son of God."[32] Bernard Ramm points out, "At this point, from the human perspective, there is only one thing for Jesus to do. He ought to deny the charge and give some reason why he healed the man on a Sabbath day. This he does not do. He says that the Jews were right. He is equal with God. In the verses that follow Jesus specifies the kind of things only God can do but yet that he can do. Hence he is equal with the Father."[33]

JESUS IS SPECIFICALLY CALLED "GOD" OR "LORD" ON MULTIPLE OCCASIONS THROUGHOUT THE NT

On more than one occasion the NT applies to Jesus the name which is unambiguously exclusive to the one God, namely, Yahweh [YHWH]. Heb 1:4 states that Jesus was exalted to the right hand of God and, as such, *"became as much better than the angels, as He has inherited a more excellent name*

---

31. Blomberg, "Matthew," 93.
32. Ali, *The Meaning*, Q. 3:55n.395.
33. Ramm, *An Evangelical*, 43.

than they." Richard Bauckham observes that this can only refer to the divine name of God, *"the name which is above every name"* (Phil 2:9), which "was bestowed on Jesus when God exalted him to the highest position."[34] Connected with this is the use of the phrase *"call on the name of the Lord."* In the OT, the phrase means to call on God by his name, YHWH (see Gen 4:26; 1 Kgs 18:24; Ps 80:18; Isa 12:4; Joel 2:32; Zeph 3:9; Zech 13:9), but the NT applies that phrase to Jesus (see Acts 2:21; 9:14; Rom 10:13; 1 Cor 1:2; 2 Tim 2:22). Other examples of Jesus' specifically being called "Lord" or "God" include the following:

- Matt 1:23: *"Behold, the virgin shall be with child and shall bear a Son, and they shall call His name Immanuel," which translated means, "God with us."*
- Matt 7:22–23: *Many will say to me on that day, "Lord, Lord . . ." Then I will declare to them, "I never knew you; depart from Me, you who practice lawlessness."*
- Luke 1:42–43: *And she [Elizabeth] cried out with a loud voice and said, "Blessed are you [Mary] among women, and blessed is the fruit of your womb! And how has it happened to me that the mother of my Lord would come to me?"*
- John 1:1, 14: *In the beginning was the Word, and the Word was with God, and the Word was God. . . . And the Word became flesh and dwelt among us, and we saw His glory, glory as of the only begotten from the father, full of grace and truth.*
- John 20:28: After being told to reach with his finger to feel the holes in Jesus' hands and side, Thomas said, *"My Lord and my God!"* Jesus did not rebuke Thomas for blasphemy but accepted those titles of deity.
- Acts 7:59–60: *They went on stoning Stephen as he called on the Lord and said, "Lord Jesus, receive my spirit!" Then falling on his knees, he cried out with a loud voice, "Lord, do not hold this sin against them!" Having said this, he fell asleep.*
- Acts 10:36: *The word which He sent to the sons of Israel, preaching peace through Jesus Christ (He is Lord of all).*
- Acts 16:31, 34: *They said, "Believe in the Lord Jesus, and you will be saved, you and your household." . . . And he brought them into his house and set food before them, and rejoiced greatly, having believed in God with his whole household.*

34. Bauckham, *God Crucified*, 34.

- Acts 20:28: *Be on guard for yourselves and for all the flock, among which the Holy Spirit has made you overseers, to shepherd the church of God which He purchased with His own blood.*

- Rom 9:5: *Whose [referring to the Israelites] are the fathers, and from whom is the Christ according to the flesh, who is over all, God blessed forever. Amen.*

- 1 Cor 2:7-8: *But we speak God's wisdom in a mystery, the hidden wisdom which God predestined before the ages to our glory; the wisdom which none of the rulers of this age has understood; for if they had understood it they would not have crucified the Lord of glory.*

- 1 Cor 11:26: *For as often as you eat this bread and drink the cup, you proclaim the Lord's death until He comes.*

- Phil 2:5-7: *Have this attitude in yourselves which was also in Christ Jesus, who, although He existed [lit. "being," hupárchōn] in the form [morphē] of God, did not regard equality with God a thing to be grasped, but emptied Himself, taking the form [morphē] of a bond-servant, and being made in the likeness of men.*[35]

- Col 2:9: *For in Him all the fullness of Deity dwells in bodily form.*

- Titus 2:13: *Looking for the blessed hope and the appearing of the glory of our great God and Savior, Christ Jesus.* In addition to being called "God," it is significant that Jesus is also called "Savior," because in the OT God specifically said, *"I, even I, am the Lord, and there is no savior besides Me"* (Isa 43:11).

- Heb 1:8: *But of the Son He says, "Your throne, O God, is forever and ever, and the righteous scepter is the scepter of His kingdom."*

- 2 Pet 1:1: *Simon Peter, a bond-servant and apostle of Jesus Christ, to those who have received a faith of the same kind as ours, by the righteousness of our God and savior, Jesus Christ.*

- 1 John 5:20: *And we know that the Son of God has come, and has given us understanding so that we may know Him who is true; and we are in Him who is true, in His Son Jesus Christ. This is the true God and eternal life.*

---

35. Zodhiates discusses the significance of the wording of these verses: "*Morphē* in Phil. 2:6-8 presumes an obj. [objective] reality. No one could be in the form (*morphē*) of God who was not God.... The fact that Jesus continued to be God during His state of humiliation is demonstrated by the pres. part. [present participle] *hupárchōn*, 'being' in the form of God. *Hupárchō* involves continuing to be that which was before." Zodhiates, *The Complete*, *morphē*, 997)

THE SAME NAMES, TITLES, AND OTHER ATTRIBUTES THAT ARE APPLIED TO GOD IN THE OT OR NT ARE APPLIED TO JESUS IN THE NT

Sometimes a passage which applied to God is alluded to or directly quoted as applying to Jesus (in the following table, [x, y, z] indicate direct quotes):[36]

Name/Title/Attribute	Applied to God	Applied to Jesus
I AM	Exod 3:13–14	John 8:24, 28, 58; 18:5–6
Lord	Isa 40:3[x]; 45:23–24[y]; Joel 2:32[z]	Mark 1:2–4[x]; Phil 2:10–11[y]; Acts 2:36; Rom 10:13[z]
God	Ps 45:6–7[x]	Heb 1:8–9[x]; John 1:1, 14, 18; 20:28; 2 Pet 1:1
First and Last	Isa 41:4; 44:6; 48:12	Rev 1:17; 2:8; 22:13
Alpha and Omega	Rev 1:8[x]; 21:5–6[x]	Rev 22:13[x]
Exalted above the heavens	Ps 57:5, 11; 108:5	Heb 7:26
Savior	Isa 43:3, 11; 1 Tim 4:10	Matt 1:21; Luke 2:11; John 4:42; Titus 2:13
Redeemer	Ps 130:7–8	1 Cor 1:30; Eph 1:7; Titus 2:13–14
Judge	Gen 18:25; Ps 50:4–6; 96:13	John 5:22; 2 Cor 5:10; 2 Tim 4:1
King	Ps 95:3	Rev 17:14; 19:16
King of Israel	Isa 43:15; 44:6; Zeph 3:15	John 1:49; 12:13
Holy	1 Sam 2:2; John 17:11	Acts 3:14; Heb 7:26
Good[37]	Ps 34:8	John 10:11
Light	Ps 27:1; Isa 60:20; Mic 7:8	John 1:4–5, 9; 3:19; 8:12; 9:5

---

36. Bickersteth, *The Trinity*, 24–90, provides overwhelming biblical data regarding the divinity of Christ and his equality with God; on pages 40–50 he lists 42 OT quotes regarding God that are applied in the NT to Jesus.

37. God's attribute of "goodness" indicates what Jesus was getting at when he asked the rich young man, *"Why do you call Me good? No one is good except God alone"* (Mark 10:18; Luke 18:19). He was not denying that he was God; rather, he was affirming his divinity by asking a rhetorical question. In effect, he was saying to the man, "Do you really know to whom you are speaking?" As Victor Babajide Cole puts it, "Jesus was not denying that he was 'good'. Rather, he was pressing the man to see the logical implication of addressing him as 'good', namely that he is God!" Cole, "Mark," 1189.

Name/Title/Attribute	Applied to God	Applied to Jesus
Rock	Deut 32:4; 2 Sam 22:32; Ps 89:26	1 Cor 10:4; 1 Pet 2:4–8
Husband	Isa 54:5; 62:5; Hos 2:16	Mark 2:18-19; 2 Cor 11:2; Rev 21:2
Shepherd	Ps 23:1; 80:1; Isa 40:11	John 10:11, 16; Heb 13:20; 1 Pet 2:25; 5:4
Creator	Gen 1:1; Ps 102:25–27^x; Isa 40:28	John 1:3, 10; Col 1:16; Heb 1:2, 10–12^x
Sustainer	Job 34:14-15; Ps 3:5; 2 Pet 3:7	Col 1:17; Heb 1:3
Giver of life	Deut 32:39; 1 Sam 2:6; Ps 36:9	John 5:22; 10:28; 11:25
Source of "living water"	Jer 2:13	John 4:10, 14; 7:37-38
Forgiver of sin	Exod 34:7; Isa 55:7; Dan 9:9	Matt 1:21; Mark 2:5; Acts 26:18; Col 2:13
The one who was pierced	Zech 12:10^x	John 19:37^x; Rev 1:7
Sovereign over all	Neh 9:6; Isa 44:24–27; 45:22–23^x	Matt 28:18; Eph 1:20-22; Phil 2:9–11^x; 3:21
Omniscient	Job 21:22; Ps 33:13–15	John 16:30; 21:17
Searches hearts & minds	1 Chron 28:9; Ps 7:9; 139:1-4, 23; Jer 17:10	Mark 2:8; John 2:24-25; Rev 2:23
Rewards according to people's deeds	Ps 62:12^x; Jer 17:10; 32:19	Matt 16:27^x; Rev 2:23

PROPHECIES AND STATEMENTS THAT PERTAIN TO GOD OR THE LORD IN THE OT ARE QUOTED AND APPLIED TO JESUS IN THE NT

- *I have set the Lord continually before me; because He is at my right hand, I will not be shaken.* (Ps 16:8; applied to Jesus in Acts 2:25)

- *Your throne, O God, is forever and ever; a scepter of uprightness is the scepter of Your kingdom.* (Ps 45:6; applied to Jesus in Heb 1:8)

- *Of old You founded the earth, and the heavens are the work of Your hands. Even they will perish, but You endure; and all of them will wear out like a garment; like clothing You will change them and they will be changed.* (Ps 102:25-26; applied to Jesus in Heb 1:10-12)

- *The stone which the builders rejected has become the chief corner stone.* (Ps 118:22; applied to Jesus in Acts 4:11)

- Isa 6:1–13: In Isa 6:5 Isaiah says, *"Woe is me, for I am ruined. . . . For my eyes have seen the King, the Lord of hosts."* In Isa 6:8–13 *"the voice of the Lord"* then commissions Isaiah to go and prophesy to the people of Israel. John 12:40 quotes Isa 6:10. John 12:41 then applies all of Isaiah 6 to Jesus by saying, *"These things Isaiah said because he saw His [Jesus'] glory, and he spoke of Him."*

- *Therefore the Lord Himself will give you a sign: Behold, a virgin will be with child and bear a son, and she will call His name Immanuel.* (Isa 7:14; applied to Jesus in Matt 1:22–23, which specifies that "Immanuel" means *"God with us"*)

- *It is the Lord of hosts whom you should regard as holy. And He shall be your fear, and He shall be your dread. Then He shall become a sanctuary; but to both the houses of Israel, a stone to strike and a rock to stumble over, And a snare and a trap for the inhabitants of Jerusalem.* (Isa 8:13–14; applied to Jesus in Rom 9:33; 1 Pet 2:8)

- *A voice is calling, "Clear the way for the Lord in the wilderness; make smooth in the desert a highway for our God."* (Isa 40:3; applied to Jesus in Matt 3:3; John 1:23)

- *My house will be called a house of prayer.* (Isa 56:7; applied by Jesus to Himself in Matt 21:13)

- *But as for you, Bethlehem Ephrathah, too little to be among the clans of Judah, from you One will go forth for Me to be ruler in Israel. His goings forth are from long ago, from the days of eternity.* (Mic 5:2; applied to Jesus in Matt 2:6. The language of the second sentence of Mic 5:2 is OT language that typically describes the eternal God in such passages as Ps 74:12; 90:2; 93:2; Isa 43:13; 63:16)

- *I will pour out on the house of David and on the inhabitants of Jerusalem, the Spirit of grace and of supplication, so that they will look on Me whom they have pierced; and they will mourn for Him, as one mourns for an only son, and they will weep bitterly over Him like the bitter weeping over a firstborn.* (Zech 12:10; applied to Jesus in John 19:37; Rev 1:7)

PEOPLE WORSHIPPED OR PRAYED TO JESUS AS GOD, AND JESUS ACCEPTED THAT WORSHIP

The Bible makes it absolutely clear that only God is to be worshipped (Exod 20:3–5; 34:14; Deut 4:19; 5:7–9; 8:19; 1 Kgs 9:6–7; Isa 42:8). Jesus himself specifically said that only God is to be worshipped (Matt 4:10; Luke 4:8). The worship of mere mortals or even angels is idolatrous and sinful (Exod 20:1–5; Deut 5:6–9; Rom 1:18–23). Jesus' disciples knew that. When Cornelius tried to worship Peter, Peter said, *"Stand up, I too am just a man"* (Acts 10:25–26). When the people in Lystra thought that Paul and Barnabas were two gods who had come to earth in human form and wanted to make sacrifices to them, Paul and Barnabas vehemently objected to this and said, *"We are also men of the same nature as you, and preach the gospel to you that you should turn from these vain things to a living God"* (Acts 14:11–18). That is the response that any monotheistic Jew would have and should have made to someone trying to worship him. Even the angels said, *"Do not do that. I am a fellow servant of yours"* when someone tried to worship them (Rev 19:10; 22:8–9).

Jesus alone was different. In Matt 2:11; 14:33; 28:9, 16–17; Luke 24:51–52; John 1:1–14; 5:22–23; 9:35–38; 20:28; Acts 2:36; 7:59–60; 20:28; Rom 9:3–5; Phil 2:5–11; Titus 2:13; Heb 1:5–10; 2 Pet 1:1; 1 John 2:23; Rev 5:1–14 people worshipped or prayed to Jesus as they would to God Himself. *Jesus accepted their worship.* The response of Jesus in accepting worship would be blasphemy and idolatry for anyone, even a prophet, if he were only a man. The fact that Jesus did not object, but accepted people's worshipping him, showed that he knew he was God who had come to earth as a man—because only by being God come to earth as a man could Jesus legitimately accept being worshipped.

In fact, the worship of Jesus was present long before the NT was even written. The universal worship of Jesus is stated in Phil 2:9–11, which is an early Christian creed that long pre-dated Paul's writing of the book of Philippians.[38] Phil 2:9–11 alludes to Isa 45:22–23 which pertains to the worship of Yahweh; this, again, shows that Jesus is equated with God.

These facts are highly significant for at least three reasons. First, it must never be forgotten that Christianity arose out of a Jewish context. At the time Jesus was on earth, Judaism sharply "distinguishing the one God absolutely from all other reality."[39] In other words, Judaism was as fiercely monotheistic as is Islam. The people who worshipped Jesus were first century

---

38. See the section in chapter 5, "The earliness of Christian creeds," below.
39. Bauckham, *God Crucified*, vii.

Jews, and the context in which they worshipped him was first century Judaism. In that context and among those people, to worship any individual was considered to be the height of blasphemy and sin. Yet they did so because Jesus had the credentials to prove to them that he was, in fact, God come to earth as a man.

Second, the last people on earth who are likely to worship someone as God are those closest to the person, i.e., family and close friends. The reason, of course, is that family and close friends know all about what the person is "really" like. They can see what a person tries to hide from the public; and they can see the unintentional "slips" of anger, pettiness, selfishness, and other character flaws that those who have more remote contact with a person cannot see. Yet those closest to Jesus worshipped him because they saw his true character, namely, that Jesus had no "slips" into anger, pettiness, selfishness, or other character flaws: he was in fact sinless in thought, word, and deed. Jesus had the character of God, because he was God come to earth as a man.

Third, although a few people throughout history may have persuaded small groups of generally marginalized people that they are "messiah"-like figures or have some aspect of divinity within them, only Jesus has convinced billions of people around the world, from all walks of life, including Jews and Muslims (who consider the worship of any individual to be blasphemy), and those who knew him best, that he is God. The only reasonable explanation for these facts is that Jesus is, in fact, God who came to earth as a man.

CONCLUSION

In *The Religions of Man,* Huston Smith observed that only two people—Buddha and Jesus—have so impressed others by the nature and quality of their lives that they "provoked this question: not 'Who are you?' with respect to name, origin, or ancestry, but '*What* are you?—what order of being do you belong to, what species do you represent?'"[40] When Buddha was approached with these questions, he specifically denied that he was a god, an angel, or a saint.[41] Jesus' response was the exact opposite. Jesus both asserted and demonstrated that he was, in fact, not just *a* god but *the* God come to earth as a man. And those who knew him first-hand, i.e., those who knew him best and from whom he could not hide his true character and identity, came to the conclusion that Jesus was indeed God come to earth

---

40. Smith, *The Religions,* 90.
41. Smith, *The Religions,* 90.

as a man—a conviction so firm that they risked and even gave their lives for that conviction. The highest possible view of Christ—identifying Jesus with God himself—was central to the Christian faith from the beginning, even before the Gospels were written. We know this because all four of the Gospels identify Jesus as God (see above). Richard Bauckham concludes, "The New Testament writers did not see their Jewish monotheistic heritage as in any way an obstacle to the inclusion of Jesus in the divine identity; they used its resources extensively in order precisely to include Jesus in the divine identity; and they saw in this inclusion of Jesus in the divine identity the fulfilment of the eschatological expectation of Jewish monotheism that the one God will be universally acknowledged as such in his universal rule over all things."[42]

Millions of people since Jesus' day have come to the same conclusion that Jesus is God who came to earth as a man—a conviction so firm that they likewise have risked or even given their lives for that conviction. Jesus' words, deeds, and character confront all of us with the same issue that confronted the first century Jews: Who is Jesus? Jesus' claims are so profound that everyone needs to look at the evidence and make a choice because, if Jesus' claims are true, then to reject Jesus *as Lord* is to reject God and thereby to miss life itself, but to have Jesus as Lord is to have God the Father as well and thereby to have eternal life (John 8:19; 1 John 2:23; 4:15; 2 John 9).[43]

---

42. Bauckham, *God Crucified*, 27.

43. Underlying the fact that Jesus could be both fully man and fully God at the same time is the Christian doctrine of the Trinity, i.e., the fact that God is one essence (Greek = *ousia*) of three persons (Greek = *hypostasis*; Father, Son, and Holy Spirit). Although the doctrine of the Trinity may not be fully understandable, the Trinity is neither incoherent (i.e., internally self-contradictory) nor illogical, and it necessarily arises from the data given us in the Bible. It is beyond the scope of this book to discuss the Trinity in detail, but the nature of the Trinity and trinitarian concepts embedded in reality are discussed in detail at Menn, *Christianity and Islam*, 115–29.

3

Jesus' Fulfillment of Prophecy

IN CHAPTER 1 WE looked at the uniqueness and reliability of the Bible and introduced the subject of biblical prophecy. Although the Bible contains prophecies relating to many nations, people, and events, here I will focus on prophecies that relate to the Messiah, i.e., Jesus Christ, since, as previously mentioned, he is the central figure of the entire Bible. With respect to the OT prophecies of Jesus Christ, recall that somewhat over 400 years existed between the last books of the OT and the advent of Jesus. Thus, there exists a period of several hundred years, up to a maximum of about 1400 years for some of the prophecies, between any prophecies relating to the Messiah and their fulfillment.[1]

The importance of prophecy is that prophecies make the claims that Jesus is the Messiah verifiable or, on the other hand, falsifiable (see Deut 18:20–22; 1 Kgs 22:28; Isa 48:5; Jer 28:9; Ezek 33:33; Zech 2:9, 11; 4:9; 6:15). Although it is possible that a few of the prophecies might be said to have been fulfilled by others, Jesus is the only one who could and did fulfill all of them. Jesus had no control over many of the prophecies (e.g., his manner and place of birth, his lineage, his betrayal, the actions of his disciples, accusers, and executioners, the manner of his death, his burial). Consequently, he could not have manipulated events to contrive to fulfill the prophecies.[2] The number and specificity of the prophecies relating to Jesus reveal that there is divine intellect and foreknowledge behind the Bible; it is not credible to contend that the prophecies just happened to be fulfilled by "chance" (as will be discussed below). The prophecies relate to all areas of Jesus' life. Prophecies relating to Jesus' identity as Messiah include:

---

1. See Geisler, *Christian Apologetics*, 341.
2. See Geisler, *Christian Apologetics*, 342–43.

Prophecy	OT Source	NT Fulfillment
1. Born of a virgin	Isa 7:14	Matt 1:18, 24–25; Luke 1:26–35
2. Son of God	Ps 2:7; 2 Sam 7:12–16; 1 Chron 17:11–14	Matt 3:17; Matt 16:16; Mark 9:7; Luke 9:35; 22:70; John 1:34, 49; Acts 13:30–33
3. Seed of Abraham	Gen 13:15; 22:17–18	Gal 3:16
4. Son of Isaac	Gen 21:12	Matt 1:2; Luke 3:23, 34
5. Son of Jacob	Num 24:17	Matt 1:2; Luke 1:33; 3:23, 34
6. Tribe of Judah	Gen 49:10; Micah 5:2	Matt 1:2; Luke 3:23, 33; Heb 7:14
7. Line of Jesse	Isa 11:1, 10	Matt 1:6, Luke 3:23, 32
8. House of David	2 Sam 7:12–16; Ps 132:11; Jer 23:5	Matt 1:1; 9:27; 15:22; 20:30–31; 21:9, 15; 22:41–46; Mark 9:10; 10:47–48; Luke 3:23, 31; 18:38–39; Acts 13:22–23; Rev 22:16
9. Born at Bethlehem	Micah 5:2	Matt 2:1, 4–8; Luke 2:4–7; John 7:42
10. Pre-existent	Micah 5:2	John 1:1–2, 30; 8:58; 17:5, 24; Col 1:17; Rev 1:17; 2:8; 22:13
11. Will be called Immanuel	Isa 7:14	Matt 1:23
12. Will be called the Lord	Ps 110:1; Jer 23:6	Matt 22:43–45; Luke 2:11
13. Will be a prophet	Deut 18:18	Matt 21:11; Luke 7:16; John 4:19; 6:14; 7:40
14. Will be a priest	Ps 110:4	Heb 3:1; 5:5–6
15. Will be a judge	Isa 11:4; 33:22	John 5:30; 2 Tim 4:1; Jas 4:12
16. Will be a king	Ps 2:6; Jer 23:5; Zech 9:9	Matt 21:5; 27:37; John 18:33–38
17. The Spirit of God would be upon him	Isa 11:2; 42:1; 61:1–2	Matt 3:16–17; 12:17–21; Mark 1:10–11; Luke 4:18, 21; John 1:32
18. Preceded by a messenger	Isa 40:3; Mal 3:1	Matt 3:1–3; 11:10; Luke 1:17; John 1:23
19. Zealous for God	Ps 69:9	John 2:15–17

Jesus' Fulfillment of Prophecy

Prophecy	OT Source	NT Fulfillment
20. Ministry to begin in Galilee	Isa 9:1	Matt 4:12–13, 17
21. Would perform miracles	Isa 32:3–4; 35:5–6	Matt 9:32–35; 11:4–6; Mark 7:33–35; John 5:5–9; 9:6–11; 11:43–47
22. Would teach in parables	Ps 78:2	Matt 13:34
23. Would enter the temple	Mal 3:1	Matt 21:12
24. Would enter Jerusalem on a donkey	Zech 9:9	Matt 21:6–11; Luke 19:35–37
25. Would be a stumbling stone to Jews	Ps 118:22; Isa 8:14; 28:16	Rom 9:32–33; 1 Pet 2:7
26. Would be a light to Gentiles	Isa 49:6; 60:3	Acts 13:47–48; 26:23; 28:28
27. Rejected by his own people	Ps 69:8; Isa 53:3	Matt 21:42–43; John 1:11; 7:5, 48
28. Hated without a cause	Ps 69:4; Isa 49:7	John 15:25
29. Would rise from the dead	Ps 2:7; 16:10; Hos 6:2	Matt 28:6; Mark 16:6; Luke 24:21, 46; Acts 2:31; 13:33
30. Would ascend to the Father	Ps 68:18	Acts 1:9; Eph 4:8
31. Seated at the right hand of God	Ps 110:1	Mark 16:19; Acts 2:34–35; Heb 1:3

Prophecies relating to Jesus' death and burial include:

Prophecy	OT Source	NT Source
1. Betrayed by a friend	Ps 41:9; 55:12–14; Zech 13:6	Matt 10:4; 26:47–50; Luke 22:19–23
2. Betrayed for 30 pieces of silver	Zech 11:12	Matt 26:15; 27:3
3. Money thrown in God's house	Zech 11:13	Matt 27:5
4. Money given for potter's field	Zech 11:13	Matt 27:6–10

Prophecy	OT Source	NT Source
5. Forsaken by his disciples	Zech 13:7	Matt 26:31, 69–74; Mark 14:27, 50
6. Silent before accusers	Isa 53:7	Matt 27:12; Acts 8:32–35
7. Beaten and spat upon	Isa 50:6; 53:5	Matt 26:67; 27:26; Mark 10:33–34
8. Mocked	Ps 22:7–8	Matt 27:31; Luke 22:63–65
9. Hands and feet pierced	Ps 22:16; Zech 12:10	Luke 23:33; John 20:25–27
10. Suffers for the sins of others	Isa 53:5–6, 8, 10–12	Rom 4:25; 1 Cor 15:3
11. Dies with transgressors	Isa 53:12	Matt 27:38; Mark 15:27–28; Luke 22:37
12. Intercedes for persecutors	Isa 53:12	Luke 23:34
13. Lots cast for his clothes	Ps 22:18	John 19:23–24
14. Friends stand far away	Ps 38:11	Matt 27:55–56; Mark 15:40; Luke 23:49
15. People wag their heads	Ps 22:7	Matt 27:39
16. People stare at Him	Ps 22:17	Luke 23:35
17. He suffers thirst	Ps 22:15; 69:21	John 19:28
18. Given gall and vinegar to drink	Ps 69:21	Matt 27:34; John 19:28–29
19. Cries out when forsaken by God	Ps 22:1	Matt 27:46
20. Commits His spirit to God	Ps 31:5	Luke 23:46
21. His bones are not broken	Ps 34:20	John 19:33
22. His side is pierced	Zech 12:10	John 19:34–37
23. Heart broken	Ps 22:14; 69:20	John 19:34
24. Darkness over the land	Gen 15:17; Amos 8:9	Matt 27:45

Prophecy	OT Source	NT Source
25. Buried in a rich man's tomb	Isa 53:9	Matt 27:57–60

Perhaps the most fascinating prophecy is found in Gen 15:1–18. There, God was ratifying the covenant he previously had made with Abraham (then known as Abram). Abram asked, *"O Lord God, how will I know that I will possess [the land God had promised him]?"* (Gen 15:8) To assuage Abram's doubt, God told Abram to bring certain animals. Abram knew that God was going to ratify a covenant with him, so he brought the animals and then cut them in two and laid the halves opposite each other. In the Ancient Near East, typically both parties then would walk through the pieces of the dead animals. What they were doing was symbolizing, "If I violate the terms of this agreement, may I become just like these dead animals here."[3] In this case, however, only God (in the symbolic form of a *"smoking oven and flaming torch,"* Gen 15:17) passed through the pieces of the dead animals.[4] By passing through the pieces of animals on his own behalf and also on behalf of Abram, God was saying, "Abram, if I violate the terms of this covenant, may I become like these dead animals." But he was also saying, "Abram, if *you* violate the terms of this covenant, by not believing me, by not following me, may *I*, not you, become like these dead animals."

This covenant which God acted out also was a prophecy (see Gal 3:16). Approximately 2000 years later, on a hill called Calvary or Golgotha, in the person of Jesus Christ, God did it for real. What makes the prophecy of Genesis 15 so amazing is the *detail* of its fulfillment. Just as the animals were killed, so was Jesus. However, the animals were not merely killed, but were cut in two. Matt 27:51 tells us that when Jesus died, *"the veil of the temple was torn in two from top to bottom."* Heb 10:19–20 tells us the meaning of that. It says, *"We have confidence to enter the holy place by the blood of Jesus, by a new and living way which He inaugurated for us through the veil, that is, His flesh."* That veil was showing that, on the cross, Jesus Christ fulfilled the Abrahamic Covenant.[5] Additionally, Gen 15:17 says, *"When the sun had set, it was very dark"* That was when the smoking oven and flaming torch

---

3. Alter, *Genesis,* 65n.8; Payne, *Encyclopedia,* 162.

4. We know that the smoking oven and flaming torch signified God himself, because later he led Israel out of captivity in Egypt (which was also prophesied in Gen 15:13-14) as a pillar of cloud by day and a pillar of smoke by night (Exod 13:21); when he appeared on Mount Sinai to give the Ten Commandments to Moses, *"Mount Sinai was all in smoke because the Lord descended upon it in fire; and its smoke ascended like the smoke of a furnace"* (Exod 19:18).

5. See Payne, *Encyclopedia,* 162.

passed through the pieces. Matt 27:45 tells us that when Jesus was on the cross, *"from the sixth hour darkness fell upon all the land until the ninth hour."* The judgment of sin is eternal separation from God, otherwise known as hell. Hell is described in various places in the Bible as *"outer darkness"* (Matt 8:12; 22:13; 25:30). The darkness of the sky when Jesus was on the cross was a sign of God's judgment on the sin that Jesus was bearing. That darkness was symbolizing the outer darkness of hell itself. Since the essence of hell is separation from God, when Jesus cried out from the cross, *"My God, my God, why have you forsaken me?"* (Matt 27:46), he was actually experiencing hell. These events did not happen by coincidence, and they could not have been "faked," since no one could control the weather or cause the veil of the temple to rip in two. The only reasonable explanation is that the God of the Bible exists, he knows *"the end from the beginning"* (Isa 46:10), and he was using prophecy and its fulfillment to demonstrate his reality, to verify who Jesus Christ is, and to confirm the truth of the gospel.

There is more to the importance of prophecy even than that. Probability analysis demonstrates that it is mathematically impossible for the multiple prophecies concerning Jesus to have been fulfilled by chance. Several years ago, mathematics and astronomy professor Peter W. Stoner took just eight of the prophecies concerning Jesus (born in Bethlehem, Micah 5:2; had a forerunner to prepare the way, Mal 3:1; entered Jerusalem on a donkey, Zech 9:9; betrayed by a friend causing wounds in his hands, Zech 13:6; betrayed for 30 pieces of silver, Zech 11:12; betrayal money cast into house of the Lord to go to a potter, Zech 11:13; oppressed and afflicted but remained silent before his accusers, Isa 53:7; and had his hands and feet pierced, Ps 22:6). A class at Pasadena City College ran a probability analysis, having first come up with reasonable and conservative estimates for the chance of one person fulfilling each of the eight prophecies. The estimates and calculations were as follows: 1 in $2.8 \times 10^5 \times 10^3 \times 10^2 \times 10^3 \times 10^5 \times 10^3 \times 10^4$ = 1 in 10^{28}.[6] The question is: What is the chance that any person might have lived from the day of those prophecies to the present time and fulfilled all eight prophecies? To answer that, one divides 10^{28} by the total number of people who have lived since the time of the prophecies, then estimated to have been approximately 88 billion. The result is that "the chance that

---

6. Stoner, *Science Speaks*, 59-62. The 2.8 number is derived from the fact that the population of the earth has averaged less than 2 billion people, and the population of Bethlehem has averaged less than 7,150. Hence, one divides 7,150 into 2 billion which results in the chance that one man in 2.8×10^5 was born in Bethlehem. Stoner, *Science Speaks*, 60.

any man might have lived down to the present time and fulfilled all eight prophecies is 1 in 10^{17}."[7]

What does that mean? Stoner wrote that if one took 10^{17} silver dollars and lay them on the face of Texas, they would cover the state two feet deep.[8] He then explained:

> Now mark one of these silver dollars and stir the whole mass thoroughly, all over the state. Blindfold a man and tell him that he can travel as far as he wishes, but he must pick up one silver dollar and say that this is the right one. What chance would he have of getting the right one? Just the same chance that the prophets would have had of writing these eight prophecies and having them all come true in any one man, from their day to the present time, provided they wrote using their own wisdom. ... This means that the fulfillment of these eight prophecies alone proves that God inspired the writing of those prophecies to a definiteness which lacks only one chance in 10^{17} of being absolute.[9]

Stoner went on to conclude, using the same principles of probability, that the human chance of fulfilling 48 of the prophecies relating to Jesus would be 1 in 10^{157}. That is equivalent to the number of electrons comprising 500 solid balls of electrons, each ball having a diameter of 6 billion light-years![10]

The implications of these data are astounding. Stoner explains, "This is not merely evidence. It is proof of the Bible's inspiration by God—proof so definite that the universe is not large enough to hold the evidence."[11] All of this leads to the conclusion that Jesus is exactly who he said he is, God

---

7. Stoner, *Science Speaks*, 63.

8. Texas is 268,597 square miles (695,660 km²) in size. It is between the size of Myanmar (261,228 square miles; 676,578 km²) and Zambia (290,586 square miles; 752,617 km²).

9. Stoner, *Science Speaks*, 63.

10. Stoner, *Science Speaks*, 64-65. In the foreword to Stoner's book, H. Harold Hartzler, Ph.D., professor of mathematics, physics, and astronomy, and secretary-treasurer of the American Scientific Affiliation, stated, "The manuscript for Science Speaks has been carefully reviewed by a committee of the American Scientific Affiliation members and by the Executive Council of the same group and has been found, in general, to be dependable and accurate in regard to the scientific material presented. The mathematical analysis included is based upon principles of probability which are thoroughly sound and Professor Stoner has applied these principles in a proper and convincing way." Hartzler, "Foreword," 4. Stoner added, "If the reader does not agree with the estimates given, he may make his own estimates and then carry them through to their logical conclusions." Stoner, *Science Speaks*, 60.

11. Stoner, *Science Speaks*, 65; see also Kaiser, *Old Testament*, 169; Van de Weghe, *Prepared*, 219–32; Reasons, *Why the Bible*, 1–4.

come to earth as a man. The implications of this are that, since he accepted and believed in the historicity of the Bible, the Bible is, in fact, correct and reliable. In short, Christianity is true. Yet one more fact demonstrates the truth that Jesus is who he says he is, the Bible is accurate and reliable, and Christianity is true, namely, the resurrection of Jesus Christ.

4

The Crucifixion and Resurrection of Jesus

Introduction

THE CRUCIFIXION AND RESURRECTION of Jesus Christ form the very heart of Christianity. Their central importance is repeatedly emphasized throughout the NT (e.g., Matt 20:28; John 10:17–18; Rom 1:4; 5:8–11; 1 Cor 15:1–4, 20–23; Phil 2:5–11; Heb 2:14–15).[1] Jesus predicted both his crucifixion and bodily resurrection (e.g., Matt 16:21; Mark 9:31; Luke 9:22; John 2:18–22). Jesus claimed to be God come to earth as a man. He came to live the life we should have lived, i.e., without sin, and to pay the price for our sin which otherwise we would have to pay but never could. In short, the primary purpose Jesus came into the world was not to heal people or teach (although those were important parts of what he did), but to die on the cross for the sake of humanity (Phil 2:6-8). Jesus' critics asked him for a sign, and he said he would give them one—his resurrection. Jesus was saying that he would prove that he is who he claimed to be by doing something (bodily rising from the dead) that is impossible for anyone who is merely a human being. It is the test by which we could know that he was telling the truth (Matt 12:38–40; 16:1–4; John 2:18–21). Such a historical test of truth is unique to Christianity.

In the Bible, the bodily resurrection of Christ is intimately linked to the crucifixion (e.g., Matt 17:22–23; Mark 10:32–34; John 2:18–22; Rom 4:24–25; 1 Cor 15:1–4; Phil 2:5–11). Since the very purpose of Christ's coming

---

1. Bruce Demarest points out that between 25%–42% of the four Gospels are devoted to the last week of Jesus' life and "in addition to the many prophetic anticipations of the Messiah's death in the OT, there are 175 direct references to his death in the NT." Demarest, *The Cross*, 166–67.

into the world was to bear the punishment for mankind's sins by sacrificing himself on the cross, the resurrection (and subsequent ascension): (1) demonstrates that God accepted Christ's sacrifice; and (2) validates who Christ is and everything Christ said and believed.[2] Even then-atheist philosopher Antony Flew acknowledged that the question of whether or not Jesus bodily rose from the dead "is of supreme theoretical and practical importance. For the knowable fact that he did, if indeed it is a knowable fact, is the best, if not the only, reason for accepting that Jesus is the God of Abraham, Isaac, and Israel."[3] The apostles Peter and Paul clearly recognized this. On one hand, Peter said that our ability to have new life and an eternal inheritance come only *"through the resurrection of Jesus Christ from the dead"* (1 Pet 1:3–4). On the other hand, in 1 Cor 15:14 Paul said, *"If Christ has not been raised, then our preaching is vain, your faith also is vain"* (see also 1 Cor 15:17). Habermas and Licona conclude, "If Jesus *did not* rise from the dead, he was a false prophet and a charlatan whom no rational person should follow. Conversely, if he *did* rise from the dead, this event confirmed his radical claim."[4]

The issues of the crucifixion and resurrection of Christ are historical ones: either he was crucified and then bodily rose from the grave or he did not. On these crucial points either the Bible's affirmation that those events took place is correct or their denial is correct. Both cannot be true. These are historical issues subject to the study of the historical evidence, not matters of "faith."[5]

---

2. Ulrich Wilckens puts it this way, "The *Cross* is the sign and symbol of what is Christian. Trust in the Cross, however, and the enormous drive and impetus which derive their power from the Cross, are ultimately based on the raising from the dead of the crucified Christ. If the meaning and direction of Christianity stand or fall with belief in the Cross of Christ, then the power of this belief stands or falls with belief in the resurrection of the crucified Christ." Wilckens, *Resurrection*, 124.

3. Flew, "Negative Statement," 3.

4. Habermas and Licona, *The Case*, 27.

5. See Habermas, *Ancient Evidence*, 21.

5

The Crucifixion of Jesus Christ Is a Historical Fact

MULTIPLE LINES OF EVIDENCE establish that Jesus did, in fact, die by crucifixion. Those lines of evidence include the following:

MULTIPLE WITNESSES

The crucifixion of Jesus was not a secret or private event. Instead, it was a public event involving Roman government officials, Jewish leaders (the Sanhedrin), and common people, both friends and foes of Jesus. Even though the disciples had fled when Jesus was arrested (Matt 26:56), Peter was a witness to his hearing before the high priest (Matt 26:69; Mark 14:54). Luke reports that Jesus' carrying the cross was accompanied by a large crowd of people, including women, who were lamenting (Luke 23:27), and Simon of Cyrene, who was made to carry the cross (Matt 27:32). Jesus' mother, Mary, and the apostle John were present at the crucifixion; from the cross, Jesus committed Mary to John's care (John 19:25–27). Also present were passersby (Matt 27:39–40), many women, some of whom were followers of Jesus, his aunt, and his acquaintances (Matt 27:55–56; Luke 23:49; John 19:25), Jewish leaders (Matt 27:41; Mark 15:31), a Roman centurion (Matt 27:54; Mark 15:39; Luke 23:47), and Roman soldiers (Matt 27:35; Mark 15:24; Luke 23:35; John 19:18, 23) who all witnessed Jesus' crucifixion.

As Jesus was being led out to be crucified, *"They pressed into service a passer-by coming from the country, Simon of Cyrene (the father of Alexander and Rufus), to bear His cross"* (Mark 15:21). The only reason to include those names is that they were known individuals who could be contacted. What Mark is saying is that "Alexander and Rufus vouch for the truth of what I am telling you, if you want to ask them"[1] The fact that Jesus' own mother, his acquaintances, and the apostle John were present at the crucifixion is significant (Matt 27:55–56; Luke 23:49; John 19:25–27). A mother knows her own son. Jesus' relatives, his friends, and his acquaintances knew who Jesus was and thus knew it was Jesus who was crucified, not someone else. The fact that the Jewish leaders were present also is significant. Their interest was in ensuring that Jesus, not some imposter, was the one who was being crucified and actually died. John, an eyewitness, specifically said, *"He who has seen has testified, and his testimony is true; and he knows that he is telling the truth, so that you also may believe"* (John 19:35). To claim that someone else was on the cross, or that Jesus did not die on the cross, is contrary to reason.

Matthew, Mark, Luke, John, the book of Acts, the epistles of Romans, 1 and 2 Corinthians, Galatians, Ephesians, Philippians, Colossians, 1 Thessalonians, 1 and 2 Timothy, Hebrews, 1 Peter, 2 Peter (implicitly), 1 John, and Revelation all record the death of Jesus; when the manner of that death is mentioned, they state it was by crucifixion. Those books were written by at least seven different authors and were all written within 20 to a maximum of 65 years after Jesus' death. That means the crucifixion was written about while many of the witnesses still were alive; in the face of that, the NT could not reasonably claim that Jesus was crucified if he had not been.[2]

THE EARLINESS OF CHRISTIAN CREEDS

As mentioned above, the books of the Bible were written early, beginning less than 20 years after the death of Jesus. However, the writers of the NT incorporated into their writings early Christian creeds *which are much older than the books in which they appear.*[3] "Such early traditions appear frequently in the New Testament and actually consist of oral teachings and proclamations which were repeated by word of mouth until recorded in the book itself. Therefore these creeds actually predate the New Testament writings in which they occur. . . . The two most common elements in these creeds concerned the death and resurrection of Jesus and his resulting deity."[4] These early creeds include 1 Cor 15:3–7 and Phil 2:6–11.[5] Both of these creedal formulas refer to Christ's death. 1 Cor 15:3–4 reports that

---

1. Keller, *The Reason*, 101.
2. See Keller, *The Reason*, 102.
3. See Habermas, *Ancient Evidence*, 119; Cullmann, *The Earliest*, 10, 22–23.
4. Habermas, *Ancient Evidence*, 33, 120.
5. Cullmann, *The Earliest*, 22–23.

"Christ died for our sins according to the Scriptures, and that He was buried." The creed recorded in Philippians specifies the manner of his death: *"even death on a cross"* (Phil 2:8). That the creed of 1 Cor 15:3-7 is early and pre-Pauline is virtually universally recognized by scholars across the theological spectrum.[6] A. M. Hunter states, "The passage [1 Cor 15:3-7] therefore preserves uniquely early and verifiable testimony. It meets every reasonable demand of historical reliability."[7]

MEDICAL EVIDENCE OF DEATH

A detailed article in the *Journal of the American Medical Association* analyzes from a medical perspective the events that led up to Jesus' crucifixion (i.e., his sweating great drops of blood in the Garden of Gethsemane, his being beaten by the Jews and then scourged by the Romans, his inability to carry his own cross), the nature of the crucifixion itself, and his being pierced by the Roman's spear with blood and water coming out of him, as described in the different biblical accounts. The authors conclude, "Clearly, the weight of historical and medical evidence indicates that Jesus was dead before the wound to his side was inflicted and supports the traditional view that the spear, thrust between his right ribs, probably perforated not only the right lung but also the pericardium and heart and thereby ensured his death. Accordingly, interpretations based on the assumption that Jesus did not die on the cross appear to be at odds with modern medical knowledge."[8]

The Roman soldier who pierced Jesus' side with his spear was making sure that Jesus was, in fact, dead (John 19:31-34). Had that soldier not been absolutely certain that Jesus was dead, either the soldiers would have broken Jesus' legs as they did to the other two men who were crucified with Jesus or they would have done something else to ensure his death. If Jesus was not truly dead, but the Roman centurion reported to Pilate that he was dead, he would have been in violation of his orders and would have been lying to his commander and therefore probably would have paid for that with his own life. Consequently, it is incredible to contend that Jesus did not die on the cross.

---

6. Habermas, *Ancient Evidence*, 124-25; see also Jeremias, *The Eucharistic Words*, 101-03.

7. Hunter, *Jesus*, 100.

8. Edwards, et al., "On the Physical Death," 1463.

JESUS' BURIAL IN A TOMB

Pontius Pilate, the Roman prefect (governor) of Judea, had ordered Jesus to be crucified (Matt 27:26; Mark 15:15; Luke 23:24–25; John 19:16). After the crucifixion, Joseph of Arimathea, a member of the Jewish Sanhedrin, requested Jesus' body in order to bury it; Pilate released the body to be buried but only after first confirming from the centurion who had been present at the crucifixion that Jesus was, in fact, dead (Matt 27:57–58; Mark 15:42–45; Luke 23:50–52; John 19:38).[9] The early creed, which pre-dates Paul and goes back essentially to the time of the crucifixion itself, includes the statement *"that He was buried"* (1 Cor 15:4). That statement is significant in that it certified that Jesus truly had died.[10] Jesus was buried in Joseph of Arimathea's own tomb; thus, the place where Jesus was buried was a known location (Matt 27:59–60; Mark 15:46; Luke 23:53; John 19:38–42). A *"large stone"* was rolled to close the entrance, the tomb was sealed, and a guard was placed at the tomb to make sure that no one could steal the body (Matt 27:60–66; Mark 15:46; 16:3–4; Luke 23:53; John 19:41–42). The official government seal, and the Roman security guard made it impossible for anyone to break into or out of that tomb.[11]

REACTION OF THE DISCIPLES

The immediate post-crucifixion events are *only* consistent with Jesus' actually dying by crucifixion. For example, John 20:19 reports that the disciples were in a room in which *"the doors were shut . . . for fear of the Jews."* That is only explicable if their leader had, in fact, been executed at the insistence of the Jewish leaders and the disciples were now afraid that the Jewish leaders would come after them. On the Sunday immediately after the crucifixion, Mark 16:10 adds that Jesus' disciples were *"mourning and weeping."* Luke 24 reports that two other disciples, one named Cleopas, were walking on the road to Emmaus. Luke 24:17 states that they were *"looking sad."* The two

---

9. Joseph of Arimathea undoubtedly was the genuine, historical individual who buried Jesus. Craig points out that "it is unlikely that early Christian believers would invent an individual, give him a name and nearby town of origin, and place that fictional character on the historical council of the Sanhedrin, whose members were well known." Craig, *The Son*, 53.

10. See Wright, *The Resurrection*, 321.

11. McDowell, *The Resurrection*, 53–61. Josh McDowell points out, "This seal on Jesus' tomb was a public testimony that Jesus' body was actually there. In addition, because the seal was Roman, it verified the fact that His body was protected from vandals by nothing less than the power and authority of the Roman Empire." McDowell, *The Resurrection*, 59.

disciples told the reason in Luke 24:20–21 when they spoke of *"how the chief priests and our rulers delivered Him [Jesus] to the sentence of death, and crucified Him. But we were hoping that it was he who was going to redeem Israel"* Again, the sadness and dashed hopes of those disciples only makes sense in light of Jesus crucifixion. The fact that one of the disciples on the road to Emmaus was named is further evidence that the account is authentic and reliable, since Cleopas could have been questioned about the events of that day.[12]

THE PREVALENCE OF SELF-DAMAGING MATERIAL

Christianity was born in a first-century Jewish context, yet all four Gospels and many other NT writings are centered on the fact that Jesus was crucified by the Romans. If the story of Jesus' life was simply made up long after the fact by his followers, the account of Jesus' crucifixion never would have been included:

> It is hard to imagine a more effective way to convince people in a first-century Jewish context that someone is *not* the Messiah than by telling them that the would-be savior was executed by Israel's military oppressors! To go further and tell them that this would-be savior died a cursed death on a tree would make the sales pitch all the worse (cf. Deut. 21:22–23). . . . Thus, the fact that the Synoptic tradition not only continues to mention the crucifixion but also makes it the centerpiece of its message must be taken as evidence that the earliest Christians, including the authors of the Synoptic Gospels, remained willing to acknowledge,

---

12. On the Sunday immediately following the burial, Mark 16:11 records that Mary Magdalene reported to the disciples the tomb was empty, Jesus had risen from the grave, and he was alive, but *"when they heard that He was alive and had been seen by her, they refused to believe it."* Likewise, Mark 16:13 reports that the two disciples to whom Jesus had appeared on the road to Emmaus *"went away and reported it to the others, but they did not believe them either."* Luke 24:10–11 similarly records that Mary Magdalene, Joanna, Mary the mother of James, and other women told the disciples what the angel at the tomb had said, *"but these words appeared to them as nonsense, and they would not believe them."* John 20:24–25 observes that when Jesus first appeared to the disciples, Thomas was not present. When the disciples told Thomas that they had seen Jesus, Thomas said to them, *"Unless I see in His hands the imprint of the nails, and put my finger into the place of the nails, and put my hand into His side, I will not believe."* All of those reports of unbelief that Jesus was alive only make sense if Jesus had, in fact, been dead and buried. The disciples knew that dead men stay dead, and bodily resurrection was unprecedented. Had these accounts been "made up" long after the fact, they probably would not have all mentioned the disciples' unbelief, since such expressions of unbelief cast the disciples in a bad light.

remember, and boldly proclaim the single most embarrassing historical fact associated with their fledgling movement. This is the very sort of self-damaging material historians typically look for in assessing the veracity of ancient works.[13]

CONFIRMATION BY HOSTILE AND NON-CHRISTIAN SOURCES

Multiple, ancient, non-Christian sources attest to the validity of the crucifixion of Jesus Christ. Celsus, a second-century Roman and virulent critic of Christianity, affirmed that Jesus was crucified and died on the cross.[14] The crucifixion was even portrayed in pictorial form. "The earliest known pictorial representation of the crucifixion of Jesus comes from Rome, found scratched into the plaster of a wall of the Paedagogium on the Palatine Hill. Known as the Alexamenos Graffito, the drawing shows Jesus on the cross with the head of a donkey, while a man standing on the ground looks up to the crucifixion victim with a raised arm. Below, an accompanying Greek inscription reads 'Alexamenos worships (his) god.'"[15] Other Roman and Jewish admissions that Jesus Christ was, in fact, crucified include the following:

1. *Babylonian Talmud.* The *Babylonian Talmud* is a central text of Rabbinic Judaism. Tractate Sanhedrin, folio 43a states, "On the eve of Passover Yeshu was hanged. For forty days before the execution took place, a herald went forth and cried, 'He is going forth to be stoned because he has practiced sorcery and enticed Israel to apostasy. Any one who can say anything in his favour, let him come forward and plead on his behalf.' But since nothing was brought forward in his favour he was hanged on the eve of the Passover!"[16] One manuscript specifies that Yeshu refers to Jesus Christ by adding "the Nasarean" after his name.[17] Most scholars conclude that this passage of the *Talmud* came from the earliest period of compilation, AD 70–200.[18] This is significant in that the *Babylonian Talmud* is an "official" work

---

13. Eddy and Boyd, *The Jesus Legend*, 411.
14. "Celsus," *Flavius Claudius Julianus,* On the Cross.
15. Kennedy, *Unearthing,* 196–97.
16. *Bab. Talmud,* Sanhedrin 43a.
17. *Bab. Talmud,* Sanhedrin 43a, n.34.
18. Habermas, *Ancient Evidence,* 97–98. The reference to "hanging" is derived from Deut 21:22–23 and is applied to Jesus' crucifixion (Luke 23:39; Acts 5:30; 10:39; Gal 3:13).

of Jewish rabbis that admits responsibility for having Jesus executed and that he died.

2. *Toledot Yeshu.* There are a number of versions of *Toledot Yeshu*, which is a derogatory version of the life of Jesus, growing out of the response of the Jewish community to Christianity. When it was compiled is unknown, the first reference to it being in the ninth century.[19] *Toledot Yeshu* confirms Jesus' execution, "Yeshu was put to death on the sixth hour on the eve of the Passover and of the Sabbath."[20] The work is also significant in that, even though it is an anti-Christian portrayal of Jesus, it confirms Jesus' ability to work miracles, including reviving the dead, and Jesus' claim that his coming had been prophesied in the OT, "Yeshu replied, 'The prophets long ago prophesied my coming: "And there shall come forth a rod out of the stem of Jesse," and I am he.'"[21]

3. *Josephus.* Josephus was born in AD 37. He became a Jewish priest and later fought against the Romans during the war of AD 66–70. After the Jews were defeated, he joined the Romans as court historian for Emperor Vespasian. In his book *Antiquities of the Jews*, written in AD 93, Josephus wrote what is called the *Testimonium Flavianum*:

> About this time there lived Jesus, a wise man, *if indeed one ought to call him a man.* For he was one who wrought surprising feats and was a teacher of such people as accept the truth gladly. He won over many Jews and many of the Greeks. *He was the Messiah.* When Pilate, upon hearing him accused by men of the highest standing amongst us, had condemned him to be crucified, those who had in the first place come to love him did not give up their affection for him. *On the third day he appeared to them restored to life, for the prophets of God had prophesied these and countless other marvelous things about him.* And the tribe of the Christians, so called after him, has still to this day not disappeared."[22]

Many people believe that a later Christian editor added the italicized portions. The vast majority of scholars agree that Josephus wrote at least the non-italicized portions of the *Testimonium*.[23]

---

19. "Toledot Yeshu," *Wikipedia*, Composition and dating.
20. *Toledot Yeshu*, text.
21. *Toledot Yeshu*, text.
22. Josephus, *Antiquities*, 18.63–64, italics added.
23. See Habermas and Licona, *The Case*, 266–70n.42.

4. *Tacitus.* Tacitus, who lived from approximately AD 55–120, is known as the "greatest historian" of ancient Rome.[24] His *Annals*, written about AD 115, confirm Jesus' death. In referring to the great fire of Rome under Emperor Nero, Tacitus states, "Nero fastened the guilt and inflicted the most exquisite tortures on a class hated for their abominations, called Christians by the populace. Christus, from whom the name had its origin, suffered the extreme penalty during the reign of Tiberius at the hands of one of our procurators, Pontius Pilatus."[25]

5. *Lucian of Samosata.* Lucian of Samosata was a Greek anti-Christian satirist. In approximately AD 165–75 he wrote *The Passing of Peregrinus*. In it, he talked of the Christians who worship "the man who was crucified in Palestine because he introduced this new cult into the world."[26]

6. *Mara Bar-Serapion.* Mara Bar-Serapion was a Stoic philosopher from Syria. He wrote between approximately AD 73–200. He wrote a letter to his son to motivate him to emulate wise teachers of the past. In that letter he said,

> For what benefit did the Athenians obtain by putting Socrates to death, seeing that they received as retribution for it famine and pestilence? . . . Or the Jews *by the murder* of their Wise King, seeing that from that very time their kingdom was driven away *from them*? For with justice did God grant a recompense to the wisdom of *all* three of them. For the Athenians died by famine; and the people of Samos were covered by the sea without remedy; and the Jews, brought to desolation and expelled from their kingdom, are driven away into Every land.[27]

The above works establish that no one in the ancient world doubted that Jesus had died by crucifixion; it had, in fact, become common knowledge.

THE FAILURE OF ALTERNATIVE EXPLANATIONS

No plausible alternative explanation has ever been advanced to explain away the crucifixion. The Qur'an's simple denial that Jesus died or was crucified (Q. 4:157) is based on no historical or factual basis whatsoever and fails for

---

24. Habermas, *Ancient Evidence*, 87.
25. Tacitus, *Annals*, 15.44.
26. Lucian of Samosata, *The Passing*, 11.
27. Mara Bar-Serapion, *Letter*, emph. in orig.

the above reasons. The same applies to the idea that someone else was "substituted" for Jesus or that he did not die on the cross but revived in the tomb.

1. *The "substitution" theory.* The majority view among Muslims is that someone else was substituted for Jesus and was crucified in his place. It cannot explain or refute the overwhelming historical evidence for the fact of Jesus' crucifixion or explain or refute the overwhelming historical evidence for the resurrection (see below). Famous Muslim commentator Sayyid Abul A'la Mawdudi admits, "So far as the trial at the court of Pilate is concerned, it was probably Jesus who was tried. Pilate sentenced him to death."[28] Jesus was in the presence of the Roman soldiers when he was sentenced and when he was handed over to them to be led out to execution; and he was continually in their presence until he was crucified and died (as well as being continually in the presence of others from the time of his arrest and trial to the crucifixion). There was no "confusion" and no opportunity in which an innocent third party could have been substituted for Jesus. Yahiya Emerick's suggests that the Romans grabbed the wrong man, "thinking all Semites looked alike."[29] However, all Semites do not look alike *to other Semites*, which in this case included Jesus' mother, his disciples, friends, acquaintances, and his enemies (who wanted to make sure that it was Jesus who was killed, not some "look-alike").

    Finally, because the historical evidence for the *resurrection* is so great (see chapter 6) the idea that "someone else was substituted for Jesus" necessitates the conclusion that the "Jesus look-alike" was resurrected from the grave! More than that, *after his resurrection* the imposter implausibly would have continued the charade by convincing everyone he was the "real" Jesus by knowing his disciples personally (John 20:11—21:24), explaining how the entire OT was all about him (Luke 24:13-49), commissioning his disciples to go to the entire world and spread the gospel of the real Jesus (Matt 28:18-20; Mark 16:15-18), and then ascending to heaven (Mark 16:19; Luke 24:50-53; Acts 1:9-11). The "substitution theory" therefore is completely incoherent.

2. *The "swoon" theory.* Perhaps the most important alternative explanation to the crucifixion that at least tried to deal with some of the facts was the so-called "swoon theory," which contends that Jesus did not die on the cross but was taken down from the cross unconscious (i.e.,

---

28. A'la Mawdudi, *Towards Understanding*, Q. 4:157n.193.
29. Emerick, *Understanding*, 224.

he "swooned") and then revived in the tomb. This was a prominent nineteenth-century "naturalistic" attempt to explain away Jesus' resurrection; it was the position of the late Muslim apologist Ahmed Deedat and is held by the Ahmadiyya sect of Muslims today.[30]

The swoon theory fails for all the reasons listed above. It is contrary to the uniform testimony of the very earliest witnesses—both the friends and foes of Christianity.[31] Additionally, the swoon theory is contrary to the physical evidence. First, "crucifixion is essentially death by asphyxiation, as the intercostals and pectoral muscles around the lungs halt normal breathing while the body hangs in the 'down' position. Therefore, faking death on the cross still would not permit one to breathe; one cannot fake the inability to breathe for any length of time."[32] Second, the swoon theory also ignores the spear thrust into Jesus' side. As the *Journal of the American Medical Association* reported, "the spear, thrust between his right ribs, probably perforated not only the right lung but also the pericardium and heart and thereby ensured his death. Accordingly, interpretations based on the assumption that Jesus did not die on the cross appear to be at odds with modern medical knowledge."[33] Third, the swoon theory does not take into account the fact that Jesus' body would not have been prepared for burial had even one spark of life remained in him and that in the tomb Jesus could not have breathed through the heavy weight of spices and gummy substance in which he was encased.[34]

Fourth, if he somehow survived the crucifixion, how could he move the heavy stone blocking the entrance to the tomb? Matt 27:60 reports that the tomb in which Jesus was laid had been hewn out of rock and a "large stone" had been rolled across its entrance. In such tombs, circular stones, probably weighing a ton (2000 pounds) or more, would have been rolled down a slightly inclined path to block the entrance to the tomb.[35] As Jason Dulle points out, "Given the structure of such tombs, it would not have been possible for Jesus to simply push the stone over from the inside of the tomb. He would have to roll the 2000+ pound stone back up the groove without having anything to grip. Such a feat would not be possible for one healthy

---

30. Habermas, *Ancient Evidence*, 56; Deedat, *Crucifixion*, passim.
31. Moule and Cupitt, "The Resurrection," 508; Maier, *First Easter*, 112.
32. Habermas, *Ancient Evidence*, 57.
33. Edwards, et al., "On the Physical Death," 1463.
34. See McDowell, *The Resurrection*, 98.
35. Dulle, "The Size," n.p.; "Rolling Stone," n.p.; McDowell, *The Resurrection*, 54.

man, yet alone a man who had just been beaten to a bloody pulp by the Romans."[36] Further, had that somehow been done, how could he have fought off the Roman guard?

Finally, the swoon theory largely was dealt its death-blow by David Strauss (an opponent of orthodox Christianity) in the latter part of the nineteenth century. Strauss pointed out,

> It is impossible that a being who had stolen half-dead out of the sepulchre, who crept about weak and ill, wanting medical treatment, who required bandaging, strengthening and indulgence, and who still, at last, yielded to his sufferings, could have given to the disciples the impression that he was a Conqueror over death and the grave, the Prince of Life, an impression which lay at the bottom of their future ministry. Such a resuscitation could only have weakened the impression which he had made upon them in life and in death, at the most could only have given it an elegiac voice, but could by no possibility have changed their sorrow into enthusiasm, have elevated their reverence into worship.[37]

CONCLUSION

The fact that Jesus died by crucifixion is strongly attested historically, and is accepted generally by scholars who are skeptical or critical of Christianity.[38] One such highly critical scholar is John Dominic Crossan who states, "That he [Jesus] was crucified is as sure as anything historical can ever be, since both Josephus and Tacitus . . . agree with the Christian accounts on at least that basic fact."[39] After assessing the evidence, Hans-Ruedi Weber concludes, "Jesus of Nazareth was crucified under Pontius Pilate—this is a fact which no one can doubt unless he willfully ignores all biblical and non-biblical accounts that have come to us."[40]

---

36. Dulle, "The Size," n.p.; see also "Rolling Stone," n.p.; Habermas, *Ancient Evidence*, 56–57.

37. Strauss, *A New Life*, 412.

38. See Habermas and Licona, *The Case*, 44, 48–49.

39. Crossan, *Jesus*, 145; see also Dunn, *Jesus Remembered*, 339; Eddy and Boyd, *The Jesus Legend*, 172.

40. Weber, *The Cross*, 12.

6

The Resurrection of Jesus Christ Is a Historical Fact

HISTORICAL DATA SIMILAR TO those that establish that Jesus died by crucifixion also establish that he bodily rose from the dead. A resurrection is the physical and bodily raising up of a dead person to new life, in Christ's case to everlasting life. Atheists, of course, do not believe in God and try to look for "natural" explanations to account for the reports of the resurrection. Atheists beg the question about whether or not miracles may occur by assuming in advance that there is no God and, hence, there cannot be miracles. However, if there is an omnipotent God such as the Bible describes, then there is nothing irrational about the possibility of miracles, including the resurrection of Jesus from the dead.[1] Science, on the other hand, can only assess natural, not supernatural, phenomena, and God and miracles, by their nature, are supernatural.[2] Further, science can only speak in terms of probabilities and cannot or should not determine *a priori* what is or is not possible. Consequently, claims of miracles should be investigated objectively.[3]

It is, of course, true that many ancient and superstitious people have believed that various events were miraculous, although we now know such events had natural causes.[4] Most ancient miracle stories do not claim to

---

1. Bahnsen, *Always Ready*, 226; Keller, *The Reason*, 86; Gilbert, *Why Trust*, 109.

2. J. Gresham Machen states that a miracle is a supernatural event "that takes place by the immediate, as distinguished from the mediate, power of God." Machen, *Christianity*, 99.

3. See Habermas, *Ancient Evidence*, 24; Lewis, "Religion," 134.

4. However, even the ancients knew that miracles were events that were exceptions to the laws of nature. C. S. Lewis points out, "The very idea of 'miracle' presupposes knowledge of the Laws of Nature; you can't have the idea of an exception until

be eyewitness accounts of actual, historical events. Instead, such stories clearly are either legends or myths or are historical events that have been embellished. Thus, it is easy for historians to conclude that such stories are not true, historical accounts. The biblical accounts of miracles fundamentally differ from other ancient miracle stories in ways that make the biblical accounts much more plausible. The biblical accounts do not on their face claim or appear to be myths, legends, or embellishments, but purport to be eyewitness accounts of real, historical events. For example, Jesus' miracles are not "tricks" like pulling a rabbit out of a hat; rather, they typically are described as "signs" (see, e.g., John 2:11, 23; 3:2). They point to who Jesus is (his walking on water and stilling a storm show his superiority over the nature that he created). His miracles also are intimately connected with his message that he has come to make right a world in which people hunger (hence, his miraculous feedings of people), suffer (hence, his miraculous healings of people), and die (hence, his raising people from the dead).[5] The historical nature of the miracles is corroborated by the real, human reactions of fear (see Matt 28:4; Mark 4:41; Luke 24:36–37) and doubt (see Matt 28:17; Mark 16:11, 13; Luke 24:10–11, 36–41; John 20:24–25) experienced by some of the people who witnessed or heard of certain miracles. In short, accounts of miracles cannot be ruled out of court *a priori*, but should be assessed as one would evaluate other purportedly eyewitness accounts of some event. This includes the account of the greatest and most important miracle: the resurrection of Jesus Christ.

Jesus' resurrection is particularly important in that it was predicted in advance, both by Jesus himself and in the OT. Jesus gave his resurrection as the test by which we could know he was telling the truth (Matt 12:38–40; 16:1–4; John 2:18–21; see also Mark 14:58; Luke 11:29–30; Rom 1:4). In the OT, Ps 2:7; 16:10; 132:11, and 2 Sam 7:12 predicted the resurrection; those predictions are quoted in Acts 2:27, 30–31, and 13:33 as being fulfilled by the fact of Jesus' resurrection. One reason these predictions of the resurrection are significant is because Karl Popper, probably the twentieth century's most important philosopher of science, pointed out that it is easy to obtain confirmations for a theory "if we look for confirmations"; but confirmations should count only if they are the result of a "risky prediction."[6] There probably could be no more "risky" prediction than the prediction of something that not only is unprecedented but is impossible for anyone who is only a

---

you have the idea of a rule." Lewis, "Christian Apologetics," 100. Thus, it is precisely because Joseph knew how babies are normally conceived that he wanted to break his engagement to Mary when he learned that she was pregnant (see Matt 1:18–20).

5. See Blomberg, *Gospels*, 104–51.
6. Popper, *Conjectures*, 36.

human being to do, namely, rise from the dead. Whether Jesus bodily rose from the dead is a factual, historical question: either he did or he did not. As professor of ancient history Edwin Yamauchi noted, "To be sure, the Resurrection of Jesus is unprecedented, but Jesus himself is *sui generis,* unique"; nevertheless, "what is at issue is whether the Resurrection of Christ is rooted in history as an objective event or is simply a creation of the subjective faith of the disciples."[7] Therefore, even though the resurrection of a man from the dead is a unique and unprecedented event, whether or not it happened can and should be determined as one would determine other claimed historical occurrences—by assessing the available evidence and using our reason to evaluate the likelihood that it did or did not occur. The following historical data demonstrate that Jesus was, in fact, bodily resurrected from the grave.

THE TOMB WAS EMPTY

The tomb in which Jesus had been buried was owned by Joseph of Arimathea (Matt 27:57–60; Mark 15:45–46; Luke 23:50–53; John 19:38–42). Thus, it was a known tomb. The women who went to the tomb on the Sunday after the burial had seen where Jesus was buried, so they knew the location of the tomb (Matt 27:61; Mark 15:47; Luke 13:55; John 20:1).

1. *The significance of the women.* On the Sunday immediately following the burial, Mary Magdalene and other women went to the tomb, found that the stone had been rolled away and the tomb was empty, and encountered the risen Christ (Matt 28:1–7; Mark 16:1–9; Luke 24:1–8; John 20:1).[8] They then reported to the disciples that the tomb was empty and that Jesus had risen from the grave and was alive (Matt 28:8; Mark 16:10–11; Luke 24:9–12; John 20:2–18). These passages are significant in that the initial appearances of Jesus following his resurrection were made to and the initial reports of the resurrection were given by women. This fact shows that the biblical accounts were not made up but are reliable. The reason is that in ancient Judaism women were considered to be unreliable witnesses; they either were not competent to act as witnesses in court or there were significant limitations on the testimony they could give.[9] Con-

7. Yamauchi, "Easter," n.p.

8. Robert Stein states, "The presence of the various Semitisms and Semitic customs in the gospel accounts of the empty tomb indicates that these accounts were early and originated most probably in a Palestinian setting." Stein, "Was the Tomb," 25.

9. "Witness," *Encyclopaedia,* Competency (1) Women; Meacham,

sequently, the disciples' disbelief of the women's reports stemmed not only from the amazing nature of what they were reporting but probably also from the fact that they were women. But that latter fact helps to authenticate that the biblical accounts are truthful because, as Paul Maier explains, since the testimony of women was considered to be unreliable, "if the resurrection accounts had been manufactured . . . women would *never* have been included in the story, at least, not as first witnesses."[10] Historian Michael Grant concurs, "The early Church would never have concocted, on its own account, the statement that this most solemn and fateful of all discoveries was made by women, including a woman with an immoral record at that."[11]

2. *The significance of the Jews.* The Jewish leaders never denied that the tomb was empty. Instead, when the Roman guard reported to the chief priests what had happened, the Jewish leaders bribed the guard and invented the story that Jesus' *"disciples came by night and stole Him away"* (Matt 28:11–15).[12] We previously quoted from Josephus, the first-century Jewish historian for the Romans. Paul Maier notes "the remarkable fact that Josephus does *not* seek to scotch the resurrection claim by any information at his disposal that Jesus' body still lay in its grave. Certainly this is an argument from silence, but the silence is especially eloquent in view of Josephus' known habit of roasting false Messiahs elsewhere in his books."[13] Justin Martyr, in his *Dialogue with Trypho,* reported c. AD 150 that "the Jewish authorities even sent specially commissioned men across the Mediterranean to counter Christian claims with this explanation of the resurrection."[14]

Additionally, Edward Bode points out that the claim that someone stole the body had to have developed early, because after a long time "too many things could have happened to explain [the tomb's] being empty."[15] He also notes that the argument of the Jewish leaders "did not contest the existence of the empty tomb; rather it admitted the fact of the empty tomb by trying to explain the emptiness through

---

"Legal-Religious," Other Laws.

10. Maier, *First Easter,* 98.

11. Grant, *Jesus,* 176.

12. The stolen body theory is discussed in more detail in section "The failure of alternative explanations," below.

13. Maier, *First Easter,* 116.

14. Maier, *First Easter,* 116–17.

15. Bode, *The First,* 163.

some manner other than Jesus' resurrection."[16] This is powerful evidence, since the Jewish leaders were the enemies of the Christians and therefore had every reason *not* to give ammunition (the admission that the tomb was, in fact, empty) in support of the disciples' proclamation that Christ had risen from the tomb.

3. *The lack of veneration of the grave.* There is another important fact that must be accounted for, namely, that there is no evidence that early Christians ever venerated the tomb in which Jesus had been laid to rest. James Dunn observes,

> This is indeed striking, because within contemporary Judaism, as in other religions, the desire to honour the memory of the revered dead by constructing appropriate tombs and (by implication) by veneration of the site is well attested. . . . Why would the first Christians not act out this pious instinct and tradition? The only obvious answer, in the light of the evidence thus far reviewed, is that they did not believe any tomb contained his body. They could not venerate his remains because they did not think there were any remains to be venerated."[17]

The lack of veneration of Jesus' tomb contrasts with the veneration of the tombs and bones of the early Christian martyrs.[18] It also contrasts with the tomb of Muhammad in Medina, which to this day remains a site of pilgrimage for Muslims. Historian Michael Grant concludes, "If we apply the same sort of criteria that we would apply to any other ancient literary sources, then the evidence is firm and plausible enough to necessitate the conclusion that the tomb was indeed found empty."[19]

THE EARLY CHRISTIANS BEGAN PROCLAIMING JESUS' RESURRECTION EVEN IN JERUSALEM

The fact that Jesus' tomb was empty and the credibility of the Christian belief in the resurrection are confirmed by the fact that the early Christians did not wait decades to proclaim Jesus' resurrection (so that the witnesses

---

16. Bode, *The First*, 163; see also Craig, *The Son*, 83–84; Wright, *The Resurrection*, 638.
17. Dunn, *Jesus*, 837–38; see also Craig, *The Son*, 63.
18. See *The Martyrdom*, 18.
19. Grant, *Jesus*, 176.

The Resurrection of Jesus Christ Is a Historical Fact 79

would be dead) but did so from the beginning.[20] As Peter and John said after having been arrested and threatened by the Jewish leaders for proclaiming Jesus' resurrection, *"We cannot stop speaking about what we have seen and heard"* (Acts 4:20). They also did not go to some remote province to proclaim Jesus' resurrection (where no one could contradict them), but began their proclamation in Jerusalem, the city where Jesus had been killed and buried and where their primary opponents, the Jewish leaders and the Romans, were most prominent (Acts 2–7).[21] Tacitus confirms that the church began in Judea.[22]

Edward Bode notes, "Given the Jewish notion of the resurrection of the body and the knowledge of the location of the tomb, it would have been impossible to preach a risen Jesus in Jerusalem if this tomb had still contained the body. With the Jewish mentality of resurrection and the availability of the tomb, someone sooner or later was bound to look for himself to see if the tomb was empty."[23] "The empty tomb could not prove the resurrection of Jesus or create faith in it. *But the contrary is not true.* If the Jewish authorities had been able to produce the body of Jesus, they would have been able finally and decisively to *disprove* the resurrection of Jesus, as the disciples believed it and were proclaiming it."[24] The Jewish leaders had the means, the motive, and the opportunity to crush the incipient Christian movement, and they easily could have and would have done so had they simply gone to the tomb, removed Jesus' dead body, and paraded it for all to see; but they did not because they could not.

The same is true with respect to the Roman authorities who, above all else, wanted to keep peace and avoid conflict among the people they governed. Terry Miethe states that "the claim was that the body was no longer there, that all the eyewitnesses were still alive, and that the church was causing so much trouble with its claim that the Roman government certainly could have put this to a rest by producing contrary evidence."[25] Thus, "If

---

20. The fact that Jesus' disciples began proclaiming his *resurrection* is itself evidence for his *crucifixion*. To proclaim that someone has risen from the dead is nonsensical unless that person first is *dead*.

21. Peter Williams itemizes the multiple and varied locations and circumstances of Jesus' post-resurrection appearances, many involving close-up encounters involving conversations. He draws the obvious conclusion, "It is hard to imagine this pattern of appearances in the Gospels and early Christian letters without there having been multiple individuals who claimed to have seen Jesus risen from the dead." Williams, *Can We Trust*, 134–35.

22. Tacitus, *Annals*, 15.44.

23. Bode, *The First*, 174; see also Craig, *The Son*, 82–83.

24. Neill, *The Interpretation*, 288, emph. in orig.

25. Miethe, *Did Jesus*, 70.

the [Jewish or Roman] authorities could have produced Jesus' corpse, they would have exploded the Resurrection faith for good; the fact that it was not exploded indicates that they did not produce the corpse, and their failure to produce it . . . shows that they could not produce it."[26] The failure of early Christianity's enemies to produce Jesus' dead body is eloquent testimony that the grave was empty—and the only plausible explanation that fits all the facts is that the grave was empty because Jesus had risen from the grave exactly as he had predicted and as the disciples were proclaiming.[27]

MULTIPLE WITNESSES

Earlier, we considered the early Christian creeds, including 1 Cor 15:3–7. That creed is particularly important since it goes back to the early AD 30s, essentially to the time of the crucifixion/resurrection itself, and was based on eyewitness testimony.[28] Verses 4–7 of that creed state, "*⁴ And that He was buried, and that He was raised on the third day according to the Scriptures, ⁵ and that He appeared to Cephas, then to the twelve. ⁶ After that He appeared to more than five hundred brethren at one time, most of whom remain until now, but some have fallen asleep; ⁷ then He appeared to James, then to all the apostles.*" A. M. Hunter points out that 1 Cor 15:3–7 "is traditional testimony to the fact of the resurrection taking us back to within half a dozen years of the crucifixion, and it has rightly been called 'the oldest document of the Christian church which we possess.' Moreover, it is 'tradition' whose *truth was open to testing*. When Paul wrote, Peter and James were still living and most of the 'five hundred brethren' yet survived and could be questioned."[29] This creed links the events it recites with the eyewitnesses and participants in those events. Habermas summarizes the importance of this, "The fact

---

26. Packer, "Response," 149.

27. "The seedbed for the first budding and growth of the church was in the city of Jerusalem itself, where, of all places, it would have been ridiculous to preach a risen Christ unless both the apostles and their hearers knew that Joseph's sepulcher was empty. Some months later, the authorities were so desperate to stop the movement that they even resorted to persecution. A far more effective tool would have been at least an elaborate counter-rumor that there was a body in Joseph's grave, but this was never attempted because by then there were apparently too many Jerusalemites who had seen for themselves that the sepulcher was empty at the time." Maier, *First Easter*, 120.

28. Habermas, "Rebuttal," 43; see also Habermas, *Ancient Evidence*, 125 and the citations therein.

29. Hunter, *Jesus*, 100, emph. in orig.

The Resurrection of Jesus Christ Is a Historical Fact 81

that it was the original eyewitnesses who reported these events indicates that legends from a later period cannot explain this initial testimony."[30]

With respect to the 500 witnesses, C. H. Dodd observes, "There can hardly be any purpose in mentioning the fact that most of the 500 are still alive, unless Paul is saying, in effect, 'the witnesses are there to be questioned.'"[31] William Lane Craig adds, *"Paul could never have said that if the event had not actually occurred."*[32] It is important to remember that Paul's letter to the Corinthians was to a church and was to be read aloud, i.e., it was a public, not a private, document. Paul's invitation to question the witnesses was a real and doable invitation, since travel throughout the Roman Empire over Roman roads and by sea was relatively safe and easy. Hence, he never could have made that invitation if the witnesses did not exist.[33]

THE EARLY CHRISTIANS' LIVES WERE CHANGED BY WHAT THEY SAW

Although Jesus had predicted his death and resurrection, the NT makes clear that his disciples did not understand him; they had no conception of a dying and rising Messiah (see, e.g., Matt 16:21–23; Mark 9:30–32; Luke 24:18–26; John 12:12–16). As mentioned earlier, the disciples did not believe the reports of the women that Jesus had risen from the tomb. Then Jesus appeared to the disciples in order to assure them that he was not just a vision, or hallucination, or spirit, or ghost; he asked them to touch his body, and he also ate with them (Luke 24:36–43; John 20:19–29; 21:9–14). That these events happened is confirmed by Ignatius, the bishop of Antioch. Ignatius was friends with Polycarp who had been "instructed by apostles, and conversed with many who had seen Christ."[34] When Ignatius was on the way to his own martyrdom about AD 110, he wrote a letter to the church at Smyrna where Polycarp was then bishop. In that letter he recounted,

> For I know that after His resurrection also He was still possessed of flesh, and I believe that He is so now. When, for instance, He came to those who were with Peter, He said to them, *"Lay hold, handle Me, and see that I am not an incorporeal spirit."* And

---

30. Habermas, *Ancient Evidence*, 126–27.
31. Dodd, "The Appearances," 128.
32. Craig, *The Son*, 94, emph. in orig.
33. Keller, *The Reason*, 204; see also Wright, *The Resurrection*, 325 ("The whole thrust of the paragraph is about evidence, about witnesses being called, about something that actually happened for which eyewitnesses could and would vouch").
34. Irenaeus, *Against Heresies*, 3.3.4.

immediately they touched Him, and believed, being convinced both by His flesh and spirit. For this cause also they despised death, and were found its conquerors. And after his resurrection He did eat and drink with them, as being possessed of flesh, although spiritually He was united to the Father.[35]

These personal appearances of Jesus in his resurrection body transformed the disciples. At and after Jesus' arrest and crucifixion, his disciples denied him, abandoned him, and hid in fear. But after his resurrection, those same disciples were transformed such that they willingly endangered themselves by proclaiming his resurrection in Jerusalem and elsewhere, endured persecution, and willingly died for the sake of the risen Christ. Clement of Rome, who is reputed to have seen the apostles,[36] wrote even at the end of the first century that their boldness in preaching was because they had "been fully assured through the resurrection of our Lord Jesus Christ."[37] If the original disciples had not seen the risen Lord, they would not have been transformed from cowards to bold witnesses of the resurrection of Jesus despite persecution and death (which most of them suffered). But for that, Christianity would not exist.

The NT frequently discusses the persecution faced by the early disciples who had seen the risen Jesus and the boldness with which they nevertheless proclaimed that Jesus had risen and was Lord (e.g., Acts 4:1–31; 5:17–42; 6:7—7:60; 2 Cor 11:23–33). This is confirmed by other ancient Christian writings.[38] Peter and Paul, among many others, were martyred for their faith.[39] Polycarp, who himself was martyred in about AD 160,[40] in his *Epistle to the Philippians* (c.110) confirms not only the suffering and deaths of Paul and the other apostles but also the source of their steadfastness—the resurrection of Christ: "For they loved not this present world, but Him who died for us, and for our sakes was raised again by God from the dead."[41]

When one considers the historical evidence, the only plausible explanation for this amazing change in the character and lives of the disciples that is also consistent with the rest of the known evidence (e.g., Jesus' death, his burial, the empty tomb) is Jesus' bodily resurrection. Origen made this

---

35. Ignatius, *Smyrnaeans*, 3.
36. Irenaeus, *Against Heresies*, 3.3.3; Tertullian, *Prescription*, 32,
37. Clement, *First Epistle*, ch. 42.
38. E.g., Clement, *First Epistle*, 5; Ignatius, *Smyrnaeans*, 1–3.
39. See Tertullian, *Prescription*, ch. 36.
40. *Martyrdom*, 9.
41. Polycarp, *Epistle*, 9.

point in AD 248, "But a clear and unmistakable proof of the fact [of Christ's resurrection] I hold to be the undertaking of His disciples, who devoted themselves to the teaching of a doctrine which was attended with danger to human life,—a doctrine which they would not have taught with such courage had they invented the resurrection of Jesus from the dead; and who also, at the same time, not only prepared others to despise death, but were themselves the first to manifest their disregard for its terrors."[42] The bold proclamation of Jesus' resurrection in the face of persecution and death thus disproves the swoon theory, the stolen body theory, or other "naturalistic" attempts to explain away the resurrection, because no one will willingly suffer and die for what he knows to be a lie.[43]

It is true, of course, that many people have willingly died for causes they sincerely believed in even if those causes proved to be untrue or evil. However, Michael Licona points out that, with respect to the early Christians who faced persecution and martyrdom for their faith, "There is an important difference between the martyred apostle and those who die for their beliefs today. Modern martyrs act solely out of their trust in beliefs passed along to them by others. The apostles died for holding to their own testimony that they had *personally* seen the risen Jesus. Contemporary martyrs die for what they *believe* to be true. The disciples of Jesus died for what they *knew* to be either true or false."[44]

THE SUDDEN CONVERSION OF PAUL, AN ENEMY OF CHRIST

The apostle Paul, first known as Saul of Tarsus, was a well-educated Pharisee (Acts 22:3; 26:4–5; Phil 3:4–5). So fanatical was he for the monotheistic Jewish faith in which he was raised and instructed that he became a zealous persecutor of Christians (Acts 7:54—8:3; 9:1–2; 22:4–5; 26:9–11; Phil

---

42. Origen, *Against Celsus*, 2:56.

43. Charles Colson has stated, "But what about the disciples? Twelve powerless men, peasants really, were facing not just embarrassment or political disgrace, but beatings, stonings, execution. Every single one of the disciples insisted, to their dying breaths, that they had physically seen Jesus bodily raised from the dead. Don't you think that one of those apostles would have cracked before being beheaded or stoned? That one of them would have made a deal with the authorities? None did. You see, men will give their lives for something they believe to be true—they will never give their lives for something they know to be false." Colson, "An UnHoly," n.p.

44. Licona, *The Resurrection*, 370; see also Dunn, *Jesus*, 861 ("It was not that some conviction regarding Jesus was subsequently cast in the form of a resurrection experience story. . . . They not only *believed* they had seen the Lord, they had *experienced* a seeing of the Lord alive from the dead.").

3:6; 1 Tim 1:13). However, even while he was in the middle of persecuting Christians, Paul was dramatically converted to Christ (Acts 9:1–22). What accounts for such a dramatic conversion—one that transformed Paul from being a persecutor to being persecuted? Paul himself describes the reason for this change as his encounter with the resurrected Christ. He adds to the early creed in 1 Corinthians 15 *"and last of all, as to one untimely born, He appeared to me also"* (1 Cor 15:8). Paul's account is credible because he himself was willing continually to suffer and ultimately die for his belief in the risen Christ. Further, the early church leaders who assessed him accounted him as authoritative as the other apostles.[45]

While many people have converted from one set of beliefs to another, Licona reminds us that people usually convert to a particular religion because they have heard or read about the religion and believed what they heard or read. Paul's conversion was different. It was based on "a personal appearance of the risen Jesus. Today we might believe that Jesus rose from the dead based on secondary evidence, trusting Paul and the disciples who saw the risen Jesus. But for Paul, his experience came from primary evidence [the direct, personal appearance of Jesus himself]."[46]

THE SUDDEN CONVERSION OF JAMES, A SKEPTIC OF CHRIST

The Bible records that Jesus had a number of brothers, one of whom was James (Matt 13:55–56; Mark 6:3; Gal 1:19). That James was Jesus' brother was also confirmed by Josephus.[47] James appears to have been a pious Jew who strictly held to Jewish laws and customs.[48] During Jesus' life, James and the other brothers did not believe that Jesus was who he claimed to be and apparently thought that he had lost his senses (Mark 3:21, 31; John 7:1–5). When he was on the cross, Jesus' committing his mother into the care of his disciple John instead of to his own brother confirms that James was not then a believer (John 19:25–27).

After Jesus' death and resurrection, as Paul recites in the ancient creed, *"then He appeared to James"* (1 Cor 15:7). Although we have less information

---

45. See 2 Pet 3:16; Polycarp, *Epistle*, 3:2; 9:1; Ignatius, *Ephesians*, 12:2; *Romans*, 4:3. Habermas and Licona note that "Paul's writings are certainly cited twenty-one times by five of the apostolic fathers and perhaps alluded to on several other occasions." Habermas and Licona, *The Case*, 280n.4.

46. Licona, *The Resurrection*, 440.

47. Josephus, *Antiquities*, 20.9.1.

48. See Gal 2:11–12; see also Eusebius, *Church History*, 2.23, quoting Hegesippus.

concerning James's conversion than we have of Paul's, the historical facts all indicate that James's conversion was just as dramatic and powerful as was Paul's. The appearance of the risen Christ to James evidently was early, because James is among those waiting in the upper room in Jerusalem for the empowering by the Holy Spirit which occurred on the day of Pentecost; that would place the appearance to James within 50 days of the resurrection (Acts 1:14). James then became a leader of the church in Jerusalem (Acts 15:13–21; Gal 1:19). He wrote one of the epistles that make up the NT. His conversion was so profound that he, like the other early disciples, died a martyr's death, which is attested by both non-Christian and Christian sources.[49]

As with Paul, the question must be asked: What best accounts for such a profound conversion and change of life of James, this former skeptic? The most plausible explanation that fits all the existing facts and that was maintained *from the beginning* (1 Cor 15:7) is the appearance to James of the resurrected Christ. As Wright puts it, "It is difficult to account for his centrality and unrivalled leadership unless he was himself known to have seen the risen Jesus."[50]

THE FORMATION AND EXISTENCE OF THE CHRISTIAN CHURCH

While Jesus was on earth, his disciples had no understanding of a dying and rising messiah; yet "at least the *belief* that Jesus rose from the dead lay at the very heart of the earliest Christian faith."[51] Where did that belief come from? Such a belief did not come from paganism. Pagans did not believe in resurrection. Some pagan cults, of course, had stories of dying and rising gods and goddesses such as Adonis, Attis, Demeter, Dionysus, Persephone, Isis, Osiris, Tammuz, and Balder, the son of the Norse god Odin. Such pagan myths manifestly were not the *source* of the Christians' belief in Jesus' resurrection, because the early Christians were all Jews, steeped in Judaism, not pagans. Worshippers of these pagan cults did not believe that actual human beings had come back to life. They knew these were metaphors for the cycles of planting and harvesting and human fertility.[52] C. S. Lewis states, "The Pagan stories are all about someone dying and rising, either every year, or else nobody knows where and nobody knows when. The Christian story

---

49. Josephus, *Antiquities*, 20.9.1; Eusebius, *Church History*, 2.23.
50. Wright, *The Resurrection*, 325.
51. Craig, *The Son*, 127.
52. See Wright, *The Resurrection*, 80–81.

is about a historical personage, whose execution can be dated pretty accurately, under a named Roman magistrate, and with whom the society that He founded is in a continuous relation down to the present day."[53] Even deceased Roman emperors who were proclaimed to be gods, or legends that human beings such as Romulus became divine, could not have been the source of belief in Jesus' resurrection, because none of those proclamations or legends involved the body or included resurrection.[54]

Since paganism could not have been the source of the disciples' belief in Jesus' resurrection, if one denies that Jesus actually rose from the grave, then he or she has to explain the disciples' belief in the resurrection either as stemming from Christian or Jewish influences.[55] Obviously, the belief in a crucified and resurrected messiah could not have come from Christian influences, because Christianity did not yet exist. This idea also could not have come from Judaism although many Jews believed in a resurrection. However, the Jewish conception of resurrection was fundamentally different from what the Christians were proclaiming in two important ways. The Christians were proclaiming that Jesus' resurrection had occurred in the middle of history and had happened to only one, specific person. In sharp contrast with that, in Jewish thought, resurrection *always*: "(1) occurred after the end of the world, not within history, and (2) concerned all the people, not just an isolated individual."[56] Consequently, Professor C. F. D. Moule concludes, "I don't for a moment think anything in the OT could have *generated* it [the belief in a resurrected messiah]. . . . I have been able to discover none [either OT passages or extra-biblical Jewish beliefs] which suggests the entry upon *eternal* life by an *individual*, *before* the wind-up of history: and it's *this* that one has to account for."[57]

---

53. Lewis, "Is Theology," 83. Lewis also notes the logical fallacy of citing such myths as a reason to discount the historical fact of Christ's resurrection. That argument assumes that Christianity is false and cites pagan myths as evidence for the already-assumed presupposition of its falsity, "just as if you started by knowing that there were no such things as crocodiles then the various stories about dragons might help to confirm your disbelief. But if the truth of Christianity is the very question which you are discussing, then the argument from anthropology is surely a *petitio* [i.e., *petitio principii*—the logical fallacy of "begging the question" in which what is to be proved is implicitly taken for granted]." Lewis, "Religion," 132.

54. See Wright, *The Resurrection*, 83.

55. See Craig, *The Son*, 129.

56. Craig, *The Son*, 129.The typical Jewish belief concerning resurrection at the end of the age is reflected in the beliefs of the Jews as indicated in the NT (see Mark 9:9–11; John 11:23–24).

57. Moule and Cupitt, "The Resurrection," 508, emph. in orig.

Nevertheless, *something* had to have occurred that accounts for the origin and rapid spread of the new worldview called Christianity. What was that "something"? The only plausible explanation for the *origin* of Christianity—which necessitated a profound theological change from previous Jewish belief—is that Jesus had, in fact, resurrected from the dead. No other explanation fits all the facts. In connection with this, Timothy Keller makes the important observation that a massive shift at the level of an entire worldview (which the belief in the bodily resurrection clearly was) "ordinarily takes years of discussion and argument in which thinkers and writers debate . . . until one side wins. That is how culture and worldviews change."[58] But Christianity and the Christian view of resurrection were not like that. The origin of Christianity and the Christian view of resurrection are absolutely unprecedented in history; they arose fully formed immediately after the death of Jesus. There was no process of discussion, argument, or debate by thinkers and writers. Instead, the followers of Jesus simply reported what they had seen and experienced. They were witnesses of an unanticipated and unique experience rather than advocates of a new philosophy. Not only does the origin of Christianity involve a massive shift at the worldview level, but the resurrection became the *focus* and central aspect of the new worldview.[59] That fact also requires a historical explanation. Again, the only plausible explanation is that Jesus did, in fact, bodily rise from the dead.

This sudden and dramatic change in belief is confirmed by certain unique aspects of Christian belief and practice, all of which began early-on:

1. *Sunday worship.* "One of the Jewish beliefs held with most tenacity is observance of the Sabbath, and yet Christian Jews transferred their worship from Saturday to Sunday [Acts 20:7; 1 Cor 16:2], which they termed 'the Lord's Day' [Rev 1:10]. Only some drastic consideration would have introduced this change: their weekly celebration of the Resurrection."[60] James D. G. Dunn adds, "Not least of relevance is the tradition that Jesus first appeared *'on the first day of the week'* (Sunday) following his crucifixion and burial. . . . Nor should we forget the striking but often neglected fact that from as early as we can trace, Sunday had become a day of special significance for Christians, 'the Lord's day', precisely because it was the day on which they celebrated the resurrection of the Lord."[61] Indeed, early church fathers

---

58. Keller, *The Reason,* 209.
59. See Wright, *The Resurrection,* 477.
60. Maier, *First Easter,* 122; see also *Didache,* 14.1.
61. Dunn, *Jesus,* 860.

Ignatius and Justin Martyr specifically refer to the resurrection as the rationale for the new day of worship.[62]

2. *Baptism.* While baptism had been practiced in ancient Judaism for proselytes to Judaism and as a sign of repentance and purification,[63] its meaning in Christianity was changed to directly relate to the death and resurrection of Jesus (Rom 6:3–5; Col 2:12). The church could have kept the old Jewish notions of baptism, but it did not. And this change in meaning occurred very early in church history.

3. *Lord's Supper.* First Cor 11:23–26 sets forth another of the ancient creeds that go back to the very beginning of Christianity in the early-to-mid-30s, in this case back to Jesus himself.[64] The celebration of the Lord's Supper specifically commemorates Jesus' death on the cross and is based on what Jesus said at the Last Supper he shared with his disciples. As we have seen, however, it is the resurrection that validates the efficacy of Jesus' sacrifice on the cross. Hence, 1 Cor 11:26 ends the formula by saying *"For as often as you eat this bread and drink the cup, you proclaim the Lord's death until he comes."* That is a recognition that Jesus is alive and will.

4. *The early writing of the NT documents, which focus on Christ and his resurrection.* We have already seen that early Christian creeds, including Phil 2:9–11 and 1 Cor 15:3–7, go back to the early AD 30s, essentially to the time of the crucifixion/resurrection itself. The apostles began writing their epistles and gospels, which became part of the NT, less than 20 years after Jesus' death and resurrection. Those documents reflect the fact that the disciples early-on industriously reflected upon Jesus, remembered what he said and did, searched through the OT to see how he fulfilled what the OT had prophesied, focused on the last days of their Lord, and began a vigorous ministry to fellow Jews in Jerusalem itself. Paul Barnett discusses the significance of this, in contrast to the reactions of others from that time period who had claimed to be messianic figures and who also had been killed:

> These activities could not have been self-generating and would not have occurred unless Jesus had been raised from the dead. Certainly no such activities occurred (so far as we know) in the

---

62. Ignatius, *Magnesians*, 9.1; Martyr, *First Apology*, 67.

63. "Baptism," *Jewish Encyclopedia*, see Matt 3:1–6; Mark 1:4; Luke 3:3; John 1:25–27.

64. Jeremias, *The Eucharistic Words*, 101, 104–5; Habermas, *Ancient Evidence*, 121.

aftermath of the death of the Teacher of Righteousness [a High Priest, messiah-like figure, of the Qumran community, depicted in the Dead Sea Scrolls] or Judas the Galilean [a would-be messiah, founder of the Zealots, who led a revolt against Rome; he is mentioned in Acts 5:37].[65]

Any theory of what happened that first Easter morning *other than the bodily resurrection of Christ* "does not even solve the problem which is here under consideration: the origin, that is, of the Christian Church by faith in the miraculous resurrection of the Messiah."[66] Consequently, Ulrich Wilckens concludes, "The history of mission in primitive Christianity and the entire history of Christian thought with its many layers, is to be understood as an effect of the original experience of the resurrection of Jesus, the preacher of love. If it were not for this experience Christianity would undoubtedly not have come into existence. Through this experience Christianity as a whole is given its basis."[67]

THE FAILURE OF ALTERNATIVE EXPLANATIONS

A number of theories that have been proposed to try to explain away the resurrection. The swoon theory, the body was stolen, the contention that Jesus didn't die so he couldn't have been resurrected, and the resurrection is a myth like the dying and rising gods and goddesses of certain pagan cults have been discussed above. Other contentions are the following:

1. *The resurrection is just a legend that developed later.* This is "the only satisfactory explanation" Islamic scholar Muhammad Asad can come up with to explain the statement in Q. 4:157 regarding the crucifixion that the Jews *"killed him not, nor crucified him, but so it was made to appear to them."*[68] Asad states,

    The story of the crucifixion as such has been succinctly explained in the Qur'anic phrase wa-lakin shubbiha lahum, which I render

---

65. Barnett, *Behind the Scenes*, 145.
66. Strauss, *A New Life*, 412.
67. Wilckens, *Resurrection*, 131.
68. Unless otherwise noted, quotations from the Qur'an are from the English translation by Yusuf Ali, *The Meaning of the Noble Qur'an*. Other versions that will be cited or quoted from (i.e., Sahih International [cited as Sahih], Pickthall, Shakir, Sarwar, al-Hilali and Khan [cited as Hilali-Khan], and Arberry) are found on the Muslim website *Quranic Arabic Corpus* (http://corpus.quran.com/); the translations by Muhammad Asad and M. A. S. Abdel Haleem will also be cited or quoted from.

as "but it only appeared to them as if it had been so" – implying that in the course of time, long after the time of Jesus, a legend had somehow grown up (possibly under the then-powerful influence of Mithraistic beliefs) to the effect that he had died on the cross in order to atone for the "original sin" with which mankind is allegedly burdened; and this legend became so firmly established among the latter-day followers of Jesus that even his enemies, the Jews, began to believe it – albeit in a derogatory sense (for crucifixion was, in those times, a heinous form of death-penalty reserved for the lowest of criminals). This, to my mind, is the only satisfactory explanation of the phrase wa-lakin shubbiha lahum, the more so as the expression shubbiha li is idiomatically synonymous with khuyyila 1i, "[a thing] became a fancied image to me", i.e., "in my mind" – in other words, "[it] seemed to me."[69]

Asad's "legend" theory is specifically directed at the issue of the crucifixion but would equally apply to the resurrection since the two are related.

Approximately 200 years ago Julius Müller made the important point that it takes considerable time for written legends to develop about historical people and events, particularly when primary sources and eyewitnesses exist. Müller wrote,

Most decidedly must a considerable interval of time be required for such a complete transformation of a whole history by popular tradition, when the series of legends are formed in the same territory where the heroes actually lived and wrought. Here one cannot imagine how such a series of legends could arise in an historical age, obtain universal respect, and supplant the historical recollection of the true character and connexion of their heroes' lives in the minds of the community, if eyewitnesses were still at hand, who could be questioned respecting the truth of the recorded marvels. Hence, legendary fiction, as it likes not the clear present time, but prefers the mysterious gloom of grey antiquity, is wont to seek a remoteness of age, along with that of space, and to remove its boldest and more rare and wonderful creations into a very remote and unknown land.[70]

Greco-Roman scholar A. N. Sherwin-White adds, "Herodotus enables us to test the tempo of myth-making, and the tests suggest that even two generations are too short a span to allow the mythical

---

69. Asad, *The Message*, Q. 4:157n.171.
70. Müller, *The Theory*, 26, quoted in Craig, *The Son*, 101.

The Resurrection of Jesus Christ Is a Historical Fact

tendency to prevail over the hard historic core of the oral tradition."[71] Not one example from all of history exists in which, within thirty years (or less) great myths or legends around an important historical individual, the central elements of which are fictitious, developed and became widely believed as true. As Müller and Sherwin-White demonstrate, several generations must pass before the "mythical tendency" can begin to prevail. That is exactly what happened concerning Jesus, as William Lane Craig observes, "The time span necessary for significant accrual of legend concerning the events of the gospels would place us in the second century A.D., just the time in fact when the legendary apocryphal gospels were born."[72]

The claims in the NT that Jesus was resurrected rule out the idea that the resurrection was a legend that developed later, because there simply was no time for "legends" of the resurrection to have developed. The four gospels—Matthew, Mark, Luke, and John, as well as the book of Acts, also written by Luke—all attest to Jesus' resurrection and were all written between approximately 40 years to a maximum of about 65 years after Jesus' resurrection. Additionally, we have the letters of Paul to the Romans, 1 and 2 Corinthians, Galatians, Ephesians, Philippians, Colossians, 1 Thessalonians, 2 Timothy, and Peter's letter of 1 Peter, all of which specifically mention the resurrection. Those letters are significant in that both Paul and Peter were martyred in the mid-60s AD, which means that their letters were written only 20–30 years after the resurrection itself. They also were eyewitnesses of Christ's post-resurrection appearances. Hence, we have public documents warren by six different individuals within the lifetime of people who were alive at the time of the resurrection, who all attest to the historicity of the resurrection. Further, as has been discussed above, some of Paul's letters contain ancient creeds that pre-date Paul's writings and go back essentially to the resurrection itself. "Since the original disciples were making the claim that Jesus rose from the dead, his resurrection was not the result of myth making. His life story was not embellished over time if the facts can be traced to the original witnesses."[73] As we have seen, the NT accounts of Christ's resurrection *can* "be traced to the original witnesses."

The resurrection of Jesus is not just a theological myth asserted long after Jesus lived. Instead, the historicity of the resurrection was

---

71. Sherwin-White, *Roman Society,* 189–90.
72. Craig, *The Son,* 101–2.
73. Habermas and Licona, *The Case,* 61–62.

asserted from the beginning and is central to the very existence of the church. "In a day when scholars have very few assured results to report from their critical study of the New Testament, it may be refreshing to know that even the more skeptical historians agree that for primitive Christianity, if not for themselves, the resurrection of Jesus from the dead was a real event in history, the very foundation of faith, and not a mythical idea arising out of the creative imagination of believers."[74] Without the actual bodily resurrection of Jesus "there would have been no Christian church and the New Testament would not have been written."[75]

2. *Psychological explanations.* It is not plausible to contend that the disciples proclaimed the resurrection of Jesus as a psychological reaction to his death. The idea that Peter, James, and the others experienced fantasies or had profound grief-related psychological reactions is based on no evidence whatsoever.[76] In fact, before the crucifixion, James did not believe that his brother Jesus was the Messiah and may even thought he was out of his mind (Mark 3:21, 31; John 7:1–5). It is not reasonable to think that a pious Jewish unbeliever like James, "who would have viewed his crucified brother as a false Messiah who had been cursed by God—was in the frame of mind to experience a life-changing hallucination of the risen Jesus, a hallucination so powerful that it would motivate him to alter his religious beliefs in an area that he believed would cost him his eternal soul if he was mistaken."[77] The same thing applies to the idea that Paul began spreading stories of the resurrection because he was consumed by guilt over his persecution of Christians. Not only is there no evidence for that, but the fact is that Paul was zealously continuing to persecute Christians up until the very moment of his encounter with the risen Christ.

Further, none of the disciples were psychologically primed to believe in Jesus' resurrection. A bodily resurrection was not something and *anyone*—including the disciples—was expecting to happen to an individual person in the middle of history.[78] In the first century there

---

74. Braaten, *History*, 78.
75. Braaten, *History*, 78.
76. See Wright, *The Resurrection*, 20.
77. Habermas and Licona, *The Case*, 107–08.

78. Wright, *The Resurrection*, 689, emph. added. This is confirmed by the first-hand accounts of the reactions of the disciples who all doubted the reports of the resurrection (see Mark 16:10–11, 13; Luke 24:10–11, 36–37, 41; John 20:24–25). Even some time later when Jesus appeared to the disciples in Galilee, Matt 28:17 states, "*When they*

were other messianic movements whose leaders had been executed by the authorities. "In not one single case do we hear the slightest mention of the disappointed followers claiming that their hero had been raised from the dead. They knew better. 'Resurrection' was not a private event.... A Jewish revolutionary whose leader had been executed by the authorities, and who managed to escape arrest himself, had two options: give up the revolution, or find another leader. We have evidence of people doing both. Claiming that the original leader was alive again was simply not an option. Unless, of course, he was."[79]

3. *Jesus' resurrection was only "spiritual."* The idea that Jesus did not rise bodily, but only rose in "spirit," cannot account for the historical data. Maier points out, "In Greece, a Platonist might have affirmed the resurrection of Jesus' spirit while his body lay moldering in an obviously occupied tomb. But for a Jew, there was no resurrection without a very physical and bodily resurrection of the flesh. The modern concept of a Christianity that would retain its validity even if the dead body of Jesus were discovered would have been philosophical nonsense to St. Paul and the early Church."[80] Such an idea both disregards the context of the disciples' own lives and cannot explain the empty tomb and the beginning of Christianity.

In the first century, Jewish burials typically took place in two stages: first, the body was laid on a slab, wrapped in cloth with spices in a cave-like tomb with a movable stone door (like Joseph of Arimathea's tomb in which Jesus was laid); second, a year or more later, after the flesh had decomposed, relatives or friends would return, collect the bones, and place them in an ossuary (bone box). "If the disciples had believed that what they called the 'resurrection' was just a 'spiritual' event, leaving the body in the tomb, someone sooner or later would have had to go back to collect Jesus' bones and store them properly. . . . But of course, if anyone had at any stage gone back to tidy up

---

saw him, they worshiped him, but some were doubtful." Had these accounts been made up long after the fact, such doubts never would have been inserted, since they would have made the disciples look like they had little faith. However, such doubts are the very thing one might expect if these events really happened, because a resurrection of an individual was completely unprecedented and was totally unexpected. Thus, the recording of these doubts is itself evidence that this is factual reporting, not after-the-fact myth-making or theologizing.

79. Wright, *Who Was*, 63.
80. Maier, "The Empty Tomb," 5.

Jesus' bones and put them in an ossuary, that would indeed have destroyed Christianity before it had even properly begun."[81]

Jesus himself specifically countered the idea that he was merely a spirit by having the disciples touch him and eat with him (Matt 28:9; Luke 24:36–43; John 20:15–17, 24–29; 21:9–14). Indeed, everyone who heard the proclamation of the resurrection knew that what was being proclaimed was the *bodily* resurrection; that is, after all, what a "resurrection" is.[82] Had that not been the case, the Jewish leaders never would have concocted the story that the body had been stolen but would have gone to the tomb and produced the body.

Not only does the idea of a "spiritual resurrection" (the very idea is an oxymoron) not explain the data, but it contradicts every biblical passage that talks about the resurrection. For example, Paul's argument in 1 Corinthians 15 explicitly concerns the "bodily" resurrection: the bodily resurrection of Jesus is the ground of his argument and constitutes the guarantee that all those who are "in Christ" likewise will be resurrected.

4. *The disciples were hallucinating or had visions.* Remember that Jesus' resurrection was completely different from any previous Jewish belief in resurrection in that (1) it occurred at a point in time in history, not at history's climax, and (2) it involved only a single individual, not humanity as a whole. Consequently, the idea that the disciples were hallucinating or saw visions assumes that Jesus' resurrection was a realistic option in the worldview of Jesus' Jewish disciples. It was not an option because hallucinations are projections of the mind; consequently, they cannot contain concepts or images that are not already in the mind.[83] In that regard, even if the disciples under the influence of the empty tomb projected hallucinatory visions of Jesus, they would never have projected him as bodily risen from the dead back to the earth. They would have seen him in "Abraham's bosom" (see Luke 16:19–31), since "that is where, in Jewish belief, the souls of the righteous go to await the final resurrection."[84]

---

81. Wright, "Grave Matters," 52.

82. See Wright, *The Resurrection*, 31. The Greek words *egeiro* and *anastasis*, which are typically translated as "resurrection" in the Bible and elsewhere, "were words in regular use to denote something specifically distinguished from non-bodily survival, namely, a return to bodily life. There is no evidence to suggest that these words were capable of denoting a non-bodily survival after death." Wright, *The Resurrection*, 330.

83. See Craig, *The Son*, 132; Keller, *The Reason*, 207.

84. Craig, *The Son*, 132.

Additionally, the hallucination or vision idea requires us to believe that multiple people—up to 500 at one time—all had the same hallucination or vision. That is not believable, since hallucinations and visions are highly individualistic. Further, such hallucinations and visions tend to occur when people are in an agitated mental state of expectancy, anticipation, or presentiment. That is the opposite of the mental and emotional state of the disciples, who were in a state of sorrow and despair and who had trouble believing in Jesus' resurrection even when he actually appeared to them. People in both the ancient and modern world have had visions of recently deceased loved ones. However, N. T. Wright makes the significant point that such visions "are a thoroughly *insufficient* condition for the early Christian belief. . . . Indeed, such visions meant precisely, as people in the ancient and modern worlds have discovered, that the person was dead, not that they were alive."[85] In short, as George Eldon Ladd succinctly summarizes, *"Faith did not create the appearances; the appearances created faith."*[86]

Finally, the post-resurrection appearances of Jesus came to an end; the appearance to the apostle Paul was the last in the series (1 Cor 15:8).[87] Had these been hallucinations rather than actual appearances of the physically-resurrected Jesus, there is no reason why they would have ended not too long after the resurrection; hallucinations could have and would have continued indefinitely, even down to the present day.[88] The idea that the disciples had hallucinations or visions or some kind of "religious experience" instead of actually seeing the resurrected Jesus therefore contradicts the facts and the actual eyewitness accounts of what happened.

5. *The body was taken or moved.* As previously discussed, the earliest response to the proclamation that Jesus had resurrected was the claim by the Jewish leaders that the disciples had stolen the body. Maier notes that the stolen-body theory faces two insurmountable obstacles, the issue of motive and the issue of execution: "To plan a tricky grave robbery of a closely guarded tomb would have required an incredibly strong incentive by a daring and extremely skillful group of men. But who had this incentive? Who had the motive and then

---

85. Wright, *The Resurrection*, 690–91, emph. in orig.
86. Ladd, *I Believe*, 138, emph. in orig.
87. Paul *distinguishes* his seeing the resurrected Jesus from visions, spiritual revelations, and other such experiences, *including his own* (see 2 Cor 12:1–5).
88. See Craig, *The Son*, 113.

the courage necessary to bring it off? Certainly not the dispirited disciples, huddling and hiding in their despair over Jesus' evident failure and in fear of the Temple authorities—hardly a pack of calculating schemers enthusiastically planning to dupe their countrymen."[89] Maier goes on to point out how far-fetched the idea of the disciples' ability to steal the body is, "The grave area was crawling with guards specifically instructed to forestall any such attempt. . . . Guards in ancient times always slept in shifts, so it would have been virtually impossible for a raiding party to have stepped over all their sleeping faces, as is sometimes claimed. The commotion caused by breaking the seal, rolling the stone open, entering the tomb, and lifting out the body was bound to awaken the guards even if they had all been sleeping."[90]

Additionally, James Dunn observes that lack of veneration of Jesus' tomb not only is evidence for the resurrection but also is evidence against the idea that the disciples had stolen the body, "For if the disciples had indeed removed the body, it is inconceivable that they would not have laid it reverently to rest in some other fitting location. In which case, it is almost as inconceivable that a surreptitious practice of veneration would not have been maintained by those in the know and that some hint of it would not have reached a wider circle of disciples."[91] Finally, for the disciples to steal the body and then claim that Jesus was alive "assumes that the disciples would expect other Jews to be open to the belief that an individual could be raised from the dead."[92] However, as we have already seen, no one in that time and culture, whether pagan or Jewish, believed that the bodily resurrection of an individual in the middle of history was even a possibility, any more than people believe in that possibility today.

Similar points apply to the idea that someone else moved the body. The Jewish leaders obviously had every incentive to make sure that the body remained exactly where it was. They are the ones, after all, who procured the guard for the tomb (Matt 27:62–66). Likewise, having no incentive to move the body were Joseph of Arimathea and Nicodemus since they are the ones who requested Jesus' body, prepared it for burial, and buried it in Joseph's own tomb. And Pontius Pilate would have been the last to disturb the body, since he is the one

---

89. Maier, *First Easter,* 109.
90. Maier, *First Easter,* 110–11.
91. Dunn, *Jesus,* 838.
92. Keller, *The Reason,* 207–8.

who had ordered the crucifixion, permitted the tomb to be guarded, and authorized the tomb to be sealed. There are no other individuals or groups who had any reason to want to remove the body, to say nothing of having to deal with the Roman seal of the tomb and the guards. In short, there is no historical evidence that anyone moved Jesus' body, or even had the motive or ability to do so. Hence, as with the other alleged alternative explanations, the idea that something happened to Jesus' body *other than his bodily resurrection* does not fit the existing historical facts.

CONCLUSION

That Jesus was crucified and bodily resurrected can be reliably determined by historical investigation in the same manner as other historical events. In other words, although Christians consider the Bible to be the Word of God, in order to investigate the truthfulness of whether or not an event happened in the ancient past, the Bible need not be looked at as the Word of God but can be looked at as one would look at other ancient writings. As we have seen, the Bible's accuracy and reliability meet the challenge of historical scrutiny.[93]

To assert an alternative explanation does not establish its validity. The alleged alternative explanations of the crucifixion and resurrection either are based on no evidence at all, do not account for all of the historical data, or contradict the historical data. The reason why the alternative explanations have been advanced does not flow from the evidence itself but is premised on philosophical or theological reasons apart from the evidence. The reason for that is because the evidence itself has implications that the holder of an alternative explanation does not want to accept, i.e., that Jesus really is the Son of God. However, to maintain any intellectual or theological credibility, it is not enough to simply dismiss the resurrection of Jesus by asserting "it didn't (or couldn't) happen."

Rather, one must face and answer several historical questions: All Jews believed that worshipping a man as God was blasphemy—what caused these people to worship Jesus as God? No Jews believed that a man in the middle of history could bodily rise from the dead—what caused these people to do so? All Jews held that the Sabbath (Saturday) was the sacred day of worship—what caused these people to begin worshipping on Sunday? And what caused their worldview to change virtually overnight? What accounts

---

93. See Habermas and Licona, *The Case,* 51–52; Blomberg, *Gospels,* 323; Gilbert, *Why Trust,* 125–26.

for people proclaiming that Jesus had risen from the dead and maintaining their witness of the resurrection in the face of extreme persecution and death?

The early Christians did not invent the idea of the empty tomb and the post-resurrection appearances of Jesus to explain a "faith" they already had, because no one was expecting this type of thing. No one thought this type of thing was even possible, except for the general resurrection of everybody at the end of history. Consequently, as N. T. Wright points out,

> no kind of conversion-experience would have generated such ideas; nobody would have invented it, no matter how guilty (or how forgiven) they felt, no matter how many hours they poured over the scriptures. To suggest otherwise is to stop doing history and to enter into a fantasy world of our own, a new cognitive dissonance in which the relentless modernist, desperately worried that the post-Enlightenment worldview seems in imminent danger of collapse, devises strategies for shoring it up nevertheless. In terms of the kind of proof which historians normally accept, the case we have presented, that the tomb-plus-appearances combination is what generated early Christian belief, is as watertight as one is likely to find.[94]

Jesus claimed to be God come to earth as a man and said he would prove it by doing something impossible for someone who is only a man, namely, he would bodily rise from his grave after being dead and buried for three days (Matt 17:22–23; 27:62–63; Mark 8:31; 9:9, 31; 10:32–34; Luke 18:31–33; 24:6–7; John 2:18–22). Whether he did so is not a question of philosophy or theology, or a matter of "faith," but of historical fact: either he did or he did not. The identity of Jesus (and thus the validity of what he said and believed) depends on the answer to that question (see 1 Cor 15:12–19). The historical evidence proves the fact of the resurrection beyond a reasonable doubt. Thus, the resurrection of Jesus Christ is the most important event in history, because it validates who Jesus is—i.e., he is the divine Son of God (see Rom 1:4)—and thereby validates everything Jesus believed, said, and did (see 1 Cor 15:1–19).[95]

Since Jesus accepted the historical reliability of the Bible as the Word of God—he endorsed the OT and authorized the NT—the resurrection validates that the Bible is more than just a historically accurate ancient

---

94. Wright, *The Resurrection*, 707.

95. One implication of this is that, as Craig Blomberg states, "If the resurrection of Jesus really happened, then none of the Gospel miracles is in principle incredible." Blomberg, *Gospels*, 150.

document but is the very Word of God. The reason, of course, is that the resurrection verifies that Jesus is who he claimed to be—God come to earth as a man. Hence, he knows what he is talking about, including his view of the accuracy of the Bible. As Gilbert summarizes, "Once you decide that Jesus really did rise from the dead, the truth and authority of the Bible follows quickly, naturally, and powerfully."[96] In short, Christianity is true.

Perhaps the most important implication of all that has been discussed—the resurrection in particular—is that it confronts everyone with the question, "What am I going to do about Jesus?" In other words, we are confronted with the gospel—the truth of who Jesus is and what he did. The gospel and what we need to do about it are set forth in Appendix 1. The stakes are incredibly high. Jesus believed in and taught about life after death, heaven, and hell (Matt 10:28; 22:29–32; 25:31–46; Mark 12:24–27; Luke 16:19–31; 20:34–38; 23:42–43; John 3:16; 5:24–29; 11:25–26; Rev 1:18). Therefore, if Jesus is who he said he is, then being rightly united with him is a matter of eternal significance. Consequently, all people—Christians, Muslims, nonbelievers of any kind—need to investigate the evidence and determine for themselves whether the Bible's account is true and then answer the question, "What am I going to do about Jesus?"

First-century Jews were not ignorant, uneducated, or superstitious; they were people just like us. Their strict monotheism and religious training made them the last people on earth predisposed or inclined to believe that Jesus, or any human being, was actually almighty God. Yet they, including those who knew him best (who thereby typically would have had even less reason to believe such a thing), came to believe that Jesus was, in fact, God come to earth as a man. Since they did so—and in light of all the other evidence that has been discussed above—on what possible basis can any of us say that they were wrong?

---

96. Gilbert, *Why Trust*, 15.

Part 2

The Impossibility of the Alternative

7

Christianity and Science

J. Gresham Machen states, "True religion can make no peace with a false philosophy, any more than with a science that is falsely so-called; a thing cannot possibly be true in religion and false in philosophy or in science. All methods of arriving at truth, if they be valid methods, will arrive at a harmonious result."[1] Before Charles Darwin published his seminal *On the Origin of Species by Means of Natural Selection* in 1859, Christianity and science had been viewed as compatible, a view that lasted well into Darwin's lifetime.[2] Allan Chapman, Oxford professor of the history of science, has written that the Judeo-Christian faith is fundamental to the rise of modern science. Indeed, Christianity brought "a radical new concept into human thought: a historical timeline. . . . And I would argue that it was this very precise relationship between monotheism and a beginning, a sequence of events, and an ending which made a scientific view of the world possible, giving as it does a potential for hard-edged objectivity."[3]

This view has been echoed by, among others, eminent non-Christian mathematician and philosopher Alfred North Whitehead. Whitehead states that the belief in the order of things, the order of nature, was indispensable to the rise of modern science.[4] However, that alone was insufficient. What was needed was "the inexpugnable belief that every detailed occurrence can be correlated with its antecedents in a perfectly definite manner, exemplifying general principles. Without this belief the incredible labours of scientists would be without hope."[5] Where did this mindset come from?

1. Machen, *Christianity*, 58.
2. Gilley and Loades, "Thomas Henry Huxley," 286–87.
3. Chapman, *Slaying*, 239–40.
4. Whitehead, *Science*, 4.
5. Whitehead, *Science*, 12.

"When we compare this tone of thought in Europe with the attitude of other civilisations when left to themselves, there seems but one source for its origin. It must come from the medieval insistence on the rationality of God, conceived as with the personal energy of Jehovah and with the rationality of a Greek philosopher."[6] C. F. von Weizsäcker concludes, "The tree on which this now floating seed of modern science has grown was Christianity."[7]

Robert Koons lists seven elements of Western theism that demonstrate not only that modern science historically was *based* on Judeo-Christian theism, but modern science was and is *necessarily dependent* on Judeo-Christian theism.[8] This dependence on, and intersection between, modern science and Christianity is both widespread and deep. Stephen Meyer surveys in some detail the necessary Judeo-Christian and biblical basis of modern science in *Return of the God Hypothesis*.[9] Philosopher Alvin Plantinga discusses multiple areas which demonstrate deep concord between Christian theism and modern science.[10] Craig Gay's survey of Christianity and the rise of modern science reveals both the cosmological and methodological affinity between modern science and Protestant Christianity in particular. Indeed, the Reformation's opposition to the quasi-magical nature of medieval religiosity and the Roman Catholic Church's dependence on Aristotelian rationalism, and John Calvin's careful and inductive approach to Scripture, provided the model for the emergence of modern empirical science but also, ironically, laid the groundwork for the "secularization" of modern science.[11]

It therefore should not be surprising that not only was Christianity foundational to the rise of modern science, but Christians have been and continue to be among the leaders of science:

> In the earlier days of science, and even discounting the numerous monk-priest scientific thinkers of the medieval centuries, one had astronomers of the standing of Nicholas Copernicus, Galileo Galilei, Johannes Kepler, Pierre Gassendi, and Isaac Newton. Then there followed Robert Boyle (of Boyle's law fame), Michael Faraday (electrical physicist), William Buckland and many other Victorian geologists (a good number in holy

---

6. Whitehead, *Science*, 12.
7. von Weizsäcker, *The Relevance*, 121.
8. Koons, "Science and Theism," 82–87.
9. Meyer, *Return*, 13–49.
10. Plantinga, *Where the Conflict*, 265–303.
11. See Gay, *The Way*, 16, 107–25, 272–73, and sources cited therein; see also Koons, "Science and Theism," 80–82.

orders), Abbot Gregor Mendel (founder of genetics), James Clerk Maxwell (mathematical physicist), and Sir Arthur Eddington and Father Georges Lemaître (both twentieth-century cutting-edge cosmologists). And those are only a selection of the illustrious dead, without reckoning those alive today.[12]

That situation—or at least the popular understanding of that situation—changed and changed radically in the decades following the publication of *Origin*. Darwin's *Origin* both augmented and epitomized a "shift in scientific framework or paradigm that was just getting under way in 1860 [but] was nearly complete by the 1890s."[13] Two principal reasons for this paradigm or worldview shift were: (1) a shift in the nature of science, the scientific endeavor, and who is to be considered a proper scientist or scientific authority; and (2) the ultimately more fundamental issue of the relationship between reason and revelation, science and scripture, naturalism versus supernaturalism, chance versus design, atheism versus theism, or, to put it succinctly, can the existence of God be acknowledged as legitimate by scientists as part of their work? In the event, the forces of "professionalism" in science, reason, atheism, chance, and naturalism triumphed over the forces of the Bible, supernaturalism, design, and theism, at least among the scientific community and the popular scientific press. The result was a profound shift in who has a lock on legitimacy when it comes to explaining the existence and development of the "natural world" and the beings that populate it.[14]

Scientific theories as they now stand either explicitly or implicitly purport to offer explanations for the existence of the universe and life that exclude God. Thus, the National Association of Biology Teachers' position statement on the teaching of evolution states that educators "should support science education by rejecting calls to account for the history of life or describe the mechanisms of evolution by invoking any non-natural or supernatural notions."[15] This is the culmination of the views and attitudes articulated by Darwin and his champion, Thomas Henry Huxley.[16] The

12. Chapman, *Slaying*, 234.
13. Stanley, "The Discussion," 1.
14. "Peer Review," n.p.
15. NABT, n.p.
16. At the time he wrote *Origin*, Darwin still believed in God as a "First Cause." However, that view weakened over time and he concluded, "The mystery of the beginning of all things is insoluble by us; and I for one must be content to remain an Agnostic." Barlow, ed., *The Autobiography*, 92–94. It was Huxley who coined the term "agnostic," and his position was similar to Darwin's, namely, that "the term 'Nature' covers the totality of that which is," and the existence of supernature or supernaturalism

contemporary situation is candidly summarized by evolutionary biologist Richard Lewontin, former Alexander Agassiz Professor of Zoology and Professor of Biology at Harvard University,

> Our willingness to accept scientific claims that are against common sense is the key to an understanding of the real struggle between science and the supernatural. We take the side of science *in spite* of the patent absurdity of some of its constructs, *in spite* of its failure to fulfill many of its extravagant promises of health and life, *in spite* of the tolerance of the scientific community for unsubstantiated just-so stories, because we have a prior commitment, a commitment to materialism. It is not that the methods and institutions of science somehow compel us to accept a material explanation of the phenomenal world, but, on the contrary, that we are forced by our *a priori* adherence to material causes to create an apparatus of investigation and a set of concepts that produce material explanations, no matter how counter-intuitive, no matter how mystifying to the uninitiated. Moreover, that materialism is absolute, for we cannot allow a Divine Foot in the door.[17]

---

has not been proved. Huxley, *Science,* 39n.1 and associated text. Although Darwin himself may have been equivocal regarding God's existence, he had made it clear that God's intervention in nature would be contrary to the principles of natural selection. See chapter 10n.173 and associated text. Hence, Charles Hodge and others correctly concluded early-on that Darwinism was atheistic. Hodge, *What is Darwinism, passim.* Now, even the idea of God as a "First Cause" is ruled out-of-court by contemporary scientific orthodoxy, which has taken Darwin's views to their logical conclusion.

17. Lewontin, "Billions," 31, emph. in orig.

8

Naturalism

Introduction

NATURALISM (ALSO KNOWN AS SCIENTIFIC or metaphysical naturalism, materialism, or physicalism) is a worldview which posits that there is no such person as God or any other supernatural being: "There is no separate realm of the supernatural, spiritual, or divine; nor is there any cosmic teleology or transcendent purpose inherent in the nature of the universe or in human life."[1] Naturalism posits a "closed system" in which "any activity must ultimately be understood as a process involving material entities and occurring within space and time."[2] Victor Reppert summarizes that, if supernatural beings do not exist,

> a consistent naturalist has to hold *1) The Closure Thesis:* Physics is a closed system; nothing other than physics explains where any particle is at any time. *2) The Mechanism Thesis:* Physics is mechanistic; purposes don't ultimately explain where the particles go, and *3) The Supervenience Thesis:* All other states in space and time (chemical, biological, psychological. sociological, economic) are the way they are because physics is the way it is.[3]

In short, there is nothing "outside" the system of nature. This entails the view that the universe in some way came into being by itself, life somehow arose from non-living matter, and everything in the universe and in this world is the result of an unguided or undirected evolutionary process that took place purely by natural means through the workings of the fundamental

---

1. Carroll, *The Big,* 11; see also Schafersman, "Naturalism," Definitions; Halverson, *A Concise,* 394–95.
2. Halverson, *A Concise,* 395; see also Simpson, *The Meaning,* 344.
3. Reppert, QCI Interview, 4.

regularities of physics and chemistry.⁴ As astronomer Carl Sagan famously put it, "The Cosmos is all that is or ever was or ever will be."⁵

The philosophy of naturalism, along with its concomitant, naturalistic Darwinian or neo-Darwinian evolution, "is the most influential idea of our time."⁶ It undergirds contemporary science, but is more: it is being pushed as "a sort of biological theory-of-everything" that applies to medicine, psychology, the humanities, law, and politics.⁷ Atheist philosopher and apologist for Darwinian evolution Daniel Dennett describes naturalistic Darwinian evolution as a "universal acid: it eats through just about every traditional concept and leaves in its wake a revolutionized world-view."⁸ Dennett was implicitly recognizing what Benjamin Wiker insightfully articulated, "Every distinct view of the universe, every theory about nature, necessarily entails a view of morality; every distinct view of morality, every theory about human nature, necessarily entails a cosmology to support it."⁹

This worldview is a frontal and direct challenge and contradiction to Christianity (and to all forms of theism). The reason is, as Phillip Johnson has said, "If naturalism is true, then humankind created God—not the other way around."¹⁰ Naturalism, and all it entails, is the ultimate adversary and alternative worldview to Christianity. As philosopher William Halverson says, "In contrast to ethical theism *and in perpetual conflict with it* stands *naturalism*."¹¹ Intelligent Design advocate William Dembski states, "Ultimately the problem is whether reality at its base is purposive and intelligent or mindless and material. This is the great divide. All ancient creation stories came down on one or the other side of this question, making blind natural forces or a transcendent purposive intelligence the fundamental reality."¹² Noted atheist and evolutionary biologist Richard Dawkins similarly says that "the only known alternative" to design is gradual evolution; the two positions "are close to being irreconcilably different."¹³ Or, as Alvin

---

4. Plantinga, *Where the Conflict*, ix–x, 24, 122; Plantinga, "Methodological," 21–22; Johnson, "Daniel Dennett's," 28–29; Behe, *Darwin's Black Box*, xi.

5. Sagan, *Cosmos*, 1.

6. Behe, *The Edge*, 1.

7. Behe, *The Edge*, 4; see also Dembski, "Foreword," ("Darwinism is essentially a moral and metaphysical crusade that fuels our contemporary moral debates").

8. Dennett, *Darwin's Dangerous*, 63; see also at 521.

9. Wiker, *Moral*, 22.

10. Johnson, *Reason*, 8.

11. Halverson, *A Concise*, 385, first emph. added.

12. Dembski, "Foreword," 11.

13. Dawkins, *The God Delusion*, 61.

Naturalism

Plantinga says, if you reject theism, naturalistic evolution is "the only game in town."[14]

Johnson summarizes the all-encompassing nature of naturalism, "Theists start with God, and scientific naturalists start with matter (perhaps virtual particles emerging from a quantum fluctuation in a vacuum) and impersonal natural laws. From the ultimate beginning to the emergence of human consciousness, according to naturalistic science, purposeless natural forces of the kind already known to our science were capable of doing, and actually did do, all the work of creating formerly credited to God."[15] This does *not* mean that science and Christianity (or science and theism in general) necessarily are in opposition to each other. As we will see below, they are not. However, the metaphysical "add-on" to empirical science of the philosophy of naturalism (materialism; physicalism)—which is not necessary for science *qua* science to exist—is opposed to Christianity and theism. It is that metaphysical worldview, not science, which is at issue here.

Most if not all of the major thinkers and movements of the last 300 years (e.g., Rousseau, Kant, Hegel and German idealism, John Stuart Mill and utilitarianism, Marx and Marxism, Nietzsche and nihilism, Freud, Sartre and existentialism) had an essentially naturalistic worldview, and most were openly hostile to Christianity. This worldview is dominant in science, Western culture, and academia; "some say it is contemporary academic orthodoxy."[16] Physicist and philosopher C. F. von Weizsäcker says, "Faith in science plays the role of the dominating religion of our time."[17] Hence, the philosophy of scientific naturalism merits discussion and critique here. Although naturalism is not as dominant in the non-Western world, as non-Western universities and scientists follow their Western counterparts (as they most probably will), this will become increasingly important throughout the world. On the other hand, if naturalism and its necessary corollary, naturalistic evolution, are untrue, then of necessity some form of theism is true; as we are endeavoring to demonstrate, that one is Christianity. If that is the case, as will be mentioned later, science should not be adversely affected at all.

---

14. Plantinga, "Methodological," 22.
15. Johnson, *Reason*, 16–17.
16. Plantinga, "Evolution vs. Naturalism," n.p.
17. von Weizsäcker, *The Relevance*, 12.

9

Naturalism Is Self-Referentially Incoherent (i.e., Self-Refuting)

NATURALISM CANNOT ACCOUNT FOR ABSTRACT UNIVERSALS

In his *An Enquiry Concerning Human Understanding* (1748), David Hume recognized that, based on experience, we all infer that similar causes will result in similar effects.[1] He observed, "As to past Experience, it can be allowed to give direct and certain information of those precise objects only, and that precise period of time, which fell under its cognizance."[2] He then added this crucial question, "But why this experience should be extended to future times, and to other objects, which for aught we know, may be only in appearance similar; this is the main question on which I would insist."[3] Hume concludes that to appeal to past examples as the basis for inferring the regularity of nature begs the question:

> For all inferences from experience suppose, as their foundation, that the future will resemble the past, and that similar powers will be conjoined with similar sensible qualities. . . . In vain do you pretend to have learned the nature of bodies from your past experience. Their secret nature, and consequently, all their effects and influence, may change, without any change in their sensible qualities. This happens sometimes, and with regard to some objects: Why may it not happen always, and with regard

1. Hume, *An Enquiry,* 4.2.16.
2. Hume, *An Enquiry,* 4.2.16.
3. Hume, *An Enquiry,* 4.2.16.

to all objects? What logic, what process of argument secures you against this supposition?[4]

Atheist philosopher Bertrand Russell agreed that arguing for the uniformity and regularity of nature based on past experience begs the very question at issue because it assumes *a priori* that nature is uniform and regular.[5] Further, Russell admitted that "the principle of induction, while necessary to the validity of all arguments based on experience, is itself not capable of being proved by experience, yet is unhesitatingly believed by every one."[6]

The point is that naturalism provides no basis or foundation or ground for assuming the regularity and uniformity of nature. Naturalism also cannot account for any abstract universals, such as the laws of logic, truth, or the laws of nature by which nature exhibits regularity and uniformity. The reason why naturalism cannot provide any such basis, foundation, or ground is that, according to naturalism, all of existence is nothing but matter and motion, with no plan, design, or purpose. Naturalism asserts that only concrete physical or material particulars exist, asserts everything that happens occurs as the result of physical forces, and denies that anything immaterial, spiritual, or supernatural exists.[7] All such abstract universals are not physical or material but are immaterial and invariant and are independent of time, space, and the physical properties of the universe; thus, if naturalistic materialism is correct, they cannot exist.[8]

---

4. Hume, *An Enquiry,* 4.2.19, 21.

5. Russell, *The Problems,* 93–108; see also Ayala, "Philosophical Issues," 477 ("Induction fails to arrive at universal truths. No matter how many regular statements may be accumulated, no universal statement can be logically derived from such an accumulation of observations."). C. F. von Weizsäcker expressed the same point this way, "Mathematical propositions are precise and their truth does not depend on time. Statements about sense-objects are ever imprecise, and what was true yesterday may be false today. . . . Now, if atoms are the only real being, how can statements about such imaginary things as mathematical spheres, triangles and so on be true knowledge? Precisely if the atomists took their philosophy in a strict sense they could not develop strict mathematics; then there cannot be a science about 'the circle' but only about circular arrangements of atoms." von Weizsäcker, *The Relevance,* 69–70.

6. Russell, *The Problems,* 109; see also "Probable Reasoning," par. 8.IV ("although the uniformity principle is the foundation of all empirical research as such, it is not itself founded on reason, demonstrative or probable").

7. See Russell, *The Problems,* 139.

8. See Bahnsen, *Always Ready,* 144. Former atheist A. N. Wilson left materialist atheism in part because, as he said, "materialist atheism is not merely an arid creed, but totally irrational. Materialist atheism says we are just a collection of chemicals. It has no answer whatsoever to the question of how we should be capable of love or heroism or poetry if we are simply animated pieces of meat." Wilson, "Religion of hatred," n.p.

But they do exist, and everybody, including naturalists, knows they do. The rules of logic are and must be universally correct and normative and actually show us which inferences are correct. If the rules of logic are merely accidents of evolution, there would be no reason to think they are truly and universally normative and correct. In other words, if naturalism is true, the rules of logic themselves are no longer normative but are believed solely because certain physical events in nature and the motions of atoms and chemical processes of our brains cause us to "believe" that our inferences are true. But if that is the case, there is and can be no such thing as "a rationally justifiable belief, including the belief in Naturalism itself."[9] Indeed, "All knowledge whatever depends on the validity of inference. If, in principle, the feeling of certainty we have when we say 'Because A is B therefore C must be D' is an illusion, if it reveals only how our cortex has to work and not how realities external to us must really be, *then we can know nothing whatever.*"[10] Thus, naturalism is irrational, cannot justify itself, and is self-defeating.

The major alternative to naturalism—pantheism—fares no better. Pantheistic ideas appear in many schools of Buddhism and Hinduism, and in the Tao–te–Ching. Pantheistic philosophies hold that God is identical with the physical world, that God is all and all is God; either everything flows from God like a flower unfolding from a seed, or God is unfolded in an evolutionary way, or finite things are modes of one infinite substance, or everything besides God is non-being.[11] Pantheistic religions hold that the entirety of reality is reducible to only one thing, i.e., "all is one."[12] Pantheistic religion holds that *Brahman* (i.e., the one, infinite-impersonal, ultimate reality; "god"; the Soul of the whole cosmos) is all that exists; the essence or soul of every person (*Atman*) is the soul of the cosmos; hence, *"Atman is Brahman."* Any diversity of reality is just a plurality of aspects or modes of

---

9. Craighead, "C. S. Lewis," 181; see also Lewis, *"De Futilitate,"* 63 ("one kind of thought—logical thought—cannot be subjective and irrelevant to the real universe: for unless thought is valid we have no reason to believe in the real universe.... This admission seems to me completely unavoidable and it has very momentous consequences. In the first place it rules out any materialistic account of thinking.").

10. Lewis, *"De Futilitate,"* 62–63, emph. added. The laws of logic, the validity of inference, and the law of noncontradiction as prerequisites for knowing anything at all are, and of necessity must be, universal. In other words, there is not such a thing as "Western logic" versus "Eastern logic" or "my logic" versus "your logic." That a circle is not a square, 2+2=4, and a person cannot be both in North America and Asia at the same time are true in the East as well as in the West, at all times, all places, and in all circumstances. These things are not matters of "opinion," but are the nature of reality itself.

11. See Geisler, *Christian Apologetics*, 151, 173.

12. See Potter, "Buddhism," n.p.; "Monism," *Wikipedia*, n.p.

the One, and anything that appears to exist but which is not part of the one, divine substance is *maya*, illusion.[13]

Such views are unaffirmable and self-refuting for at least four reasons: First, if "all is one" and all distinctions between premises and entities are an illusion, we could not know it, because such a state is contrary to the laws of logic and, hence, of reality. If that were the case, one could not justify or even explain pantheism itself. Second, if existence is the emanation of an absolute spirit, then reality is not ultimately predictable or empirically provable. Third, Norman Geisler points out that "a strict pantheist must affirm, 'God is but I am not.' But this is self-refuting, since one must exist in order to affirm that he does not exist."[14] Fourth, if God is all there is and is coextensive with the universe, then pantheism is equivalent to atheism, since both hold that either God (pantheism) or the material universe (atheism) is all that exists. "The only difference is that the pantheist decides to attribute religious significance to the All and the atheist does not. But philosophically the Whole is identical, namely, one eternal self-contained system of reality."[15]

In contrast to both naturalism and pantheism, theism in general and Christianity in particular provide a coherent and reasonable explanation for abstract universals and the regularity and uniformity of nature. Theism in general and Christianity in particular *can* account for abstract universals and the regularity and uniformity of nature, because the God of theism, unlike the "god" of pantheism, is outside of the cosmos (not identical to it) and is the creator of nature and all of existence. Greg Bahnsen points out, "God's mind gives both diversity and order to all things, thus guarantying the reality of particulars (multiplicity) [i.e., diversity of reality is real, not *maya*] and yet assuring that they are intelligible (unity)."[16] Heb 1:3 tells us that the eternal Son of God *"upholds all things by the word of his power."* The Greek word for "upholds" is *pherō*, which in that verse implies a continuous action. In other words, the universe is being "upheld, sustained, and carried along to its appointed end by the very same orderly God who has fixed the order of the heavens and set the course of all things from eternity past (Isa 46:10; Jer 31:35). In a universe governed by such a God, uniformity of nature is to be expected, and as a result of this expectation, the scientific method and the scientific enterprise are both possible and valuable."[17]

---

13. Sire, *The Universe*, 144–45; see also Smith, *The Religions*, 82–84.
14. Geisler, *Christian Apologetics*, 187.
15. Geisler, *Christian Apologetics*, 190; see also Smith, *The Religions*, 121–22.
16. Bahnsen, *Always Ready*, 49.
17. Laskaris, "The New Atheist," 444; see also Meyer, *Return*, 441–43.

Naturalism assumes abstract universals such as the laws of logic, truth, the laws of nature, and the regularity and uniformity of nature; however, by its very nature, naturalism cannot account for any of these things. In short, naturalism cannot justify itself but, rather, *assumes the theistic worldview as the precondition for understanding anything.*[18] Therefore, naturalism is, and of necessity must be, false.

THE ARGUMENT FROM REASON AND THE EVOLUTIONARY ARGUMENT AGAINST NATURALISM

The self-contradictory nature of naturalism is even worse than as discussed above. The reason is that, although naturalists argue and reason to support their position, naturalism cannot account for mind or reason itself. According to naturalism, all thoughts and reasons are simply the result of the motions of atoms in the brain, which are simply the result of the laws of chemistry and physics. Nevertheless, naturalists assume *a priori* the laws of logic and assume objective human rationality, even though rationality and logic cannot be accounted for and are contrary to naturalism itself. Stephen Hawking admitted this and called it "a fundamental paradox."[19] In short, naturalists cannot live in accordance with their own worldview but must assume the theistic and Christian worldview even to argue their case for naturalism. Hence, naturalism is self-referentially incoherent, i.e., it is self-refuting.

The Argument from Reason

In his book *Miracles,* C. S. Lewis articulated what is known as the argument from reason.[20] Lewis explains that all possible knowledge is based and depends on our ability to validly reason: "Unless human reasoning is valid no science can be true. It follows that no account of the universe can be true

---

18. This is admitted by theoretical physicist Paul Davies who states that "even the most atheistic scientist accepts as an act of faith the existence of a law-like order in nature that is at least in part comprehensible to us. So science can proceed only if the scientist adopts an essentially theological worldview." Davies, "The Appearance," 148.

19. Hawking, *A Brief History,* 12–13.

20. The literature on this issue is vast. Perhaps the best discussion of this is Victor Reppert, *C. S. Lewis's Dangerous Idea* (Downers Grove, IL: InterVarsity, 2003). See also Moreland, *Scaling,* 77–103; Taylor, *Metaphysics,* 114–19. Lewis summarized the essence of this argument in a number of his books: see Lewis, "Is Theology," 91–92; "Answers," 52–53; and *Miracles* 17–36.

unless that account leaves it possible for our thinking to be a real insight."[21] Naturalism, however, applies to everything, including the mind and the reasoning of the mind, because naturalism is "the view that the universe is an ultimately homogeneous mechanical system in which everything that happens, human thought and action included, depends on something else that is happening within the system and ultimately on the whole system of completely interlocking events."[22]

If everything that exists is all part of a closed, material, system of nature, then physical forces cause everything, i.e., there is an unbroken chain of physical, chemical occurrences that cause all events, including human thoughts and action, that stretch back to the origin of the universe; hence, determinism must be true.[23] However, that cannot possibly be the case, since determinism is self-refuting. J. R. Lucas points out, "He [a determinist] does not hold his determinist views because they are true, but because he has such-and-such a genetic make-up, and has received such-and-such stimuli. . . . Determinism, therefore, cannot be true, because if it was, we should not take the determinists' arguments as being really arguments, but as being only conditioned reflexes."[24]

According to naturalism, "mind" is nothing more than neurological impulses in physical tissue (the brain); yet at the same time, naturalism posits that this very organ—the same physical instrument that generates the impulses—is supposed to be able to independently verify the "truth" or "falsehood" of the "thoughts" generated by those impulses. Evolutionist J. B. S. Haldane admitted, "It seems to me immensely unlikely that mind is a mere by-product of matter. For if my mental processes are determined wholly by the motions of atoms in my brain I have no reason to suppose that my beliefs are true. They may be sound chemically, but that does not make them sound logically. And hence I have no reason for supposing my brain to be composed of atoms."[25] Later he similarly said, "If materialism is true, it seems to me that we cannot know that it is true. If my opinions are the result of the chemical processes going on in my brain, they are determined by the laws of chemistry, not those of logic."[26] Haldane was anticipating Lewis who pointed out that, if all our thoughts are the "accidental by-product of the

21. Lewis, *Miracles*, 21.
22. Schutte, "The Refutation," 481.
23. Halverson, *A Concise*, 394; see also at 385; Hawking, *A Brief History*, 12–13; Moreland, *Scaling*, 89–90; Wiker, *Moral*, 139–41.
24. Lucas, *The Freedom*, 114–15; see also Moreland, *Scaling*, 90–96.
25. Haldane, *When I am*, 219–20.
26. Haldane, "Some Consequences," 162. Although Haldane subsequently recanted his statements, they still remain true. See Haldane, "I Repent," 7, 29.

movement of atoms," then "I see no reason for believing that one accident should be able to give me a correct account of all the other accidents. It's like expecting that the accidental shape taken by the splash when you upset a milk-jug should give you a correct account of how the jug was made and why it was upset."[27]

Lewis distinguishes necessity (cause and effect) from inference (ground and consequent) and points out that we can "know" nothing at all unless our reasoning, inferences, and insights are true and valid.[28] Acts of thinking and reason concern matters outside of or other than themselves; further, thoughts and reasons can be true or false. In both particulars, thoughts and reason are unlike all other types of events.[29] By its very nature, reasoning is not and cannot be based on naturalism, because acts of reasoning, inference, and insight are not part of the rest of the total interlocking physical-chemical system of nature. Lewis uses the example of how a machine's parts are all connected with each other physically, but when one thinks about a machine, one's thoughts are not connected with the machine in the same way as the parts of the machine are connected with each other; one's thoughts of the machine are not part of the machine itself. Thus, our thoughts, reasoning, inferences, and insights are not a part of nature *per se*, but are, in a sense, beyond nature.[30] As Ronald Nash puts it, although naturalism excludes the possibility of anything outside of or other than nature, "the process of reasoning requires something that exceeds the bounds of nature."[31] Because naturalism necessitates that thoughts are simply physical or chemical processes that are as connected to the rest of the interlocking parts of nature as are the parts of a machine, naturalism "leaves no room for the acts of knowing or insight on which the whole value of our thinking, as a means to truth, depends."[32] In short, the fact of being able to validly reason is contradictory to, cannot be explained by, and therefore precludes naturalism.

---

27. Lewis, "Answers," 53; see also Lewis, "Religion," 136–38.
28. Lewis, *Miracles*, 26.
29. See Lewis, *Miracles*, 25–26; Taylor, *Metaphysics*, 116–19.
30. Lewis, *Miracles*, 37–38.
31. Nash, *Faith*, 258.
32. Lewis, *Miracles*, 27. Truth and true propositions require the existence of mind. Humans and their minds are finite, temporal, and changeable. However, truth is unchanging and everlasting. Therefore, its ground must be unchanging and everlasting, unlike human minds. The only adequate ground for truth can be the eternal mind of God. The necessary conclusion is that "should every human mind cease to exist, truth would continue to exist because of its relation to the mind of God. But if (impossible though it may be) no mind including God's mind existed, truth would cease to exist." Nash, *Faith*, 166.

Naturalism Is Self-Referentially Incoherent (i.e., Self-Refuting) 117

Naturalism gives no basis to think that our reasoning is valid. Philosopher Richard Purtill notes, "Only conscious minds can have plans or purposes, so there is no plan or purpose that will ensure that [if naturalism is true] our reasoning will attain truth. Forces that are without mind *might* happen to give us powers of valid reasoning, but they equally *might* happen to give us defective or invalid reasoning powers."[33] Since, according to naturalism, everything occurs by means of chance, determinism, and/or non-purposeful, nonteleological, nonrational laws or forces, the result is "to destroy our confidence in the validity of any reasoning—including the reasoning that may have led us to adopt these [naturalistic] theories!"[34] Naturalism, of necessity, entails that mindless forces produced mind, irrational forces produced reason, material forces produced things immaterial (reasons, ideas, numbers), concrete particulars produced abstract universals (laws of logic, truth, the content of propositions), and a closed, interlocking system with nothing outside it produced something that, by its very nature, is "outside" the system (our minds and reason). In short, naturalism is self-referentially absurd. In other words, the only way a person can rationally justify his or her acceptance of naturalism is by rejecting the central tenet of naturalism itself.[35]

Naturalistic evolution also cannot account for logical insight, reasoning, and truth, because, although natural selection may tend to eliminate harmful biological characteristics and augment those that increase an organism's chances of survival, natural selection cannot turn a organism's characteristics and responses into true "insights," any more than the fact that, while physical vision is a more useful response to light than a light-sensitive cell, neither physical vision nor any other physical improvement can bring an organism any nearer to having a knowledge of light.[36] Indeed, any alleged naturalistic, evolutionary explanation of how people think, reason, and draw inferences begs the very question at issue, because it cannot explain how anyone's reasons, inferences, and conclusions could be *justified* as being true and valid. As Lewis points out, by inferring or coming to the conclusion that one's reason, inference, or conclusion is a mere phenomenon of nature (as naturalism contends), you are claiming to have arrived at an objective "truth" that is not bound by the mere physical and chemical

---

33. Purtill, *Reason*, 44.
34. Purtill, *Reason*, 44.
35. See Nash, *Faith*, 259.
36. Lewis, *Miracles*, 28–29; see also Taylor, *Metaphysics*, 118.

processes of nature. In short, you have stepped "outside" of nature, but "there is then no way, except by begging the question, of getting inside again."[37]

In short, naturalism is fatally flawed. Naturalism holds that all of our thoughts are the products of purely physical or mechanical forces. But naturalism is not a physical force or object that can be weighed, measured, or presented to the senses. The theory itself has been arrived at through reason. If the theory is true, there is no basis to believe that reason is trustworthy. Because the premises of naturalism give us no ground for trusting reason, if naturalism is true it gives us no ground to believe in its truthfulness. Consequently, there is no basis to believe that naturalism is true. But naturalists believe that naturalism is true. Which means that they have to presuppose the falsity of their own theory even to assert it. Hence, "either Naturalism is false or, if it is true, we could never know it to be true. We must, therefore, on both counts, assume the falsity of Naturalism."[38]

Existence is rational and understandable only if our rational capacities have a non-physical, non-mechanical, non-accidental, non-blind, intelligent source. Richard Taylor gives two examples to illustrate this. First, if you are riding on a train and see several white stones on a hillside arranged in a pattern resembling the letters "The British Railways Welcomes You To Wales" and you conclude from this that you are, in fact, entering Wales, "it would be irrational for you to regard the arrangement of the stones as evidence that you were entering Wales, and at the same time to suppose that they might have come to have had that arrangement accidentally, that is, as the result of the ordinary interactions of natural or physical forces."[39] Second, suppose a stone was found with interesting marks on it which, on further examination, resembled the characters of an ancient alphabet that said, "Here Kimon fell leading a band of Athenians against the forces of Xerxes." Again, if on the basis of the stone itself one were to conclude that a man named Kimon fell in battle as described on the stone, then one cannot rationally conclude that that the marks on the stone are the result of purposeless forces of nature. On the contrary, one of necessity would have to "assume that they were inscribed there by someone whose purpose was to record an historical fact. If the marks had a purposeless origin, as from volcanic activity or whatnot, then they cannot reveal any fact whatever except, perhaps, certain facts about themselves or their origin. It would, accordingly, be irrational for anyone to suppose *both* that what is seemingly

---

37. Lewis, *Miracles*, 31–33; see also Taylor, *Metaphysics*, 119; Wiker, *Moral*, 139–41.
38. Craighead, "C. S. Lewis," 173.
39. Taylor, *Metaphysics*, 115.

expressed by the marks is true, and *also* that they appeared as the result of nonpurposeful forces."[40]

Taylor is pointing out two things: first, meaning comes *only* from a rational agent (the corollary is that if the stones did not come from a rational agent, they could have *no meaning*); second, meaning must exist in the mind of the rational agent *before* the stones were arranged or the marks made on the stone; it was the meaning that *determined the order* in which the stones were arranged and the marks made. Thus, meaning cannot be identified with the stones, nor can it emerge from the stones.[41] Craighead states the ultimate, necessary conclusion,

> Any view holding that the ultimate constituent(s) of reality are mental and that ultimate explanations go to the decision(s) of mind is some kind of supernaturalism.... We must presuppose a benevolent creator. If a malign genie is "behind the scenes," then our rational capacities are no more trustworthy than they would be if blind, naturalistic forces were the ultimate causes. If reason is what we think it is, then it is that solely by chance or its ultimate creator is a benevolent intelligence.[42]

Naturalism cannot rationally account for reason, logic, meaning, and truth; the only viable explanation is a benevolent, supernatural creator.

The Evolutionary Argument Against Naturalism

Alvin Plantinga has articulated a similar argument he calls the "Evolutionary Argument Against Naturalism" (EAAN), in somewhat more philosophical terms.[43] Beginning with a doubt expressed by Darwin concerning whether the convictions of man's mind are trustworthy if that mind has been developed from that of lower animals,[44] and noting that evolution is interested only in adaptive *behavior* rather than true *belief*, Plantinga formed the equation "P(R/N&E) is low": R is the proposition that our cognitive faculties are reliable; N is naturalism; E is the proposition that we and our cognitive faculties have come to be in the way proposed by the contemporary

---

40. Taylor, *Metaphysics*, 116.
41. See Moreland, *Scaling*, 511–52.
42. Craighead, "C. S. Lewis," 185.
43. His argument has appeared in a number of places, including Plantinga, *Warrant and Proper*, 219–37; "Naturalism Defeated," 1–54; *Warranted Christian*, 227–40; "Introduction," 1–12; and *Where the Conflict*, 307–50. In *Warranted Christian*, 237n.28 he acknowledges the similarity of his argument to those set forth by Lewis and Taylor.
44. See Barlow, ed., *The Autobiography*, 93.

scientific theory of evolution; P(..../____) is shorthand for "the probability of...given____."[45]

Virtually all naturalists hold that beliefs either "are in fact no more than the behaviour of a vast assembly of nerve cells and their associated molecules" (this is known as "reductive materialism"),[46] or that the neurophysical properties of the brain necessarily determine one's mental beliefs (this is known as "nonreductive materialism").[47] In other words, according to materialism/naturalism, all thoughts and beliefs are simply material events of material structures. The ultimate (and fatal) question for naturalism is, "How does this neuronal event *have* a content *at all?*"[48] They cannot, since a material structure or event cannot have a "content" like a belief has; hence, naturalism cannot rationally account for reason, logic, meaning, and truth.

According to naturalistic evolutionary theory, animals clearly have cognitive faculties ("indicators") that are correlated to their environment so that they can obtain food and mates and flee predators, but those activities do not require true beliefs. As Plantinga states, "Indication is one thing; belief content is something else altogether; and we know of no reason (given materialism) why the one should follow the other."[49] British philosopher Hastings Rashdall adds, "Error and delusion may be valuable elements in Evolution; to a certain extent it is undeniable, from any metaphysical standpoint, that they have actually been so"[50] This has been echoed by other

---

45. Plantinga, *Where the Conflict*, 317; see also Plantinga, "Introduction," 4. Plantinga develops his argument, and the bases for it, in considerable detail in Plantinga, *Warrant and Proper*, 216-37 and Plantinga, *Warranted Christian*, 227-40. In *Warrant and Proper*, 218-28, 231-33, Plantinga goes into some detail why, according to evolutionary theory, E does not entail R.

46. Crick, *The Astonishing*, 3, quoted in Plantinga, *Where the Conflict*, 322-23.

47. Plantinga, *Where the Conflict*, 322-25.

48. Plantinga, *Warranted Christian*, 233n.50, emph. in orig.

49. Plantinga, *Where the Conflict*, 331. Einstein made a similar point concerning the fact that there is a logical gap between sensory experience and concepts or propositions, "In thinking we use, with a certain 'right,' concepts to which there is no access from the materials of sensory experience, if the situation is viewed from the logical point of view. As a matter of fact, I am convinced that even much more is to be asserted: the concepts which arise in our thought and in our linguistic expressions are all—when viewed logically—the free creations of thought which cannot inductively be gained from sense-experiences. This is not so easily noticed only because we have the habit of combining certain concepts and conceptual relations (propositions) so definitely with certain sense-experiences that we do not become conscious of the gulf—*logically unbridgeable*—which separates the world of sensory experiences from the world of concepts and propositions." Einstein, "Remarks," 286-87, emph. added.

50. Rashdall, *The Theory*, 2:209.

Naturalism Is Self-Referentially Incoherent (i.e., Self-Refuting) 121

evolutionists.[51] Experimental psychologist Justin Barrett summarizes that it is "epistemologically dubious" to think that natural selection has "designed" our brains and their functions so that we can trust them to tell us the truth: "Just because we can successfully survive and reproduce in no way ensures that our minds as a whole tell us the truth about anything—especially when it comes to sophisticated thinking. . . . Psychologists have proven repeatedly that our minds are *not* naturally tuned to represent truth. Even in basic perception we get things wrong all the time by selectively attending to and distorting information as it comes in. What a completely naturalistic view of the human mind may safely embrace is merely that our minds were good for survival *in the past*."[52] Evolutionary biologist David Lack concludes that "the scientist must be able to trust the conclusions of his reasoning. Hence he cannot accept the theory that man's mind was evolved wholly by natural selection if this means, as it would appear to do, that the conclusions of the mind depend ultimately on their survival value and not their truth, thus making all scientific theories, including that of natural selection, untrustworthy."[53]

Since no one can know the truth of the content of any belief if naturalism is true, Plantinga sensibly assumes the probability is about .5. The question then arises, what is the probability that the cognitive faculties so produced are *reliable*? Plantinga proposes that at least 75% of beliefs produces should be true for the cognitive faculty to be considered "reliable." Given these premises, if one has a thousand independent beliefs, the probability that about three quarters of those beliefs are true is "less than 10^{-58}. . . . [With] only one hundred beliefs, the probability that three-quarters of them are true, given that the probability of any one's being true is one half, is very low, something like .000001."[54] In short, evolutionary naturalism and materialism are contradictory to and cannot account for the reliability of one's beliefs; in fact, according to naturalistic evolution, we have significant reason to *doubt* the reliability of our minds and the truthfulness of what

---

51. Wright, *The Moral*, 265 ("our accurate depiction of reality—to others, and sometimes, to ourselves—is not high on natural selection's list of priorities"); Trivers, "Foreword," xx ("the conventional view that natural selection favors nervous systems which produce ever more accurate images of the world must be a very naïve view of mental evolution"); Churchland, "Epistemology," 548–49 ("The principal function of nervous systems is to get the body parts where they should be in order that the organism may survive. . . . Truth, whatever that is, definitely takes the hindmost").

52. Barrett, *Why Would Anyone*, 19n.19, emph. in orig.

53. Lack, *Evolutionary Theory*, 104.

54. Plantinga, *Where the Conflict*, 331–33.

we believe. Therefore, naturalism and naturalistic evolution cannot be rationally accepted.[55] Hence, naturalism itself should be rejected as untrue.

On the other hand, the traditional theist has no reason to doubt that our brains and neurological systems produce true beliefs. The reason, of course, is that God has created human beings in his image, and that includes the ability to think true thoughts, reason, and make correct inferences, extrapolations, and conclusions that correspond to reality. Christian epistemology (i.e., how we can know anything) is therefore warranted in a way that is impossible under naturalism; indeed, it is impossible to warrant epistemology under naturalism at all.[56]

CONCLUSION

Naturalism and naturalistic evolution *cannot* logically bridge the material/sensory-concept/proposition gap, and the naturalist-materialist has no logical basis whatever for rationality and reason. Naturalism is self-refuting because it "cannot seriously claim to be *supported by rational argument*."[57] On the other hand, theism, particularly Christian theism, is not self-refuting and has no such internal contradiction. The reason is that God has a mind (1 Cor 2:16), he has made mankind in his image (Gen 1:26), and he gives us the ability to reason (Isa 1:18). God is a rational God and is necessarily so; hence, logic is necessary and ultimately is based in God's eternal nature. Phillip Johnson states, "If our minds are created in the image of the maker – the maker of the entire universe – we have a reason for confidence in our own rationality."[58] Further, Christianity holds that human beings are not purely physical; rather, we are body-soul unities. That is important, because "the soul—being immaterial in nature—transcends the physical realm, allowing us to transcend the determinism inherent to physical reality. When faced with prior physical forces acting on our physical stuff, we are not forced to react in a manner determined by those factors. Through the soul we are enabled to step back from the cause and effect cycle to adjudicate, deliberate, and then decide what we will believe or do. We can adjudicate between competing views based on the merits of the views themselves, independent

---

55. Plantinga, *Where the Conflict*, 344–45; see also Plantinga, "Foreword," 11.

56. It is important to note that, as James Bielby points out, "while it is true that the natural conclusion of Plantinga's argument *is* that theism is logically superior to naturalism, the truth of theism is nowhere among the premises in Plantinga's argument." Beilby, "Is evolutionary naturalism," 75–76.

57. Popper, "Is Determinism," 104, emph. in orig.

58. Provine and Johnson, "Debate," 11.

Naturalism Is Self-Referentially Incoherent (i.e., Self-Refuting)

of prior physical forces."[59] Thus, only theism, particularly Christianity, allows even the *possibility* of bridging the material world (the world of sensory experience) and the world of logical content, concepts, and propositions.

Christianity is supported by rational argument, is consistent with, and can explain and account for both the nature of the world, abstract universals, the laws of logic, and humanity's cognitive abilities. Victor Reppert concludes,

> Materialist accounts of reasoning typically presuppose the existence of the very thing that they are trying to explain. According to materialism, the universe begins with no mental states and somehow evolves them into existence through the shuffling and reshuffling of material particles. Suppose, however, . . . the universe were the result of the activities of a rational being. If that were the case, then we could understand how such a rational being could bestow beings in the universe with a measure of its rationality. . . . Explaining reason in terms of reason is no more question-begging than explaining physical states in terms of physical states. [But] explaining reason in terms of unreason explains reasoning away, and undercuts the very reasoning on which the explanation is supposed to be based.[60]

---

59. Dulle, "You Can't Know," A Soul is Required. See also J. P. Moreland, "Neuroscience," 53–69 for compelling arguments for the existence of the soul and why neuroscience is generally irrelevant in addressing the ontological nature of consciousness and the soul.

60. Reppert, "The Argument," 6–7; see also Reppert, "Several Formulations," 10–11.

10

Naturalistic Evolution Is Contrary to the Facts of Nature

IN THE MORE THAN 160 years since Darwin's *Origin* was published, Darwin's theory itself has evolved, and other scientific and philosophical theories have been developed that address the issues of existence. Darwin's principle of natural selection has been combined with the principles of genetics and genetic inheritance (first discovered by Augustinian abbot Gregor Mendel in the 1860s), resulting in the modern evolutionary synthesis (sometimes called neo-Darwinism). The modern synthesis is based on a number of core principles: "(1) genetic variation is the source of phenotypic variation; (2) this variation arises due to mutations that are random with respect to fitness; (3) accumulated mutations selected over time are the basis of evolution within a taxon (gradualism); (4) adaptation is solely the result of natural selection; and (5) evolution occurs at the population level."[1] This has become the scientifically normative explanation for animate existence and development, although various modifications have been proposed. For example, in the 1970s Niles Eldredge and Stephen Jay Gould challenged the cardinal tenet of Darwinism and neo-Darwinism, evolutionary gradualism (which they said is not borne out in the fossil record), with their theory of "punctuated equilibrium," i.e., that most species remain in a state of stasis, but the bulk of evolutionary change occurs in punctuated bursts.[2] At the grandest level—how and why the universe exists at all and in the form it is—much of the classical Newtonian physics of Darwin's day has been

---

1. Hancock, Lehmberg, and Bradburd, "Neo-darwinism," 1245.
2. Eldredge and Gould, "Punctuated"; Gould and Eldredge, "Punctuated."

significantly changed by Einstein's theories of special and general relativity, the development of quantum mechanics, and now string theories and M-theory.

Despite their scientific orthodoxy, naturalism and the theory of evolution which naturalism entails, are not able to scientifically and factually account for existence as it is. Among other things, naturalistic evolution asserts that, at all foundational levels of existence, existing conditions gave rise to their very opposites, e.g., something came from nothing, variation came from uniformity, order came from disorder, life came from non-life, intelligence, mind, and reason came from non-intelligence, non-mind, and non-reason. Both Christian and many non-Christian scientists and philosophers have raised issues that go to the heart of explanatory power and even the validity of the non-theistic theories of evolution.[3] These issues go to every aspect of neo-Darwinian naturalism. Only a few such issues will be able to be discussed here.

Before getting to the scientific issues concerning neo-Darwinism, however, there is a fundamental foundational or presuppositional problem, at least insofar as neo-Darwinian evolution is said to apply to human beings. A primary basis for Darwin's entire theory is the supposed "Struggle for Existence," which he derived from a theory first articulated by Thomas Malthus in *An Essay on the Principle of Population* (1798). Darwin claimed that this struggle for existence applies "amongst all organic beings throughout the world, which inevitably follows from their high geometrical powers of increase.... This is the doctrine of Malthus, applied to the whole animal and vegetable kingdoms. As many more individuals of each species are born than can possibly survive; and as, consequently, there is a frequently recurring struggle for existence, it follows that any being, if it vary however slightly in any manner profitable to itself, under the complex and sometimes varying conditions of life, will have a better chance of surviving, and thus be naturally selected."[4] David Stove has wittily and engagingly devoted an entire book to demonstrating that this foundational proposition is false. If it were true, then the population of every species, including humanity, would tend to increase beyond the size of the food available to support it. There would be "a competition to survive and reproduce which is so severe that

---

3. The multiple scientific and other inadequacies, problems, and contradictions of the neo-Darwinian theory of evolution at all levels have been exhaustively collated by W. R. Bird in his encyclopedic two-volume work, *The Origin of Species Revisited: The Theories of Evolution and of Abrupt Appearance* (New York: Philosophical Library, 1989).

4. Darwin, *Origin*, 23; see also at 79.

few of the competitors in any generation can win."⁵ That manifestly is not the case. Hence, as Stove concludes:

> This principle is not true without exception even in the case of other species, but in the case of our own it is extravagantly wide of the truth. . . . Darwin's explanation of evolution, then, contains as an essential element a proposition which is false in the case of man. . . . [I]t means that Darwin's explanation of evolution, even though it is (as I said earlier) still the best one available, is not true.⁶

With respect to the scientific evidence pertaining to neo-Darwinian evolution, we shall consider the fossil evidence, the microbiological evidence, and the impossibility of mutations + natural selection to create new organs, forms, functions, and organisms.

THE FOSSIL RECORD

French zoologist Pierre-Paul Grassé, who was Chair of Evolutionary Biology of the Faculty of Paris, has observed that "the process of evolution is revealed only through fossil forms"; therefore, "only paleontology can provide . . . the evidence of evolution."⁷ Concerning the fossil evidence, in *Origin*, Darwin himself stated,

> Why, if species have descended from other species by fine gradations, do we not everywhere see innumerable transitional forms? Why is not all nature in confusion, instead of the species being, as we see them, well defined? . . . By this theory innumerable transitional forms must have existed, why do we not find them embedded in countless numbers in the crust of the earth? . . . If my theory be true, numberless intermediate varieties, linking closely together all the species of the same group, must assuredly have existed; . . . But just in proportion as this process of extermination has acted on an enormous scale, so must the number of intermediate varieties, which have formerly existed, be truly enormous. Why then is not every geological formation and every stratum full of such intermediate links? Geology assuredly does not reveal any such finely-graduated organic chain;

---

5. Stove, *Darwinian Fairytales*, 29.
6. Stove, *Darwinian Fairytales*, 29.
7. Grassé, *Evolution*, 4; see also Løvtrup, *Darwinism*, 7 (the fossil record "is the only direct and tangible evidence we have" for testing the reality of the theory of evolution).

and this, perhaps, is the most obvious and serious objection which can be urged against the theory.[8]

Darwin also acknowledged, "The abrupt manner in which whole groups of species suddenly appear in certain formations, has been urged by several palaeontologists—for instance, by Agassiz, Pictet, and Sedgwick—as a fatal objection to the belief in the transmutation of species. If numerous species, belonging to the same genera or families, have really started into life at once, the fact would be fatal to the theory of evolution through natural selection."[9]

The Cambrian Explosion and the absence of transitional fossils

The "abrupt manner in which whole groups of species suddenly appear" was particularly true during the so-called "Cambrian explosion," which refers to "an interval of time approximately 538.8 million years ago in the Cambrian Period when practically all major animal phyla started appearing in the fossil record"; before the Cambrian explosion, "most organisms were relatively simple, composed of individual cells, or small multicellular organisms, occasionally organized into colonies."[10] There are only three animal phyla in the pre-Cambrian period, but twenty new phyla appear during the Cambrian, with only four other new phyla appearing in post-Cambrian periods; the Cambrian explosion saw a tremendous number of new forms of organisms and body parts that have little or no resemblance to pre-Cambrian fossils.[11] This makes no sense on a Darwinian, evolutionary basis, since

---

8. Darwin, *Origin*, 178, 179, 184, 333–34.

9. Darwin, *Origin*, 354–55.

10. "Cambrian explosion," *Wikipedia*, Introduction. Hoyle and Wickramasinghe point out, however, "Although we may care to think of fossil bacteria and fossil algae and microfungi as being simple compared to a dog or horse, the information standard remains enormously high. Most of the biochemical complexity of life was present already at the time the oldest surface rocks of the Earth were formed. Thus, we have no clue, even from evidence which penetrates very far back in time, as to how the information standard of life was set up in the first place, and so the evolutionary theory lacks a proper foundation." Hoyle and Wickramasinghe, *Evolution*, 8.

11. Meyer, *Darwin's Doubt*, 32, 34, 84–86; see also Meyer, "The Origin," The Cambrian Explosion (at least 19 and perhaps as many as 35 phyla made their initial appearance during the Cambrian explosion). Phyla are the major groups of plants and animals in which "all members of the phylum share a number of distinct morphological features, which are known as the **body plan** of that phylum. Thus, by studying the defining features of various animal phyla, you are also studying the fundamental features that define animal diversity." McCauley, "Animal Phyla," What is an animal phylum?, bold emph. in orig.

"many late Precambrian depositional environments actually provide *more* favorable settings for the preservation of fossils than those present in the Cambrian period."[12]

Darwin was aware of this and said that, if his theory was true, "it is indisputable that before the lowest Cambrian stratum was deposited, long periods elapsed, as long as, or probably far longer than, the whole interval from the Cambrian age to the present day; and that during these vast periods the world swarmed with living creatures. Here we encounter a formidable objection; for it seems doubtful whether the earth, in a fit state for the habitation of living creatures, has lasted long enough."[13] Further, he acknowledged that "the almost entire absence, as at present known, of formations rich in fossils beneath the Cambrian strata,—are all undoubtedly [objections to my theory] of the most serious nature,"[14] and "The case at present must remain inexplicable; and may be truly urged as a valid argument against the views here entertained."[15] He also admitted, "To the question why we do not find rich fossiliferous deposits belonging to these assumed earliest periods prior to the Cambrian system, I can give no satisfactory answer."[16]

Thus, Darwin himself was stating one basis upon which his theory could be falsified. His only answer to the lack of pre-Cambrian fossils and the absence of numerous transitional or intermediate fossils links throughout all the ages of the fossil record, "mainly lies in the record being incomparably less perfect than is generally supposed.... The explanation lies, as I believe, in the extreme imperfection of the geological record."[17] But he also admitted, "He who rejects this view of the imperfection of the geological record, will rightly reject the whole theory."[18]

In the over 160 years since *Origin* was published, millions of fossils have been recovered. The geologic record is no longer in a state of "extreme imperfection" but is now "mature."[19] However, the fossil record reveals the *exact opposite* of what Darwin predicted would be the case when more fossils were discovered. David Raup, Dean of Science at the Field Museum of Natural History in Chicago, points out, "We have even fewer examples of

---

12. Meyer, *Darwin's Doubt*, 69.
13. Darwin, *Origin*, 359.
14. Darwin, *Origin*, 363.
15. Darwin, *Origin*, 361.
16. Darwin, *Origin*, 360.
17. Darwin, *Origin*, 179, 334.
18. Darwin, *Origin*, 392.
19. Foote, "Sampling," 181; see also Meyer, *Darwin's Doubt*, 71.

evolutionary transition than we had in Darwin's time. By this I mean that some of the classic cases of Darwinian change in the fossil record, such as the evolution of the horse in North America, have had to be discarded or modified as a result of more detailed information – what appeared to be a nice simple progression when relatively few data were available now appears to me much more complex and much less gradualistic."[20] In short, the "innumerable transitional forms" have not been unearthed because they do not exist.

Darwin's only attempted explanation for the lack of pre-Cambrian fossils and the lack of intermediate "transitional" fossils throughout the fossil record ("the extreme imperfection of the geological record") was, in fact, *not* an answer at all. The reason is not the imperfection of the fossil record, but the *selective* incompleteness of the fossil record, i.e., the "gaps" in the fossil record "always happen to be incomplete at the nodes connecting major branches of Darwin's tree of life."[21] In other words, the fossil record itself is clear and contradicts—at the fundamental point—Darwin's idea that one kind of creature "transitioned" through intermediate steps and forms into another kind of creature.

The problem of a lack of "transitional" fossils is not limited to the lack of any precursors for the plethora of life forms that appear during the Cambrian explosion but applies to all life forms throughout the entire fossil record. Famous Harvard biologist Stephen Jay Gould stated that the remarkable diversity among the different kingdoms of plants and animals may appear to reflect progress in the history of life, "But the paleontological record supports no such interpretation. There has been no steady progress in the higher development of organic design."[22] Elsewhere he admitted, "All paleontologists know that the fossil record contains precious little in the way of intermediate forms; transitions between major groups are characteristically abrupt," and he added that we cannot even "invent a tale of continuity in most or all cases."[23] Paleontologist George Gaylord Simpson remarked, "Gaps among known orders, classes, and phyla are systematic and almost always large."[24] Francisco Ayala and James Valentine add, "There are about 25 major living subdivisions (phyla) of the animal kingdom alone, all with gaps between them that are not bridged by known intermediaries. . . . In fact, there are no extinct fossil groups known that are the common ancestors

---

20. Raup, "Conflicts," 25; see Gish, *Evolution*, 189–97 regarding the horse.
21. Meyer, *Darwin's Doubt*, 24.
22. Gould, "The Five," 37.
23. Gould, "The Return," 24, 28; see also Gould, "Is a new," 127.
24. Simpson, "The History," 149.

of two or more living phyla, and the common ancestral stocks of only a few classes (out of many score) have been found. Most taxa at these high levels appear abruptly in the fossil record, and we do not know their immediate ancestors."[25] Paleontologist Steven Stanley puts it this way, "The known fossil record fails to document *a single example of phyletic evolution* accomplishing a major morphological transition and hence offers *no evidence* that the gradualist model can be valid."[26]

Dr. E. S. Russell, Scottish biologist and philosopher of biology, summarizes, "Each of the great phyla of animals is built upon a structural plan quite different from that of the others. Their origin is unknown; between them there exist no true connecting links, and there is no likelihood of the direct transformation of one into another."[27] In fact, Gould states, "The extreme rarity of transitional forms in the fossil record persists as the trade secret of paleontology."[28] Grassé concludes, "The lack of direct evidence leads to the formation of pure conjectures as to the genesis of the phyla; we do not even have a basis to determine the extent to which these opinions are correct."[29]

Not only are there virtually no alleged "transitional forms" in the fossil record, but the fossil record as it exists exhibits a pattern directly opposite to what should be the case if evolution were true. Gould states that the fossil record includes two features "particularly inconsistent with gradualism": "1. *Stasis*. Most species exhibit no directional change during their tenure on earth. They appear in the fossil record looking much the same as when they disappear; morphological change is usually limited and directionless. 2. *Sudden appearance*. In any local area, a species does not arise gradually by the steady transformation of its ancestors; it appears all at once and 'fully formed.'"[30] Gould and Niles Eldredge more recently added that stasis, i.e., the absence of evolutionary change, is "the most common of all paleontological phenomena" and "stability dominates the fossil record."[31] Further, "because species often maintain stability through such intense climatic change as glacial cycling, stasis must be viewed as an active phenomenon,

---

25. Ayala and Valentine, *Evolving*, 258.

26. Stanley, *Macroevolution*, 39, emph. added; see also Hoyle and Wickramasinghe, *Evolution*, 77–97; Løvtrup, *Darwinism*, 352–53 ("the fossil record stubbornly fails to deliver one single bit of evidence in support of the 'phyletic gradualism', which is supposed to be a prediction of the micromutation theory").

27. Russell, *The Diversity*, 58; see also at 130.

28. Gould, "Evolution's Erratic," 14.

29. Grassé, *Evolution*, 31.

30. Gould, "Evolution's Erratic," 14; see also Raup, "Conflicts," 23–24.

31. Gould and Eldredge, "Punctuated equilibrium comes," 223.

not a passive response to unaltered environments."³² As a result, Gould and Eldredge admit, "Many leading evolutionary theorists . . . have been persuaded by punctuated equilibrium that maintenance of stability within species must be considered as a major evolutionary problem."³³

The Cambrian explosion directly contradicts Darwin's theory in yet another way. Darwin's theory posits that new animal forms emerged from a common ancestor. Hence, they would at first be quite similar to each other; large differences between the evolving forms of life would only occur later as more mutations occur and accumulate.³⁴ In fact, the fossil record *directly contradicts* Darwin's theory. Geophysicist and philosopher of science Stephen Meyer states that the disparity in the large differences between forms of the animals that appeared suddenly in the Cambrian explosion, "arose *before*, not after, the diversification of many representatives of lower taxonomic categories (such as species or genera)."³⁵ Michael Denton summarizes regarding both the Cambrian explosion and the entire so-called tree of life, "Nature is clearly a *discontinuum*," which is the exact opposite of what Darwinian evolution posits and predicts.³⁶

Gould and Eldredge's theory of punctuated equilibrium was an attempt to save the idea of evolution in light of the fact that, if evolution were true, there should be innumerable transitional forms in the fossil record. Punctuated equilibrium contends that speciation (i.e., the formation of new species) does not arise within large populations but within small or tiny populations, peripherally isolated or even cut off from the main or parental stock, where "favorable variations spread quickly."³⁷ The first problem with punctuated equilibrium is that it explains too little. Denton, who was senior research fellow in the Biochemistry Department at the University of Otago, Dunedin, New Zealand, pointed out that Gould and Eldredge's model could possibly explain relatively trivial gaps between species such as dog/fox or rat/mouse but cannot account for the gaps which exist between the larger classes of animals. Denton states, "Such major discontinuities simply could not, unless we are to believe in miracles, have been crossed in geologically short periods of time through one or two transitional species occupying restricted geographical areas."³⁸ More basically, the theory of punctuated

---

32. Gould and Eldredge, "Punctuated equilibrium comes," 223.
33. Gould and Eldredge, "Punctuated equilibrium comes," 223–24.
34. Meyer, *Darwin's Doubt*, 34, 39, 41–44, 74–75.
35. Meyer, *Darwin's Doubt*, 40.
36. Denton, *Evolution: Still*, 112.
37. Gould, "Evolution's Erratic," 16.
38. Denton, *Evolution: A Theory*, 193.

equilibrium is based, not on evidence but on a *lack* of evidence. It simply begs the question by assuming that evolution is a fact, instead of objectively seeing the lack of transitional forms as evidence against the theory of evolution.

The further fatal flaw of punctuated equilibrium is that it has no mechanism for generating new traits. In other words, there is no biological basis that the alleged speciation occurring within small, isolated populations can cause changes in the form and functions of plants or animals or of their parts or organs.[39] Gould conceded in 1982, and reiterated in his last major work in 2002, "Punctuated equilibrium is not a theory of macromutation ... it is not a theory of any genetic process."[40] Rather, it essentially is only "a paleontological observation" of the state of the fossil record.[41] In fact, Gould and Eldredge stated that punctuated equilibrium "*represents no departure from Darwinian mechanisms*, but only the previously unrecognized mode of operation for natural selection at hierarchical levels higher than the local population."[42] They acknowledge that "continuing unhappiness [with the theory of punctuated equilibrium], justified this time, focuses upon claims that speciation causes significant morphological change, for no validation of such a position has emerged."[43]

Other inconsistencies and anomalies

Three other aspects of the fossil record are inconsistent with the supposed evolution of all life from a common ancestor. First, multiple different taxa (groups of different types of plants or animals) all have distinct, unique, "taxa-defining novelties" that appear fixed and immutable and for which there are no "transitional" antecedents in earlier, putative ancestral forms. Such taxa-defining novelties include the pentadactyl limb of all terrestrial vertebrates, the three-part insect body plan, the four, nested, concentric whorl pattern of angiosperm flowers, the amniotic membrane, and many, many others.[44] Entomologist William Thompson adds that "the last thing we should expect on Darwinian principles is the persistence of a few common fundamental structural plans. Yet this is what we find. The animal world, for example, can be divided into some ten great groups or phyla,

---

39. See discussion at Meyer, *Darwin's Doubt*, 136–51.
40. Gould, *The Structure*, 1010; see also Meyer, *Darwin's Doubt*, 146–48.
41. Bohlin, "The Quiet," n.p.
42. Gould and Eldredge, "Punctuated equilibria," 139, emph. added.
43. Gould and Eldredge, "Punctuated equilibrium comes," 227.
44. Denton, *Evolution: Still*, 43–57.

Naturalistic Evolution Is Contrary to the Facts of Nature

all of which are . . . stable and definable entries from the taxonomic standpoint. All identifiable animals that ever have existed can be placed in these groups."[45] In short, if evolution, with its innumerable transitional forms of antecedent structures, is true, these taxa-defining novelties should not exist.

Second, the situation is far more damaging to evolutionary theory than the fact that the phyla are stable, well-defined, and distinct. The fact is, many types of individual species, from bacteria through all the different classes of organisms to mammals, have not evolved at all since their origin. Grassé lists scores of such creatures, including animals such as opossums, which live in widely different environments and therefore are the beneficiaries of environmental conditions theoretically favorable to evolution, yet they do not evolve.[46] He concludes by asking, "How does the Darwinian mutational interpretation of evolution account for the fact that the species that have been the most stable—some of them for the last hundreds of millions of years—have mutated as much as the others do?"[47] The answer is, it does not and cannot.

Third, the fact is that many fossils appear in the "wrong" order according to evolutionary theory. Evolutionary biologist Richard Dawkins states, "Evolution makes the strong prediction that if a *single* fossil turned up in the *wrong* geologic stratum, the theory would be blown out of the water."[48] On the other hand, creationist Dr. Carl Werner states, "*If* evolution did not occur (animals did not change significantly over time) and *if* all of the animals and plants were created at one time and lived together (humans, dinosaurs, oak trees, roses, cats, wolves, etc), then one should be able to find fossils of at least *some* modern animals and modern plants alongside dinosaurs in the rock layers."[49] Werner tested his thesis by looking at fossils found in dinosaur dig sites "so that scientists who support evolution could not suggest that the fossils we looked at were not 'old'. All of the fossils we used for comparisons were found in dinosaur rock layers (Triassic, Jurassic and Cretaceous)."[50] Werner

---

45. Thompson, "A Critique," 6.
46. Grassé, *Evolution*, 78.
47. Grassé, *Evolution*, 87.
48. Dawkins, *The God Delusion*, 127; see also Thomson, "Marginalia," 529.
49. Werner, quoted in Batten, "Living fossils," Introduction, emph. in orig.
50. Werner, quoted in Batten, "Living fossils," Introduction. The following table shows the geologic ages and time periods, from the Cambrian era to the present, as supposed by old-earth scientists (see "Geologic time scale," *Wikipedia*):

Name	Time Span
Quaternary	2.6 to 0 million years ago
Neogene	23 to 2.6 million years ago

was amazed at his findings. In the supposed "dinosaur" rock layers, he found "fossilized examples from *every* major invertebrate animal phylum living today"; additionally, he found cartilaginous fish (sharks and rays), boney fish (sturgeon, paddlefish, salmon, herring, flounder and bowfin), and jawless fish (hagfish and lamprey) "and they look the same as modern forms"; modern-appearing frogs and salamanders and "all of today's reptile groups have been found in the dinosaur layers and they look the same or similar to modern forms"; further, "modern types of birds, including: parrots, owls, penguins, ducks, loons, albatross, cormorants, sandpipers, avocets, etc." have been found at the dinosaur dig sites, as have "fossilized mammals that look like squirrels, possums, Tasmanian devils, hedgehogs, shrews, beavers, primates, and duck-billed platypus"; Werner observes, "Few are aware of the great number of mammal species found with dinosaurs. Paleontologists have found 432 mammal species in the dinosaur layers; almost as many as the number of dinosaur species. These include nearly 100 *complete* mammal skeletons"; Werner concludes, "In the dinosaur rock layers, we found fossils from *every* major plant division living today including: flowering plants, ginkgos, cone trees, moss, vascular mosses, cycads, and ferns. Again, if you look at these fossils and compare them to modern forms, you will quickly conclude that the plants have not changed."[51]

Gary Bates and Lita Sanders give several other examples of fossils in the "wrong geologic stratum," including: • "pollen fossils—evidence of flowering plants—were found in the Precambrian strata. According to evolutionists, flowering plants first evolved 160 mya [million years ago], but the Precambrian strata is older than 550 mya." • "Dinosaurs are supposed to have evolved into birds. But Confuciusornis was a true beaked bird that pre-dates the 'feathered' dinosaurs that it allegedly came from. It also has been found in the stomach of a dinosaur." • "Grass which has been found in

Paleogene	66 to 23 million years ago
Cretaceous	145 to 66 million years ago
Jurassic	201.4 to 145 million years ago
Triassic	251.9 to 201.4 million years ago
Permian	298.9 to 251.9 million years ago
Carboniferous	358.9 to 298.9 million years ago
Devonian	419.2 to 358.9 million years ago
Silurian	443.8 to 419.2 million years ago
Ordovician	485.4 to 443.8 million years ago
Cambrian	538.8 to 485.4 million years ago

51. Werner, quoted in Batten, "Living fossils," *passim*, emph. in orig.

fossilized dinosaur coprolites (fossilized dung). But grass is not supposed to have evolved until at least 10 million years after the dinosaurs went extinct."
- "A dog-like mammal fossil was found with remains of dinosaurs in its stomach—but no mammals large enough to prey on dinosaurs were supposed to exist alongside them."[52] There is also a set of human-appearing footprints found at Laetoli, Tanzania and dated as approximately 3.7 million years old. One of the scientists involved said,

> Make no mistake about it. . . . They are like modern human footprints. If one were left in the sand of a California beach today, and a four-year-old were asked what it was, he would instantly say that somebody had walked there. He wouldn't be able to tell it from a hundred other prints on the beach, nor would you. The external morphology is the same. There is a well-shaped modern heel with a strong arch and a good ball of the foot in front of it. The big toe is straight in line. It doesn't stick out to the side like an ape toe, or like the big toe in so many drawings you see of australopithecines in books.[53]

There is dispute over who made the footprints. Some attribute them to true humans, *homo sapiens*;[54] many attribute the footprints to the hominid *Australopithecus afarensis*.[55] If they were made by true *homo sapiens*, however, that would absolutely contradict evolution.

One of the most interesting and perhaps significant findings is that of nuclear physicist Robert Gentry. Gentry's work concentrated on polonium halos, which are minute, spherical areas of discoloration of minerals found in Precambrian granite, resulting from the radioactive decay of polonium. Polonium-218 has a half-life of only 3 minutes. The significance is that "according to evolutionary geology, the granites now containing these special halos had originally formed as hot magma slowly cooled over long ages. On the other hand, the radioactivity responsible for these special halos had such a fleeting existence that it would have disappeared long before

---

52. Bates and Sanders, "Are there," Lots of inconvenient fossils; see also Doyle, "Precambrian rabbits," A real Precambrian rabbit scenario (secular literature documents "pollen found in Precambrian metamorphic rock from the Roraima formation in South America 'dated' at 1.7 Ga [billion years] old. In the orthodox evolutionary timeline, pollen is supposed to be *over 1 Ga* younger than these rocks supposedly are."); Oard, "Are fossils"; Oard, "Origin," 10–11; Oard, "Evolution," 171–72; Woodmorappe, "Anomalously Occurring," Anomalously Occurring Fossils (table of over 200 published instances of anomalously occurring fossils); Wysong, *The Creation-Evolution*, 365–83.

53. Johanson and Edey, *Lucy*, 250.

54. Gish, *Evolution*, 274–76.

55. Hatala, Demes, and Richmond, "Laetoli footprints," 1–9.

the magma had time to cool and form the granite rocks."[56] If the granite in which the polonium halos were found is, in fact, "primordial," i.e., are representative of the Earth's crust at the time of its formation, that would indicate that the Earth was created instantaneously, in a cool condition, in accordance with the biblical view and not according to naturalistic theories. Gentry did further research on radiohalos in coalified wood specimens taken from three different geologic time periods (Triassic, c.200–250 mya; Jurassic, c.145–200 mya; and Eocene, c.35–60 mya). The data included polonium halos and also halos from the radioactive decay of uranium. The data implied "a single uranium infiltration occurred nearly simultaneously in all the wood specimens."[57] This means that the three geologic formations containing the coalified wood specimens were not laid down millions of years apart but, instead, evince "a rapid deposition of them all."[58] Gentry's findings are consistent with the biblical creationist view and contradict the naturalist evolutionary view.[59]

Conclusion

Darwin himself said that if the fossil record does not reveal innumerable transitional forms, his theory would be falsified. The fossil record no longer is imperfect as Darwin thought and reveals the exact opposite of what Darwin's theory predicted: the "innumerable transitional fossils" which evolution posits do not exist; large disparities of basic forms appeared suddenly and before the diversification of "lower" forms; multiple organisms of all types have "refused" to evolve; and multiple organisms of all types and radiohalos are found in the "wrong" geologic strata. Thus, Darwin's theory, by his own tests, is false. Even Gould says that the neo-Darwinian synthesis, which replaced Darwinism *per se*, "is effectively dead, despite its persistence as textbook orthodoxy."[60] Although punctuated equilibrium—the alternative to Darwinian gradualism—recognizes the lack of transitional forms in the fossil record, it cannot account for the gaps between larger classes of animals and therefore provides no solution to that fatal problem for naturalistic

---

56. Gentry, *Creation's Tiny*, 2.
57. Gentry, *Creation's Tiny*, 57–58.
58. Gentry, *Creation's Tiny*, 58.
59. See Snelling, "Radiohalos" (3-part series of articles); "Fingerprints," *Earth Science Associates*.
60. Gould, "Is a new," 120.

evolution or, for that matter, of the issue of the non-evolved "living fossils" and out-of-sequence fossils.[61]

Naturalistic evolution is *inconsistent* with and cannot account for the evidence of the fossil record; Christianity is *consistent* with and can account for the evidence of the fossil record. The reason, of course, is that the Bible reveals what actually happened, namely, God created plants and animals and designed them to reproduce *"after their kind"* (Gen 1:1, 11–12, 20–21, 24–25). In other words, there are limits to the variations that occur within each "kind." The issue here is not a "religious" one, but a factual one: which view comports with the evidence and which one does not? The answer is obvious.

THE MICROBIOLOGICAL EVIDENCE: PATTERNS AND STATISTICS

In addition to the fossil record, in the years since Darwin, the molecular biological revolution has dramatically given us the ability to compare organisms at the more fundamental biochemical level. In light of this new knowledge, the only thing necessary to demonstrate evolutionary relationship among different organisms is to "examine the proteins in the species concerned and show that the sequences could be arranged into an evolutionary series."[62] The biochemical and molecular evidence has completely failed to substantiate Darwin's theory; in fact, molecular biology contradicts what evolution would predict. Beginning in the 1960s multiple biochemical and molecular studies have been performed, and they all "reaffirm the traditional view that the system of nature conforms fundamentally to a highly ordered hierarchic scheme from which all direct evidence for evolution is emphatically absent. Moreover, the divisions turned out to be more mathematically perfect than even the most die-hard typologists would have predicted."[63]

No evolutionary biochemical relationships

Denton provides a table of thirty-three comparisons between cytochrome C of bacteria and a wide variety of non-bacterial organisms, including multiple and different yeasts, plants, insects, fish, amphibians, reptiles, birds,

---

61. Meyer, *Darwin's Doubt*, 148–49.
62. Denton, *Evolution: A Theory*, 275, 277.
63. Denton, *Evolution: A Theory*, 278.

and mammals.[64] The result is that, at the molecular level, there is no ascending hierarchy as one goes from yeasts to plants to insects, fish, amphibians, reptiles, birds, and mammals. In fact, at the molecular level, "when the vertebrates are compared with non-vertebrate organisms, all types are equidistant apart" from each other.[65]

This same phenomenon applies throughout the animal kingdom. For example, the lungfish is a "living fossil," virtually identical to fossil lungfish dated as 350,000,000 years old; however, lungfish proteins are no more or less far away from the proteins of lamprey as are the proteins of any other fish, amphibian, or mammal.[66] At the molecular level, each class of organism is unique and not linked to "intermediate" species. All of this means that, at the molecular level, no class of organism is more "primitive" than or "ancestral" to others or more "advanced" than others. In short, the molecular evidence, like the fossil evidence, not only does not confirm the evolutionary teaching that one type of being evolved into another via a chain of intermediate forms, but it positively contradicts that idea.[67]

In a speech to the American Museum of Natural History in 1981, Dr. Colin Patterson, then senior paleontologist of the British Museum of Natural History, reported on the microbiological evidence of a recent experiment. Famous evolutionist Ernst Mayr had predicted that, in a comparison of crocodiles, birds, and reptiles, "the proportion of genotypes shared by C, the crocodile and B, another reptile [would] be greater than proportion shared by C, the crocodile and D, the bird. He predicts that in some shared genotypes BC will be greater than CD."[68] Here is what was studied and these were the findings: "The prediction is that the amino acids common to B the viper, C the crocodile and D the chicken, that BC would be greater than CD. And here of course are his findings: BC: 8 out of 143 – 5.6%; CD: 25 out of 143 – 17.5%; BD: 15 out of 143 – 10.5%."[69] Patterson concluded, "Here we are. The theory makes a prediction, we've tested it and the prediction is falsified precisely. CD far outweighs BC so something is wrong with the prediction. Something is wrong with the theory."[70] Patterson also reported

---

64. A cytochrome is any of a group of hemoprotein cell components that, by readily undergoing reduction and oxidation [gain and loss of electrons] with the aid of enzymes, serve a vital function in the transfer of energy within cells.

65. Denton, *Evolution: A Theory*, 280–81, 284–86; at the molecular level, human beings are as close to lamprey eels as are fish!

66. Denton, *Evolution: A Theory*, 302.

67. See Denton, *Evolution: A Theory*, 290–91.

68. Patterson, "Speech," 7.

69. Patterson, "Speech," 7–8.

70. Patterson, "Speech," 8.

Naturalistic Evolution Is Contrary to the Facts of Nature 139

on other, similar studies, none of which were in accord with what the evolutionary belief in descent from a common ancestor would have predicted.

Similar facts contradict what the theory of evolution would predict at virtually every level of the microbiological data. For example, Grassé states that, if naturalistic evolution were true, the quantity of DNA should be proportional to the number of genes; more complex organisms should have more DNA. However, contrary to what evolution would predict, this is not the case. "The nuclei of many protozoans and protophytes and of the lower metazoans contain just as much if not more DNA than those of birds and mammals."[71]

Gene duplication is the primary hypothesis of how new forms and functions could evolve. However, "the theory predicts a positive correlation between organismal complexity and gene number, genome size and/or chromosome number. All of these predictions are contradicted by the evidence."[72] Thus, humans have about 25,000 genes, but rice has about 50,000; regarding chromosome number, "the descending rank order of diploid numbers for a selection of animals is as follows: *Cambarus clarkii* (a crayfish) 200, dog 78, chicken 78, human 46, *Xenopus laevis* (South African clawed frog) 36, *Drosophila melanogaster* (fruit fly) 8, *Myrmecia pilosula* (an ant) 2," and "the largest known genome does not occur in man, but rather in a bacterium! *Epulopiscium fishelsoni* carries 25 times as much DNA as a human cell, and one of its genes has been duplicated 85,000 times yet it is still a bacterium."[73] In short, the genetic data not only does not support, but is the exact opposite of, what the theory of evolution would predict.

No "tree of life"

Most basically, evolution posits a "tree of life" in which a common ancestor gives rise to multiple, diverse descendants branching from it like a tree's branches and twigs diverge from the trunk. The molecular data do not support this at all. One gene or protein gives one branching pattern and one "tree of life," while another gene or protein gives a contradictory branching pattern and "tree of life."[74] Graham Lawton states, "The problems began in the early 1990s when it became possible to sequence actual bacterial and

---

71. Grassé, *Evolution*, 189.

72. Bergman, "Does gene duplication," 100.

73. Bergman, "Does gene duplication," 100–101; see also Orgel and Crick, "Selfish DNA," 604 (the DNA found in certain species such as lilies and salamanders "may amount to as much as 20 times that found in the human genome")

74. See Luskin, "A Primer," n.p.; Meyer, *Darwin's Doubt*, 119–21.

archaeal genes rather than just RNA. Everybody expected these DNA sequences to confirm the RNA tree, and sometimes they did but, crucially, sometimes they did not. RNA, for example, might suggest that species A was more closely related to species B than species C, but a tree made from DNA would suggest the reverse."[75]

Lawton goes on to cite a study of 2000 genes that are common to humans, frogs, sea squirts, sea urchins, fruit flies, and nematodes. According to evolutionary theory, one should have been able to construct an evolutionary tree showing the relationships between the six types of organisms. However, "different genes told contradictory evolutionary stories. This was especially true of sea-squirt genes. Conventionally, sea squirts–also known as tunicates–are lumped together with frogs, humans and other vertebrates in the phylum Chordata, but the genes were sending mixed signals. Some genes did indeed cluster within the chordates, but others indicated that tunicates should be placed with sea urchins, which aren't chordates"; approximately 50% of its genes showed one evolutionary history and 50% another.[76] Lawton concludes, "Today the project lies in tatters, torn to pieces by an onslaught of negative evidence. Many biologists now argue that the tree concept is obsolete and needs to be discarded. 'We have no evidence at all that the tree of life is a reality,' says [French evolutionary biologist Eric] Bapteste. That bombshell has even persuaded some that our fundamental view of biology needs to change."[77]

The same is true when anatomy (morphological data) and DNA sequences (molecular data) are compared. In a major study of living hominoids, including gorillas, chimpanzees, orangutans, humans, and Old World monkeys, including baboons, mangabeys, and macaque, "the molecular and morphological trees could not be made to match."[78] As a result, the study concluded, "existing phylogenetic hypotheses about human evolution are unlikely to be reliable."[79] In short, at virtually every level, the molecular and microbiological facts contradict what naturalistic evolution would hypothesize should be the case.

The problem exists even at the most basic cellular level. There are two kinds of single-celled forms: prokaryotes and eukaryotes. Prokaryotes are smaller and simpler and their DNA is diffusely distributed; they are represented by bacteria and blue-green algae. Eukaryotes are larger and their

75. Lawton, "Why Darwin," quoted in Luskin, "A Primer," n.p.
76. Lawton, "Why Darwin," quoted in Luskin, "A Primer," n.p.
77. Lawton, "Why Darwin," quoted in Luskin, "A Primer," n.p.
78. Gura, "Bones," 232; see also Schwartz and Maresca, "Do Molecular Clocks," 357.
79. Gura, "Bones," 232.

DNA is concentrated in one or more nuclear regions; single-celled algae (excluding blue-greens), microfungi, protozoa, and multi-celled plants and animals are made up of eukaryotic cells. Most biologists had assumed that eukaryotes evolved from prokaryotes. However, recent discoveries in microbiology to not support that idea. Sir Fred Hoyle states,

> The genes of [prokaryotes] are continuous sequences of bases on the DNA, whereas the genes of eukaryotes are built characteristically from several disjointed segments of DNA. There is evidently a major chasm between the modes of gene expression in the two kinds of cell. A similar conclusion might have been reached long ago from the fact that photosynthesis in prokaryotes does not use water as in eukaryotes, a remarkable difference.[80]

In fact, eukaryote cells are found in the world's oldest known rocks, equivalently dated with, or even pre-dating, rocks in which prokaryote cells are found.[81] This is all fatal to evolution.

THE DEVELOPMENT OF NEW ORGANS, FORMS, FUNCTIONS, AND ORGANISMS

Darwin also raised the issue he called "organs of extreme perfection and complication." In *Origin* he admitted, "To suppose that the eye with all its inimitable contrivances for adjusting the focus to different distances, for admitting different amounts of light, and for the correction of spherical and chromatic aberration, could have been formed by natural selection, seems, I freely confess, absurd in the highest degree. . . . If it could be demonstrated that any complex organ existed, which could not possibly have been formed by numerous, successive, slight modifications, my theory would absolutely break down."[82]

---

80. Hoyle, "The Big Bang," 70–72.
81. Hoyle and Wickramasinghe, *Evolution*, 70–75.
82. Darwin, *Origin*, 190, 194. Darwin devoted four-and-a-half pages in *Origin* to the eye. He supposed that, somehow, a nerve became sensitive to light, and he looked at different types of eyes in different creatures, concluding "we must suppose" and "may we not believe" that the eye could be formed by natural selection working on genetic mutations over a long period of time. Darwin, *Origin*, 194.

Textbook cases of evolution

What evidence is there that genetic mutations combined with natural selection can produce new organs, forms, functions, and organisms? The "textbook case" is that of the famous peppered moths (*Biston betularia*): when pollution from the Industrial Revolution darkened tree trunks, the lighter moths stood out, so birds more readily ate them; therefore, the proportion of dark moths increased dramatically. Later, as pollution was cleaned up, the lighter moths became predominant again. However, Carl Wieland points out, "The textbook story demonstrates nothing more than gene frequencies shifting back and forth, by natural selection, within one created kind. It offers nothing which, even given millions of years, could add the sort of complex design information needed for ameba-to-man evolution."[83] Even evolutionists admit that this type of phenomenon is relatively "trivial" or "superficial" and does not demonstrate evolution in action.[84] In other words, this is not evolution but simply a color change back and forth within a stable species. Biologist M. W. Ho and mathematician P. T. Saunders conclude, "The successes of the [neo-Darwinian] theory are limited to the interpretation of the minutiae of evolution, such as the adaptive change in coloration of moths; while it has remarkably little to say on the questions which interest us most, such as how there came to be moths in the first place."[85]

Similarly, one of the most studied, experimented-on, and mutated creatures is the fruit fly (*Drosophila melanogaster*). Nevertheless,

> a mutant *Drosophila melanogaster* remains recognizably a *melanogaster*. It is true that some mutations affect the course or the rate of development of certain organs and may thus bring about considerable changes, but these are generally in an adverse direction, leading to arrests and abnormalities of development—as for instance in the series of crippled wings which appear in *Drosophila* mutants. . . . Gene mutation never produces a new organ; it produces merely deviations from the norm, which, if

---

83. Wieland, "Goodbye," 56.

84. Denton, *Evolution: A Theory*, 81; Grassé, *Evolution*, 84; Matthews, "Introduction," xi ("all the moths remain from beginning to end *Biston betularia*"); Grene, "The Faith," 193–97.

85. Ho and Saunders, "Beyond neo-Darwinism," 589; see also Grene, "The Faith," 193 ("The colour of moths or snails or mice is clearly controlled by visibility to predators; but 'evolution'? Do these observations explain how in the first place there came to be any moths or snails or mice at all? By what right are we to extrapolate the pattern by which colour or other such superficial characters are governed to the origin of species, let alone of orders, classes, phyla of living organisms?").

large are definite abnormalities that are unlikely to survive for long or be perpetuated, and if small are comparatively trivial variations which in no way affect or alter the structural plan of the species.[86]

As Arthur Koestler states, "none of the mutations observed in millions of *Drosophila* have produced offspring showing any evolutionary advantage."[87]

On the Galapagos Islands in the Pacific Ocean, there are a variety of different finches, which vary in the shape and size of their beaks. Darwin studied these finches, which have been called "the emblems of evolution."[88] Researchers at Harvard Medical School "found a molecule that regulates genes involved in shaping the beaks of Darwin finches."[89] As with peppered moths and fruit flies, however, the finches are still finches, with no evidence that they are evolving into anything else. Ornithologist Robert Zink recently reported, "The various ground finches don't differ significantly in ways that usually differentiate bird species, such as plumage patterns or song."[90] The predominance of larger and smaller finches has simply cycled back and forth depending upon dry or wet environmental conditions.[91] As one science writer stated, Darwin's finches are "a prime example of the limits of natural selection,"[92] and "it appears to be clear that no macroevolution is happening in 'Darwin's finches' on the Galápagos Islands."[93]

To a large degree, Darwin based his theory on an analogy between natural selection and the artificial selection used by breeders who artificially select particular characteristics of plants or animals.[94] That is a false analogy:

> Man has an aim or an end in view; "natural selection" can have none. Man picks out the individuals he wishes to cross, choosing them by the characters he seeks to perpetuate or enhance. He protects them and their issue by all means in his power, guarding them from the operation of natural selection, which

---

86. Russell, *The Diversity*, 103; see also Behe, *The Edge*, 200–201.
87. Koestler, *Janus*, 183.
88. Cromie, "How Darwin's finches," n.p.
89. Cromie, "How Darwin's finches," n.p.
90. Breining, "Are Darwin's finches," No New Species; see also Wells, "Misrepresenting," B. Hybridization and Extrapolations ("no new species have been observed to originate from selection on finch beaks").
91. See Johnson, *Darwin*, 25; Gibbs and Grant, "Oscillating," 511–12.
92. Lönnig, "Galapagos Finches," n.p.
93. Lönnig, "Darwin's Finches," n.p.
94. Darwin, *Origin*, 25–57; see Grene, "The Faith," 195.

would speedily eliminate many freaks; he continues his active and purposeful selection from generation to generation until he reaches, if possible, his goal. Nothing of this kind happens, or can happen, through the blind process of differential elimination and differential survival which we miscall "natural selection".[95]

Additionally, tame animals that have reverted to the wild state quickly lose the characteristics artificially bred into them.[96] Artificial selection does not result in the creation of new species but simply demonstrates the narrow limits within which species can vary. It does not amount to "evolution" at all.[97]

None of the above examples, whether in the wild (peppered moths or finches) or domestically mutated and selected (fruit flies and other animals), have resulted in the generation of any new organs, forms, functions, or organisms. Swedish embryologist Søren Løvtrup has stated that "nobody has ever demonstrated that natural selection can bring about anything but events that are trivial from an evolutionary perspective."[98] Indeed, Michael Behe notes, "There has never been a meeting, or a book, or a paper on the details of the evolution of complex biochemical systems"—even a cell—let alone an organ, form, function, or organism.[99] The above are all examples of what is often called "microevolution," i.e., variations within an existing kind or type of organism, as opposed to "macroevolution," i.e., the development of new organs, forms, functions, and organisms that result in amoebas ultimately evolving into human beings.[100] The issue, however, is whether the naturalistic processes of genetic mutations + natural selection are even capable of generating the form and functional transformations macroevolution requires. The evidence conclusively demonstrates that such macroevolution is biologically impossible.

---

95. Russell, *The Diversity*, 124; see also Matthews, "Introduction," xi.

96. Grassé, *Evolution*, 124, 225.

97. Grassé, *Evolution*, 125–26; see also Bergman, "Some Biological Problems," 147–49.

98. Løvtrup, *Darwinism*, 4.

99. Behe, *Darwin's Black Box*, 179.

100. It should be noted that biblical creationism agrees with the concept of so-called "microevolution": "Contemporary creationists work with a model of original created design subsequently modified by secondary causes (linked to natural selection, mutation, genetic drift, etc.). Thus, many of the cases of imperfect design (blind cave fish, for example) are rightly interpreted as degenerative descent with modification." Tyler, "Darwinism's theological," n.p.

The impossibility of mutations + natural selection to create new organs, forms, functions, and organisms

The eye is only one of multiple organs that could not possibly have evolved incrementally by undirected natural selection acting upon genetic mutations over time. With respect to the eye, R. L. Wysong observes, "To form the eye, a combination of beneficial mutations would have to occur. These mutations would not involve simple rearrangements of a few bases in DNA, but would first of all have to form sufficient DNA to work with, then mutations of this DNA would have to be integrated with other segments of DNA controlling the nervous, vascular, skeletal, muscular, and endocrine systems."[101] A supposed "light-sensitive nerve" or cell must become a light-sensitive organ; it then must become a cup-like depression that has focusing capacity, which necessitates muscle changes; it then must become a lens; then focusing must become imaging (and that does not just happen in one place but in two places in the same part of the body); then there must be nerve connections to the brain, which reverses or interprets a reverse image (how could that have any selective advantage?); and the visual cortex is at the back of the brain, whereas the eyeballs are at the front of the head, and the right side of the visual cortex is associated with the left-hand field of vision and *vice versa*. All of this would have required *thousands* of favorable mutations which would have to take place *simultaneously*; and none of this could have any "selective advantage" until it was all properly in place.[102] To all of this must be added the molecular structure and the chemistry of a complex organ would need to be significantly rearranged; this was never considered either by Darwin or contemporary evolutionists.[103]

Wysong further notes, "The bony orbits must be 'mutated' to house the globe of the eye. The bone must have appropriate holes (foramina) to allow the appropriate 'mutated' blood vessels and nerves to feed the eye.... Each of the gross features of the eye would be under the control of many genes (Drosophila—fruit fly—eye color is under the control of some 15 genes). Each gene consists of thousands of nucleotides. The spontaneous mutation of sufficient DNA to code just the lens of the eye would be roughly equivalent to the formation of a chapter in a book from an explosion of letters [he then lists multiple other specifics]."[104] Grassé concludes, "Moreover, during

---

101. Wysong, *The Creation-Evolution*, 306; see also Grassé, *Evolution*, 105; Taylor, *The Great*, 94–103; Schützenberger, "Interview," 11, 13–14)

102. See Behe, *Darwin's Black Box*, 18–22, 38–39; Grassé, *Evolution*, 106.

103. See Grassé, *Evolution*, 105.

104. Wysong, *The Creation-Evolution*, 306–9.

phylogenetic organogenesis, natural selection must be capable of foresight. . . . But the choice cannot take place without predicting the future role of the incipient organ. Without such prescience, the coordination of successive states is incomprehensible."[105] However, the necessity of foresight is directly contrary to what "natural selection" actually is and does. Dawkins points out that natural selection "has no purpose in mind. It has no mind and no mind's eye. It does not plan for the future. It has no vision, no foresight, no sight at all. If it can be said to play the role of watchmaker in nature, it is the blind watchmaker."[106] In short, undirected naturalistic evolution is not even a *possible* means for the creation of the eye or any other "organs of extreme perfection and complication."

As another example, consider the supposed evolution of sexual reproduction. The supposed first cellular forms of life would have reproduced asexually by some means of cellular division.[107] However, at some point, sexual reproduction is said to have evolved. As with (or even more than) the eye, the evolution of sexual reproduction necessitates an enormous series of coordinated mutations, only this time in two separate individuals, not one. A partially-developed sex organ could have no "survival value"; indeed, a species with partially-developed sex organs could not reproduce and, therefore, could not survive at all. To evolve sexual reproduction, mutations must lead to the evolution of both male and female genitalia, in different organisms, both with all the attendant components (penis, sperm, testicles, vas deferens; eggs, uterus, fallopian tubes, vagina), all fully-developed and coordinated. Further, the male and female must evolve at the same time and same place! Natural selection is said to favor those that leave the most viable offspring. Asexual reproduction "does not involve the union of gametes, which accordingly results in a much faster rate of reproduction compared to sexual reproduction, where 50% of offspring are males and unable to produce offspring themselves."[108] Consequently, sexual reproduction could not have evolved at all, because it is contrary to a fundamental tenet of evolution itself.

Jeremy Rifkin summarizes, "One could draw up a list of tens of thousands of other complex biological systems that utterly defy the idea of gradual development by way of natural selection. In fact, upon close examination, virtually every fully operational system that exists within living things works only as an integrative unit, and the individual parts that make

---

105. Grassé, *Evolution*, 106.
106. Dawkins, *The Blind*, 5; see also Ayala and Valentine, *Evolving*, 322.
107. See Wolchover, "How Did Life."
108. "Evolution of sexual reproduction," *Wikipedia*, Introduction.

Naturalistic Evolution Is Contrary to the Facts of Nature

it up appear to exhibit absolutely no value on their own in advancing the survival of the individual or the species."[109] Arthur Koestler concludes, "The doctrine that the coming together of all requisite changes was due to a series of coincidences is an affront not only to common sense but to the basic principles of scientific explanation."[110]

There is another aspect of this that is rarely considered. That is, while most people think of the evolution of new forms and physical structures, Koestler adds the significant fact that evolution supposedly creates "not only new shapes; it also creates new types of behaviour, new instinctual skills which are innate and hereditary. If the forces behind the evolution of new structures are obscure, those behind the evolution of innate skills are shrouded in total darkness."[111] Those innate and instinctual skills and behaviors include bird and butterfly migration and the convoluted reproductive procedures of certain wasps.[112] Insofar as human beings are concerned, human language (articulate speech) is restricted to human beings. There are no known or even hypothetical sequence of simple forms of communication leading up to articulate speech that has ever been proposed.[113] In short, "Neo-Darwinism does not possess the theoretical tools to tackle the problem" of the development of new types of behavior, new instinctual skills, and human language.[114]

Irreducible complexity

In his 1996 book *Darwin's Black Box: The Biochemical Challenge to Evolution*, biochemist Michael Behe discussed the issue of "irreducible complexity," i.e., "a single system composed of several well-matched, interacting parts that contribute to the basic function, wherein the removal of any one of the parts causes the system to effectively cease functioning."[115] He pointed out that an irreducibly complex system "cannot be produced directly (that is, by continuously improving the initial function, which continues to work by the same mechanism) by slight, successive modifications of a precursor system, because any precursor to an irreducibly complex system that is missing a

---

109. Rifkin, *Algeny*, 140.
110. Koestler, *Janus*, 176.
111. Koestler, *Janus*, 177.
112. Koestler, *Janus*, 177–78; see also Macbeth, *Darwin Retried*, 71–72.
113. Denton, *Evolution: Still*, 198–99.
114. Koestler, *Janus*, 177.
115. Behe, *Darwin's Black Box*, 39.

part is by definition nonfunctional."[116] He used a common mousetrap as an example of an irreducibly complex system: all of its parts (spring, hammer, catch, platform, holding bar) must be present, must be the proper kind and shape, and must be in their proper places simultaneously, or the mousetrap is worthless. He then discussed in detail the fact that the cilium and flagellum within a cell are irreducibly complex systems that could not have been produced by random mutations and natural selection.[117] He reached the same conclusion with respect to the mechanism for blood clotting.[118]

Cells are more than irreducibly complex systems. They evince clearly purposeful activity, which is a hallmark of design. In the generation of protein chains (which initiate and sustain growth), "each codon [a DNA or RNA sequence of three nucleotides (a trinucleotide) that forms a unit of genomic information] instructs the cell to start the creation of a protein chain, to add a specific amino acid to the growing protein chain, or to stop creation of the protein chain. For instance, a messenger RNA codon, GCA, signals the addition of the amino acid alanine to the protein chain. The messenger RNA stop codon, UAG, signals the end of that protein's production."[119] I. L. Cohen discusses the significance of this:

> The fact that this system includes a STOP – GO signal has significant implications. It indicates a predetermined purposefulness of action, a knowledge of an expected future necessity within an enormously complex, yet perfect, system. Purposefulness is clearly a reflection of sophistication or intelligence. These are not characteristics that we can attribute to unthinking chemical atoms and molecules. . . . It reflects a level of intelligence far higher than anything we are familiar with – certainly far superior to our own level of intelligence and knowledge.[120]

Ten years after *Darwin's Black Box*, Behe returned to the cilium and flagellum. He pointed out that, in the ten years since his first book, knowledge of the molecular world of the cilium and flagellum has increased exponentially. We now know that the cilium and flagellum are part of a complex cellular construction machinery. The cilium, among other things, is "a sophisticated chemical sensor involved in a wide array of biological processes"

---

116. Behe, *Darwin's Black Box*, 39.
117. Behe, *Darwin's Black Box*, 59–73.
118. Behe, *Darwin's Black Box*, 74–97.
119. "Codon," *National Human*, n.p.
120. Cohen, *Darwin*, 60.

Naturalistic Evolution Is Contrary to the Facts of Nature 149

which is connected with an intraflagellar transport mechanism that builds and maintains the cilium.[121] Cilia and flagella

> are not only stupendously complex systems in their own right, but they have complicated systems dedicated to their construction, and genetic control systems coordinating that construction, whose intricacy science is only now beginning to appreciate. . . . Such coherent, complex, cellular systems did not arise by random mutation and natural selection, any more than the Hoover Dam was built by the random accumulation of twigs, leaves, and mud.[122]

The effect of natural selection on mutations

The traits upon which natural selection is said to operate arise from random mutations and variations. However, mutations + natural selection, *by their very nature*, are *not* designed to create new organs, forms, functions, or organisms. The reason is that natural selection acts on species and characteristics that *already* exist and *eliminates* the less fit, as opposed to generating new or novel parts or characteristics to aid in the "struggle for existence." Thus, natural selection tends to conserve the form and function of an organism rather than transform it.[123]

The mutations upon which natural selection acts are like copying errors. Hence, they tend to be harmful, not beneficial, to the organism. Over time the accumulation of mutations tends to degrade genetic information and, far from producing new functions, "eventually and typically result in the *loss* of function."[124] This is especially, perhaps invariably, true with respect to mutations of the genes necessary to effect macroevolution, i.e., the development of new organs, forms, functions, and organisms. Evolutionary biologist Wallace Arthur explains, "Those genes that control early developmental processes are involved in the establishment of the basic body plan.

---

121. Behe, *The Edge*, 85–94.

122. Behe, *The Edge*, 102; see also at 146–47. Later in the book he discusses the genetic regulatory network (called a "kernel") for the construction of a tissue called endomesoderm in sea urchins. When drawn schematically, it looks like a complex electronic or computer-logic circuit. Interference with expression of any one kernel gene destroys the kernel's function altogether, which means that the kernel is irreducibly complex and could not possibly have been created by a step-by-step, unguided, evolutionary process. Behe, *The Edge*, 196–97.

123. Meyer, *Darwin's Doubt*, 147; Løvtrup, *Darwinism*, 120; Koestler, *Janus*, 171; Grassé, *Evolution*, 115, 119, 121.

124. Meyer, *Darwin's Doubt*, 236; Grassé, *Evolution*, 115.

Mutations in these genes will usually be extremely disadvantageous, and it is conceivable that they are *always* so."[125] That was confirmed by Christiane Nüsslein-Volhard and Eric Wieschaus who generated thousands of mutations in *Drosophila melanogaster* (fruit flies) to investigate their genome. They induced mutations in the genes that regulate embryonic development and won a 1995 Nobel Prize for their work. One finding was that, *without exception*, the mutants died as deformed larvae long before reaching reproductive age.[126] In further experiments with fruit flies after their Nobel Prize, Nüsslein-Volhard and Wieschaus again found that, in all cases in which mutations in the regulatory genes that affect body-plan formation occur early in the in the development of the organism, embryonic death of the organism inevitably occurred.[127] The significance is that, since mutating the genes that regulate body-plan construction destroys the organism as it develops embryonically, mutations combined with natural selection *could not possibly* build the body plans in the first place or develop new body plans.

As if that were not enough, researchers have demonstrated the mathematical impossibility of mutations and natural selection to create new organs, forms, functions, and organisms. Biochemist Michael Behe and physicist David Snoke assessed the plausibility of naturalistic evolution generating two or more coordinated mutations (since developing new forms and functions requires more than just one mutation or one new protein or gene).[128] Behe and Snoke found that "mutation and selection could generate two coordinated mutations in 1 million generations. However, that only occurred in a population of 1 trillion or more multicellular organisms, *"a number that "exceeds the size of the effective breeding populations of practically all individual animal species that have lived at any given time."*[129] On the other hand, two coordinated mutations could occur in a population of only 1 million organisms, but for that to occur it would take *10 billion generations* to do so, which, assuming only one year for each generation, would equate to *10 billion years*, or more than twice the age of the earth as estimated by most scientists.[130] Even those numbers were looking at the generation of only two coordinated mutations as being necessary to build a new gene; if three or more coordinated mutations are necessary (as is undoubtedly the

---

125. Arthur, *The Origin*, 14, emph. in orig.; see also Schützenberger, "Algorithms," 74–75; Meyer, *Darwin's Doubt*, 171–72.
126. Meyer, *Darwin's Doubt*, 255–57.
127. Meyer, *Darwin's Doubt*, 260–61.
128. See Behe and Snoke, "Simulating," Abstract.
129. Meyer, *Darwin's Doubt*, 245, emph. in orig.; see also Behe and Snoke, "Simulating."
130. Meyer, *Darwin's Doubt*, 245.

case), the length of time and/or population of organisms necessary would be astronomically greater.[131] Again, the means suggested (or required) by naturalistic evolution to generate new forms, functions, organs, and organisms are not just implausible, but impossible. Similar conclusions regarding the mathematical impossibility of the neo-Darwinian theory of evolution to explain the phenomenon of evolution on the basis of the known laws of biology, physics, and chemistry have been reached by multiple other scientists in different scientific specialties.[132]

The genetic evidence

Plant and animal development is controlled at the genetic level. However, there is no plausible or even possible mechanism at the genetic level to create the changes necessary to transform one type of structure or organism into another. With respect to the genetic mechanism of gene duplication, which is the primary hypothesis of how new forms and functions could evolve, Jerry Bergman states, "Gene duplication does occur. For example, chromosomal recombination can result in the loss of a gene on one chromosome and the gain of an extra copy on the sister chromosome. Gene duplication can involve not only whole genes, but also parts of genes, several genes, parts of a chromosome, or even entire chromosomes."[133]

The problem is that, while gene duplication plays a role in variation within kinds of organisms, it does not play a role in transforming one kind of form or function into another. Behe points out, "Randomly duplicating a single gene, or even the entire genome, does not yield new complex machinery; it only gives a copy of what was already present."[134]

Perhaps more fundamentally, DNA contains the genetic information that allows all organisms to live, develop, function, grow, and reproduce. DNA is something like a computer code. It conveys functional information for building proteins or RNA molecules. Even Richard Dawkins acknowledges that our genetic system is like a computer and "digital to the core. . . . Genes are pure information—information that can be encoded, recoded and decoded, without any degradation or change in meaning. . . .

---

131. Meyer, *Darwin's Doubt*, 247.

132. See Eden, "Inadequacies," 5–12; Ulam, "How to Formulate," 21–28; Schützenberger, "Algorithms," 73–75; Salisbury, "Natural Selection," 342–43; see also Cohen, *Darwin*, 64–73; Denton, *Evolution: A Theory*, 308–25; Meyer, *Darwin's Doubt*, 170–77.

133. Bergman, "Does gene duplication," 99.

134. Behe, *The Edge*, 74; see Lynch and Conery, "The evolutionary," Abstract; Bergman, "Does gene duplication," 101–4.

DNA characters are copied with an accuracy that rivals anything modern engineers can do."[135] As evolution is said to occur, the organisms become more complex. This increasing complexity in organs, forms, function, and organisms necessitates more cell types to perform their more diverse functions which, in turn, requires new and specialized proteins.[136] This requires a vast increase in genetic information. Denton asks the obvious question, "Is it really credible that random processes could have constructed a reality, the smallest element of which – a functional protein or gene – is complex beyond our own creative capacities, a reality which is the very antithesis of chance, which excels in every sense anything produced by the intelligence of man?"[137]

Eric Davidson of the California Institute of Technology has studied the genetic regulatory basis of animal development in more detail than probably any other researcher. All organisms body plans are controlled, not by single genes, but by developmental gene regulatory networks (dGRNs). However, Davidson states that a dGRN "is very impervious to change, except for catastrophic loss of the body part or loss of viability altogether."[138] He adds, "There is always an observable consequence if a dGRN subcircuit is interrupted. Since these consequences are always catastrophically bad, flexibility is minimal, and since the subcircuits are all interconnected, the whole network partakes of the quality that there is only one way for things to work. And indeed the embryos of each species develop in only one way."[139]

To develop new organs, forms, functions, or organisms would require changing the dGRN of an organism which could not occur without multiple, coordinated mutations (which, as we saw with the cilium and flagellum and as Davidson's research proves, is impossible). In short, our understanding of genetics and microbiology—of which Darwin knew nothing and which was virtually unknown when the neo-Darwinian synthesis was developed—have rendered naturalistic evolution biologically impossible. Davidson concludes that neo-Darwinian evolution

> erroneously assumes that change in protein coding sequence is the basic cause of change in developmental program; and it erroneously assumes that evolutionary change in body plan morphology occurs by a continuous process. All of these assumptions are basically counterfactual. This cannot be surprising, since the

---

135. Dawkins, *River*, 17–19.
136. See Meyer, *Darwin's Doubt*, 161–68.
137. Denton, *Evolution: A Theory*, 342; see Meyer, *Darwin's Doubt*, passim.
138. Davidson, "Evolutionary," 38.
139. Davidson, "Evolutionary," 40.

neo-Darwinian synthesis from which these ideas stem was a pre-molecular biology concoction focused on population genetics and adaptation natural history, neither of which have any direct mechanistic import for the genomic regulatory systems that drive embryonic development of the body plan.[140]

In fact, observational and experimental evidence at the molecular level prove mathematically that mutations + natural selection cannot have caused the development of new organs, forms, functions, and organisms. New animals require new organs and cell types; new cell types require new proteins to service them.[141] Proteins comprise at least three distinct levels of structure; the tertiary structure is called a "protein fold." In order to perform new functions, proteins require new protein folds.[142] Because new protein folds are "the *smallest unit of structural innovation* in the history of life," they are the smallest unit of structural innovation that natural selection could select; in short, "the ability to produce new protein folds represents the *sine qua non* of macroevolutionary innovation."[143] Meyer summarizes the experimental research of protein scientist Douglas Axe and others concerning this very area. Axe's experiments in mutating genes to produce new folds and functions found that the gradual transformation of one functional protein fold into another did not happen at all.[144] In short, naturalistic evolutionary processes do not have the ability to transform even the smallest unit of structural innovation in living beings.

Michael Behe points out that because of its "enormous population, rate of reproduction, and our knowledge of the genetics, the single best test case of Darwin's theory is the history of malaria," with confirmatory evidence from the study of *E. coli* and HIV.[145] Over the course of time, the interaction between malaria parasites and human beings has resulted in certain mutations both within the malaria parasites (which have helped malaria parasites to be resistant to chloroquine) and human beings to be resistant to malaria (e.g., if they have the sickle hemoglobin or hemoglobin C mutations). However, when chloroquine is no longer used to treat malaria patients in an area, the resistant strain of the malaria parasite declines and the original strain returns.[146] With respect to human resistance to malaria,

140. Davidson, "Evolutionary," 35–36.
141. See Meyer, *Darwin's Doubt*, 161–63.
142. Meyer, *Darwin's Doubt* 189.
143. Meyer, *Darwin's Doubt*, 190, emph. in orig.
144. See Meyer, *Darwin's Doubt*, 196–97.
145. Behe, *The Edge*, 12–13.
146. Behe, *The Edge*, 50–51.

both sickle hemoglobin or hemoglobin C mutations are harmful mutations. Further, the mutations do not act to develop a more complex, interactive biochemical system. In short, "the mutations are neither making a new system nor even adding to an established one.... They are all damaging. Some are worse than others, but all are diminishments; none are constructive."[147]

More importantly, by considering the number of human beings versus malarial parasites through history and what we now know of the human and malaria genomes, "for humans to achieve a mutation like this [i.e., equivalent of the kind required for malaria to become resistant to chloroquine] by chance, we would need to wait a hundred million times ten million years."[148] That is many times the age of the universe! In other words, the likelihood that such a mutation could arise even once in the entire course of human existence is zero: it is beyond any reasonable doubt that mutations + natural selection *cannot* cause the construction of new, complex, interactive structures, organs, functions, or organisms.[149]

Naturalistic evolution entails the claim that, given enough chances, unguided mutations and natural selection can build the sort of complex machinery we see in the cell as well as new organs, forms, functions, and organisms. Intelligent design/biblical creation holds that mutation and natural selection can account for small changes within strict limits but cannot account for the creation of the complex machinery of the living cell or new organs, forms, functions, or organisms. Behe summarizes the scientific data, "Darwin and design hold opposite, firm expectations of what we should find when we examine a truly astronomical—a hundred billion billion—number of organisms [i.e., the intensive studies of malaria discussed in Behe's book]. Up until recently, the magnitude of the problem precluded a definitive test. But now the results are in. Darwinism's most basic prediction is falsified."[150]

The above demonstrates that so-called "microevolution," i.e., mutations and changing gene frequencies within a species, does not and cannot lead to "macroevolution," i.e., the transformation of one type of organ, form, function, or organism into another: bacteria do not become mollusks which then become fish, amphibians, reptiles, birds, mammals, and ultimately human beings.[151] Frank Salisbury of the plant science department of Utah State University stated, "Modern biology is faced with two ideas which seem to

---

147. Behe, *The Edge*, 33–34, 38.

148. Behe, *The Edge*, 61.

149. See Behe, *The Edge*, 137–47, 152–62, 200 for a comparison of the trivial effects of mutations in malaria, HIV, and *E. coli*.

150. Behe, *The Edge*, 235.

151. Gilbert, Opitz, and Raff, "Resynthesizing," 361 ("Microevolution looks at adaptations that concern only the survival of the fittest, not the arrival of the fittest").

me to be quite incompatible with each other. One is the concept of evolution by natural selection of adaptive genes that are originally produced by random mutations. The other is the concept of the gene as part of a molecule of DNA, each gene being unique in the order of arrangement of its nucleotides. If life really depends on each gene being as unique as it appears to be, then it is too unique to come into being by chance mutations."[152] In fact, "the results of the last 20 years of research on the genetic basis of adaptation has led us to a great Darwinian paradox," namely, "the kind of mutations the evolutionary process would need to produce new animal body parts—namely, beneficial regulatory changes expressed early in development—don't occur. Whereas, the kind that it doesn't need—viable genetic mutations in DNA generally expressed late in development [that affect only minor aspects of form or function]—do occur."[153] In short, it is impossible to extrapolate from microevolution to macroevolution, as even many evolutionists now recognize.[154] Consequently, naturalistic evolution cannot be true.

Conclusion

Darwin himself cited the complexity of organs as a ground for falsification of his theory of naturalistic evolution. In looking at the evidence, one must ask: Which view is more reasonable—which view better fits the facts—that the eye, other such organs, and the variety of different organisms evolved by undirected natural selection playing upon chance mutations or that such organs and organisms were designed by God for a purpose? At the Wistar Institute's April 1966 symposium on mathematical challenges to the neo-Darwinian interpretation of evolution. Dr. Stanislaw Ulam's presentation showed that it was mathematically impossible for evolution to have taken place, given the millions of favorable mutations in the right direction necessary in the short span of a billion years. In response, evolutionists C. H. Waddington, Peter Medawar, and Ernest Mayr said, "It is, indeed, a fact that the eye has evolved" and we know "that evolution has occurred";[155] therefore, they concluded "you have got the question upside down."[156] The same was true after Dr. Marcel-Paul Schützenberger reached a conclusion similar

---

152. Salisbury, "Natural Selection," 342.

153. McDonald, "The Molecular Basis," 92–93; see also Meyer, *Darwin's Doubt*, 262.

154. See Gould, "The Return," 23; Gould, "Is a new," 120–21, 124–25; Grassé, *Evolution*, 88, 96–97, 170, 211–28, 243–46; Manser, "The Concept," 28; Russell, *The Diversity*, 102–5, 121–23.

155. Ulam, "How to Formulate," 29–30.

156. Ulam, "How to Formulate," 29.

to Dr. Ulam's.[157] Dr. Waddington responded, "Your argument is simply that life must have come about by special creation."[158] Waddington, Medawar, and Mayr were basing their conclusions on their *pre-existing presupposition that evolution had to have occurred*, not on the mathematical and scientific facts. Waddington, Medawar, and Mayr could not conceive of or allow any alternative to the worldview of naturalism and naturalistic evolution. Phillip Johnson observed that these Darwinists "know" that "the mutation-selection mechanism can produce wings, eyes, and brains not because the mechanism can be observed to do anything of the kind, but because their guiding philosophy assures them that no other power is available to do the job. The absence from the cosmos of any Creator is therefore the essential starting point for Darwinism."[159] Whatever else may be said, their response certainly is not scientific or in the spirit of free, rational inquiry. Although it has been decades since the Wistar symposium took place, the facts presented by Drs. Ulam and Schützenberger have not changed; unfortunately, neither have the presupposition-based responses of evolutionary naturalists.

This highlights one issue raised at the beginning of this book, namely, the primary issue is not so much the facts themselves (which are largely undisputed), but the *interpretation* of and conclusions drawn from those facts. Where facts are generally agreed upon, differences of interpretation stem from differences in one's underlying fundamental philosophical or worldview presuppositions. Re-evaluating and changing one's fundamental underlying presuppositions is difficult for many if not most people. Nevertheless, as Johnson states, "Evidence must be evaluated independently of any assumption about the truth of the theory being tested."[160] Until that happens, the dominance of the naturalistic evolutionary worldview will continue, not because of the facts but in spite of them.

One of the other questions we are raising in this book is, "Which view better comports with the facts: naturalism or Christianity?" God's creation is not just of the outward form of different creatures but extends to (indeed, is based on) the molecular level. Darwin formulated his theory without being aware of the molecular and genetic basis of life, the significance and amazing intricacy of which has only recently been unlocked. We have seen that both at the morphological (phenotype) level and at the molecular (genotype) level, naturalistic evolution is inconsistent with and cannot account

---

157. Schützenberger, "Algorithms," 75.
158. Schützenberger, "Algorithms," 80.
159. Johnson, *Darwin*, 115.
160. Johnson, *Darwin*, 73.

for the scientific facts. On the other hand, Christianity is consistent with the scientific facts and can account for them.

This does not mean or imply that science is not important and that scientific investigation of nature is irrelevant or should not take place. It is relevant, important, should take place, and can lead to tremendous breakthroughs in knowledge and technology. The fact that the current underlying worldview of naturalism and evolution is false should not affect the scientific enterprise at all, except to redirect one's fundamental underlying presuppositions and, hence, one's conclusions concerning the meaning and significance of one's scientific findings. That is exemplified by famous anatomist Richard Owen and other scientists, who based their views of science on their Christian understanding of God and the Bible, which are consistent, not inconsistent, with how reality actually is structured.[161] The only thing capable of design is a mind—an intelligent agency. That is the only position consistent with science, since mind alone, as opposed to any materialistic cause, "is the only known cause of the origin of large amounts of functionally

---

161. Owen (1804–1892) is only one of a host of scientists whose research was based on the Bible, not contemporary naturalistic evolution. Henry Morris provides brief biographies of 101 such scientists in his *Men of Science—Men of God* (1988). Such scientists include Carolus Linnaeus (1707–1778), the father of biological taxonomy, whose classification system was his attempt to equate his "species" with the "kinds" mentioned in Genesis 1; Georges Cuvier (1769–1832), founder of the science of comparative anatomy; Matthew Maury (1806–1873), founder of modern hydrology and oceanography, whose search to find the paths in the seas (ocean currents) was based on his understanding of Ps 8:8; James Simpson (1811–1870), a founder of gynecology, whose motivation for research leading to the discovery of chloroform was based on the "deep sleep" of Adam in Gen 2:21; Louis Pasteur (1822–1895), whose research invalidated the theory of spontaneous generation; James Clerk Maxwell (1831–1879), whose research regarding electromagnetic field theory, thermodynamics, and other areas was based on God's mandate in Gen 1:26–28; Edward Maunder (1851–1928), founder of the British Astronomical Association, who wrote on the Bible's accuracy and insights in astronomical matters; William Ramsay (1851–1939), the great archaeologist, who was converted to Christianity because of the archaeological accuracy of the Bible and wrote many books providing archaeological support and illumination for the NT; Douglas Dewar (1875–1957), an ornithologist who wrote many books and papers on the scientific basis of creationism; L. Merson Davies (1890–1960), a geologist and paleontologist who wrote a book defending the scientific accuracy of the Bible. Not included in Morris's book, but one who is "acknowledged to be the foremost expert in the field of radio-halos," is Robert Gentry, whose research into polonium radio-halos was based on his belief in young-earth creationism. Taylor, *In the Minds*, 311; see Gentry, *Creation's Tiny*, 1–3. I mention these particular scientists because their research specifically was motivated by various statements in the Bible, and/or they wrote on the compatibility of science and the Bible. They demonstrate that a biblical, creationist viewpoint is not antithetical to science or scientific research but can, in fact, facilitate or spur scientific research.

specified information."¹⁶² As the work of Owen and others demonstrates, rejecting the worldview of naturalistic evolution should not adversely affect science or scientific research at all. "Medical science, for example, remains a very useful discipline whether or not there are instances of miraculous cures that are in principle beyond scientific explanation."¹⁶³ Freeing scientific research from the baggage of an invalid presupposition and theory should enable it to pursue the truth untrammeled, just like astronomy was freed when it abandoned the Ptolemaic system for the Copernican.

THE THEORY OF NATURALISTIC EVOLUTION IS NOT EVEN A PROPER SCIENTIFIC THEORY

"Science" is typically defined as a system of knowledge of the physical world and its phenomena obtained through the "scientific method," i.e., "principles and procedures for the systematic pursuit of knowledge involving the recognition and formulation of a problem, the collection of data through observation and experiment, and the formulation and testing of hypotheses."¹⁶⁴ The Science Council similarly defines science and the scientific method as follows, "Science is the pursuit and application of knowledge and understanding of the natural and social world following a systematic methodology based on evidence. Scientific methodology includes the following: • Objective observation: Measurement and data (possibly although not necessarily using mathematics as a tool) • Evidence • Experiment and/or observation as benchmarks for testing hypotheses • Induction: reasoning to establish general rules or conclusions drawn from facts or examples • Repetition • Critical analysis • Verification and testing: critical exposure to scrutiny, peer review and assessment."¹⁶⁵

Karl Popper, perhaps the twentieth century's most influential philosopher of science, noted that any method that appeals to observation and experiment, even if it had apparent explanatory power and was verified by confirming instances, is not thereby scientific. The reason is that astrology, Freud's psychoanalysis, and Marx's theory of history all meet those criteria. Consequently, Popper stated that *"the criterion of the scientific status of a theory is its falsifiability, or refutability, or testability."*¹⁶⁶ He went on to point

---

162. Meyer, *Return*, 211.
163. Johnson, *Reason*, 92; see also Alston, "Divine Action," 49–50.
164. *Merriam-Webster*, science; scientific method.
165. Science Council, "Our definition of science."
166. Popper, *Conjectures*, 37, emph. in orig.; see also Ayala, "Philosophical,"476 ("A hypothesis that is not subject to the possibility of rejection by observation and

Naturalistic Evolution Is Contrary to the Facts of Nature 159

out that it is easy to obtain confirmations for a theory "if we look for confirmations," but confirmations should count only if they are the result of risky predictions, i.e., "if, unenlightened by the theory in question we should have expected an event which was incompatible with the theory—an event which would have refuted the theory"; the reason is that "a theory which is not refutable by any conceivable event is non-scientific."[167] Additionally, "Confirming evidence should not count except which it is the result of a genuine test of the theory; and this means that it can be presented as a serious but unsuccessful attempt to falsify the theory."[168]

Popper's point has profound implications for the integrity of science because it goes directly to the truthfulness or falsity of any scientific hypothesis or theory. Popper's point directly assails Darwin's theory of naturalistic evolution because Darwin's work "mostly consisted in searching the literature for corroborating, not falsifying evidence."[169] But more than that, Darwin was not approaching matters objectively, neutrally, or in the spirit of attempting to determine the truth of origins on an empirical basis. Rather, as Søren Løvtrup observes, "From his notebooks and his correspondence, and less distinctly in his publications, it appears that Darwin's primary goal was to oppose Creationism."[170] Thus, in a letter to Professor Asa Gray in May 1863, Darwin said, "Personally, of course, I care much about Natural Selection; but that seems to me utterly unimportant, compared to the question of Creation *or* Modification."[171] Robert Young concludes that Darwin had to keep his account at a certain level of abstraction, because "He could neither show evolution at work nor provide a complete example of the stages by which it had worked. The former process was too slow while the record of its having occurred was too fragmentary."[172] Darwin's task underlying all of this, therefore, "was to explain *away* the *lack* of evidence while repeatedly stressing the greater plausibility of his theory over that of special creation."[173]

---

experiment cannot be regarded as scientific.").
167. Popper, *Conjectures*, 36.
168. Popper, *Conjectures*, 38.
169. Løvtrup, *Darwinism*, 405.
170. Løvtrup, *Darwinism*, 402.
171. Darwin, ed., *The Life*, 2:371.
172. Young, *Darwin's Metaphor*, 98.
173. Young, *Darwin's Metaphor*, 98, emph. in orig. Darwin made clear his view of the antipathy between natural selection and God. Darwin wrote to Charles Lyell on October 20, 1859, "I have reflected a good deal on what you say on the necessity of continued intervention of creative power. I cannot see the necessity; and its admission, I think, would make the theory of Natural Selection valueless." Darwin, ed., *The*

As we discussed above, in all of the most important areas, unguided biological evolution cannot stand up to objective, scientific critique: the explanations of how it supposedly works are in conflict with reality and cannot solve the extraordinary problems involved.[174] Many scientists are pointing out something more fundamental, namely, that Darwin's theory is not a proper scientific theory at all. For example, because the neo-Darwinian theory of evolution is basically a theory of historical reconstruction, it cannot be either directly observed or verified experimentally. As an explanation of how the species that exist now came into being, it amounts to a theory of a series of unique events which, by their very nature, cannot be repeated. As such, the theory cannot be scientifically validated.[175]

Canadian entomologist William Robin Thompson, in his introduction to the 1956 edition of Darwin's *Origin*, referred to French biologist Jean Louis Armand de Quatrefages' critique of Darwinism, saying that "de Quatrefages cited Darwin's explanation of the manner in which the titmouse might become transformed into the nutcracker, by the accumulation of small changes in structure and instinct owing to the effect of natural selection; and then proceeded to show that it is just as easy to transform the nutcracker into the titmouse. The demonstration can be modified without difficulty to fit any conceivable case. It is without scientific value, since it cannot be verified."[176]

The theory of naturalistic evolution in any of its forms (Darwinism, neo-Darwinism, or any other variant) cannot predict which organisms will survive and on what basis and cannot be tested or falsified, yet it is tenaciously held to, not for scientific reasons, but for non-scientific, philosophical or worldview reasons.[177] Indeed, as David Raup points out, "It is not always clear, in fact it's rarely clear, that the descendants were actually better adapted than their predecessors. . . . If we allow that natural selection works, as we almost have to do, the fossil record doesn't tell us whether it was responsible for 90 percent of the change we see, or 9 percent, or .9 percent. . . . On the other hand, it may be that a great many of the differences that

---

Life, 2:174. Further, Darwin "rejected the idea that God had miraculously inserted the human soul in an animal body, and set a challenge for his argument. 'I would give absolutely nothing for [the] theory of natural selection if it required miraculous additions at any one stage of descent.'" Keynes, *Darwin*, 256.

174. See Grassé, *Evolution*, 202.

175. See Denton, *Evolution: A Theory*, 75; Peters, "Tautology," 3.

176. Thompson, "A Critique," 4; see also Birch and Erlich, "Evolutionary History," 352.

177. Lewontin, "Billions," 31 ("materialism is absolute, for we cannot allow a Divine Foot in the door").

Naturalistic Evolution Is Contrary to the Facts of Nature   161

we observe within major animal groups are differences which do not have much effect on fitness. We are thus talking about the survival of the lucky as well as the survival of the fittest."[178]

Stephen Jay Gould admits that Darwin's theory is not strictly a "scientific" theory at all but is fundamentally a "big idea," a "truly large theory," a "comprehensive world view," an "historical hypothes[i]s" or "historical inquiry"; it cannot be "seen or derived by experiment" and cannot "proceed by canonical methods of direct experiment and repetition," but "is based on analogy, not observation" and could only be judged "by seeking concordance of pattern among large sets of independent criteria."[179] Daniel Dennett similarly acknowledges that the theory of natural selection is not and never was an attempt to prove how (pre)history actually was but is "only the power to prove how it could have been," given what we know about how things are.[180] Thus, Karl Popper concludes that Darwinism, in both its original and modern forms, "is not a testable scientific theory, but a metaphysical research programme."[181] Pierre-Paul Grassé and Sir Fred Hoyle call it a "pseudoscience."[182]

The situation is even more damning than that. Yale biology professor Keith Thomson points out that the traditional paleontological "proof" of "finding ancestors" in the fossil record

> cannot be tested by assembling nice series of fossils without discontinuities, because the evolutionary hypothesis is superficially so powerful that any reasonably graded series of forms can be thought to have legitimacy. In fact, there is circularity in the approach that first assembles some sort of evolutionary relatedness and then assembles a pattern of relations from which to argue that the relatedness must be true. This interplay of data and interpretation is the Achilles' heel of the second meaning of evolution [i.e., that organisms are related by descent through common ancestry].[183]

---

178. Raup, "Conflicts," 23, 26; see also Koestler, *Janus*, 171–72.
179. Gould, "Soapy," 22–24.
180. Dennett, *Darwin's Dangerous*, 319.
181. Popper, *Unended*, 168; see also at 171.

182. Grassé, *Evolution*, 6; Hoyle and Wickramasinghe, *Evolution*, 131; see also Løvtrup, *Darwinism*, 385 (the assertion of the "fitness" and "adaptation" of animals to their environment amounts to merely either "an affirmation of the fact that they exist, or else a metaphysical proposition").

183. Thomson, "Marginalia," 529–30; see also Patterson, *Evolution*, 109 ("Fossils may tell us many things, but one thing they can never disclose is whether they were ancestors of anything else.").

In other words, the theory of naturalistic evolution is merely a tautology, i.e., a circular argument, something defined in terms of itself.[184] Thus, Robert Henry Peters, professor of biology at McGill University, found "A number of popular ecological tenets, including natural selection, competitive exclusion, and parts of succession, species diversity, and spatial heterogeneity . . . lack the predictive and operational qualities which define scientific theories. Consequently, they must be termed tautologies."[185] Tautological statements cannot be falsified and, therefore, cannot be scientific. Hence, "the tautology/circularity charge, if true, is fatal to natural selection as a theory of how biological change occurs."[186]

CONCLUSION

Although evolution is not logically inconsistent with theism *per se*, it *is* inconsistent with historic, biblical Christianity. The reasons are two-fold and have been so from the beginning: (1) Darwinism is an all-encompassing worldview, not merely a theory of biological development. Michael Ruse (himself a leading evolutionist) acknowledges that "from the first it [Darwinism] has functioned as a secular religion, in opposition to the Christian religion of which it is the bastard offspring."[187] Physicist H. S. Lipson

---

184. E.g., "survival of the fittest": Who survives? The fittest. Who are the fittest? Those who survive. Or "the fittest individuals in a population leave the most offspring": Who are the fittest? Those who leave the most offspring. Who leave the most offspring? Those who are the fittest.

185. Peters, "Tautology," 11; see also Manser, "The Concept," 18–34; Eden, "Inadequacies," 5; Koestler, *Janus*, 170–73; Brady, "Natural Selection," 600–621.

186. Hunt, "Reconsidering," 4.

187. Ruse, "Is Darwinism," abstract. Elsewhere, Ruse noted, "Evolution is promoted by its practitioners as more than mere science. Evolution is promulgated as an ideology, a secular religion – a full-fledged alternative to Christianity, with meaning and morality. . . . This was true of evolution in the beginning, and it is true of evolution still today." Ruse, "Is Darwinism," n.p. In his book *Darwinism as Religion*, Ruse makes this point by looking at a number of areas including God, origins, humans, race and class, morality, sex, sin and redemption, and showing how, through Darwinian-influenced literature and other means, Darwinism speaks to these issues as "a religion, or if you want to speak a little more cautiously a 'secular religious perspective'" Ruse, *Darwinism*, ix. Coming from a different perspective, Allan Chapman similarly identifies six "religious" premises and structures which characterize modern science Chapman, *Slaying*, 170–71. Chapman states, "In short, modern science, instead of driving religious and 'meaning' questions out of the picture, has brought them centre stage and under the spotlight." Chapman, *Slaying*, 164. The similarities between evolution and a religious sect were noted as early as 1873 by T. S. Baynes. Baynes, "Darwin," 502–7. Perhaps this should not be surprising, since Momme von Sydow, in an interesting essay, shows that Darwin based his theory of evolution "on metaphysical tenets, which initially appeared

Naturalistic Evolution Is Contrary to the Facts of Nature

agrees and observes, "Evolution became in a sense a scientific religion: almost all scientists have accepted it and many are prepared to 'bend' their observations to fit in with it."[188] (2) The Darwinian worldview is based on pure naturalism/materialism; there is no room for God or the supernatural; instead, the process of evolution is claimed to be unplanned, undesigned, undirected, accidental, and blind.

Even naturalistic evolutionists admit that particularly living organisms appear to be designed,[189] and "seem to have purpose written all over them."[190] They attribute this appearance of design to the power of natural selection.[191] However, as we have seen above, naturalistic evolution is contrary to the fossil and microbiological evidence and, both mathematically and scientifically, cannot account for life in all of its diversity and complexity.

If naturalistic, unguided, unplanned evolution cannot account for the development of organs, forms, functions, and organisms, the *only* logical conclusion is that the biological organs, forms, function, and organisms we see today and that are revealed in the fossil record do not merely have the "appearance" of design but were, in fact, planned, designed, and caused to exist by an intelligent being of immense knowledge and power.[192] In a lengthy article, Swedish professor of information science Steinar Thorvaldsen and professor of mathematical statistics Ola Hössjer elaborated on basic information from DNA sequences, proteins, protein complexes, signaling pathways and networks. They conclude, "Fine-tuning is a clear feature of biological systems. Indeed, fine-tuning is even more extreme in biological systems than in inorganic systems. It is detectable within the realm of scientific methodology. . . . We have enough evidence to demonstrate that fine-tuning and design deserve attention in the scientific community as a conceptual tool for investigating and understanding the natural world."[193] In

---

to him to have a strong ethical and religious appeal." von Sydow, "Charles Darwin," 155.

188. Lipson, "A Physicist," 64.

189. Dawkins, *The God Delusion*, 79; see also at 116, 157–58.

190. Dawkins, *River*, 97.

191. Dawkins, *The God Delusion*, 79, 113–14, 116, 121, 157–58; Dawkins, *River*, 98.

192. Statements that some things "appear to be designed" presuppose and imply that people know that there is a difference between appearance and reality (real design) and also presuppose that there is a way of determining which is which in any particular case. That fact alone should mean that intelligent design/biblical creationism should not be rejected *a priori*; it also makes intelligent design/biblical creationism legitimate *as science* to the extent that the conclusion that a particular organ or organism has been designed is a conclusion based on the factual record.

193. Thorvaldsen and Hössjer, "Using statistical," 7; see also Axe, *Undeniable*, passim; Meyer, *Scientific*, 1–15.

short, intelligent design/creation is a scientific inference from the molecular and biological data.[194]

Behe points out that "the conclusion of intelligent design flows naturally from the data itself. . . . It comes simply from the hard work that biochemistry has done over the past forty years, combined with consideration of the way in which we reach conclusions of design every day."[195] The process of coming to such a conclusion is what is known as "abduction," which is "a form of logical inference that starts with a set of observations and seeks to find the simplest and most likely explanation for the observations [i.e., the inference to the best explanation]" which has even been called "the inference that makes science."[196]

Creation by an intelligent creator is the only adequate explanation of the origin and nature of life in all of its variety and complexity, because only a purposive designer and creator has the necessary powers that mutations + natural selection lack; only an intelligent creator has the ability to arrange complex matter and information with a goal in mind. Such a creator customarily is referred to as God.[197] The tremendous profusion of new animal

---

194. See Denton, *Evolution: A Theory*, 341 ("The inference to design is a purely *a posteriori* induction based on a ruthlessly consistent application of the logic of analogy. The conclusion may have religious implications, but it does not depend on religious presuppositions.").

195. Behe, *Darwin's Black Box*, 193.

196. Thorvaldsen and Hössjer, "Using statistical," 3; see also Meyer, *Darwin's Doubt*, 346–49.

197. There are four primary positions with respect to the interaction of God and the created order: (1) "Intelligent design" proponents, such as attorney Phillip Johnson, biochemist Michael Behe, and geophysicist and philosopher of science Stephen Meyer, do not begin with the Bible and do not mention or identify the intelligent designer. They accept that the universe is billions of years old and the common descent of all living creatures; they view the existence of design, and therefore a designer, as the necessary inference from the scientific facts alone, given the impossibility of naturalistic evolution to account for the creation of life, new organs, forms, functions, and organisms. The specifics of how the intelligent designer brought such organs, forms, functions, and organisms into existence is left unclear. Only in his 2021 book *The Return of the God Hypothesis* did Meyer actually name the intelligent designer as God. (2) "Theistic evolution" proponents, such as geneticist Francis Collins, believe that the Bible is a reliable source of information about God and spiritual matters but is not a reliable source of information about scientific matters such as the creation of the universe and of living things. They accept the mainstream scientific beliefs concerning the age of the earth, the common descent of all living creatures, and the neo-Darwinian evolutionary process. They believe that God used the process of evolution to create living things, including humans; in some way God guided the evolutionary process, by programing or endowing existence with the ability to select the "right" mutations to result in existence as it now is. (3) "Old earth creationism" proponents, such as astronomer Hugh Ross, believe that the Bible and science are both reliable sources of information regarding the

forms that arose during the "Cambrian explosion" were unique and without any evident antecedents. They arrived on the scene complete with their own, unique genetic digital codes. No unplanned, unguided, mindless process has ever been demonstrated—or is even known—to be able to create such specifically organized, information-based living systems. Purposeful design is the cause of every other instance in which we encounter any other object manifesting any of the key features, i.e., the specified information and circuitry, of the Cambrian animals (and, for that matter, all other forms of life). Consequently, we may infer that the purposeful design and creation of the Cambrian animals by an intelligent and powerful creator is the best and most rational explanation for their creation and existence.[198] Although biologist Francisco Ayala adheres to the naturalistic evolution view, he concedes, "The apparent strength of the argument-from-design to demonstrate

---

creation of the universe and the earth and that, when rightly interpreted, science and the Bible are compatible. They accept that the universe is billions of years old and hold that, although quite a bit of evolution may have happened, humans and (at least some) other major forms of life were separately created by God. (4) "Young earth creationism" proponents, such as biochemist Duane Gish and nuclear physicist Robert Gentry, begin with the Bible and hold that the Bible indicates that the universe is not billions of years old but is 10,000 years old or less. They hold that God specially created the different "kinds" of living creatures and accept "microevolution," i.e., variation within the different "kinds"; however, they reject macroevolution, i.e., that one kind of organism can evolve into another kind. These different views are discussed and explained in a series of online articles by Ted Davis, "Science and the Bible" (2019).

There are two other positions taken by some biblical scholars concerning the creation accounts in the book of Genesis. Both of these views contend that God created the world and everything in it (i.e., metaphysical naturalism is ruled out) but that neither the book of Genesis nor any other passage in the Bible indicates the *timing or method* God used in creation. The "framework view" holds that the creation account of Gen 1:1—2:3 is predominantly shaped by theological and literary concerns independent of the empirical study of origins. Irons and Kline, "The Framework," 217–53. The "cosmic temple" view holds that Genesis 1 is not a description of the *material* origin of the universe at all but is an account, using an Ancient Near East conceptual framework, of the *functional* origins and purposes of an already-materially-existing cosmos so that it would function as God designed it for people made in his image, namely, as a temple. Walton, *The Lost World*, 33–167. Both views are consistent with either an "old earth" or a "young earth" position and with either a creationist or a theistic evolution position. As Walton says regarding the cosmic temple view, "science cannot offer an unbiblical view of material origins, because there is no biblical view of material origins aside from the very general idea that whatever happened, whenever it happened, and however it happened, God did it." Walton, *The Lost World*, 112. The same could be said regarding the framework view (with the possible exception of the creation of humanity). See Hagopian, ed., *The Genesis Debate* and Walton, *The Lost World* for the interaction between the framework and cosmic temple views and those views which contend that the Bible does provide an account of the material origins of the cosmos and its inhabitants.

198. See Meyer, *Darwin's Doubt,* 81.

the existence of a Creator is obvious. Wherever there is a function or design we look for its author. A knife is *made* to cut and a clock is *made* to tell time; their functional designs are contrived by a knifemaker and a watchmaker. The structures, organs, and behaviors of living beings are directly organized to serve certain functions. Thus the fundamental design, or teleology, of organisms and their features would seem to argue for the existence of a designer."[199]

Given the historical relationship between Christianity and science, it is neither fair nor reasonable to view, as Thomas Henry Huxley did, theology in general and Christianity in particular as being the "natural and irreconcilable enemies of Science."[200] Important and valid issues, including the fundamental issue of the adequacy or inadequacy of scientific "naturalism" or materialism, are being debated today by Christian and non-Christian, Darwinian and non-Darwinian, scholars.[201] Behe gives multiple examples, from evolutionists themselves, not only of how basic features of life were totally unpredicted by Darwin's theory and how reasoning based on Darwin's theory led even eminent biological scientists to conclusions the opposite of reality.[202]

If the dominant scientific establishment would, at minimum, look more objectively at the contributions Christian philosophers and scientists continue to make to the advancement of knowledge, understanding, and science, not reject the concept of God *a priori*, and open peer-reviewed mainstream science journals to theistic scientists, the goal of science itself would be advanced, namely, the pursuit of truth wherever that truth may be. Ironically, opening mainstream science and scientific journals to creationist scientists actually would be in accord with what even Darwin advocated in the introduction to the sixth edition of *Origin*, "I am well aware that scarcely a single point is discussed in this volume on which facts cannot be adduced, often apparently leading to conclusions directly opposite to those at which I have arrived. A fair result can be obtained only by fully stating and balancing the facts and arguments on both sides of each question."[203]

---

199. Ayala, "Philosophical," 496, emph. in orig.

200. Huxley, "Letter," 15:106.

201. See, e.g., Buell and Hearn, eds., *Darwinism*; Manson, ed., *God and Design*; Dennett and Plantinga, *Science and Religion*; Rasmussen and Leon, *Is God*.

202. Behe, *The Edge*, 188–91. Behe also points out that most biochemistry textbooks either ignore evolution completely or virtually never even mention it, i.e., evolution is irrelevant to biochemistry as it is actually studied, researched, and taught. Behe, *Darwin's Black Box*, 180–83.

203. Darwin, *Origin*, 6th ed., 2.

11

Naturalism Cannot Account for Existence as It Is

NATURALISM CANNOT ACCOUNT FOR CONSCIOUSNESS AND MIND

Because the premise of metaphysical naturalism underlies the theory of naturalistic evolution, it follows that "impersonal, unintelligent, purposeless forces must have been capable of doing all the work of creation, because there wasn't anything else. Purpose and intelligence could not come into existence until they evolved through unintelligent and purposeless processes."[1] The uniqueness of humanity, particularly human consciousness, mind, and the ability to reason, remains a major stumbling-block to evolutionary materialism. Famous evolutionist Theodosius Dobzhansky acknowledged, "Human self-awareness obviously differs greatly from any rudiments of mind that may be present in nonhuman animals. The magnitude of the difference makes it a difference in kind, and not one of degree."[2] Philosopher and evolutionist Daniel Dennett simply asserts, "An impersonal, unreflective, robotic, mindless little scrap of molecular machinery is the ultimate basis of all the agency, and hence meaning, and hence consciousness, in the universe."[3] However, not only does the theory of evolution not even attempt to prove how consciousness or mind could arise from non-conscious matter, but everything we know about physics and chemistry indicates that

---

1. Provine and Johnson, "Debate," 6.
2. Dobzhansky, "Evolution," 453.
3. Dennett, *Darwin's Dangerous*, 203.

consciousness and mind *cannot* arise from non-conscious matter. Chemist and philosopher Michael Polanyi recognizes this,

> Hydrochloric acid will never dissolve platinum by mistake.... We speak of the thoughts Shakespeare had while writing his plays and not of the thoughts of hydrochloric acid dissolving zinc, because men think and acids don't. It is obvious, therefore, that the rise of man can be accounted for only by other principles than those known today to physics and chemistry.... And so long as we can form no idea of the way a material system may become a conscious, responsible person, it is an empty pretense to suggest that we have an explanation for the descent of man.[4]

Additionally, as we previously discussed, to assert that naturalism produced mind and reasoning that we know to be *reliable* is logically self-refuting. The only answer theoretical physicist and cosmologist Stephen Hawking can give is to assert that, pursuant to Darwin's principle of natural selection, "we might expect" that our ability to reason would be valid.[5] That assertion does not and cannot solve the problem, because Darwin's theory gives us no such expectation, for the following reasons. First, recall the logically unbridgeable gulf between the world of sensory experiences and the world of concepts and propositions that Einstein referred to.[6] That unbridgeable gulf means that hydrochloric acid can dissolve zinc (a sensory experience) for millions of years, but it will never develop the ability to think about what it is doing (the world of concepts and propositions). Second, "Darwinian selection rewards only success in leaving offspring, and the presumption that abstract mental powers cause their possessor to leave more viable offspring than creatures who are more modestly endowed is neither borne out by experience or even remotely plausible."[7] Third, since

---

4. Polanyi, *Personal*, 389–90. Polanyi's point is strongly echoed by eminent atheist philosopher Thomas Nagel in *Mind & Cosmos: Why the Materialist Neo-Darwinian Conception of Nature is Almost Certainly False* (Oxford: Oxford University Press, 2012). Nagel discusses in some detail the implausibility of there being a naturalistic explanation for human consciousness, cognition (thought, reason, and evaluation), and value (good and bad, right and wrong). The recent anthology edited by Angus Menuge, Brian Krouse, and Robert Marks, *Minding the Brain* (Seattle: Discovery Institute, 2023), provides compelling evidence from multiple specialties, including philosophy, neuroscience, biology, medicine, computer science, and mathematics, that the mind is more than the brain and that naturalism (physicalism, materialism) cannot account for, among other things, the mind, the unity of mind in split-brain patients, the unity of one's visual field, and personal identity over time.

5. Hawking, *A Brief*, 13.

6. Einstein, "Remarks," 286–87.

7. Johnson, *Reason*, 62.

natural selection is simply the operative principle of the closed system of the binding, universal, natural laws of nature, all thoughts would be the result of "the chemical processes going on in my brain, ... determined by the laws of chemistry, not those of logic."[8] That is not strictly "mind" or "consciousness" at all.

Fourth, natural selection does not lead to validity in reasoning and cannot account for logical insight, reasoning, and truth, because natural selection may eliminate harmful characteristics and augment those that enhance one's chances of survival, but it cannot get outside of the interlocking physical system of nature to create "insight" that can be known to be true.[9] As we saw earlier, the adaptive abilities to flee predators, obtain food, and find mates require cognitive processes connected with an organism's muscles and connected with certain features of the environment, but these adaptive abilities do not require "true beliefs," and the latter do not follow from the former.[10] Thus, evolutionary naturalism's account of mind and reasoning is what is known as a "self-referential absurdity," i.e., a theory which defines truth that it *itself* fails to meet. Therefore, it refutes itself. Nancy Pearcey explains that an example of self-referential absurdity is the theory that contends that "the human mind is a product of natural selection. The implication is that the ideas in our minds were selected for their survival value, not for their truth-value. But what if we apply that theory to itself? Then it, too, was selected for survival, not truth — which discredits its *own* claim to truth. Evolutionary epistemology commits suicide."[11]

Finally, Hawking's assertion about natural selection giving us valid reasoning abilities is a circular argument and begs the very question at issue. Charles Darwin himself expressed this doubt, "Can the mind of man, which has, as I fully believe, been developed from a mind as low as that possessed by the lowest animal, be trusted when it draws such grand conclusions?"[12] Multiple Christian and non-Christian philosophers have demonstrated that Darwin's doubt is valid and, therefore, is fatal to naturalism.[13]

---

8. Haldane, "Some Consequences," 162.

9. See Lewis, *Miracles*, 28–29; Taylor, *Metaphysics*, 118.

10. See chapter 9n.49 and associated text; see also Wright, *The Moral*, 265; Trivers, "Foreword," xx; Churchland, "Epistemology," 548–49; Lack, *Evolutionary*, 104; Rashdall, *The Theory*, 2:209.

11. Pearcey, "Why Evolutionary Theory," n.p.

12. Barlow, ed., *The Autobiography*, 93.

13. See Taylor, *Metaphysics*, 118–19; Churchland, "Epistemology," 548–49; Nagel, *The View*; Plantinga, *Warrant and Proper*, 219–37; Plantinga, *Warranted Christian*, 227–40; Plantinga, "Introduction," 1–12; Stroud, "The Charm," 28; Plantinga, *Where the Conflict*, 312–50.

There is another aspect to this that is completely contrary to the idea that humanity's mental abilities developed by a naturalistic evolutionary process. That is the fact that human beings of every culture and whatever level of education have mental abilities far beyond that which is necessary for survival. Humans have musical, artistic, and mathematical abilities and the capacity for abstract thought such that, although not every individual human being has the intellectual ability of an Einstein, Newton, Michelangelo, or Mozart, that potentiality is innate in the human brain in general.[14] If people from one culture and language group move to another culture, they can learn to speak a new language and learn and excel in all the higher intellectual abilities and styles of the new culture. That suggests that these innate abilities have always been present in human beings despite the different races, cultures, and language groups being separate for tens or hundreds of thousands of years.

Alfred Russel Wallace, co-founder with Darwin of the theory of evolution through natural selection, recognized this in Darwin's lifetime. He observed, "A brain slightly larger than that of the gorilla would, according to the evidence before us, fully have sufficed" for the mental needs of prehistoric humanity.[15] Wallace added, "The large brain he actually possesses could never have been solely developed by any of those laws of evolution, whose essence is, that they lead to a degree of organization exactly proportionate to the wants of each species, never beyond those wants."[16] Not only the size of the human brain but its capabilities far exceed that which naturalistic evolution could account for. Wallace recognized that even humans from remote, undeveloped, and nontechnological cultures possess "a brain capable, if cultivated and developed, of performing work of a kind and degree far beyond what he ever requires it to do . . . and from the fact that all the moral and intellectual faculties do occasionally manifest themselves, we may fairly conclude that they are always latent."[17] Susumu Ohno, geneticist and evolutionary biologist, who was a seminal researcher in the field of molecular evolution, concurred, "Did the genome of our cave-dwelling predecessors contain a set or sets of genes which enable modern man to compose music of infinite complexity and write novels with profound meaning? One is compelled to give an affirmative answer. . . . It looks as though the early Homo was already provided with the intellectual potential

---

14. See Denton, *Evolution: Still*, 196.
15. Wallace, *Contributions*, 343.
16. Wallace, *Contributions*, 343.

17. Wallace, *Contributions*, 340–41. Wallace therefore concluded that natural selection was not an all-sufficient cause of the evolution of man, particularly regarding the higher human faculties. Wallace, *Contributions*, 343.

which was in great excess of what was needed to cope with the environment of his time."[18]

Regarding this, Denton asks the important question, "How could our love and capacity for abstract thought, for language, for mathematics, for music, and for art have been of utility in that unforgiving [prehistoric] environment, *millennia before their ability was manifest?* Such intellectual abilities seem absurdly powerful, beyond any conceivable utility for hunter-gatherers on that ancient savanna, and hence beyond any functionalist explanation."[19] In short, humanity's higher mental abilities cannot be explained by naturalism and are contradictory to naturalistic evolution. Hoyle and Wickramasinghe call this one fact "a *reductio ad absurdum* disproof of [Darwin's] theory."[20]

Plantinga contends that "there is superficial conflict but deep concord between theistic religion and science, but superficial concord and deep conflict between naturalism and science."[21] We have seen this deep conflict between naturalism and science in that naturalism cannot even account for itself. The deep concord between Christian theism and science stems from God's providentially creating and governing the world in which things do not happen by "chance," but display reliability, predictability, and the regularity of natural law.[22] That deep concord also stems from God's creating humanity in his image such that we can have true knowledge. Even atheist philosopher Thomas Nagel concludes, "Evolutionary naturalism provides an account of our capacities that undermines their reliability, and in so doing undermines itself," whereas "A theistic understanding . . . would leave intact our natural confidence in our cognitive faculties."[23] Being created in God's image entails that humanity's musical and artistic abilities and the ability to grasp and practice mathematics of depth and complexity are far beyond what is required for survival and reproduction. Being created in God's image also gives humanity the ability to inductively infer, reason, learn from experience, and understand abstract universals, which enables science to be possible in the first place. Christian theism gives us reason to expect that our cognitive abilities will match the world. Naturalism gives us no reason at all to expect such a match and, therefore, should be rejected.

---

18. Ohno, *Evolution*, 144.
19. Denton, *Evolution: Still*, 196, emph. in orig.
20. Hoyle and Wickramasinghe, *Evolution*, 103.
21. Plantinga, *Where the Conflict*, 265.
22. The nature and character of scientific law as having divine attributes, reflecting the fact that God is their creator, is discussed at Poythress, "Why Scientists," 111–23.
23. Nagel, *Mind*, 27, 26.

NATURALISM CANNOT ACCOUNT FOR MORALITY AND HUMAN RIGHTS

Benjamin Wiker has pointed out that "because nature and human nature are necessarily connected, there is no way to escape the interrelationship of science and ethics"; indeed, "every distinct view of the universe, every theory about nature, necessarily entails a view of morality."[24] In a naturalistic or materialistic framework, it is impossible to determine that anything is morally good or evil.[25] The reason is that, according to naturalism, only mass, energy, and other physical and chemical properties exist. As such, "Materialism is a form of philosophical monism which holds matter to be the fundamental substance in nature, and all things, including mental states and consciousness, are results of material interactions."[26] In other words, no "moral values" are inherent in existence. Physical nature is all there is, and there is nothing "outside" of nature—no supernatural realm, God, or anything else—to give meaning to existence, or to prescribe or account for morals, good, or evil.[27] The ideas of universal "human rights" and equality are bound up with this. The idea of human rights and equality do not and cannot come from—indeed, are contradictory to—the philosophy of naturalism and the concept of evolution. It is illogical to the point of being laughable to say, "Creatures in a pointless universe gradually evolved by devouring and out-reproducing each other; therefore, we all have equal value, equal rights, and should love each other."

Stephen Jay Gould acknowledges, "Nature has no automatically transferable wisdom to serve as a basis of human morality."[28] William Provine, a biologist, historian of science, and naturalistic evolutionist, makes this very clear, "No purposive principles exist in nature. . . . Humans and other animals make choices frequently, but these are determined by the interaction of heredity and environment and are not the result of free will. No inherent moral or ethical laws exist, nor are there absolute guiding principles for human society. The universe cares nothing for us and we have no ultimate meaning in life."[29] Elsewhere he said, "There is no ultimate foundation for ethics, no ultimate meaning in life, and no free will for

---

24. Wiker, *Moral*, 22.

25. Probably the best overall discussion of the moral implications of naturalism and the historical development of naturalism is Benjamin Wiker, *Moral Darwinism: How We Became Hedonists* (Downers Grove, IL: InterVarsity, 2002).

26. "Materialism," *Wikipedia*, Introduction; see also Menuge, "Declining," 26.

27. See Rashdall, *The Theory*, 2:211–12.

28. Gould, *An Urchin*, 225.

29. Provine, "Scientists," 1.

humans, either."³⁰ Richard Dawkins similarly recognizes there is no design or purpose to the universe, so nothing can be either evil or good;³¹ elsewhere he added, "Science has no methods for deciding what is ethical."³² Albert Einstein similarly said that "science can only ascertain what *is*, but not what *should be*, and outside of its domain value judgments of all kinds remain necessary."³³ As Wiker concludes, "If design in nature is the result of the Blind Watchmaker, that Watchmaker is also *morally* blind."³⁴

Neuroscientist Sam Harris believes that science *can* determine human values, but he simply asserts the general principle of "maximizing the well-being of conscious creatures."³⁵ That value, however, does not stem from science but is a philosophical proposition that is "just talking about what's conducive to the flourishing of sentient life on this planet."³⁶ William Lane Craig points out, "Since it's possible that human well-being and moral goodness are not identical, it follows necessarily that human well-being and moral goodness are not the same."³⁷ Although Harris decries "moral relativism," he provides no basis in atheism why objective moral values can exist at all. In fact, he admitted that if evil and goodness were equally reliable paths to "happiness" (which, apparently, is equivalent to "well-being"), then there would be "a continuum of well-being, upon which saints and sinners would occupy equivalent peaks."³⁸ Harris himself epitomizes the fact that atheism and naturalism cannot provide objective, universal moral values or obligations. He said in an interview that, in order to harm a political candidate he did not like, it was perfectly "warranted" to engage in a conspiracy, censor an important and true media story, claimed that the then President of the United States was "more despicable" than Islamic terrorist Osama bin Laden, and said that he "would not have cared" if the son of the candidate he favored had "the corpses of children in his basement."³⁹ If all that is justifi-

30. Provine and Johnson, "Debate," 9.

31. Dawkins, *River*, 133.

32. Dawkins, *A Devil's*, 34; see also atheist Julian Baggini who admits, "In an atheist universe, morality can be rejected without external sanction at any point, and without a clear, compelling reason to believe in its reality, that's exactly what will sometimes happen." Baggini, "Yes, life," n.p.

33. Einstein, *Ideas*, 45, emph. in orig.; see also Dawkins, "Obscurantism," 397; Campbell, "Naturalism," 495.

34. Wiker, *Moral*, 299.

35. Harris, *The Moral*, 1, 11–13.

36. Craig, "Navigating," n.p.

37. Craig, "Navigating," n.p.

38. Harris, *The Moral*, 190.

39. Kew, "Corpses."

able simply for an election, what limits would there be in Harris's "morality" for more important matters?

Further, Harris says that "maximizing the well-being of conscious creatures . . . must at some point translate into facts about brains."[40] He cited neuroimaging studies which indicate that "there are mental states and capacities that contribute to our general well-being (happiness, compassion, kindness, etc.) as well as mental states and capacities that diminish it (cruelty, hatred, terror, etc.)."[41] If "science" (as opposed to moral philosophy and theology) has a particular role to play in maximizing well-being, "perhaps the future of happiness, then, is not peace, love, and justice, but massive doses of the neurochemicals that activate the brain faculties involved in producing experiences of happiness and removing misery."[42]

Atheist philosopher William Halverson explains why there are and can be no moral absolutes according to atheism and naturalism, "The 'ultimate realities,' according to naturalism, are not the alleged objects of the inquiries of theologians; they are the objects of investigation by chemists, physicists, and other scientists. To put the matter very simply: materialism is true. . . . Everything that occurs is ultimately explicable in terms of the properties and relations of the particles of which matter is composed. Once again the point may be stated simply: determinism is true."[43] The necessary implication of this is, "Moral responsibility is not compatible with universal determinism; and I hold that universal determinism is true. I conclude, therefore, that man is not in fact morally responsible."[44]

The end result is that, on naturalistic grounds, there is no objective and absolute ground of morality; morality must be subjective, i.e., to be

---

40. Harris, *The Moral*, 11; see also at 191.

41. Harris, *The Moral*, 64.

42. Arnold, "Book review," 395. That is not a farfetched application of Harris's position. Harris gives an example, "If, for instance, a preference for chocolate ice cream allowed for the most rewarding experience a human being could have, while a preference for vanilla did not, we would deem it *morally important* to help people overcome any defect in their sense of taste that caused them to prefer vanilla—*in the same way we currently treat people* for curable forms of blindness [medication? surgery?]." Harris, *The Moral*, 196, emph. added. And this "treatment" would be applied (mandated? imposed?) simply to force people to prefer chocolate ice cream over vanilla so that they would have a "rewarding experience" (shades of *Brave New World*). Timothy Keller adds, "Someone may retort that social science can measure happiness and it can tell us how to live life in order to maximize happiness. But that leads to the question—Why believe that human beings should live for happiness? Science cannot answer that question. It requires a moral or philosophical argument." Keller, *Making Sense*, 261n.11.

43. Halverson, *A Concise*, 394; see also at 385; Hawking, *A Brief*, 12–13; Moreland, *Scaling*, 89–90; Wiker, *Moral*, 139–41.

44. Halverson, *A Concise*, 251.

determined by each individual or individual culture. C. S. Lewis called this is a "fatal superstition." Writing in the context of the Holocaust of World War II, Lewis pointed out,

> Everyone is indignant when he hears the Germans define justice as that which is to the interest of the Third Reich. But it is not always remembered that this indignation is perfectly groundless if we ourselves regard morality as a subjective sentiment to be altered at will. Unless there is some objective standard of good, over-arching Germans, Japanese and ourselves alike whether any of us obey it or no, then of course the Germans are as competent to create their ideology as we are to create ours. If "good" and "better" are terms deriving there sole meaning from the ideology of each people, then of course ideologies themselves cannot be better or worse than another. Unless the measuring rod is independent of the things measured, we can do no measuring.[45]

This was brought home in a dialogue between humanists (i.e., nontheists) on humanist ethics. Paul Kurtz stated that "ethics need not be derived from any theological or metaphysical proposition about the nature of ultimate reality" and spoke of "general principles" that are "only approximate guides for behavior," but then said that "these are general prescriptions, rules, and policies that we ought to observe."[46] Mihailo Markovic responded by observing, "It remains quite unclear where this ought comes from. It is one thing to describe a *variety* of actual historical patterns of conduct and moral habits. It is a completely different thing to make a *choice* among them and say that we *ought* to observe some of them. Why some and not others?"[47] In his reply, Kurtz admitted, "I can find no ultimate basis for ought."[48]

To try to bring moral sense to the moral emptiness of naturalism and atheism, Darwin said, "A man who has no assured and ever present belief in the existence of a personal God or a future existence with retribution and reward, can have for his rule of life, as far as I can see, only to follow those impulses and instincts which are the stronger or which seem to him the best ones."[49] However, one's "impulses and instincts" do not, of themselves, tell a person which one is "right." As C. S. Lewis pointed out, "If two instincts are in conflict, and there is nothing in a creature's mind except those two

---

45. Lewis, "The Poison," 73.
46. Kurtz, "Does Humanism," 11, 22.
47. Markovic, "Comment," 33.
48. Kurtz, "Reply," 34.
49. Barlow, ed., *The Autobiography*, 94.

instincts, obviously the stronger of the two must win."[50] Nancy Pearcey observes that for a person to yield to one's strongest impulse is simply "self-interest, not ethics."[51] Darwin himself believed that "the highest satisfaction is derived from following certain impulses, namely the social instincts" such as acting "for the good of others.[52]" However, Lewis notes, "You might think love of humanity in general was safe [as a rule you ought to follow], but it is not. If you leave out justice you will find yourself breaking agreements and faking evidence in trials 'for the sake of humanity,' and become in the end a cruel and treacherous man."[53]

The only basis naturalism ultimately can give for morality and ethics is survival itself. B. F. Skinner said, "Survival is the only value according to which a culture is eventually to be judged, and any practice that furthers survival has survival value by definition."[54] Since natural selection is said to operate at the genetic level, altruism and morality, according to the naturalistic evolutionary worldview, may have been programed into our genes but only for the purpose of increasing the number of progeny for the race/tribe/clan/nation, i.e., survival value.[55] As Michael Ruse and Edward O. Wilson put it, "Morality, or more strictly our belief in morality, is merely an adaptation put in place to further our reproductive ends.... In an important sense, ethics as we understand it is an illusion fobbed off on us by our genes to get us to cooperate. It is without external grounding."[56] Dawkins also sees altruism as evolutionarily based on genetic survival; he believes that feelings of altruism toward those outside of our own group are based on a "misfiring" or "Darwinian mistake."[57]

Whether the supposed "good" is "maximizing the well-being of conscious creatures" (Harris), "survival" (Skinner), "furthering our reproductive ends" (Ruse and Wilson), or any other proposed value, naturalism inconsistently contradicts itself by surreptitiously sneaking in an absolute, universal standard of ethics, despite the fact that there is no absolute or universal basis for ethics and morality that can possibly arise from naturalism

---

50. Lewis, *Mere Christianity*, 23.
51. Pearcey, "The Influence," 168.
52. Barlow, ed., *The Autobiography*, 94.
53. Lewis, *Mere Christianity*, 24.
54. Skinner, *Beyond Freedom*, 130.
55. See Simon, "A Mechanism," 1665.
56. Ruse and Wilson, "The Evolution," 310.
57. Dawkins, *The God Delusion*, 214–22.

itself.⁵⁸ Further, the fact that naturalistic evolution establishes no moral obligations at all is exposed by David Bentley Hart, who points out

> that certain fortuitously acquired behaviors may have proved evolutionarily advantageous in the past entails no binding demand upon any person to adopt those behaviors in the present. Quite the opposite, in fact. . . . What may have been generally beneficial to the species over many ages may not be particularly beneficial to an individual in the present, after all, and if morality is really a matter of benefit rather than of spiritual obligations transcending personal concerns, no one has any sound motive to act in accord with anything other than private prudence.⁵⁹

In other words, people, animals, and other organisms can act on the basis of what they want and what they think is in their own best interest, not the interest of having lots of future progeny.⁶⁰

Indeed, if moral attitudes and actions are simply genetically-based habits adapted for fostering reproduction, they really aren't "moral" or ethical at all. *Any behavior*—however cruel, self-centered, or unjust—that helps one survive would be morally "good" in a world based on naturalistic evolutionary principles. As Deane-Peter Baker states, moral beliefs and principles based on naturalism

> are "good" only in that they happen to have contributed to our survival and proliferation. This contingency of the good shows that if things had turned out differently then a different set of beliefs would be the ones we'd now be calling "good". If, for example, Hitler had won World War II, then presumably hating Jews would contribute greatly to one's survival and one's potential to breed. Under such circumstances, from an evolutionary perspective, we'd have to say that anti-Semitism was morally good.⁶¹

Pearcey goes to the root of the matter when she observes that "survival" or longevity does not mean that an individual or a society is morally better than others: "Sheer survival is not an automatic good. Indeed, survival is often aided by unethical behavior, such as disloyalty, cruelty, or

---

58. See Lewis, "The Poison," 74–75.
59. Hart, *The Experience*, 252.
60. See Plantinga, "Methodological," 26n.5; see also Stove, *Darwinian Fairytales*, 79–224 for evisceration of the view of Dawkins and sociobiologists that humans are essentially slaves of their "selfish genes."
61. Baker, "Dawkins' Moral," 82.

selfishness."[62] B. F. Skinner himself, after stating that survival is naturalism's "only value," answered the question of why anyone should be concerned about the survival of one's culture by saying, "The only honest answer to that kind of question seems to be this: 'There is no good reason why you should be concerned, but if your culture has not convinced you that there is, so much the worse for your culture.'"[63] In other words, naturalism and naturalistic evolution are morally vacuous.

More fundamental is the fact that, if nature—this world; the cosmos—is all there is, it cannot provide *any* basis for morality, because "Nature operates by mechanical, physical laws, not by moral imperatives."[64] Pearcey concludes with two inherent problems of any naturally-based morality: First, since nature is amoral and we are merely the by-products of natural forces, inherently we should be amoral like the rest of nature; second, "If we can be wholly explained by physical, chemical laws, then we are completely determined.... We have no more freedom of choice than a river or an insect.... What, then, becomes of moral choice? ... Physical determinism denies the existence of choice, and thus undercuts the very possibility of moral behavior.[65]

No one actually believes that or acts on that basis. Everyone believes and acts on the basis that "good and bad, virtue and evil are real in a deep sense, not contingently dependent on whether they lead to some survival-enhancing outcome."[66] Charles Taylor observes that our sense of what is admirable "is never simply defined in terms of [survival and group flourishing], and sometimes even runs athwart them.... That admiration and its opposites are such an ineradicable part of the human life form testifies to the centrality of values that are seen as essentially higher, more worthy."[67] Greg Koukl then goes to the heart of the issue, "To say something is evil is to make a moral judgment, and moral judgments make no sense outside of the context of a moral standard.... Evil can't be real if morals are relative.

---

62. Pearcey, "The Influence," 169.

63. Skinner, *Beyond Freedom*, 131.

64. Pearcey, "The Influence," 169.

65. Pearcey, "The Influence," 169; see also Noebel, *Understanding*, 193–210.

66. Baker, "Dawkins' Moral," 83. As we saw earlier, naturalism cannot justify itself but has to assume the theistic worldview as the precondition for understanding anything; morality is another example of this. In other words, atheists, naturalists, and relativists cannot justify good and evil, right and wrong on their own philosophical presuppositions but must and do implicitly assume a theistic view of morality as the basis for their lives. See Budziszewski, *What We*, 186–87; Lewis, "The Poison," 74–75.

67. Taylor, "Ethics," 310.

Evil is real, though. That's why people object to it. Therefore, objective moral standards must exist as well."[68]

With respect to the different possible *sources* of moral standards, good and evil, "a morally perfect God is the only adequate standard . . . that makes sense of the existence of evil to begin with."[69] William Lane Craig summarizes,

> If God does not exist, then objective moral values do not exist. When I speak of objective moral values, I mean moral values that are valid and binding whether anybody believes them or not. Thus, to say, for example, that the Holocaust was objectively wrong is to say that it was wrong even though the Nazis who carried it out thought that it was right and that it would still have been wrong even if the Nazis had won World War II and succeeded in exterminating or brainwashing everyone who disagreed with them."[70]

Even non-Christian philosopher and ethicist Richard Taylor admits, "The modern age, more or less repudiating the idea of a divine lawgiver, has nevertheless tried to retain the ideas of moral right and wrong, without noticing that, in casting God aside, they have also abolished the conditions of meaningfulness for moral right and wrong as well. . . . The concept of moral obligation [is] unintelligible apart from the idea of God."[71]

On the other hand, Wiker observes that once the amoral view of nature, which is inherent in naturalism, is accepted, then there is no *theoretical* objection an atheist or naturalist can make to any practice, no matter how evil it may be; and once the theoretical or principled objection to certain behavior has been removed, then all practical objections, in turn, will tend

---

68. Koukl, "Evil," n.p.; Rashdall, *The Theory*, 2:212; see also Leff, "Unspeakable," 1249.

69. Koukl, *Tactics*, 138; see also Koukl, "Evil"; Lewis, "The Poison," 79–81; Lewis, *Mere Christianity*, 45–46; Craig, "The Indispensability," 9–12; Rashdall, *The Theory*, 2:212–13.

70. Craig and Sinnott-Armstrong, *God?*, 17. Law professor Arthur Leff put it this way, "It is of the utmost importance to see why a God-grounded system has no analogues. Either God exists or He does not, but if He does not, nothing and no one else can take His place. . . . There is no one who can be said a priori to have that power [the power to establish and determine, oughtness, rightness, and goodness] unless the question being posed is also being begged. Except, as noted, God. . . . God's will is binding because it is His will that it be. Under what other circumstances can the unexamined will of anyone else withstand the cosmic 'says who' and come out similarly dispositive?" Leff, "Unspeakable," 1231, 1232.

71. Taylor, *Ethics*, 2–3, 84; see also Barnett, "Four Problems," Perry, *Toward a Theory*, 3–29; Plantinga, "A Christian," 72–73; Leff, "Unspeakable," 1231–32.

to be overridden.[72] Wiker correctly concludes that, since "moral conflicts are ultimately rooted in cosmological conflicts," resolution of the overall scientific and philosophical issues of naturalism versus theism is the only way to resolve the moral conflicts about human nature and the moral conflicts in society.[73] Or, as political scientist Glenn Tinder puts it, "We cannot give up the Christian God—and the transcendence given other names in other faiths—and go on as before. We must give up Christian morality too. If the God man is nothing more than an illusion, the same is true of the idea that every individual possesses incalculable worth."[74] Tinder is echoing what Friedrich Nietzsche presciently said approximately 100 years previously, "When we give up Christian belief, we thereby deprive ourselves of the right to maintain a stand on Christian morality. This is not at all obvious of itself; we have again and again to make this point clear. . . . Christianity is a system, a view of things, consistently thought out and complete. If we break out of its fundamental idea, the belief in God, we thereby break the whole into pieces: we have no longer anything determined in our grasp."[75]

Since, therefore, only theism can account for morality, the question of "Which God?" becomes paramount. The god of Islam, Allah, cannot be the basis for morality; nor can the "god" of pantheistic monism:

The *nature* of Allah is such that it (he) cannot be the source of morality. The Hadith says that Allah "created" mercy when he created the world: "Allah created one hundred (parts of mercy) and He distributed one amongst His creation and kept this one hundred excepting one with Himself (for the Day of Resurrection)."[76] Because it is "created," mercy is not an intrinsic part of Allah's essential being. Another hadith says, "Allah created Satan, and he created good and created evil."[77] Because it is "created," goodness is not an intrinsic part of Allah's essential being. Consequently, if Allah were the source of morality and the moral law, they would only be because he decreed or commanded them. However, as C. S. Lewis points out, "If good is to be *defined* as what God [Allah] commands, then the goodness of God Himself is emptied of meaning and the commands of an omnipotent fiend would have the same claim on us as those of the 'righteous Lord.'"[78] The

---

72. Wiker, *Moral*, 288, 296–301.
73. Wiker, *Moral*, 316.
74. Tinder, "Can We," 80.
75. Nietzsche, *Twilight*, 42.
76. Muslim, *Sahih*, 2752b; see also 2753c; al-Bukhari, *Sahih*, 6469; at-Tirmidhi, *Jami' at-Tirmidhi*, 3541; Ibn Majah, *Sunan*, vol. 5, book 37, no. 4294.
77. Abi Dawud, *Sunan*, 4618.
78. Lewis, "The Poison," 79.

only other alternative would be that Allah would be "the mere executor of a law somehow external and antecedent to His own being."[79] Either way, Allah could not be the source of morality and the moral law.

Additionally, the *character* of Allah is antithetical to the very nature of morality in at least four ways:

(A) By his own admission, Allah is not trustworthy. Allah calls himself a "deceiver." Q. 3:54 says, *"And (the unbelievers) plotted and planned, and Allah too planned, and the best of planners is Allah"* Pickthall translates that last portion of Q. 3:54 as *"Allah is the best of schemers."* The root word is *makr*, based on the root letters Miim-Kaf-Ra. According to the "Study Qur'an" Islamic website, Miim-Kaf-Ra means, "To practice deceit or guile or circumvention, practice evasion or elusion, to plot, to exercise art or craft or cunning, act with policy, practice stratagem."[80] This is not the only verse where Allah deceives (see Q. 4:88; 8:30; 11:34; 14:4; 15:39; 86:15–16; see also Q. 4:142; 7:16, 99; 8:43–44; 9:115; 13:42; 27:50; 68:45). Muhammad recognized Allah's deceptiveness.[81] Sam Shamoun concludes, "Muhammad's deity is a deceiver who cannot be trusted since he lies without hesitation. A Muslim may contend that Allah only deceives unbelievers who deserve it. The problem with this assertion is that the Muslim scripture teaches that Allah doesn't merely deceive unbelievers but also his followers."[82] Consequently, on what basis could anyone have any confidence that what Allah says is true?

(B) Q. 4:88 (Hilali-Khan) states that Allah is the one who actually causes people to go astray without hope or remedy: *"Do you want to guide him whom Allah has made to go astray? And he whom Allah has made to go astray, you will never find for him any way (of guidance)."* Q. 14:4 (Hilali-Khan) adds, *"Allah misleads whom He wills and guides whom He wills"* (see also Q. 16:93). Allah also actively guarantees that those who go astray and will fall further into sin. Allah himself caused Satan to sin: *"Then Satan said, 'Because you have made me go astray, I shall certainly try to seduce people into straying from the right path'"* (Q. 7:16, Sarwar). Allah also attaches demons to people as intimate companions: *"If anyone withdraws himself from remembrance of (Allah) Most Gracious, We appoint for him an evil one, to be an intimate companion to him. Such (evil ones) really hinder them from the Path, but they think that they are being guided aright!"* (Q. 43:36–37)

---

79. Lewis, "The Poison," 79.
80. *Study Quran*, Miim-Kaf-Ra.
81. At-Tirmidhi, *Jami' at-Tirmidhi*, 3551.
82. Shamoun, "Greatest Deceiver," n.p.; see also Cornelius, "Allah," n.p.

(C) Allah's "morality" is such that Muslims are commanded *not* to take non-Muslims, even their own family members, as friends (Q. 3:28, 118; 4:89, 144; 5:51; 9:23); they are to be *"severe against disbelievers, and merciful among themselves"* (Q. 48:29, Hilali-Khan; see also Q. 5:54; 66:9); and they are to wage war and kill their enemies and non-Muslims in general (Q. 2:191; 4:89; 9:5, 29, 123, 193). Violating these commands has eternal consequences. Islamic scholars Dr. Naajeh Ibrahim, Sheikh 'Aasim 'Abdul Maajid, and Sheikh 'Esaam-ud-Deen Darbaalah state that Islam "determines the position a Muslim should take against the disbelievers, namely hatred, animosity and roughness, and nothing else other than that. There should be no inclination towards the disbelievers, nor should there be any compromises with them. . . . Islam considers both inclination towards the disbelievers and making compromises with them forbidden acts. . . . Hidden loyalty to the disbelievers (that is with the heart) is deemed *kufr akbar,* or major disbelief which definitely takes one out of the fold of Islam, whether or not one expresses it openly."[83] This results in a "the end justifies the means" approach to lying and deception versus being truthful. In fact, Islam has developed a doctrine of deception called *taqiyya,* which is particularly prevalent among Shi'ah Muslims;[84] the Sunni equivalent is called *muda'rat.*[85] All of the above aspects of Islamic "morality" are directly contrary to the "universally accepted standard of right and wrong" which even Muslims admit exists "as part of our innate constitution."[86]

(D) Some lines of Islamic thought hold that Allah chooses to forgive or not forgive for reasons only he knows, without justice being a consideration. For example, in one hadith Muhammad said, "Seventy thousand people of my Ummah would be admitted into Paradise *without rendering any account.*"[87] Another hadith says, "He [Allah] laughs at two men, one of whom killed the other, then they both entered Paradise."[88] For Allah to "just forgive" amounts to saying that there is no difference between sin and righteousness, good and evil, or justice and injustice, guilt or innocence, being a murderer or being a victim. Hence, under Allah there is no moral law and no basis for morality at all.

---

83. Ibrahim, Maajid, and Darbaalah, *In Pursuit,* 137–38, citing Q. 2:120, 217; 3:28, 118; 11:113; 58:22; 61:8; 68:9.
84. See Sookhdeo, *Understanding,* 89–92.
85. "Some Islamic Doctrines," *Faith Freedom,* n.p.
86. Emerick, *Understanding,* 195.
87. Muslim, *Sahih,* 218a, emph. added.
88. An-Nasa'i, *Sunan,* 3165.

Pantheistic, monistic philosophies or religions likewise cannot be the basis of morality. Monism holds that the entirety of reality is reducible to only one thing, i.e., "all is one."[89] In pantheism, "the heavens, the earth, and everything in them are all just manifestations of Brahman, the eternal, impersonal, divine essence which is the only being that truly exists."[90] Consequently, there is no basis for any meaningful moral standard at all. In other words, "You can't look at other people as separate persons with distinct motivations doing individual things. You can't hold them to a standard outside themselves. There can be no such standard. All is one."[91]

Additionally, if all is divine and all is one, there can be no distinction between good and evil: "Each bacteria is as much a manifestation of the divine as you or I. Who am I to slay thousands or even millions of sacred lives to save only one dying infant? I am one with the parasite every bit as much as I am one with the child."[92] In short, "Theft is as divine as giving. Murder is as holy as rescue."[93]

The monistic view that the universe forms an ultimate harmonious unity further suggests that "evil is only apparent and would be recognized as good if we could but see it in its full cosmic context."[94] In Hermann Hesse's novel *Siddhartha*, which was based on pantheistic thought, Siddhartha explained to Govinda, "a person is never entirely holy or entirely sinful. It does really seem like this, because we are subject to deception, as if time was something real. Time is not real, Govinda, I have experienced this often and often again. And if time is not real, then the gap which seems to be between the world and the eternity, between suffering and blissfulness, between evil and good, is also a deception."[95]

Finally, karma is the notion that one's present life and state is the result of one's past actions, especially one's actions in a prior life; karma is thus tied to the idea of reincarnation.[96] James Sire describes the implications of this, "The basis for doing good is not so that the good will be done or so that you benefit another person. Karma demands that every soul suffer for its past 'sins,' so there is no value in alleviating suffering. The soul so helped will have to suffer later. So there is no agape love, giving love, nor would any

---

89. See Potter, "Buddhism," n.p.; "Monism," *Wikipedia*, n.p.
90. Wayne, "The Ethical," Introduction.
91. Wayne, "The Ethical," Moral incoherence; see also Fennell, "A moral challenge."
92. Wayne, "The Ethical," Moral incoherence; see also Fennell, "A moral challenge."
93. Wayne, "The Ethical," Moral incoherence; see also Fennell, "A moral challenge."
94. Hick, *Evil*, 15.
95. Hesse, *Siddhartha*, Govinda.
96. See Smith, *The Religions*, 77–78, 122–23.

such love benefit the recipient. One does good deeds in order to attain unity with the One. Doing good is first and foremost a self-helping way of life."[97] In sum, self-centeredness is at the heart of karma and pantheistic monism.

Christianity alone is different and provides the sufficient basis for morality and for inherent, universal human rights.[98] The Bible reveals that God is holy, just, righteous, and good (Gen 18:25; Exod 34:6–7; Lev 11:44; Job 34:10–12; Ps 5:4; 136:1; 145:17; Hab 1:13; Rom 1:18; Jas 1:13). God himself is the source of the moral law, sometimes called "God's law" or "natural law."[99] God's moral law reflects his own holy, just, righteous, and good character. Because God himself is morally holy and perfect, that is the standard to which he holds us (Matt 5:48).[100] In God's Law, "you find the 'real' or 'correct' or stable, well-grounded directions for living," precisely because "they are based on the very nature of things and the very nature of God. . . . He enjoins what is good because it is good, because he is good. Hence His laws have *emeth* 'truth', intrinsic validity, rock-bottom reality, being rooted in His own nature, and are therefore as solid as that Nature which He has created."[101] Hence, to sin is to offend "against our own highest welfare as well as against the authority and love of God."[102]

God's moral law is seen in such biblical passages as the Ten Commandments (Exod 20:1–17; Deut 5:6–21), the "Golden Rule" (*"Do unto others as you would have them do unto you,"* Matt 7:12; Luke 6:31), Psalm 19, and Rom 1:18—2:16. It is summarized in two commandments, *"You shall love the Lord your God with all your heart, and with all your soul, and with all your mind,"* and *"You shall love your neighbor as yourself."* Jesus said that those two commandments are the foundation for the entire Bible (Matt 22:36–40; Mark 12:28–34; Luke 10:25–28). J. Budziszewski, in perhaps the most comprehensive discussion of this, states that these expressions of God's law "appear in the Bible; yes, the Bible illuminates them; but the knowledge of them is anterior to the Bible [see, e.g., Gen 4:3–10; 6:5–6; and Rom 5:12–14], and they can be recognized as true apart from it. . . . This does not make the Bible dispensable. It explains why the Bible is believable."[103]

---

97. Sire, *The Universe*, 153.

98. That Christianity did, in fact, provide the basis for inherent, universal human rights is set forth by Nicholas Wolterstorff in *Justice: Rights and Wrongs* (Princeton: Princeton University Press, 2008).

99. See Lewis, "The Poison," 79–81; Budziszewski, *What We*, 12–15.

100. How this plays out is discussed in Appendix 1—The Gospel.

101. Lewis, *Reflections*, 60–61.

102. Stott, *The Cross*, 90.

103. Budziszewski, *What We*, 50; see also Lewis, *The Problem*, 88; Lewis, "The Poison," 72–81; Lewis, *Mere Christianity*, 17–26; Jepson, *Don't Blame*, 64.

God's law is basic to all civilization. C. S. Lewis explains that "without it, the actual laws of the state become an absolute. . . . They cannot be criticized because there is not norm against which they should be judged."[104] The Christian idea that, in Christ, all people are equal, regardless of religious background, race, tribe, sex, or socio-economic condition (see Gal 3:28; Col 3:11) was unique and unprecedented in the history of the world. The reason for this is that Christianity affirms that the ultimate nature of reality is personal—that "God's essential being consists in the absolutely personal communion of Father, Son, and Holy Spirit" and that "the world was created and destined to participate in the divine nature and to share in personal communion with the Father, through the Son, and in the power of the Holy Spirit eternally."[105] As a result, "no other religion, ancient or modern, has ever dared to place as much emphasis upon the person as Christianity. Indeed, personal existence is Christianity's distinctive glory; and to the extent that our culture still appreciates such things as the rights of conscience, individual responsibility, and the dignity of persons, this is largely the legacy of Christian theology."[106]

This uniqueness of Christianity is recognized by Chinese scholar Zhou Xinping, who discusses how the Christian concept of transcendence differs from Confucian, Taoist, Buddhist, and traditional Chinese ideas. He observes that "Christian principles of otherworldly transcendence and the equality of all before God accord to the state and civil society's other institutions only a relative significance" and "is not idle talk or an empty idea but is closely connected with actual reform and progress. It is a guiding principle for the human pursuit of truth, goodness and beauty in this world."[107] He concludes, "Only by accepting this understanding of transcendence as our criterion can we understand the real meaning of such concepts as freedom, human rights, toleration, equality, justice, democracy, the rule of law, universality, and environmental protection."[108]

104. Lewis, "We have," 318.
105. Gay, *The Way*, 282–83.
106. Gay, *The Way*, 283.
107. Xinping, "The Significance," 35)
108. Xinping, "The Significance," 36. Xinping is echoed by the late "deconstructionist" philosopher Jacques Derrida, "Today the cornerstone of international law is the sacred, what is sacred in humanity. You should not kill. You should not be responsible for a crime against this sacredness, the sacredness of man as your neighbor, your brother. . . . In that sense, the concept of crime against humanity is a Christian concept and I think there would be no such thing in the law today without the Christian heritage, the Abrahamic heritage, the biblical heritage. That is why I do not think there is anything secular in international law today. The idea of crime against humanity is a religious law." Derrida, "On Forgiveness," 70.

When assessing the validity of any theory or view of life, one should ask such questions as: "Is it true to reality?" and "Can people actually live it out?" The naturalist view of morality is contrary to how everyone—naturalist and theist alike—actually thinks and lives.[109] Monism (whether materialistic or pantheistic) denies the distinction between good and evil, but monists do not and cannot live that way. Islam and its Allah prescribe attitudes and behavior contrary to what even Muslims acknowledge to be the "universally accepted standard of right and wrong" which are "part of our innate constitution."[110] All such views are contrary to the uniform position of all people, in all cultures, in all times, who act on the basis that good and evil exist and that some actions are moral and others immoral. Christianity alone provides a sufficient ground for morality (God himself), a universal moral standard which is at least implicitly and intuitively understood and accepted by people of every tribe, tongue, and nation (love of God and love of your neighbor), the example of Jesus Christ, and the means (a new heart, the mind of Christ, and the indwelling Holy Spirit) by which people can actually meet the "universally accepted standard of right and wrong" which are "part of our innate constitution."

NATURALISM CANNOT ACCOUNT FOR THE ORIGIN OF LIFE ITSELF

Behind these issues is the issue of how, in a purely materialistic universe, life itself could have arisen from non-living matter. Michael Denton states, "Between a living cell and the most highly ordered non-biological system, such as a crystal or a snowflake, there is a chasm as vast and absolute as it is possible to conceive.[111] Michael Behe's study of cilia and flagella showed us that cells are not primitive or simple, but are incredibly complex construction systems. Despite their tiny size, each cell amounts to being a "veritable micro-miniaturized factory containing thousands of exquisitely designed pieces of intricate molecular machinery, made up altogether of one hundred thousand million atoms, far more complicated than any machine built by

---

109. Michael Ruse and Edward O. Wilson admit the utter moral bankruptcy of naturalism: in positing the naturalistic, evolutionary development of ethics and morality, they deny that any "genuinely objective external ethical premises" exist; but at the same time, they state that "human beings function better *if they are deceived by their genes into thinking* that there is a disinterested objective morality binding upon them, which all should obey." Ruse and Wilson, "Moral Philosophy," 186, 179, emph. added.

110. Emerick, *Understanding*, 195.

111. Denton, *Evolution: A Theory*, 249–50.

Naturalism Cannot Account for Existence as It Is 187

man and absolutely without parallel in the non-living world."[112] Geneticist William Stansfield says that there are two basic ideas concerning the origin of life: "(1) life is produced from nonliving components of the environment by natural processes (the theory of *spontaneous generation*), and (2) life is produced by supernatural (vitalistic) powers (the theory of special creation)."[113] Sir Fred Hoyle, who formulated the theory of stellar nucleosynthesis, wrote, "The combinatorial arrangement of not even one among the many thousands of biopolymers on which life depends could have been arrived at by natural processes here on Earth."[114] He concluded, "Now imagine 10^{50} blind persons[115] each with a scrambled Rubik cube and try to conceive of the chance of them all *simultaneously* arriving at the solved form. You then have the chance of arriving by random shuffling at just one of the many biopolymers on which life depends. The notion that not only the biopolymers but the operating programme of a living cell could be arrived at by chance in a primordial soup here on Earth is evidently nonsense of a high degree."[116] Dr. David Green of the Institute for Enzyme Research at the University of Wisconsin and Dr. Robert Goldberger, chief of the Biosynthesis and Control Section, Laboratory of Chemical Biology, U.S. National Institutes of Health similarly state, "The macromolecule-to-cell transition is a jump of fantastic dimensions which lies beyond the range of testable hypotheses. In this area all is conjecture. The available facts do not provide a basis for postulating that cells arose on this planet."[117]

Stephen Meyer discusses other probability calculations: one set calculated the maximum number of events that actually could have taken place during the history of the observable universe by, among other things, calculating the number of elementary particles in the observable universe

---

112. Denton, *Evolution: A Theory*, 250.

113. Stansfield, *The Science*, 50.

114. Hoyle, "The Big Bang," 526.

115. I.e., 100 billion, billion, billion, billion, trillion blind persons.

116. Hoyle, "The Big Bang," 527, emph. in orig. Elsewhere, Hoyle calculated the odds of life originating on earth by chance at one in $10^{40,000}$ which he characterized as "an outrageously small probability that could not be faced even if the whole universe consisted of organic soup." He added, "If one is not prejudiced either by social beliefs or by a scientific training into the conviction that life originated on Earth, this simple calculation wipes the idea entirely out of court." Hoyle and Wickramasinghe, *Evolution*, 24; see also Major, "Big enough." The situation is even worse than that, because "It is highly unlikely that biochemical compounds in the primitive oceans ever reached the consistency of a 'thick soup' as so many 'popular science' books intimate." Stansfield, *The Science*, 56. In short, there is no positive evidence that a "prebiotic soup" ever existed. See Denton, *Evolution: A Theory*, 261.

117. Green and Goldberger, *Molecular*, 406–7.

(10^{80}), the amount of time since the big bang (10^{16} seconds), and the number of interactions per second (10^{43}). Based on all of this, the only logical conclusion is, "The complexity of the events that origin-of-life researchers need to explain exceeds the probabilistic resources of the entire universe. In other words, the universe itself does not possess the probabilistic resources necessary to render probable the origin of biological information by chance alone."[118]

Additionally, the issue for the origin of life is not only the extreme improbability of natural processes simultaneously creating all the necessary components to create a living cell, but the fact that the DNA and genetic systems upon which all life is based are computerlike, digital, information storage and replication systems.[119] In other words, in addition to matter and energy, *information* is a fundamental necessity for life to exist.[120] Moreover, the information must be *functionally specific*, i.e., "the bases in DNA convey instructions for building proteins—and do so in virtue of their *specificity of arrangement*."[121] However, no materialist model or undirected chemical or physical process has ever been able to generate the functionally specific information necessary to create even one living cell.[122] Scientific consultant Dr. David Foster augments this by noting, "The specificity of the DNA of the T4 bacteriophage is represented by the number $10^{78,000}$ so that there is only one chance in $10^{78,000}$ of it actually occurring by random shufflings."[123] Foster describes the significance of this, "These figures have to be set against the fact that the universe is only 10^{18} seconds, old, and so there is no possibility whatsoever of life having evolved through Darwin's theory of natural selection operating on chance mutations."[124]

The underlying problem is even greater than the above facts indicate. Even the simplest living cell "employs the same genetic code and the same mechanism of translation as do, for example, human cells. . . . The code is meaningless unless translated. The modern cell's translating machinery consists of at least fifty macromolecular components *which are themselves encoded in DNA: the code cannot be translated otherwise than by products of translation*."[125] In other words, DNA contains the instructions an organism

118. Meyer, *Signature*, 215–19.
119. See Dawkins, *River*, 17–18.
120. Meyer, *Return*, 188.
121. Meyer, *Return*, 173.
122. Meyer, *Darwin's Doubt*, vi; Meyer, *Return*, 187.
123. Foster, *The Philosophical*, viii.
124. Foster, *The Philosophical*, viii.
125. Monod, *Chance*, 142–43, emph. in orig.

needs to develop, live, and reproduce but cannot operate unless it is fully formed and functional; hence, we cannot begin to guess, on naturalistic grounds, how DNA could have come into existence in the first place. Karl Popper put it like this, "What makes the origin of life and of the genetic code a disturbing riddle is this: the genetic code is without any biological function unless it is translated; that is, unless it leads to the synthesis of the proteins whose structure is laid down by the code. . . . [But] the code cannot be translated except by using certain products of its translation"; he called this a "vicious circle" which faces us with "the possibility that the origin of life (like the origin of the universe) becomes an impenetrable barrier to science, and a residue to all attempts to reduce biology to chemistry and physics."[126]

Darwin's theory which, both in its original and contemporary forms, pronounces the naturalistic ability to create and evolve life from non-living matter, simply is an assertion which it cannot prove. In fact, evolutionary theorists nowhere endeavor to prove it.[127] In light of Popper's "vicious circle" and the other scientific facts we have surveyed, the Darwinian belief in the naturalistic origin of life is, to put it mildly, a very peculiar inference from the known scientific facts, an inference for which there is no logical or rational justification, except that, as Richard Lewontin stated earlier, it keeps the Divine foot outside the door.

126. Popper, "Scientific Reduction," 270.

127. The closest things to "proof" have been attempts, commencing with the Miller-Urey experiment in 1952, to create organic compounds from a simulated early-earth atmosphere of methane, ammonia, hydrogen, and water vapor; electrical sparks were fired into the mixture to simulate lightning. In Miller-Urey and similar experiments, as long as oxygen was excluded from the mixture, amino acids and other organic compounds have resulted. See "Miller-Urey experiment," *Wikipedia*; see also Thaxton, Bradley, and Olsen, *The Mystery*, 22–41 for descriptions of Miller-Urey and similar experiments.

However, not even one living cell—the simplest form of "life"—was created by these experiments, and how to traverse the tremendous difference between amino acids and actual living cells has never even been hinted at. Thaxton, Bradley, and Olsen point out that, not only is "there is no known geological evidence for organic pools . . . ever existing on this planet," but evidence indicates that the early earth's atmosphere was oxidizing, which would have prevented any chemical generation of organic compounds; further, most prebiotic simulation experiments owe their "success" to the illegitimate role of the investigators. Thaxton, Bradley, and Olsen, *The Mystery*, 66, 182–85; see also Behe, *Darwin's Black Box*, 166–70. In an updated and expanded version of Thaxton, Bradley, and Olsen's work, one commentator observes that, given the vast amount of knowledge we have gained regarding DNA and other matters since Miller-Urey, "one could argue that origin-of-life research is even more befuddled now than it was in 1952 since more questions have evolved than answers, and the voluminous new data regarding the complexity within a cell makes the target much more daunting than it used to be." Tour, "We're Still," 324; see also Dose, "The Origin," Abstract.

This does not mean that all we can do is throw up our hands and conclude that no one can know how life came to be. Although no *material* cause based on chemical or physical processes is able to create functioning digital codes (which, as we have seen, DNA and genes essentially are) one type—and only one type—of cause has the ability to produce this type of information: intelligence/mind. Consequently, "the discovery of digital information in even the simplest living cells indicates the prior activity of a designing intelligence at work in the origin of the first life."[128]

Fred Hoyle concurs. After considering the details of polymer chemistry and stellar nucleosynthesis, he concluded, "A common sense interpretation of the facts suggests that a superintellect has monkeyed with physics, as well as with chemistry and biology, and that there are no blind forces worth speaking about in nature. The numbers one calculates from the facts seem to me so overwhelming as to put this conclusion almost beyond question."[129] In short, scientifically, logically, and biblically, life could not have come into existence through naturalistic processes; the most plausible explanation is that it had to be and was created by God.

NATURALISM CANNOT ACCOUNT FOR THE EXISTENCE OF THE UNIVERSE

Behind all of these issues is the foundational issue of how the earth and the universe came into being at all, or "why is there something rather than nothing?" Martin Heidegger called that "the fundamental question of metaphysics."[130] The reason is that everything that does not *have to exist* requires a cause.[131] Christianity holds that *"In the beginning God created the*

---

128. Meyer, *Darwin's Doubt*, vi.

129. Hoyle, "The Universe," 12; see also Hoyle and Wickramasinghe, *Evolution*, 148. Hoyle's own answer to the issue of where life on earth came from and the identity of the "superintellect" that produced it is that the first life on earth began in space, spreading through the universe via panspermia. Hoyle and Wickramasinghe, *Evolution*. That answer, however, only takes the question of how life arose back one step but does not answer it.

130. Heidegger, *An Introduction*, 7–8.

131. In addition to the original coming into being of the universe, the necessity of God's current, sustaining causality applies to the continued existence of the universe and everything in it. Norman Geisler points out, "The cause of all contingent existence, such as I am, cannot in itself be contingent. If it were contingent then it would not be the *cause* of the contingent; it too would be an *effect*. . . . As long as there is a dependent [i.e., contingent] being in the universe [which includes the universe itself], there must be something independent on which it depends. If there is an existing effect, something must be effecting or causing it. No effect exists without its cause. If something existed

heavens and the earth" (Gen 1:1). Evolutionist William Stansfield admits that "science cannot account for the primary origin of matter or energy."[132] Indeed, as Nobel prize winner Sir Peter Medawar points out, by its very nature, the question of how everything began cannot, *even in principle*, be answered by science, since "there can be no empirical awareness of nothingness, so that if any such frontier [between being and nothingness] exists it cannot exist in the domain of discourse of science and common sense."[133] Nevertheless, scientists have done their best to come up with naturalistic explanations for why the universe exists at all.

In the early 1970s Stephen Hawking, Roger Penrose, and George Ellis demonstrated that the universe began to exist at a finite point in time, beginning from nothing temporal or material.[134] This is known as a "singularity" at which point time is said to begin and the laws of physics cease.[135] Theoretical physicist Paul Davies states, "An initial cosmological singularity therefore forms a past temporal extremity to the universe. We cannot continue physical reasoning, or even the concept of spacetime, through such an extremity. For this reason most cosmologists think of the initial singularity as the 'beginning' of the universe. On this view the big bang represents the creation event; the creation not only of all the matter and energy in the universe, but also of spacetime itself."[136]

The predominant view of how the universe came into existence is the "Big Bang" theory, which says that "the universe as we know it started with an infinitely hot and dense single point that inflated and stretched—first at unimaginable speeds, and then at a more measurable rate—over the next

---

without a cause then it would not be an effect; it would be self-caused or uncaused. But since I [or the universe itself] am not self-caused or uncaused . . . then my existence must be effected or caused by a cause. Hence, my existence demands a current here-and-now cause of its continuing *be-*ing." Geisler, *Christian Apologetics*, 245, 253. This is echoed by philosopher Mortimer Adler who states, "To bring into existence out of nothing that which, without such creative action, would not exist is to exnihilate. To preserve in existence that which, without such preservative action, would cease to exist and be reduced to nothingness is also to exnihilate. Neither form of exnihilating action is within the power of natural causes. Hence we are led to conclude that a supernatural cause exists to accomplish either result." Adler, *How to Think*, 146. Adler's conclusion is significant in that, when he wrote that, he was a self-described pagan writing for other pagans. Adler, *How to Think*, 19.

132. Stansfield, *The Science*, 53.
133. Medawar, *The Limits*, 88.
134. See Meyer, *Return*, 115–17.
135. Hawking, *A Brief*, 49–50; Davies, "Space-Time," 49–50.
136. Davies, "Space-Time," 78–79.

13.8 billion years to the still-expanding cosmos that we know today."[137] That theory is consistent with the existence of cosmic microwave background radiation, the fact that the universe appears to be expanding, and other phenomena.[138] Some scientists did not like the ideas of a singularity and that time has a beginning, "probably because it smacks of divine intervention."[139] That implication is valid, since a singularity implies that space, time, energy, and matter "*first* arose at the beginning of the universe"—before that time nothing would have existed that could have caused the universe (space, time, energy, and matter) to come into being.[140]

The beginning of the universe, M-theory, and the multiverse

Various issues and questions with respect to the Big Bang theory have led scientists to posit other theories, or refinements of the Big Bang, including "string theories," the latest development of which is M-theory.[141] One of those scientists is Hawking himself. Hawking and Leonard Mlodinow describe M-theory as predicting that multiple universes were created naturally out of nothing: "Because gravity shapes space and time, it allows space-time to be locally stable but globally unstable. . . . Because there is a law like gravity, the universe can and will create itself from nothing. . . . Spontaneous creation is the reason there is something rather than nothing."[142] They add that this was a "quantum event" (i.e., it could not happen according to the laws of classical [non-quantum] physics) in which the universe was "a billion-trillion-trillionth of a centimeter," and gravity "warped" time such that "time behave[d] like another dimension of space"[143] At some point, this infinitesimal "universe" spontaneously expanded faster than the speed of light.[144] In short, "quantum fluctuations" are said to lead to the creation of

137. Howell, "What is," n.p.; see also "Big Bang," *Wikipedia*. Many Christians accept the big bang as implying how God began the creation of the universe. "Religious interpretations," *Wikipedia*; Ball, "A Christian Physicist."

138. Siegel, "Surprise."

139. Hawking, *A Brief*, 46. It was the scientific evidence for a "creation event" that led famous astronomer Allan Sandage, who had been an agnostic with a materialist philosophy of science, to convert to Christianity. See Meyer *Return*, 107–9.

140. Meyer, *Return*, 117.

141. See, e.g., Wolf, *Parallel*; Craig, "The Ultimate"; Craig, "Creation ex nihilo"; Tate, "Alternatives"; Siegel, "Surprise."

142. Hawking and Mlodinow, *The Grand*, 8–9, 180.

143. Hawking and Mlodinow, *The Grand*, 131, 134; see also Davies, "The Appearance," 150–51.

144. Hawking and Mlodinow, *The Grand*, 129; see also Cleaver, "Multiverse," 72–73.

multiple universes out of nothing, some of which then expand in an inflationary manner, forming stars and galaxies, and, in at least one case, "beings like us."[145] In such a hypothesized universe, Hawking says, "there would be no boundary to space-time" and so there would be no need to specify the behavior at the boundary. There would be "no singularities at which the laws of science broke down"; instead, the universe "would neither be created nor destroyed. It would just BE."[146]

Hawking was quite explicit about the theological reason behind his theory. He acknowledges, "So long as the universe had a beginning, we could suppose it had a creator"; however, if the universe is completely self-contained and has no boundary or edge, then, he asserts, it would not have a beginning, but "it would simply be. What place, then, for a creator?"[147] Several years later he added that the beginning of the universe was governed by the laws of science, which "fully determines both the future and the past. This would exclude the possibility of miracles or an active role for God."[148] In his last, posthumous, book, Hawking again said that "there is no God. No one created the universe and no one directs our fate"; he added, "I think the universe was spontaneously created out of nothing, according to the laws of science."[149]

Hawking admitted that his "no boundary" proposal cannot be deduced from anything.[150] Major problems exist with it. First, the only "laws of science" we know are those which came out of the "big bang." We cannot even remotely hope to know or model what laws were in operation *before* the big bang occurred and cosmic inflation was set in motion. Consequently, on evidential grounds, all such speculation is not one whit better than the supposedly outdated "God hypothesis."[151] Second, Hawking substituted *imaginary* time for *real* time to come up with his proposal; he called this "a mathematical device (or trick)."[152] However, his imaginary time has no correspondence to the properties of real space and time.[153] Hawking then interpreted "a mathematical expression [imaginary time] with no physical

---

145. Hawking and Mlodinow, *The Grand*, 137. M-theory posits that there may be as many as 10^{500} different universes, each with its own set of physical/scientific laws. Hawking and Mlodinow, *The Grand*, 118.

146. Hawking, *A Brief*, 136.

147. Hawking, *A Brief*, 141.

148. Hawking and Mlodinow, *The Grand*, 135, 30.

149. Hawking, *Brief Answers*, 38, 29.

150. Hawking, *A Brief*, 136.

151. See Chapman, *Slaying*, 156–57.

152. Hawking, *A Brief*, 135.

153. Meyer, *Return*, 507n.18; 352.

meaning as if it had physical and metaphysical significance."[154] Hawking admitted that only in imaginary time are there no singularities or boundaries between space and time; he further admitted, "In real time, the universe has a beginning and an end at singularities that form a boundary to space-time and at which the laws of science break down."[155] In short, the singularity (the temporal beginning of the universe), which is inherent in real time and in reality, renders his "no boundary" proposal as imaginary as the imaginary time upon which it is based.

Third, the claim that the universe was spontaneously created out of nothing pursuant to the laws of science represents a fundamental "category error." Causes and scientific laws are not the same thing. Causes are events that precede other events and act, happen, or exist in such a way to produce an effect. Laws, on the other hand, are simply descriptions of nature, its components, and their relationships; however, as descriptions, laws do not and cannot cause events to occur.[156] Thus, the "law of gravity" and the "laws of science" do not *cause* space, energy, or anything else to come into existence, but simply *describe* how they interact with each other once they already exist.[157] Hawking's explanation of how the universe was "created out of nothing" is therefore no explanation at all.

More fundamentally, David Darling, former Dean of the College of Education at the University of New Mexico, points out the sleight-of-hand behind the naturalistic pronouncements made by people such as Hawking,

> What is a big deal—the biggest deal of all—is how you get something out of nothing. Don't let the cosmologists try to kid you on this one. They have not got a clue either—despite the fact that they are doing a pretty good job of convincing themselves and others that this is really not a problem. "In the beginning," they will say, "there was nothing—no time, space, matter or energy. Then there was a quantum fluctuation from which . . ." Whoa! Stop right there. You see what I mean? First there is nothing, then there is something. And the cosmologists try to bridge the two with a quantum flutter, a tremor of uncertainty that sparks it all off. Then they are away and before you know it, they have pulled a hundred billion galaxies out of their quantum hats. I don't have a problem with this scenario from the quantum

---

154. Meyer, *Return*, 366.
155. Hawking, *A Brief*, 138–39.
156. See Meyer, *Return*, 371.

157. See Meyer, *Return*, 371; see also Lewis, "The Laws," 77 ("*the laws of Nature have never produced a single event.* They are the pattern to which every event must conform, provided only that it can be induced to happen.").

fluctuation onward. Why shouldn't human beings build a theory of how the Universe evolved from a simple to a complex state. But there is a very real problem in explaining how it got started in the first place. You cannot fudge this by appealing to quantum mechanics. Either there is nothing to begin with, in which case there is no quantum vacuum, no pre-geometric dust, no time in which anything can happen, no physical laws that can effect a change from nothingness into somethingness; or there is something, in which case that needs explaining.[158]

Indeed, contrary to Hawking's position that modern physics permits an atheistic view of the origin of the universe, quantum mechanics actually points decisively *against* atheism and naturalism. According to quantum mechanics, at the subatomic level everything is truly probabilistic and not determined; further, the presence of an observer (either a conscious being or an instrument used by a conscious being) somehow determines "an after-the-fact reality based solely on the act of observing."[159] In light of that, biochemist Sy Garte states that since we now know that "the subatomic world of atoms, photons, and other elementary particle is ruled by quantum physics, which requires an irrational kind of interaction or dialogue between the particles, their surroundings, and the person studying them. . . . Such strange phenomena that are part of the reality of nature at the smallest and most fundamental level make it difficult to maintain philosophical materialism as the one legitimate way to view reality."[160] The logical candidate for the one who designed the laws of science and formed the materials and forces that constitute the universe is God.

Hawking admitted that, although proposals like his may be put forward "for aesthetic or metaphysical reasons," the real test for a truly scientific theory is "whether it makes predictions that agree with observation."[161] David Lindley points out that modern particle physics "is grounded not in the tangible and testable notions of objects and points and pushes and pulls but in a sophisticated and mathematical language of fields and interactions and wavefunctions . . . [which are] ultimately meaningless because the objects of the mathematical manipulations are forever beyond the access of experimentation and measurement. . . . But what is the use of a theory that looks attractive but contains no additional power of prediction, and makes

---

158. Darling, "Forum," 49.
159. Garte, *The Works*, 34.
160. Garte, *The Works*, 36–37.
161. Hawking, *A Brief*, 136–37.

no statements that can be tested?"[162] Even Hawking acknowledges that his model, or any such model, cannot calculate predictions.[163]

In light of this, astrophysicist Luke Barnes asks, "Could a multiverse proposal ever be regarded as scientific?" The answer is "No." He explains, "We cannot observe any of the properties of a multiverse . . . as they have no causal effect on our universe. We could be completely wrong about everything we believe about these other universes and no observation could correct us. The information is not here. The history of science has repeatedly taught us that experimental testing is not an optional extra. The hypothesis that a multiverse actually exists will always be untestable."[164] In short, as Phillip Johnson points out, the "no boundary/no beginning point" proposal "is a mathematical construct that has no empirical basis, makes no predictions and generates no research agenda. Its sole purpose is to support the metaphysical principle that nature is self-contained and effectively eternal."[165] Paul Davies adds the salient point that "the existence of a mathematical scheme for a universe is not the same thing as the actual existence of that universe" but amounts to a mathematical proposal that there is a nonzero possibility that such a universe could exist.[166] Consequently, the "no boundary/no beginning" proposal can have no evidential value in proving the naturalistic explanation for the universe or the non-existence of God.

Finally, any supposed naturalistic beginning of the universe is contradicted by the laws and findings of science themselves. First, "the law of conservation of energy, also known as the first law of thermodynamics, states that the energy of a closed system must remain constant—it can neither increase nor decrease without interference from outside. The universe itself is a closed system, so the total amount of energy in existence has always been the same."[167] The Second Law of Thermodynamics states that "in converting

---

162. Lindley, *The End*, 18–19.

163. Hawking, *A Brief*, 137.

164. Barnes, "the Fine-Tuning," 58; see also Garte, *The Works*, 52 (the multiverse theory "has the problem of being unprovable, since information cannot travel between universes").

165. Johnson, *Reason*, 226; see also Thorvaldsen and Hössjer, "Using statistical," 4 ("This multiverse hypothesis is not backed up with any empirical support, and may be regarded as a rather speculative idea"). Christian physicist Don Page lists a number of common scientific, philosophical, and theological objections to multiverse ideas. Page, "Does God," 19–22; for other objections to multiverse ideas see also Davies, "A Brief"; Behe, *The Edge*, 220–27; Ellis, "Does the Multiverse"; Craig, "Creation ex nihilo"; Maudlin, "Distilling," 461–62; Cleaver, "Multiverse," 77.

166. Davies, *The Mind*, 69.

167. Moskowitz, "Fact," n.p.; see also Meyer, *Return*, 220–21 ("Naturalism regards

one form of energy to another, some of it is lost as unusable heat. *Entropy* is the thermodynamic quality of randomness or disorder within a system. The Second law therefore implies that as energy is being transformed throughout the universe, entropy is increasing."[168] Any form of naturalism means that the universe began in a state of randomness with a terrific explosion but, instead of becoming more random as the second law of thermodynamics would dictate, the universe, through no known means, progressively became more organized and complex! As such, any proposal that the universe came into existence by itself is contrary to the first and second laws of thermodynamics. This also means that the universe, of necessity, had a beginning: "The Second Law inevitably forces upon us is the following: If, given enough time, the universe will reach heat death, then why is it not in a state of heat death now, if it has existed forever, from eternity? If the universe did not begin to exist, then it should now be in a state of equilibrium. Like a ticking clock, it should by now have run down."[169] Even though he is an evolutionist, Stansfield admits, "These Laws argue strongly for a created universe."[170]

Second, from a factual standpoint, in 2003 Arvind Borde, Alan Guth, and Alexander Vilenkin developed a proof "that all cosmological models in which expansion occurs [which includes our expanding universe]—including inflationary cosmology, multiverses, and the oscillating and cosmic egg models—are subject to the BGV theorem" which holds that the universe must have had a starting point or beginning.[171] Hence, director of the Tufts Institute of Cosmology Alexander Vilenkin says, "With the proof now in place, cosmologists can no longer hide behind the possibility of a past-eternal universe. There is no escape; they have to face the problem of a cosmic

---

nature as an orderly system of cause and effect within a closed system"). With respect to quantum mechanics, "Einstein objected fervently to the idea that quantum mechanics defied energy conservation. And it turns out he was right. After physicists refined quantum mechanics a few years later, scientists understood that although the energy of each electron might fluctuate in a probabilistic haze, the total energy of the electron and its radiation remained constant at every moment of the process. Energy was conserved." Moskowitz, "Fact," n.p.

168. Stansfield, *The Science*, 57.

169. Craig, "Creation ex nihilo," The Thermodynamics.

170. Stansfield, *The Science*, 57. The second law of thermodynamics would also rule out an oscillating universe, because there are no known means for the universe to repeatedly converge into a dimensionless point and then expand again with 100% efficiency, i.e., the universe could not be infinitely old but would have ceased contraction-expansion ages ago. See Moreland, *Scaling*, 33–34.

171. Meyer, *Return*, 124–28.

beginning."[172] Hawking made explicit the implication of this, "A point of creation would be a place where science broke down. One would have to appeal to religion and the hand of God."[173]

Fine-tuning (the Anthropic Principle)

Evidence of God's design is seen in the nature of the universe and its relationship to humanity. Francis Collins, head of the Human Genome Project who is both an MD and has a PhD in physics, observes, "There are 15 constants – the gravitational constant, various constants about the strong and weak nuclear force, etc. – that have precise values. If any one of those constants was off by even one part in a million, or in some cases, by one part in a million million, the universe could not have actually come to the point where we see it. Matter would not have been able to coalesce, there would have been no galaxy, stars, planets or people. That's a phenomenally surprising observation. It seems almost impossible that we're here."[174] This is known as the anthropic principle or the "fine-tuning" of the universe. Astrophysicist Martin Rees considers just six numbers[175] and says that "if any one of them were to be 'untuned', there would be no stars and no life."[176] The details necessary for life to exist on earth extend to the distance of the earth from the sun (not too close to make it too hot or too far away to cause everything to freeze) and the fact that the earth is not too close to or far away from the center of the galaxy (which would result in high doses of X-rays

---

172. Vilenkin, *Many Worlds,* 176; see Grossman, "Death," 7.

173. Grossman, "Death," 6. It is important to understand that God is not only the *temporal* "first cause" of the existence of the universe, but is also the *logical* first cause of the existence of the universe. By that we mean that the Christian notion of creation includes more than that the universe had a beginning in time. It also includes the idea that the continued existence of the world is dependent upon God. In other words, God's creative activity also involves his continually sustaining existence. Col 1:17; see n.131, supra. To put it another way, "God minus the world equals God. The world minus God equals nothing." Nash, *Faith,*125.

174. Paulsen and Collins, "The believer," n.p.

175. (1) The number of spatial dimensions we live in – 3; (2) The relative strength of the electrostatic to the gravitational force between two protons – approximately 10^{36}; (3) The fraction of mass converted to energy when hydrogen is fused to form helium – approximately 0.007; (4) The average matter density of the universe, rather than being expressed in kilograms per cubic meter, it is expressed in units where the critical density (10^{-26} kilograms per cubic meter) is equal to one – approximately 0.32; (5) The average dark energy density of the universe, also expressed in units where the critical density is equal to one – 0.68; (6) How tightly bound the large clusters and supercluster of galaxies are. On the scale used in Rees's book it has the value 10^{-5}.

176. Rees, *Just Six,* 4.

and affect element formation).¹⁷⁷ Michael Behe adds that "the 'anthropic coincidences' needed for life in this universe extend beyond the basic physical laws and constants, well into chemistry," including such things as the fact that water, unlike almost all other liquids, expands when it freezes and, at the molecular level, the particular strength of the electric charge allows both the strong and weak chemical bonds which are necessary for proteins to work.¹⁷⁸ There may be 100 fine-tuning parameters, which are "like a panel that controls the parameters of the universe with about 100 knobs that can be set to certain value."¹⁷⁹ As Thorvaldsen and Hössjen point out, "The chances that the universe should be life permitting are so infinitesimal as to be incomprehensible and incalculable."¹⁸⁰

Rees asks, "Is this tuning just a brute fact, a coincidence? Or is it the providence of a benign Creator?"¹⁸¹ This fine tuning is the opposite of what we would expect if naturalism were true. Stephen Hawking admits that, even assuming that the universe was formed through some type of "big bang" or expansion from an infinitesimal point, the initial state of the universe in terms of its temperature, rate of expansion, etc. "must have been very carefully chosen"; hence, it is very difficult to explain why the universe began and exists in the way it does "except as the act of a God who intended to create beings like us"¹⁸² Elsewhere he adds that the universe and its laws "appear to have a design that is both tailor-made to support us and, if we are to exist, leaves little room for alteration."¹⁸³

The fine-tuning of the universe represents more than just an extremely improbable set of minutely calibrated constants. Fine-tuning also involves what Stephen Meyer calls "functional significance" and mathematician William Dembski calls "specification," i.e., extremely improbable events "that also exhibit 'an *independently recognizable* pattern.'"¹⁸⁴ It is like the example used earlier about the stones that have the pattern "The British Railways Welcomes You To Wales." The stones represent an extremely improbable pattern but also are independently recognizable as signifying a particular meaning. As Dembski says, "Specification is the only means available to us for distinguishing choice from chance, directed contingency from blind

177. Behe, *The Edge*, 210–12.
178. Behe, *The Edge*, 208–9, 214.
179. Thorvaldsen and Hössjen, "Using statistical," 4.
180. Thorvaldsen and Hössjen, "Using statistical," 4.
181. Rees, *Just Six*, 4.
182. Hawking, *A Brief*, 126–27.
183. Hawking and Mlodinow, *The Grand*, 162.
184. Meyer, *Return*, 157, emph. in orig.; see also Meyer, *Signature*, 360–63.

contingency."[185] In other words, improbable patterns that also exhibit functional significance or specification "*invariably* result from intelligent causes, not chance or physical-chemical laws."[186] Meyer observes, "The fine-tuning of the universe exhibits precisely those features—extreme improbability and functional specification—that invariably trigger an awareness of, and justify an inference to, intelligent design," and "the observation of fine-tuning confirms precisely what we might well expect if a purposive intelligence . . . had acted to design the universe and life."[187]

That the fine-tuning of the universe points to God is clearly indicated by: (1) "features that need to be in place *before* the universe can be said to exist and operate," which means that any intelligent designer could not have been within or a part of the cosmos itself but had to have been a being outside of and pre-existing the universe; and (2) "Like a Bach fugue, the Universe has a beautiful elegance about it, governed by laws whose mathematical precision is meted out to the metronome of time. These equations of physics are finely balanced, with the constants of nature that underpin the equations tuned to values that allows our remarkable Universe to exist in a form where we, humanity, can study it."[188] The only being who conceivably could have designed and engineered this is God. Thus, "theism can account for (1) the origin of the universe in time (i.e., at a beginning), (2) the fine-tuning of the universe from the beginning of time, and (3) the origin of the specified information that arises after the beginning of time that is necessary to produce the first living organism."[189] It is this extremely improbable but also functionally significant fine-tuning that shook the atheism of Fred Hoyle and caused other physicists, including Henry Margenau, distinguished Yale professor of quantum physics, to embrace theism.[190]

Rees, Hawking, and Richard Dawkins try to escape the force of this by appealing to the concept of the "multiverse." The reason is that, in a multiverse, fine-tuning parameters likely would arise somewhere in some universe, since multiple universes would greatly increase the number of opportunities for generating a universe friendly to life.[191] However, Meyer

---

185. Dembski, *The Design*, 64.
186. Meyer, *Return*, 158, emph. in orig.
187. Meyer, *Scientific*, 20, 274.
188. Thorvaldsen and Hössjen, "Using statistical," 4.
189. Meyer, *Scientific*, 25–26.
190. See Meyer, *Return*, 130–31, 142–46. For good overall discussions of fine-tuning and the history of its discovery, see Meyer, *Return*, 130–63 and Plantinga, *Where the Conflict*, 193–224.
191. See Meyer, *Scientific*, 17–18; Dawkins, *The God Delusion*, 145; Rees, *Just Six*, 4, 148–61; Hawking and Mlodinow, *The Grand*, 164–65.

Naturalism Cannot Account for Existence as It Is 201

points out that the speculative cosmologies proposed for generating such alternative universes "invariably invoke mechanisms that themselves require fine-tuning, thus begging the question as to the origin of that prior fine-tuning."[192]

Alvin Plantinga responds to the gratuitous "it-just-so-happens" nature of the "multiverse" defense by considering the example of a cowboy in the Old West town of Tombstone or Dodge City who just "happens" to always deal himself four aces and a wild card in a game of poker. As the other players reach for their six-shooters the dealer says, "I know it's a leetle mite suspicious that every time I deal I git four aces and a wild card, but have you considered the following? Possibly there is an infinite succession of universes, so that for any possible distribution of possible poker hands, there is a universe in which that possibility is realized; we just happen to find ourselves in one where someone like me always deals himself only aces and wild cards without ever cheating."[193] That kind of argument will have no effect on the other card players. Although it is technically possible that the man just happened always to deal himself four aces and a wild card, Plantinga explains that "the probability of that distribution [of dealt cards] is much greater on the hypothesis that I am cheating than on the hypothesis that the cards have been dealt fairly.... The same thing goes for the fine tuning arguments; the probability of fine tuning on the proposition that God has created the universe is much greater than on the proposition that the universe has not been created."[194]

The proposal of the multiverse does not and cannot deal with or answer the question of God's existence and active involvement. Mathematician and cosmologist George Ellis points out, "Scientists proposed the multiverse as a way of resolving deep issues about the nature of existence, but the proposal leaves the ultimate issues unresolved. All the same issues that arise in relation to the universe arise again in relation to the multiverse. If the multiverse exists, did it come into existence through necessity, chance or purpose? That is a metaphysical question that no physical theory can answer for either the universe or the multiverse."[195]

The length that some scientists go in order to try to shore up naturalism is another example of Richard Lewontin's admission (quoted earlier) that much of science is not driven by the evidence in a search for truth

---

192. Meyer, *Scientific*, 19–20; see also Meyer, *Return*, 326–47 for an overall discussion of fine-tuning and its relation to multiverse concepts.
193. Plantinga, "Dennett's Dangerous," 35.
194. Plantinga, "Methodological," 27n.25.
195. Ellis, "Does the Multiverse," Too Much Wiggle Room.

but will accept ideas plainly *contrary* to the scientific evidence, because of a pre-existing commitment to the philosophical presupposition of naturalism.[196] The irony of the current situation is that scientists today are speaking about matters that go far beyond the purview of science.[197] The multiverse idea, or any view of the origin of the cosmos, describes a singularity, since how and why the universe exists are not subject to observation, testing, experiment, or replication.[198] The claims that the universe came into being "naturally" (i.e., without God) and that evolution is not guided or directed by anyone but takes place by chance, not teleology, are not part of scientific theory as such, but are metaphysical or theological propositions that cannot be demonstrated "scientifically."[199] On the other hand, as one reviewer of Rees's book stated, the view that "divine providence, in tuning the universe so that human life can exist, *is just as valid a scientific proposition*—though likewise it cannot be subject to scientific validation."[200] Thus, it is perfectly legitimate for a scientist like Gerald Cleaver, a Christian and physicist at Baylor University whose area of work is with M-theory, to contend that M-theory reveals "a Christian God whose creative ability is much larger than we ever could imagine before."[201] In fact, as theoretical physicist Paul Davies acknowledges, the validity of the Christian worldview is implicitly conceded by all scientists, because "even the most atheistic scientist accepts as an act of faith the existence of a law-like order in nature that is at least in part comprehensible to us. So science can proceed only if the scientist adopts an essentially theological worldview."[202]

---

196. Lewontin, "Billions," 31.

197. Theoretical physicist Paul Davies, who himself would prefer that the laws governing the cosmos "should have an explanation from within the universe and not involve appealing to an external agency," nevertheless recognizes that "until science comes up with a testable theory of the laws of the universe, its claim to be free of faith is manifestly bogus." Davies, "Taking Science," n.p.

198. See Cleaver, "Multiverse," 77–80.

199. See Plantinga, *Where the Conflict*, 309; Cleaver, "Multiverse," 77–80.

200. Roberts, "Review," n.p.; see also Garte, *The Works*, 52 ("While scientists typically reject any supernatural explanations, it must be said that the God hypothesis is not any *more* removed from testing or scientific confirmation than the multiverse").

201. Persaud, "Christ of the," 47, quoting Cleaver. Elsewhere, Cleaver lists a number of other Christian scientists and philosophers who accept M-theory and the "multiverse" concept and also a number who oppose those ideas. Cleaver, "Multiverse," 81–84.

202. Davies, "The Appearance," 148.

Conclusion

The existence of the universe and natural laws not only do not preclude either God's existence or his being the creator of the universe, but are consistent with and point to God. Hawking spoke of the universe being "spontaneously created out of nothing, according to the laws of science." The existence of such laws themselves points to the necessity of God as the creator. The reason is that such laws and the mathematics behind quantum theory and the existence of the universe can only exist (A) in the human mind, (B) independently in an immaterial realm of pure ideas, or (C) in a pre-existing transcendent mind (i.e., the mind of God).[203] The third option makes the only logical sense, for at least two reasons: First, options one and two necessarily make such laws and ideas a part of the universe, not something that pre-existed the universe; as such, they could not have created the universe itself. Second, although mathematics and "scientific laws" can *describe* the universe, they cannot *create* material reality. Our uniform experience of the relationship between mathematical and other ideas or principles and creation is that such immaterial concepts begin in the mind and by acts of intelligent design and volition produce entities that embody those ideas. Therefore, "*if* a realm of mathematical ideas and objects must preexist the universe, as quantum cosmology implies, then those ideas must have a transcendent mental source—they must reflect the contents of a pre-existing mind."[204]

Natural laws also do not preclude God's ongoing "active role" in the universe, including miracles. There are at least two reasons for this. First, the physical "laws of science" only apply in a "closed system." However, God's active role in the universe and any miracles he chooses to perform indicate that the universe is not a closed system; hence, God's intervention in the universe would not contravene natural law, because natural laws do not speak to the issue of what happens when the universe is not closed.[205] The fact that the universe had a temporal beginning means that the things of nature and the universe itself are not eternal. That alone indicates that the universe is not a "closed system."[206] Second, the realization that the universe is not a closed system is augmented by the development of quantum mechanics, which has changed scientific understanding and the "determinism" implied by the classical laws of physics. "Through QM [quantum mechanics] the

---

203. See Meyer, *Return*, 374.
204. Meyer, *Return*, 375.
205. Plantinga, *Where the Conflict*, 82–83; 130; Alston, "Divine Action," 50.
206. See Wiker, *Moral*, 293.

future of a system is not inherently predictable; there is profound freedom in the physical universe, and future states of a system can only be predicted with probability."[207] Because QM only assigns probabilities to the possible outcomes for a given set of initial conditions rather than determining specific outcomes, "even the most stunning miracles are not clearly inconsistent with the laws promulgated by science."[208] It is not contradictory to believe that an infinite power (God) can bring into existence that which did not previously exist; but it is contradictory to believe that nothing can cause something. In short, whereas naturalism is incapable of accounting for the existence and fine-tuning of the universe, Christian theism can. The existence and fine-tuning of the universe are succinctly summarized in Gen 1:1, "In the beginning God created the heavens and the earth."

NATURALISM CANNOT ACCOUNT FOR SUPERNATURAL EXPERIENCES

By definition, naturalism holds that there is no supernatural realm to existence; therefore, miracles and other supernatural phenomena such as direct communication from or manifestations of God or angels cannot occur. However, that begs the question of whether or not miracles and other supernatural experiences may occur by assuming in advance that there is no God or supernatural realm. Science has not and cannot prove any of this, because science can only assess natural, not supernatural, phenomena. If there is a creator God, then nothing is illogical about the possibility of miracles.

The Bible contains multiple accounts of miracles and other supernatural experiences. The biblical accounts of miracles fundamentally differ from other ancient miracle stories in ways that make the biblical accounts much more plausible. The biblical accounts do not on their face claim or appear to be myths, legends, or embellishments, but purport to be eyewitness accounts of real, historical events. We previously looked at Jesus' miracles, particularly his resurrection from the dead. Jesus' miracles are described as "signs" (see, e.g., John 2:11, 23; 3:2) that point to who Jesus is. It will not do to claim that the people in Jesus' day were ignorant or superstitious: they knew, just like we do, that dead men stay dead. The historical nature of the resurrection (and other miracles recorded in the Bible) is corroborated by the real, human reactions of fear (see Matt 28:4; Mark 4:41) and doubt (see

---

207. Cleaver, "Multiverse," 70.

208. Plantinga, *Where the Conflict*, 96; at pages 113–21 Plantinga proposes a means by which God regularly could act in special ways consistent with QM. See also Lewis, "Religion," 133; Cleaver, "Multiverse," 70.

Matt 28:17; Mark 16:11, 13; Luke 24:10–11, 36–41; John 20:24–25) experienced by some of the people who witnessed or heard of them. Yet even though the resurrection was contrary to their own personal experience and everything those early disciples had been taught and were predisposed to believe, they could not deny what they themselves saw and experienced. As a result, many of them ultimately suffered and died because of their testimony, without recanting, because they knew it was true.

The point is that if Jesus is who he says he is, i.e., God himself come to earth as a man, that fact validates the miracle accounts recorded in the Bible, because Jesus validated the OT, including its miracles, as the historically accurate and reliable word of God and authorized the same level of authority of the NT which was about to be written.[209] Consequently, we can know that God and the supernatural are real, and miracles and other supernatural experiences really do occur.

Miracles and supernatural phenomena are not limited to the Bible. If God exists, it is reasonable to assume that he will manifest himself from time to time to different people in different ways. In fact, an important reason why naturalism and atheism are untrue is the existence of multiple, credible accounts of supernatural manifestations and occurrences. These have been observed, experienced, and reported by millions of people of all walks of life, across the globe, throughout history. The only response that naturalists can make is that everyone—all those millions of people of every background—who claimed to witness or experience a miracle or some other supernatural event is either lying, hallucinating, or otherwise mistaken. As Keith Campbell puts it, "Naturalism requires that religious experience, and in particular mystical experience, be given a reductionist interpretation. Such experiences are regarded as unusual states of mind that have their own causes and consequences within the natural world, but do not provide any contact with, or insight into, a supernatural realm."[210] That is exactly Richard Dawkins' tactic to try to discount every claimed supernatural experience as madness, optical illusions, hallucinations, or the "simulation software in the brain" at work.[211] *Everyone? Every such experience?* That, like so many naturalistic explanations we have seen, strains credibility beyond the breaking point.[212] The only people who are skeptical about the existence of miracles or other supernatural phenomena are people who have never experienced

---

209. See Geisler, *Christian Apologetics,* 368–71; Corduan, "Why I Believe," 186–87; Gilbert, *Why Trust,* 134–42; Carter, "What Did Jesus."

210. Campbell, "Naturalism," 493.

211. Dawkins, *The God Delusion,* 87–92, 347–52.

212. See Moreland, *Scaling,* 231–40.

them. It is understandable to be skeptical about something completely outside of one's personal experience, but it is not a logical inference to thereby conclude that miracles or other supernatural phenomena do not exist and cannot occur. Again, such an inference or conclusion is begging the question by its *a priori* rejection of the possibility of the supernatural.

British philosopher C. D. Broad points out,

> The practical postulate which we go upon everywhere else is to treat cognitive claims as veridical [i.e., truthful; corresponding to facts; not illusory; real; actual; genuine] unless there be some positive reason to think them delusive. This, after all, is our only guarantee for believing that ordinary sense-perception is veridical. . . . I think it would be inconsistent to treat the experiences of religious mystics on different principles. So far as they agree they should be provisionally accepted as veridical unless there be some positive ground for thinking that they are not.[213]

The credibility of many of the accounts of supernatural experiences is seen, first, in their diversity: they are not limited to the uneducated and the poor, and they are not limited to one particular type of experience. Instead, supernatural phenomena are experienced by people of all educational and social levels all over the world, and the types of such experiences are likewise diverse. Second, probably most of the people who have had supernatural experiences were neither seeking them nor were they predisposed to believe in such things. Third, many people have paid a price for such experiences, but have not renounced or recanted their testimonies even though it would have been easy and to their advantage to do so.

Examples of all three of these characteristics are seen in the fact that "God is visiting . . . Muslims through dreams, visions, and answered prayers in the name of Jesus. Virtually everyone who has worked in ministry to Muslims can attest to the pervasive presence of the Holy Spirit."[214] David Garrison recounts one example of a Muslim man who had experienced a particular dream. One of Garrison's colleagues opened his Bible to the account of Christ's transfiguration which records that *"His face shone like the sun, and his clothes became as white as the light"* (Matt 17:1-2). The Muslim was startled and said, "That's the guy, the guy in my dreams! Who is this?"[215] Surveys of Muslims who have become Christians report that anywhere from approximately 25-60% of Muslim converts had had a supernatural experience such as a vision, dream, miraculous healing, specific answer to prayer,

---

213. Broad, *Religion*, 197.
214. Garrison, *A Wind*, 242.
215. Garrison, *A Wind*, 243.

Naturalism Cannot Account for Existence as It Is 207

or other supernatural communication.[216] These Muslim converts often pay the price of persecution, yet they maintain their testimony and faith.

Normal people of sound mind in all walks of life and circumstances have had supernatural experiences they were not expecting. The experiences are as varied as the circumstances. Many Christians have had a post-conversion deeper experience of God of being *"filled with the Spirit"* (Eph 5:18) or *"baptized with the Holy Spirit"* (Acts 1:5; see also Acts 2:1–4; 4:31; 10:44–47; 19:1–6). This experience has given them a joy, depth of character, and stability they had never previously known.[217] This experience of the Holy Spirit has occurred all over the world throughout the last 2000 years and has resulted in various supernatural manifestations of the Holy Spirit that have been experienced and observed by millions of people, many of whom had no predisposition to believe in such things.[218] For example, a businessman did not believe that miraculous healings or the supernatural gift of *"speaking in tongues"* (1 Cor 12:10) apply today; nevertheless, he received those gifts, and they changed his life. He paid the price for it in his church, which did not believe they apply today.[219]

Other supernatural manifestations of the Holy Spirit (and otherwise) are well-documented. A Russian soldier was forced to stand outside for four hours in -25° C. cold weather wearing only a summer uniform; his face became blue from the cold, and though "it was impossible that he did not freeze and beg for mercy," miraculously he was kept warm.[220] In a concentration camp during World War II, a small bottle of liquid vitamins continued to produce drops of vitamin every day long after it was physically possible to do so; it only stopped when the prisoners were provided vitamins from another source.[221] A woman was miraculously enabled to see and describe to the police people who were trapped, even though she had never met them and it was physically impossible for her to have seen them.[222] A soldier was able to call for help on his radio, which was heard and responded to, even though every component of the radio had just been destroyed by a

---

216. See Abdulahugi, "Factors," 157–66; Dunning, "Palestinian," 285–86; Greenham, "A Study," 166–67; *The Camel,* 2007: 50, 79–91; Naja, "A Jesus Movement," 27–29; Naja, "Sixteen Features," 155–60; Straehler, "Coming," 211; Woodberry and Shubin, "Muslims tell," I have had a dream.

217. See Lawson, *Deeper.*

218. See Lloyd-Jones, *Joy*; Frisbee and Sachs, *Not by Might.*

219. Hunt, *Confessions.*

220. Grant, *Vanya,* 54–59. The soldier, Ivan Moiseyev, had many other miraculous and supernatural experiences until he was finally martyred by his atheist superiors.

221. ten Boom and Sherrill, *The Hiding,* 184–85.

222. Editors, *His Mysterious,* 16–17.

grenade.²²³ During surgery, a four-year-old boy had a supernatural experience of leaving his body in which, among other things, he saw Jesus and heaven and learned things about people, living and dead, of which he had no previous knowledge and which he could not possibly have known any other way.²²⁴ A disembodied voice told a Muslim man in a Muslim-dominated country, which had only three known Christians in its 24-million people group, to "find Jesus, find the gospel." The man had never heard of Jesus and didn't know if "*Jesus* might be a fruit or a rock or a tree." He was then told, "Get out of bed, go over the mountains, and walk down the coast to _____ (a city where he had never been). When you get to that city at daybreak, you will see two men. When you see those men, ask them where _____ street is. They will show you the way. Walk up and down the street and look for this number. When you find the number, knock on the door. When the door opens, tell the person why you have come." He did so and was met by one of the only three Christians out of 24 million people, who explained the gospel and discipled the man, which changed his life in startling ways."²²⁵ Craig Blomberg includes multiple sources that catalogue or discuss thousands of documented miracles or other supernatural manifestations.²²⁶

Francis MacNutt reports thousands of cases of divine healings in response to prayer. He notes, "Many of these healings taken individually are ambiguous as proof; they can be explained in a variety of ways. . . . But I do believe that anyone who would come with me on retreat after retreat would see so many blessed by healings that he would see a cumulative body of evidence all pointing in the direction of an extraordinary power present, of a number of healings taking place well beyond the realm of chance occurrence."²²⁷ Blomberg personally witnessed two miraculous healings in response to prayer and reports that dozens of his friends and close acquaintances have experienced the same. He concludes, "It is less rational to affirm by a kind of religious faith, in spite of the empirical evidence, that all of us were lying or deceived, than to acknowledge the reality of the miracles."²²⁸ He also quotes British medical doctor Rex Gardner, who collected numerous instances of miraculous healings which were verified by eyewitnesses and medical documentation and concluded that if one is not prepared to

223. Editors, *His Mysterious*, 44–45.
224. Burpo, *Heaven*, 60–123.
225. Ripken, *The Insanity*, 266–68.
226. See Blomberg, *New Testament*, 663–715.
227. MacNutt, *Healing*, 22.
228. Blomberg, *New Testament*, 673n.26.

accept any evidence such as this, "then you had better face the fact that you have abandoned logical enquiry."[229]

Additionally, many people have had encounters with angels. Angels often convey God's message, comfort, or protect someone; the recipient of the angelic encounter may receive temporary extraordinary abilities; sometimes the person him- or herself does not see the angel, but others do.[230] For example, a girl who ran into the street in front of a speeding car was lifted up and gently placed unharmed on the other side of the street in a neighbor's yard; the couple in the car "told all the people who gathered on the lawn that they had seen Susan lifted into the air and over their car."[231] In another incident, a three-year-old child was standing on railroad tracks as a train approached; as the mother "raced from the house screaming her daughter's name, she suddenly saw a striking figure clothed in pure white, lifting Lisa off the tracks."[232] These events cannot be explained away as madness, optical illusions, hallucinations, or the working of the "simulation software in the brain." As we have seen in so many other areas, naturalism has no plausible explanation for the facts. The best explanation, and the only logical explanation, is that these truly are supernatural manifestations of God and/or supernatural beings.

Dawkins quotes David Hume that "no testimony is sufficient to establish a miracle, unless the testimony be of such a kind, that its falsehood would be more miraculous, than the fact, which it endeavours to establish."[233] Hume's and Dawkins' opinion is based on Hume's statement that "a miracle is a violation of the laws of nature; and as a firm and unalterable experience has established these laws, the proof against a miracle, from the very nature of the fact, is as entire as any argument from experience can possibly be imagined."[234] In other words, Hume and Dawkins only reject the possibility of miracles and supernatural experiences because they *a priori* accept naturalism and *a priori* reject the existence of the supernatural. Hence, their view really only begs the question. On the other hand, Ronald Nash points out, "The laws of nature are not rules that prescribe how God must act; they are simply expressions of how God has willed to act. When exceptional events occur, it means only that God has willed something different, but to compare this to what happens when a human being breaks a law is to set up

---

229. Garder, *Healing*, 165, quoted by Blomberg, *New Testament*, 673.
230. See MacDonald, *When Angels*, 43; Editors, *His Mysterious*.
231. MacDonald, *When Angels*, 86.
232. MacDonald, *When Angels*, 3.
233. Dawkins, *The God Delusion*, 91, quoting Hume, *An Enquiry*, 10.1.13.
234. Hume, *An Enquiry*, 10.1.13.

a false analogy."[235] Indeed, to God, there are no "miracles" at all. It takes no more effort for God to miraculously heal someone or even raise the dead than to do anything else. If one is not close-minded to considering the evidence, like Hume and Dawkins are, the logical conclusion is that the *absence* of the possibility and existence of miracles "would be more miraculous" than the existence of miracles themselves. As Hamlet said, "*There are more things in heaven and earth, Horatio, than are dreamt of in your philosophy.*"[236]

NATURALISM CANNOT ACCOUNT FOR POST-DEATH EXPERIENCES

Given the principles of naturalism, William Provine states, "Humans are complex organic machines that die completely with no survival of soul or psyche."[237] Elsewhere he added, "There is no life after death. When I die I am absolutely certain that I am going to be dead. That's the end of me. . . . I don't have any kind of soul. My brain is a physical, chemical bundle of material stuff, and when it ceases to have its blood supply, my consciousness and my awareness will disappear. I will never be conscious again at that point. I'll just die, I'll just rot and that will be the end of it."[238] Stephen Hawking agreed, "I think belief in an afterlife is just wishful thinking. There is no reliable evidence for it, and it flies in the face of everything we know in science. I think that when we die we return to dust."[239]

What Provine and Hawking say has to be true if naturalism is true. However, as with every other subject we have discussed, naturalism is not true. Even ancient Greek philosopher Epicurus who, as with Provine and Hawking, believed that death amounted to annihilation of the person, reportedly admitted, "If we could be sure that death was annihilation, then there would be no fear of it. . . . But we cannot be totally sure there is annihilation, for what people fear most is not that maybe death is annihilation, but that maybe death is not."[240] Philosopher William Rowe (a nonbeliever) uses the analogy of a person enclosed in a room with only one window; he points out, "The mere fact that the mind is dependent on the functioning of the brain *while it (the mind) is associated with a living body* is no more proof that the mind will cease functioning at bodily death than is the fact that the

---

235. Nash, *Faith*, 243; see also Plantinga, *Where the Conflict*, 82–83, 130.
236. Shakespeare, "Hamlet," act 1; scene 5.
237. Provine, "Scientists," 1.
238. Provine and Johnson, "Debate," 9, 1.
239. Hawking, *Brief Answers*, 38.
240. Simmons III, "The Eternal," n.p.

person is dependent on the window *while she is in the room* proof that when the room and window are no more the person will cease having experiences of the outside world."[241]

There have been hundreds of accounts of "near-death" experiences (NDEs). One recent study, led by researchers at NYU Grossman School of Medicine at 25 hospitals in the US and UK, looked at over 500 people whose hearts stopped beating while hospitalized, were seemingly unconscious, and were on the brink of death. According to the study, "Survivors reported having unique lucid experiences, including a perception of separation from the body, observing events without pain or distress, and a meaningful evaluation of life, including of their actions, intentions and thoughts toward others. The researchers found these experiences of death to be different from hallucinations, delusions, illusions, dreams or CPR-induced consciousness."[242] Tests identified measurable electrical signs of lucid and heightened brain activity. Lead investigator Sam Parnia, MD, PhD said "These lucid experiences cannot be considered a trick of a disordered or dying brain, but rather a unique human experience that emerges on the brink death."[243] This is at least circumstantial evidence of *something* beyond this existence.

Beyond "near death" experiences, there is good, direct evidence of actual post-death experiences. Judy Bachrach states in her book *Glimpsing Heaven: The Stories and Science of Life After Death* (2014), "On this subject—the issue of recollections of incidents or images or encounters that could only have occurred or been seen during clinical death—there are simply, as some of the doctors and scientists I've interviewed point out, too many experiencers and too many experiences to discount."[244] These accounts are from "tens of thousands of reported cases" of people who have not simply had "near-death" experiences but "those who have actually died, however briefly," those who have observed the dead and then heard and confirmed as accurate their stories after the dead person came back to life, and those who examine and research the subject of what occurs after life is extinguished.[245]

241. Rowe, *Philosophy*, 159, emph. in orig.

242. NYU Grossman, "Lucid," n.p. Professor of Neurological Surgery and Pediatrics, Michael Egnor, similarly notes that, although multiple materialistic explanations for NDEs have been posited, none of them is credible, each accounts for only a small part of the experience of many individuals, and each is inconsistent with many aspects of the experience; he concludes that the explanation "most consistent with the data available on NDEs, is that some of these experiences are manifestations of persistence of mind despite cessation of brain activity." Egnor, "Neuroscience," 256. In short, the mind is not limited to the physical brain; thus, materialism is false.

243. NYU Grossman, "Lucid," n.p.; see also Moody, *Life*, 16, 21–23, 156–77.

244. Bachrach, *Glimpsing*, 18; see also the documentary film *After Death* (2023).

245. Bachrach, *Glimpsing*, 18, 19.

As is true with those who have had supernatural experiences, those who had conscious experiences after actually dying "weren't delusional or crazy, although a lot of them were concerned their old friends would think them so. They had been pretty ordinary, most of them, until their unplanned travels led them elsewhere."[246]

Bachrach's book (there are other, similar books) recounts many instances of the conscious experiences of people who had, in fact, died. These reports are from men, women, and children, from different backgrounds and different religions, including atheists, who had died in different ways (during surgery, hit by lightning, drowning, etc.), had been dead for varying periods of time, and had varying post-death experiences. One example is a Dutch man who, according to his doctor, arrived at the hospital "clinically dead: 'blue—cold, no breathing, no gag reflexes, no blood pressure, no brain stem reflexes, his eyes didn't react to light.'"[247] Nevertheless, the hospital staff intubated him, a 90-minute surgery was performed, and he was transferred to the intensive care unit, where he remained in a coma for a week. Surprisingly, he recovered (which his doctor called a "miracle") and even was able to accurately describe where the nurse had stashed his dentures after she had removed them in order to intubate him when he was dead.[248] Dr. Raymond Moody (who coined the term "near-death experience") adds that "several doctors have told me . . . that they are utterly baffled about how patients with no medical knowledge could describe in such detail and so correctly the procedures used in resuscitation attempts, even though these events took place while the doctors knew the patients involved to be 'dead.'"[249]

The International Association for Near-Death Studies, Inc. (IANDS) has thousands of such reports, as has the Near-Death Experience Research Foundation (NDERF). Jeffery Long, MD reports on a study of hundreds of near-death and post-death experiences of people from non-Western countries and cultures and from different religions. He states, "Near-death experiences occur at a time when the person is so physically compromised that they are typically unconscious, comatose, *or clinically dead.* Considering NDEs from both a medical perspective and logically, it should not be possible for unconscious people to often report highly lucid experiences that are clear and logically structured."[250] He adds, "The high percentage of accurate out-of-body observations during near-death experiences does

---

246. Bachrach, *Glimpsing*, 20.
247. Bachrach, *Glimpsing*, 85.
248. Bachrach, *Glimpsing*, 85–86.
249. Moody, *Life*, 99.
250. Long, "Near-Death," Results suggesting, emph. added.

not seem explainable by any possible physical brain function as it is currently known."251 Long concludes, "Multiple lines of evidence point to the conclusion that near-death experiences are medically inexplicable and cannot be explained by known physical brain function. Many of the preceding lines of evidence would be remarkable if they were reported by a group of individuals during conscious experiences. However, NDErs [near-death experiencers] are generally unconscious *or clinically dead* at the time of their experiences and should not have any lucid organized memories from their time of unconsciousness."252

Bachrach concludes, "A 21st-century evolutionary argument doesn't hold much water here. After all, evolution is about thriving, succeeding in life. What advantage is there in having a pleasurable journey into death? Also, not all death experiences are pleasant. . . . Science finds itself up against experiences that cannot be observed or measured."253 These multiple near- and post-death experiences demonstrate that consciousness and personhood exist and continue after a person dies. As such, they absolutely contradict naturalism.

CONCLUSION

We have seen that, at every level, naturalism cannot account for reality; in fact, naturalism is contradictory to existence as it is. Naturalism is self-referentially incoherent—in other words, it is self-refuting and cannot even account for itself. Although a large number of scientists have a completely naturalistic or materialistic worldview, naturalistic science cannot account for the origin of the universe, the origin of life, the origin of mind, or morality. It cannot account for the thousands of plausible cases of supernatural experiences and conscious post-death experiences. Such experiences directly contradict the naturalistic or materialistic worldview.

Since, as we have seen, naturalism or materialism cannot account for existence, only supernaturalism can. There must, therefore, have been a supernatural creator outside of space, time, and the material universe, who brought creation into existence. What must be the characteristics of the one who brought existence into being? William Lane Craig points out that, if the universe did not create itself but was created by causal agency outside of

---

251. Long, "Near-Death," Line of Evidence #2.
252. Long, "Near-Death," Conclusion of Study, emph. added.
253. Bachrach, *Glimpsing*, 98; see also Gary Habermas's detailed analysis of 300 documented and corroborated cases of NDEs, including cases where the heart and brain were non-functional or had flatlined. Habermas, "Evidential," 323–56.

time, space, and matter, there are certain features that such a creator must possess. These include changelessness and immateriality ("since timelessness entails changelessness, and changelessness implies immateriality"), being uncaused and beginningless, and unimaginable power. Further, such a being must be a personal being with mind, because

> If the cause of the origin of the universe were an impersonal set of necessary and sufficient conditions, it would be impossible for the cause to exist without its effect. For if the necessary and sufficient conditions of the effect are timelessly given, then their effect must be given as well. The only way for the cause to be timeless and changeless but for its effect to originate *de novo* a finite time ago is for the cause to be a personal agent who freely chooses to bring about an effect without antecedent determining conditions. Thus, we are brought, not merely to a transcendent cause of the universe, but to its personal creator.[254]

The universe includes both non-living and living matter, impersonal beings and personality (i.e., beings that have consciousness, perception, self-awareness). Additionally, unity (with an underlying rationality that can be perceived and studied) and diversity (particularity, individuation) are found at all levels of the universe. That is true for living and non-living beings and from the atomic level to the largest star systems in the universe. This in turn raises the issue of the origin and relationship of unity and diversity (or as it is also called, "the one and the many"), including such questions as: How do we know the many do not exist simply as unrelated particulars? and How can we obtain a unity that does not destroy the particulars?

The pantheistic notion of the divine cannot account for existence. Pantheism is based on the philosophy of monism which holds that "all is one." Pantheistic religion or philosophy holds that "the metaphysical and the real are thoroughly merged. It upholds the unity of the macrocosm and the microcosm."[255] In other words, pantheistic monism asserts that the "divine" is not a supernatural being outside of space, time, and the universe, but that the divine "god" (*Brahman*) is essentially *impersonal*, and the divine and nature (the universe and all its components) are one.[256] Consequently, pantheism cannot explain the origin and nature of the universe for reasons that similarly eliminate naturalism as an adequate explanation. First, because the "god" of pantheism is a part of and, indeed, is coextensive with, the

---

254. Craig, "The Ultimate," The Supernaturalist Alternative; see also Moreland, *Scaling*, 41–42.

255. Vohra, "Metaphysical," 94.

256. See Ferm, ed., *An Encyclopedia*, 557–58.

physical universe, such a god could not bring the physical universe into being from nothing physical, since such a god is not independent of the physical universe.[257] Second, the fact that the universe is finite and had a temporal beginning also rules out pantheism as the cause. The reason is that, if at some point in time the physical universe did not exist, the god of pantheism would not have existed, because such a god is part of and coextensive with the physical universe. Hence, if such a god did not exist, it could not cause the physical universe to exist.[258]

Third, pantheism cannot account for the "fine-tuning" of the universe. Fine-tuning was established at the beginning of the universe. This would require a *pre-existent* intelligent cause. However, pantheism's "god" is impersonal and does not pre-exist the universe, since *Brahman* and the universe are one. Since the "god" of pantheism is not a pre-existing intelligence, such a god is inadequate to have brought the finely-tuned universe into existence.[259] Fourth, pantheistic monism cannot account for personality because Brahman is "a formless, abstract, eternal being without personal attributes."[260] Finally, pantheistic monism also cannot coherently account for diversity-particularity-the many. In fact, pantheistic monism asserts that diversity-particularity-the many is an illusion (*maya*), since "all is one."[261]

Islam's Allah also cannot account for existence as it is. First, the basic Islamic confession is that Allah is "one." However, his "oneness" is a simplistic, monolithic singularity. This necessarily means that Allah is an *insufficient being who is dependent upon creation*. The reason is that Allah would have *needed* to create other beings in order to have any sort of relationship. The fact that Allah is only a "bare unity" that lacks intrinsic plurality necessarily means that he "cannot function without the supplementation supplied by the plurality of the world."[262] As a simplistic singularity Allah could account for unity within the universe but is inconsistent with diversity.

Second, Allah is an *impersonal* being (like a force or a force-field), not a personal one. This flows in part from his single, solitary nature. Because of his simplistic unitary nature, Allah did not and *could not have any relationship* until he created other beings with whom he could then be in relationship; he could not *experience or express* any "personal" or "relational"

---

257. See Meyer, *Return*, 257.
258. See Meyer, *Return*, 257.
259. See Meyer, *Return*, 277.
260. Van de Weghe, *Prepared*, 358; see also Smith, *The Religions*, 121–22.
261. See Smith, 1958: 82–84.
262. Frame, *Cornelius Van Til*, 64; see also Schaeffer, *He Is There*, 289 (Allah "needed to create in order to love and communicate"; consequently, Allah "needed the universe as much as the universe needed [him]").

attribute unless and until he created the world. Consequently, none of the "personal" or "relational" attributes *are, or could be, an intrinsic part* of Allah's being. A force or force-field or any impersonal entity *cannot create, relate to, or have relationship with "personality" or "personal" beings.* The Hadith reflects the impersonality of Allah by saying that Allah "created" mercy when he created the world.[263] Because it is "created," mercy is not an intrinsic part of Allah's essential being. Thus, while each surah except surah 9 begins by calling Allah "merciful," those statements are not telling us anything about Allah's essential nature. Another hadith says, "Allah created Satan, and he created good and created evil."[264] Because it is "created," goodness is not an intrinsic part of Allah's essential being (nor is evil intrinsic to his essential being). The fact that neither good nor evil are intrinsic to Allah's essential being confirms that intrinsically he is an *impersonal* being, since both good and evil, as well as mercy, are inherently personal attributes.

Additionally, the Islamic teaching that Allah is unknowable is a reflection of his impersonal nature. Abu Ḥamid Muḥammad ibn Muḥammad Al-Ghazali (1058–1111), one of the most famous Islamic theologians and philosophers, wrote extensively on the subject of the utter uniqueness and difference of Allah, saying, "He is not like anything nor is anything like Him"; "His attributes are unlike those of any creature just as His Essence unlike the essence of any created thing"; "(one must) deny similarity (between God and other things) absolutely"; "God's knowledge is absolutely unlike that of His creatures"; "These Names [of Allah] are like the corresponding attributes of Adam (i.e. man) in name only, the uttered word"; and Allah's attributes are "above [men's] attributes of perfection just as He is above their attributes of imperfection, nay of every attribute conceivable by men, as well as what is like it (the attribute) or similar to it."[265] Professor Fadlou Shehadi, who has analyzed Ghazali's work in depth, concludes,

> If God [Allah] is a unique kind of being unlike any other being in any respect, more specifically, unlike anything known to man, it would have to follow by Ghazali's own principles that *God is utterly unknowable.* For, according to Ghazali, things are known by their likenesses, and what is utterly unlike what is known to man cannot be known. Furthermore, God would have to be unknowable, completely unknowable, not only to the 'man in the

---

263. Muslim, *Sahih*, 2752b; see also 2753c; al-Bukhari, *Sahih*, 6469; at-Tirmidhi, *Jami' at-Tirmidhi* 3541; Ibn Majah, *Sunan*, vol. 5, book 37, no. 4294.

264. Abi Dawud, *Sunan*, 4618.

265. Shehadi, *Ghazali's Unique*, 17–18, quoting various works of Ghazali.

street', but to prophets and mystics as well. This is a conclusion that Ghazali states very explicitly and not infrequently.[266]

As Muslim apologist Yahiya Emerick admits, "He [Allah] does not reveal Himself to people."[267] Personality cannot come from impersonality. In short, as an essentially impersonal being, Allah cannot account for the personality of human beings, since human beings are "personal" beings.

Christianity alone, unlike the atheism of naturalism, the "god" of pantheism, or the Allah of Islam, provides a coherent account of epistemology, existence, and ethics. The God of the Bible meets all of the requirements of a creator as listed above by William Lane Craig. Additionally, as we have discussed, the God of the Bible meets the requirements to provide the basis for by which we can trust our minds and also provides the only adequate ground for morality. Finally, the God of the Bible is Trinity, i.e., one God in three persons (Father, Son, and Holy Spirit).[268] This is unlike the "god" of pantheism and the Allah of Islam and is important, because only such a God can create and explain existence as it is. The reason is that, to account for existence as it is, consisting of unity and diversity along with personality, the cause must be at least as great as the universe and its components.[269] Cornelius Van Til points out that, because he is Trinity, "In God the one and the many are equally ultimate. Unity in God is no more fundamental than diversity, and diversity in God is no more fundamental than unity. The persons of the Trinity are mutually exhaustive of one another. The Son and the Spirit are ontologically [i.e., in the nature of their existence or being] on par with the Father."[270]

Christianity alone can account for abstract universals and the regularity and uniformity of nature, because God is the creator of nature and all of existence. God is truth (John 14:6), he knows the end from the beginning (Isa 46:10), and he is not a God of confusion (1 Cor 14:33). Francis Schaeffer puts it like this: in order to have a cause sufficient to account for existence, "we need two things. We need a personal-infinite God (or an infinite-personal God), and we need a personal unity and diversity in God."[271] Only "the Judeo-Christian content to the word *God* as given in the Old and New Testaments does meet the need of what exists—the existence of the universe in its complexity and of man as man. And what is that content? It relates to

---

266. Shehadi, *Ghazali's Unique*, 21–22, emph. in orig.
267. Emerick, *Understanding*, 49.
268. See chapter 2, n.30.
269. Wood, *The Trinity*, 22–23.
270. Van Til, *The Defense*, 25.
271. Schaeffer, *He Is There*, 286.

an infinite-personal God, who is personal unity and diversity on the high order of Trinity.... Without the high order of personal unity and diversity as given in the Trinity, *there are no answers.*"²⁷² Only the triune God of the Bible is an adequate cause for and explanation of existence as it is, including its unity, diversity, and personality. Unlike Allah, the Trinity "is not a blank unity, which would be impersonal. Rather, he is a unity of persons."²⁷³ As Nathan Wood says, "Triunity in the image of the Triune God is the principle and explanation of the universe. It is the organizing principle of all things. It is the structure and pattern of the universe."²⁷⁴ "The truth of Christianity is that it is true to what is there."²⁷⁵

In short, as philosopher Richard Swinburne points out, scientists, historians, and detectives all observe and analyze evidence to determine what account best explains the data. Using those same criteria, we see that the existence of God explains all that we observe, not simply some of the data. As Swinburne observes, the existence of God

> explains the fact that there is a universe at all, that scientific laws operate within it, that it contains conscious animals and humans with very complex intricately organized bodies, that we have abundant opportunities for developing ourselves and the world, as well as the more particular data that humans report miracles and have religious experiences. In so far as scientific causes and laws explain some of these things (and in part they do), these very causes and laws need explaining, and God's action explains them. The very same criteria which scientists use to reach their own theories lead us to move beyond those theories to a creator God who sustains everything in existence.²⁷⁶

Recognizing that the triune God of the Bible is the one who designed, fine-tuned, and called the universe into existence and created the different kinds of living organisms on earth does not represent a "science stopper." The issue is not (and should not be) what naturalistic or materialistic hypothesis best explains the existence of the universe and life as we know them, but "What actually caused the universe and its fine tuning, and life and its fine tuning, to come into existence?"²⁷⁷ Isaac Newton's belief in God

---

272. Schaeffer, *He Is There*, 287–88, emph. in orig.
273. Frame, *Cornelius Van Til*, 65.
274. Wood, *The Trinity*, 103.
275. Schaeffer, *He Is There*, 290.
276. Swinburne, *Is There*, 2.
277. This question is fundamental and goes to the essential nature of science itself and the difference between science and "scientism," i.e., "the opinion that science and

Naturalism Cannot Account for Existence as It Is 219

as the source and sustainer of mathematically describable order in the universe and the intelligent designer of living organisms and the solar system inspired his scientific research and led him to formulate his theory of universal gravity, to discover the three laws of motion, invent the calculus, construct the first reflecting telescope, develop the binomial theorem, infer the oblate shape of the sphere of the earth, and conduct a detailed study of the nature of light.[278] There is no reason to believe that explicitly recognizing the necessary existence of God and his role in creating and sustaining the universe will threaten science or scientific research today. On the contrary, for scientists to recognize the necessary existence of God should "inspire deeper interest in discovering more about the intricacy, order, and design of the universe, just as it did for Newton himself."[279]

---

the scientific method are the best or only way to render truth about the world and reality." "Scientism," *Wikipedia*, Introduction; see also Gay, *The Way*, 88–89. On the other hand, as Lewis Mumford has stated, "what the physical sciences call the world is not the total object of common human experience: it is just those aspects of this experience that lend themselves to accurate factual observation and to generalized statements." Mumford, *Technics*, 46–47.

278. See again chapter 10n.161 regarding the many famous scientists whose research specifically was motivated by various statements in the Bible, and/or wrote on the compatibility of science and the Bible.

279. Meyer, *Return*, 430.

Part 3

The Problem of Evil

12

The Problem of Evil

God's Sovereignty, Humanity's Responsibility, and the Existence of Sin and Evil

IN HIS *DIALOGUES CONCERNING NATURAL RELIGION*, David Hume stated the classic "problem of evil" concerning God: "Is he willing to prevent evil, but not able? then is he impotent. Is he able, but not willing? then is he malevolent. Is he both able and willing? whence then is evil?"[1] Or, to put it in the form of a logical syllogism: "[1] If God exists, then he is omnipotent and perfectly good; a perfectly good being would eliminate evil as far as it could; there is no limit to what an omnipotent being can do; therefore, if God exists, there would be no evil in the world; [2] there is evil in the world; [3] therefore, God does not exist."[2] This leads to the issue of theodicy

---

1. Hume, *Dialogues*, part 10, 186.

2. Sherry, "Problem," The problem; see also Erlandson, "A New Perspective," The Anti-theist Cannot Generate. This is what is known as the logical problem of evil. Leading atheist spokesman William Rowe admits, however, that "no one, I think, has succeeded in establishing such an extravagant claim. Indeed, . . . there is a fairly compelling argument for the view that the existence of evil is logically consistent with the existence of the theistic God." Rowe, "The problem," 10n.1. Other prominent atheists agree: Draper, "Pain," 26n.1 ("I agree with most philosophers of religion that theists face no serious logical problem of evil"); Gale, "Some Difficulties," 206 ("Almost everyone now believes that adequate defenses have now been devised to neutralize this challenge"); Mackie, *The Miracle*, 150 ("There is no explicit contradiction between the statements that there is an omnipotent and wholly good god and that there is evil"), 154 ("The problem of evil does not, after all, show that the central doctrines of theism are logically inconsistent with one another"). Patrick Sherry notes that the logical argument against God "does not recognize cases in which eliminating one evil causes another to arise or in which the existence of a particular evil entails some good state of affairs that morally outweighs it. Moreover, there may be logical limits to what an omnipotent being can or cannot do. Most skeptics, therefore, have taken the reality of evil as evidence that

or "justifying God," i.e., explaining how God can be perfectly good, omniscient, and omnipotent and yet ordain and permit evil.[3]

God is sovereign over all of creation; he is omniscient and infinitely wise. Therefore, he knows infinitely more than we do about how everything is fitting together. Since he is eternal and his plan takes everything into account, his timeframe and scope of reference are vastly greater than ours. Nonbelieving philosophers start with the fact of rampant evil and ask, "How can God—if there is a God—ordain or allow this?" Even raising the "problem of evil" indicates that the person has abandoned orthodox Christian beliefs for an essentially secular worldview. Indeed, the "problem of evil" never had the appeal it has to many today before the Enlightenment with its non- and anti-theistic presuppositions and worldview.[4] On the other hand, by putting God first—and by putting *what we know to be true about God* as our starting point—we can understand, by faith-based-on-fact, that God's existence, omnipotence, omniscience, wisdom, and goodness are all

---

God's existence is unlikely rather than impossible." Sherry, "Problem," The problem. This latter view, known as the "inductive" or "evidential" problem of evil, claims that the existence of evil, while not logically incompatible with the existence of an omnipotent and good God, is evidence that God "probably" does not exist. "It is now acknowledged on (almost) all sides that the logical argument is bankrupt, but the inductive argument is still very much alive and kicking" Alston, "The Inductive," 97.

3. Technically, a theodicy purports to give the actual reason why God has ordained and allowing evil to exist. A defense gives only possible reasons why God may have ordained and allowed evil to exist instead of preventing it. "As long as that possible explanation does remove the alleged inconsistency internal to the theist's system, the theist meets the demands of the logical form of the problem of evil." Feinberg, *The Many Faces*, 19; see also Keller, *Walking*, 95. In such a case, the heaviest burden of proof is on the atheist, since he or she began the debate by attacking and trying to prove something about theism; on the other hand, if the theist attempts to prove a full theodicy, he or she will bear a heavier burden than simply mounting a defense. Feinberg, *The Many Faces*, 205, 283–84; Keller, *Walking*, 95–96. It should be noted that some writers use the term "theodicy" to refer both to full theodicies and to defenses.

From a biblical standpoint, however, the entire "problem of evil" is actually backwards. The real issue is not "How can God's allowing sin and evil be justified to people?" but "How can sinful, evil people be justified to a holy God?" God's holiness is foundational. Sin is incompatible with his holiness. Indeed, "God is not indifferent to our immoral thoughts and behaviour. On the contrary, his holy nature is deeply offended by such things. As a perfect God, he cannot ignore anything evil. The smallest lie is an offense to the One who is truth. The tiniest feeling of animosity towards another person is repulsive to the One who is love. Due to his holy and perfect nature God cannot turn a blind eye to perverse human behaviour as if it does not matter." Alexander, *From Eden*, 130. Consequently, God will judge all evil and evildoers. See Rom 2:16; 2 Cor 5:10; Heb 9:27; Rev 20:10–15.

4. See Keller, *Walking*, 86–87; Erlandson, "A New Perspective," Countering Objections ("The only way in which evil provides counter-evidence to the God of the Bible is through prior acceptance of anti-theistic presuppositions.").

still intact and are not affected by the existence of widespread evil, suffering, and injustice. That being said, let us deal with the problem of evil and the issue of theodicy in somewhat more detail, since these are profoundly important issues.

A GOOD, OMNIPOTENT GOD IS NECESSARY TO EVEN TALK COHERENTLY ABOUT GOOD AND EVIL

God is holy, just, righteous, and good (e.g., Gen 18:25; Exod 34:6–7; Lev 11:44; Job 34:10–12; Ps 136:1; 145:17; Hab 1:13; Jas 1:13), yet sin and evil exist. Many people find it difficult to reconcile how God can be entirely good and absolutely sovereign yet reign over a world containing sin and evil. However, the argument against God assumes that some things are, in fact, objectively evil: "To say something is evil is to make a moral judgment, and moral judgments make no sense outside of the context of a moral standard. . . . Evil can't be real if morals are relative. Evil is real, though. That's why people object to it. Therefore, objective moral standards must exist as well."[5]

With respect to the different possible *sources* of moral standards, good and evil, "a morally perfect God is the only adequate standard . . . that makes sense of the existence of evil to begin with."[6] In other words, there needs to be an adequate standard for determining whether something is good or evil, right or wrong, moral or immoral—and the only adequate ground and standard is God.[7] Even atheist, Marxist, existentialist philosopher Jean-Paul Sartre recognized this:

> The existentialist . . . finds it extremely embarrassing that God does not exist, for there disappears with Him all possibility of finding values in an intelligible heaven. There can no longer be any good *a priori* [i.e., a general truth valid in the mind independent of observation or experience], since there is no infinite and perfect consciousness to think it. It is nowhere written that "the good" exists, that one must be honest or must not lie, since we are now upon the plane where there are only men. Dostoevsky

---

5. Koukl, "Evil as Evidence," The presence of evil.

6. Koukl, *Tactics*, 138; see also Koukl, "Evil as Evidence," One remaining Answer; Lewis, *Mere Christianity*, 45–46; Craig, "The Indispensability," 9–12.

7. On the other hand, prolific author and atheist professor Richard Dawkins frankly states that "nature is not cruel, only pitilessly indifferent. This is one of the hardest lessons for humans to learn. We cannot admit that things might be neither good nor evil, neither cruel nor kind, but simply callous—indifferent to all suffering, lacking all purpose." Dawkins, *River*, 96, 133.

> once wrote: "If God did not exist, everything would be permitted". . . . Everything is indeed permitted if God does not exist, and man is in consequence forlorn, for he cannot find anything to depend upon either within or outside himself. . . . Nor, on the other hand, if God does not exist, are we provided with any values or commands that could legitimise our behaviour. Thus we have neither behind us, nor before us in a luminous realm of values, any means of justification or excuse.[8]

Non-Christian philosopher and ethicist Richard Taylor similarly admits, "The modern age, more or less repudiating the idea of a divine lawgiver, has nevertheless tried to retain the ideas of moral right and wrong, without noticing that, in casting God aside, they have also abolished the conditions of meaningfulness for moral right and wrong as well. . . . The concept of moral obligation [is] unintelligible apart from the idea of God."[9]

The consequences of this are twofold: (1) By casting aside God and his Word, i.e., the only adequate basis for right and wrong and moral obligation, we have brought sin and evil on ourselves, and God rightly holds us accountable for it. (2) The "problem of evil" is a far greater problem for atheists and other unbelievers in the God of the Bible than it is for Christians. Nonbelievers have no rational, adequate, and coherent (i.e., internally consistent; not self-contradictory) basis to claim that *any* human law or action is truly, objectively, or universally unjust, wrong, or evil—however much they oppose it and however harmful, exploitative, selfish, or deadly such a law or action may be. Thus, nonbelievers may believe and speak as though certain activities (racism; child abuse) are wrong in-and-of-themselves. However, they also—inconsistently—profess the underlying belief that the individual (or the culture) can determine ethical values for themselves. This underlying belief vitiates the idea that those who are racists or child abusers are actually doing anything wrong, since they are merely acting in conformity with the values their have chosen for themselves.

The unbeliever thus is both internally inconsistent and supplies the premises that permit and condone the very acts which the unbeliever condemns as evil. The only way that the unbeliever can think and contend that some acts are evil and wrong in-and-of-themselves is to

> secretly *rely upon* the Christian worldview in order to make sense of his argument from the existence of evil which is *urged against* the Christian worldview! Antitheism presupposes theism to make its case. The problem of evil is thus a logical

---

8. Sartre, "Existentialism,": n.p.
9. Taylor, *Ethics*, 2–3, 84.

problem for the unbeliever, rather than the believer.... The non-Christian's worldview (of whatever variety) eventually cannot account for such moral outrage. It cannot explain the objective and unchanging nature of moral notions like good or evil. Thus the problem of evil is precisely a philosophical problem for unbelief.[10]

Paradoxically, therefore, the existence of evil actually is an argument *for* the existence of God. In a debate with an atheist, William Lane Craig put this in the form of a logical syllogism: "1. If God does not exist, objective moral values do not exist. 2. Objective moral values do exist. 3. Therefore, God exists."[11] Christian philosopher Alvin Plantinga summarizes, "A naturalistic way of looking at the world ... has no place for genuine moral obligation of any sort; a fortiori, then, it has no place for such a category as horrifying wickedness.... Accordingly, if you think there really is such a thing as horrifying wickedness (that our sense that there is, is not a mere illusion of some sort), and if you also think the main options are theism and naturalism, then you have a powerful theistic argument from evil [i.e., that God exists]."[12]

C. S. Lewis recognized that this issue goes far beyond atheism's inability to account for the existence of right and wrong, good and evil, and moral obligations but strikes at the very heart of atheism itself. In *Mere Christianity* Lewis (himself a former atheist) wrote, "My argument against God was that the universe seemed so cruel and unjust. But how had I got this idea of *just* and *unjust*? A man does not call a line crooked unless he has some idea of a straight line.... Of course I could have given up my idea of justice by saying it was nothing but a private idea of my own. But if I did that, then my argument against God collapsed too—for the argument depended on saying

---

10. Bahnsen, "The Problem," 15–16, emph. in orig. C. S. Lewis pointed out that even dualism, i.e., two equal, uncreated powers, one good and the other bad, does not provide an adequate ground for objective right and wrong, good and evil, and moral obligation. The reason is that "Dualism gives evil a positive, substantive, self-consistent nature, like that of good.... In what sense can the one party be said to be right and the other wrong? If evil has the same kind of reality as good, the same autonomy and completeness, our allegiance to good becomes the arbitrarily chosen loyalty of a partisan." Lewis, "Religion," 22–23. W. Gary Crampton adds, "In actuality, the philosophic system called dualism is absurd. If there were two co-eternal and co-equal deities, we could not say that one was good and one evil. That is, without a superior standard to determine what is good and evil, good and evil cannot be predicated of anything. But if there is such a superior standard (that is, something above the two deities), then there is no ultimate dualism." Crampton, "A Biblical," 2n.6. Only Christian monotheism provides an adequate basis for good and evil.

11. Craig and Sinnott-Armstrong, *God?*, 19.

12. Plantinga, "A Christian Life," 73.

that the world was really unjust, not simply that it did not happen to please my private fancies."[13] Thus, atheism is self-refuting.

If there is no supernatural existence, i.e., if the physical universe is all there is and we are merely products of physical and chemical reactions (usually called naturalism, materialism, or physicalism)[14]—which atheism inherently entails—then this view of existence "breaks down at the problem of knowledge. If thought is the undesigned and irrelevant product of cerebral motions, what reason have we to trust it?"[15] Lewis elaborated that elsewhere: "If naturalism were true then all thoughts whatever [including all ideas that anything is good, evil, right, or wrong] would be wholly the result of irrational causes. Therefore, all thoughts would be equally worthless. If it is true, then we can know no truths. It cuts its own throat."[16] Similar views have been expressed by others, including notable Christian and non-Christian scientists and philosophers.[17]

THE INVALIDITY OF THE ATHEISTIC ARGUMENTS FROM THE EXISTENCE OF EVIL

The Christian can have confidence that the existence of evil is not evidence against either God's existence *or his goodness,* because God has a morally sufficient reason for ordaining and permitting every act of evil even though he may not have revealed that reason to us. As Greg Bahnsen states, because the Christian presupposes that, as the Bible states, God is perfectly holy and good, "when the Christian observes evil events or things in the world, he can and should retain consistency with his presupposition about God's goodness by now *inferring* that God has a *morally good reason* for the evil that exists. . . . God has planned evil events for reasons which are morally commendable and good."[18] Or, as Doug Erlandson puts it, "A being is not

---

13. Lewis, *Mere Christianity,* 45–46.

14. J. P. Moreland defines naturalism as follows: "The three major components to naturalism are 1) scientism — the belief that scientific knowledge is either the only form of knowledge or a vastly superior form of knowledge; 2) the belief that the atomic theory of matter and the theory of evolution explain all events; and 3) the belief that non-physical things don't exist and that the world isn't here for any purpose." Moreland, "What is," n.p.

15. Lewis, "The Laws," 21.

16. Lewis, "Religion," 137; see also Lewis, *Miracles,* 17–36.

17. See Lucas, *The Freedom,* 114–16 (see at 116n.1 for others who have articulated the same point); Moreland, *Scaling,* 77–103; Nagel, *Mind,* 71–95; Polanyi, *Personal,* 389–90; Reppert, *C. S. Lewis's Dangerous, passim*; Willard, "Knowledge," "Reflections."

18. Bahnsen, "The Problem," 19, emph. in orig.

morally culpable in allowing preventable evil if he has a 'morally sufficient reason' for so doing."[19] Thus, the answer to David Hume's and similar logical syllogisms is: (1) A totally good God will prevent all the evil he can *unless he has a morally sufficient reason* for permitting its existence; (2) Evil exists; (3) Therefore, God has a morally sufficient reason for permitting the existence of evil. Abraham had this view when he said, *"Shall not the Judge of all the earth do right?"* (Gen 18:25, NKJV) Paul had the same view when he said *"Let God be found true, though every man be found a liar"* (Rom 3:4). Additionally, although God has a morally sufficient reason for permitting the existence of evil now, it follows from God's infinite goodness and omnipotence that we can have confidence that one day evil will be defeated and eliminated.

In light of this and in light of certain defenses that various Christians have proposed, we have already seen that even atheists admit that "the existence of evil is logically consistent with the existence of the theistic God."[20] This admission is also fatal to the so-called inductive or evidential problem of evil. Because both theists and atheists agree that the existence of evil is *consistent* with the existence of God, i.e., since both God and evil can logically exist at the same time, how can it be shown that "evil *does not* fit with God and thus is evidence that makes His existence improbable?"[21]

Atheists typically point to the great quantity of evil in the world, the intensity of much evil (e.g., torture; extremely painful diseases), the apparent gratuitousness (pointlessness) of much evil (e.g., a fawn dying in a forest fire; the rape and murder of a child), and/or natural evils (floods; earthquakes; diseases) in making their inductive or evidential arguments for the improbability of God's existence. The problem, however, is that the atheists' arguments are based on the hidden premise that God does not have a morally sufficient reason for allowing these sorts of evil; but that is just an assertion that cannot be proven. There is another hidden premise inside the first hidden premise. That second hidden premise is, "If *I* can't see a reason for God's ordaining or allowing some instance of evil then God does not have a sufficient reason for ordaining or allowing it." But that second hidden premise is obviously false. Since God is omniscient and infinitely wise, he clearly could have reasons we cannot think of.[22] God is under no obligation to tell us his reasons for ordaining and allowing evil in general or any specific evil in particular. It may be that his reason is too complicated

---

19. Erlandson, "A New Perspective," The Anti-theist Cannot Generate.
20. Rowe, "The Problem," 10n.1; see n.2, above.
21. Feinberg, *The Many Faces,* 290, emph. in orig.; see also at 164.
22. See Keller, *Walking,* 98.

for us to understand, or he may have some other reason for not revealing his reason. Since atheists are unable to prove that God has *no* morally sufficient reasons for allowing various evils, their inductive or evidential "probability" arguments of necessity must fail.

A multitude of other reasons show that these inductive or evidential arguments cannot get off the ground:

In making any inductive argument or judgment as to the probability of something (i.e., the existence of God), it is necessary to incorporate all evidence that is relevant to the issue, because what may be improbable given one set of data may be probable given additional data. In other words, in order to make any argument asserting the non-existence or probable non-existence of God in the face of the existence of evil, it is necessary to advance good reasons *apart from the existence of evil itself* that God does not or probably does not exist; without doing that, one is simply appealing to a pre-existing conclusion, i.e., essentially is begging the question.[23] This fact essentially renders the atheist's argument from evil invalid, because atheists typically do *not* incorporate background information or evidence relevant to God's existence, but only discuss the existence of evil itself.

The background information or evidence that is needed in order to make a valid argument or probability judgment concerning God's existence would include but not be limited to: the uniqueness of the Bible; the implausibility of the universe coming into existence by itself; the implausibility of life coming from non-living matter; the implausibility of mind and consciousness coming from non-sentient beings; the inability of non-sentient forces to account for abstract universals like logic, truth, values, right and wrong; evidence of design throughout the universe; fulfilled prophecy; the resurrection of Jesus Christ; evidence of miracles; and experiences of divine and supernatural encounters. This other information makes the likelihood of God's existence so high that the existence of evil cannot make it improbable.[24] However, the atheists' failure to factor in any of this evidence and background information makes it impossible to even begin an argument concerning the probability of the existence of God. The fact of evil, standing alone, has no evidential value whatsoever in trying to assess the probability of God's existence.

The importance of considering background evidence concerning God's existence in answering the problem of evil is relevant for another important reason. One should ask the atheist to specify "which God" he or she is attacking based on the existence of evil, because unless one knows the

---

23. See Feinberg, *The Many Faces*, 182.
24. See Feinberg, *The Many Faces*, 164.

nature and characteristics of the God being attacked or defended, it will be difficult, if not impossible, to assess the adequacy of the attack or defense.[25] If the atheist is attacking the existence of the God of the Bible (and that is the only God Christians should defend), it is legitimate to look to the Bible and the data contained in the Bible concerning both God and evil. This is particularly true since the atheist's contention has its source, at least in part, in biblical revelation (i.e., the concept of an omnipotent, omniscient, and good God). K. Scott Oliphint states, "Since the objector presents the problem as one intrinsic to Christianity, there is no fallacy or logical breach if one answers the objection from the same source in which the alleged problem itself, including the characteristics of God, is found."[26] The objector's own beliefs about what he or she thinks God is like and what he or she thinks God would or should do about evil are completely irrelevant.[27]

The atheist's argument is also invalid for a related reason: it is nothing but an assertion of what God would or should do, or, to put it another way, it postulates that, if God exists, reality would or should be considerably different from what it is. None of that is based on any empirical or observed data at all. Although we can observe many different kinds, amounts, and intensities of evil in the world, those instances of evil do not in themselves indicate how to evaluate them, e.g., Is this an instance of gratuitous evil? Is this excessive evil under all the relevant circumstances? What is God's purpose for ordaining and allowing this instance of evil?[28] As Bruce Reichenbach puts it, "The atheologian's argument seems to proceed along the illicit lines that since *we* could have prevented the suffering, *God* could have prevented the suffering."[29] The arrogance of such a claim is astounding, particularly since "they cannot provide the evidence needed to show that God could have prevented the suffering without losing a greater good."[30] In short, the entire atheistic argument amounts to a hypothesis of what the atheist thinks

---

25. See Feinberg, *The Many Faces*, 285.

26. Oliphint, *Reasons*, 174–75. It is for that reason that Oliphint proposes the proposition, "Adam responsibly and freely chose to disobey God, to eat the forbidden fruit, after which time he and all of creation fell," to resolve the alleged incompatibility between the existence of an omnipotent, omniscient, good God and the existence of evil, instead of the more generic proposition, "God has a morally sufficient reason for allowing evil." Oliphint, *Reasons*, 172. The *Westminster Confession of Faith* speaks of Adam's ability to freely choose as follows: "Man, in his state of innocency, had freedom, and power to will and to do that which was good and well pleasing to God; but yet, mutably, so that he might fall from it." *Westminster*, 9.2.

27. Feinberg, *The Many Faces*, 18; Oliphint, *Reasons*, 175.

28. Feinberg, *The Many Faces*, 288.

29. Reichenbach, *Evil*, 37–38; see also Feinberg, *The Many Faces*, 178.

30. Reichenbach, *Evil*, 37.

God would or should do and various auxiliary assumptions the atheist assumes to be true (e.g., there is too much evil; there is pointless or gratuitous evil; God should remove evil; God could remove evil without forfeiting a greater good or causing greater harm). The atheist's hypothesis and auxiliary assumptions are all inherently subjective and inferential and none of them is based on any empirical facts or known truths at all!

The fact is, God has *infinitely* greater knowledge than we have, has an *infinitely* greater vision and frame of reference, and is *infinitely* wiser than we are. Stephen Wykstra analogized our understanding of God's reasons for allowing evil and suffering to the likelihood of a one-month-old infant trying to understand his parents' purposes in allowing him to experience pain, which is to say it is not likely at all. The gap between our abilities and understanding compared to God's is actually infinitely greater than that between a one-month-old infant and his or her parents. Wykstra's point is that "the disparity between our cognitive limits and the vision needed to create a universe gives us reason to think that if our universe is created by God it is expectable that . . . if there are God-purposed goods [connected to evil and suffering], they would often be beyond our ken."[31] Biblically, this is certainly true inasmuch as *"the secret things belong to the Lord our God"* (Deut 29:29), now *"we walk by faith, not by sight"* (2 Cor 5:7), and *"now we see in a mirror dimly, but then face to face; now I know in part, but then I will know fully just as I also have been fully known"* (1 Cor 13:12).

William Alston elaborates this; after discussing many possible reasons why God might allow evil and suffering, he states,

> Even if we were fully entitled to dismiss all the alleged reasons for permitting suffering that have been suggested, we would still have to consider whether there are further possibilities that are undreamt of in our theodicies. Why should we suppose that the theodicies thus far excogitated, however brilliant and learned their authors, exhaust the field? . . . Even if . . . my opponent could definitively rule out all the specific suggestions I have put forward, she would still face the insurmountable task of showing herself to be justified in supposing that there are no further

---

31. Wykstra, "Rowe's Noseeum," 139–40; see also Plantinga, "Epistemic," 75–76 ("An evil is *inscrutable* if it is such that we can't think of any reason God (if there is such a person) could have for permitting it. . . . If theism is true we would expect that there would be inscrutable evil. Indeed, a little reflection shows there is no reason to think we could so much as grasp God's plans here, even if he proposed to divulge them to us. But then the fact that there is inscrutable evil does not make it improbable that God exists.").

possibilities for sufficient divine reasons. That point by itself would be decisive.[32]

Timothy Keller observes that, since God has an all-comprehensive plan for the universe which includes all of history and all the events of history, "it would be folly to think we could look at any particular occurrence and understand a millionth of what it will bring about"[33] Logically, theists do not even need a hypothesis as to why God ordains or permits evil but can simply rest on the facts that God has a good and sufficient reason but has not explicitly revealed it to us. To do this is not irrational. John Feinberg notes that "we often rationally continue to believe something without knowing how to explain it. For example, one may reasonably trust the laws of chemistry, even if a particular experiment went awry and one cannot explain why."[34]

Even David Hume, the originator of the modern "problem of evil," admitted that it is likely we would *not* know God's reasons for allowing evil and suffering: "such a limited intelligence must be sensible of his own blindness and ignorance, and must allow, that there may be many solutions of those phenomena [evil and suffering], which will for ever escape his comprehension."[35] The book of Job alone should tell us that it is nonsensical to think that the finite human mind could comprehend all the reasons God might have for ordaining and allowing any instance of evil, pain, and suffering, let alone all instances of evil, pain, and suffering. Since that is the case, it is impossible for an atheist to make a valid argument that the existence, quantity, intensity, and apparent gratuitousness of evil renders God's existence improbable.

Concerning natural evils (e.g., earthquakes, floods, genetic malfunctions, diseases), ultimately the natural order went awry because of humanity's fall into sin (Gen 3:17–19; Rom 8:20–22). John Frame states, "Natural evil is a curse brought upon the world because of moral evil. It functions as punishment to the wicked and as a means of discipline for those who are righteous by God's grace. It also reminds us of the cosmic dimensions of sin and redemption [see Col 1:20]."[36] In other words, neither human beings nor the natural order are in the "very good" state in which God made them (Gen 1:31) but are corrupted and disordered because of humanity's

---

32. Alston, "The Inductive," 119.
33. Keller, *Walking*, 101.
34. Feinberg, *The Many Faces*, 3rd ed., 288.
35. Hume, *Dialogues*, part 11, 200.
36. Frame, "The Problem," 142.

disobedience to God. It is, therefore, disingenuous to blame God for natural evils and disasters.

Beyond that, God created a world in which human beings and other creatures can live and function adequately. The world is run by various natural processes that fit the creatures God placed in it. Sometimes these natural processes produce harmful effects. However, it makes no sense to object to such a world because sometimes things go awry. It is particularly illogical to claim that, because sometimes natural processes produce harmful effects, therefore, God does not exist. That would be like saying that, because sometimes certain medicines cause adverse side effects, medical science does not exist. In this regard, Richard Swinburne points out that multiple instances of natural evils need to occur in order for people to induce what is likely to happen in the future, what causes evil, and how to prevent evil. For example, how can people know where to build cities along earthquake belts "unless they know where earthquakes are likely to occur and what their probable consequences are? And how are they to come to know this, unless earthquakes have happened due to natural and unpredicted causes, like the Lisbon Earthquake of 1755?"[37]

Further, the very thing that is beneficial about natural phenomena can also be detrimental, e.g., water is necessary for life but one can drown in it; gravity is necessary but can result in injury or death when someone falls or avalanches occur. The beneficial aspects are so essential to life as we know it that to change these phenomena and processes would fundamentally change life and the world itself. Bruce Reichenbach observes that to alter natural laws to preclude the possibility of injury or death would fundamentally change the nature of all existence:

> What would it entail to alter the natural laws regarding digestion so that arsenic or other poisons would not negatively affect the human constitution? Would not either arsenic or the human physiological composition or both have to be altered such that they would, in effect, be different from the present objects which we now call arsenic or human digestive organs? . . . Fire would no longer burn or else many things would have to be by nature non-combustible. . . . The introduction of different natural laws affecting human beings in order to prevent the frequent instances of natural evil would entail the alteration of human beings themselves.[38]

---

37. Swinburne, *The Existence*, 208.
38. Reichenbach, *Evil*, 110–11.

Concerning the apparent gratuitousness or pointlessness of much evil, the claim that such instances of evil are pointless is an appeal to ignorance, since we do not have God's perspective. We may not see the point of such evil, but we cannot know that there is not point to it. The claim that evil is gratuitous also begs the question by *assuming* that there is no point to such instances of evil, but such a claim does not and cannot demonstrate that there truly or genuinely is no point to such suffering.[39] Even atheist William Rowe admits, "It would seem to require something like omniscience on our part before we should lay claim to knowing that there is no greater good connected to [an apparently pointless instance of suffering] that an omnipotent, omniscient being could not have achieved that good without permitting that suffering or some evil equally bad or worse."[40]

Concerning the quantity of evil, as with the assertion that some evils are "pointless," given our cognitive finiteness (especially compared to God), the assertion that there is "too much" evil is just that—an assertion, an opinion, but does not constitute evidence. Such an assertion permits no inference against the existence of a justifying reason that God may have. Hence, it is no evidence against the probability that God exists. From our perspective, less evil might seem possible and preferable; but from God's perspective, with his knowledge and wisdom of how specific instances of evil and the amount and nature of evil as a whole interact with good fit into his overall plan, and how the ultimate result would be changed if the amount of evil were reduced, it is impossible for us to say that there is "too much evil."[41] Further, different instances of evil of the same kind might be

39. See Reichenbach, *Evil*, 38; Trau, "Fallacies," 485–89; Feinberg, *The Many Faces*, 180. Keith Yandell states, "That there are evils whose morally sufficient points, ends, or purposes, if any, are not apparent does not entail that they have no such point, end, or purpose, because it is false that if they have such ends that fact would be apparent to us. It does not entail that they probably have no such point, for it is not the case that if they had a point, that fact probably would be apparent to us. It does not follow that it is reasonable to believe that they do not have a point, because it is false that it is reasonable to believe that they have no point because it is the case that it is not apparent to us that they have one." Yandell, "Gratuitous," 19–20.

40. Rowe, "The Problem," 4.

41. See Feinberg, *The Many Faces*, 308. There is a related point concerning the quantity and intensity of pain and suffering. Although we might try to imagine the sum total of suffering by all animals and humans everywhere and throughout history, the fact is that "such a sum of suffering does not and cannot exist. Pain is not accumulable . . . for that composite pain cannot be found in anyone's consciousness. There is no such thing as 'a sum of suffering' for the simple reason that no one suffers it." Boyd, *Why Doesn't God*, 98–99. The only one who knows and suffers the sum of the anguish of this world is God Himself. "He knows each of His children and all of His creatures with an immediacy more instant and acute than their own consciousness of themselves, and feels their suffering more deeply than they do in their own person. . . . [Yet we] hold

justified in entirely different ways. The consequence of this is that "evils we think are surplus or too much may not at all be, because they may have a different purpose and explanation than we think."[42]

Finally, God was not required to create any world at all. In light of this, we really have no standing to condemn the Creator (or, more illogically, claim that he does not even exist) because we do not like certain aspects of creation. Michael Peterson asks "whether our moral structures can condemn the very being who makes it possible for us even to exist, to be able to apprehend moral values in the first place, and to have the significance of life which is lived within their ambit. Of course, we morally condemn those who lie, steal, and murder, but it is not at all clear that we must likewise condemn God for creating the context in which such evils can happen."[43] God is under no obligation, moral or otherwise, to tell us why he decides to do or not do something. Our focusing on instances of evil in the world often blinds us to God's ever-present grace which, among other things, enables the world and life (including us) to continue to exist (Col 1:17; Heb 1:3). As discussed earlier, when he ordains and allows evil to take place, all that is required is that he has a morally sufficient reason for doing so—and, as we have seen, we can never say that that is not the case.

The Bible indicates that one day God will create a world in which there is no longer any pain, suffering, evil, death, or curse (Rev 21:1, 4; 22:3). So why didn't he start with that world since that world would be better than ours? The answer is similar to the question of why God ordains and permits evil. God clearly had a number of things he wanted to accomplish by creating this world. He evidently intended to create a world populated by non-glorified human beings (not superhumans or subhumans or "glorified" humans) and put them in a world where they could function. All of our experiences here in this world are necessary and in some sense preparations for the next world. As we have seen, to prevent moral evil would require vast changes in the nature of human beings, and to prevent natural evil would entail significant changes in the natural order, such that God's plan of creating human beings like us in a natural world such as ours would be thwarted.[44] God was not wrong to have these other goals and thus create this world with its inhabitants and characteristics, since this world and

---

it against Him as a reason for unbelief while all the time it is He who carries it in love and redeems it by an infinite compassion." Boyd, *Why Doesn't God*, 99; see Isa 53:3–12.

42. Feinberg, *The Many Faces*, 308–9.

43. Peterson, *Evil*, 127.

44. See Feinberg, *The Many Faces*, 130–36, 149–54, 309–10.

its inhabitants and characteristics are not evil in themselves.[45] John Hick concludes that, by focusing on the amount of evil in the world, "Such critics as Hume are confusing what heaven ought to be, as an environment for perfected finite beings, with what this world ought to be, as an environment for beings who are in process of becoming perfected."[46]

THE RELATIONSHIP BETWEEN A GOOD GOD AND THE EXISTENCE OF SIN AND EVIL

There are several facets to God's relationship with sin and evil which must be borne in mind when we consider that God is omnipotent, omniscient, and totally good, yet has ordained and permitted sin and evil to exist.

God is sovereign over everything, and is actively at work accomplishing his plan

The Bible depicts God as sovereign over everything and actively involved in all aspects of the life of the world: his plan is absolute and comprehensive, and he decrees and acts to bring that plan to completion (see 1 Chron 29:11-12; Job 12:13-25; Ps 103:19; Isa 40:21-26; 46:9-11; Dan 4:35; Acts 4:27-28; Rom 9:14-24; Eph 1:11; Rev 17:14-17). This is known as the doctrine of God's *providence*, i.e., "that continued exercise of the divine energy whereby the Creator preserves all His creatures, is operative in all that comes to pass in the world, and directs all things to their appointed end."[47] For example, he creates mountains, creates wind, and makes dawn into darkness (Amos 4:13); he makes wind blow and water flow (Ps 147:18); he governs the sun, moon, and stars, and stirs up the sea (Jer 31:35); he governs the growth of plants (Isa 41:19-20); he governs the animals (Job 39). God is also sovereign over and active in the affairs of people. Thus, he is ultimately in charge of life and death, including birth defects, sickness, and death, including death of the "innocent" (Gen 20:17-18; Exod 4:11; 2 Sam 12:15; Neh 9:6; Job 12:9-10; Isa 44:24; Ezek 24:15-18); he raises some up and puts others down (1 Sam 2:7); he rules over the nations (2 Chron 20:6; Ps 33:10-11; Isa 40:23-25); He stirs up people's spirits, puts thoughts in their minds, and turns their hearts (Ezra 6:22; Neh 2:12; 7:5; Ps 105:25; Isa 44:28; Hag 1:14). His sovereignty includes sovereignty even over the sinful

---

45. See Feinberg, *The Many Faces*, 142.
46. Hick, *Evil*, 257-58.
47. Berkhof, *Systematic*, 181.

decisions of people (Gen 45:5–8; Luke 22:22; Acts 2:23–24; 4:27–28; 13:27; Rev 17:17). Consequently, the Bible tells us, *"Whatever the Lord pleases, he does, in heaven and in the earth"* (Ps 135:6). God states that he *"declare[s] the end from the beginning, and from ancient times things which have not been done, saying, 'My purpose will be established and I will accomplish my good pleasure.... Truly I have spoken; truly I will bring it to pass. I have planned it, surely I will do it.'"* (Isa 46:10–11)

God's sovereignty over events includes his sovereignty over sin and evil but not in a way that makes him sinful or evil

God did not create the world and people and then just let them act on their own; instead, he is actively involved in the world and in the lives of the people he created. At no time are creatures independent of the will and power of God, because *"in Him we live and move and exist"* (Acts 17:28).

> This divine activity accompanies the action of man at every point, but without robbing man in any way of his freedom. The action remains the free act of man, an act for which he is held responsible. This simultaneous concurrence does not result in an identification of the *causa prima* [primary cause] and the *causa secunda* [secondary cause]. In a very real sense the operation is the product of both causes.... Bavinck illustrates this by pointing to the fact that wood burns, that God only causes it to burn, but that formally this burning cannot be ascribed to God but only to the wood as subject.[48]

Typically, God acts *through* his creatures, not immediately and directly. Berkhof puts it like this, "God causes everything in nature to work and to move in the direction of a pre-determined end. So God also enables and prompts His rational creatures, as second causes, to function, and that not merely by endowing them with energy in a general way, but by energizing them to certain specific acts."[49] At the same time

> God's presence does not mean either divine micromanagement or a divine will that is irresistible.[50] ... The world retains its integrity as creature even while filled with the presence of the

---

48. Berkhof, *Systematic*, 189.

49. Berkhof, *Systematic*, 189.

50. There are different senses to the meaning of God's "will." His revealed or preceptive will may, indeed, be resisted by people; however, his secret or decretive will cannot be resisted.

Creator. . . . God—who is other than the world—works relationally from within the world, and not on the world from without. . . . That is, both God and the creatures have an important role in the creative enterprise, and their spheres of activity are interrelated in terms of function and effect. . . . But, even more, God gives human beings powers and responsibilities in a way that *commits God* to a certain kind of relationship with them. This commitment entails a divine constraint and restraint in the exercise of power within the creation. For example, God will not do the procreating of animals or the bearing of fruit seeds in any unmediated way.[51]

Given this relationship between God and human beings, the Bible repeatedly presents a *dual explanation* for events: God is sovereign and has ordained all events (that, in one sense, is a full explanation for all events); yet that is compatible with and does not in any way diminish people's responsibility for the choices they make and the things they do (that, in another sense, is also a full explanation for all events).[52] This is known as the doctrine of *concurrence*, i.e., "the co-operation of the divine power with all subordinate powers, according to the pre-established laws of their operation, causing them to act and to act precisely as they do."[53] This doctrine implies two things: "(1) That the powers of nature do not work by themselves, that is, simply by their own inherent power, but that God is immediately operative in every act of the creature. This must be maintained in opposition to the deistic position. (2) That second causes are real, and not to be regarded simply as the operative power of God. . . . This should be stressed over against the pantheistic idea that God is the only agent working in the world."[54] In keeping with this dual explanation of events, Paul tells Christians to *"work*

---

51. Fretheim, *God and World*, 23–24, 26–27; see also Berkhof, *Systematic*, 188–90; Walton, *The Lost*, 18, 121.

52. K. Scott Oliphint remarks, "It is difficult to see how one thing, like God's condescending providence, could bring together both the decree of God and the free act of Adam as a part of that decree. But surely, in a world in which God, in Christ, takes on a human nature all the while remaining God, it is no conceptual stretch to assert such a thing of God and his providence. That is, just as the person of Christ combines the divine and human without losing the essential properties of each, so also providence combines the divine (decree) and human (decision) in such a way that no essential properties are lost in each of them." Oliphint, *Reasons*, 301.

53. Berkhof, *Systematic*, 187. Appendix 2 is a table showing multiple examples from the Bible of the same events being attributed both to God and to secondary agents.

54. Berkhof, *Systematic*, 187; see *Westminster*, 5.2.

out your salvation with fear and trembling, for it is God who is at work in you, both to will and to work for His good pleasure" (Phil 2:12-13).[55]

Let us explain this specifically as it relates to the existence of evil and sin. Many people try to shield God from *any* involvement with sin or evil (they attribute all evil either to Satan or to the individual sinner). However, the Bible presents a more nuanced and complex picture. On one hand,

---

55. Philosophically, the term that describes the God-human relationship is "compatibilism": God is absolutely sovereign, but His sovereignty never functions in such a way that human responsibility is minimized or eliminated (i.e., human beings are not turned into robots or puppets); likewise, human beings are morally responsible creatures who can make real choices and actions, including rebelling against the revealed will of God, and are rightly held accountable for such choices and actions, but this never functions so as to make God absolutely contingent. In other words, God is able to foreordain all things with certainty; human beings do what they want and choose to do (i.e., God does not force them to act against their desires and wills), but they do not have the *absolute* power to act contrary to God's foreordained plan. See Carson, *Divine*, 163-67, 201-22; Carson, *How Long*, 199-227; Feinberg, *No One*, 625-796; Alcorn, *If God*, 258-69. As Feinberg states, "Each person, though causally determined to do what she does, still has the ability and opportunity to choose otherwise than she has. And when she chooses evil, she does so in accord with her wishes. Compatibilistic freedom is still freedom; it is not compulsion." Feinberg, *The Many Faces*, 3rd ed., 183.

Some philosophers and theologians have proposed a defense to the problem of evil called the "free will defense," which is based on another view of free will called libertarian or incompatibilistic free will. The leading proponent of this is Alvin Plantinga. Although the free will defense does counter the logical problem of evil, the notion of incompatibilistic free will is not biblical. Plantinga defines free will as follows: "If a person is free with respect to a given action, then he is free to perform that action and free to refrain from performing it; no antecedent conditions and/or causal laws determine that he will perform the action, or that he won't. It is within his power, at the time in question, to take or perform the action and within his power to refrain from it.... Now God can create free creatures, but He can't *cause* or *determine* them to do only what is right." Plantinga, *God*, 29. This means that "in order for libertarian freedom to be affirmed, a full-orbed sovereignty must be denied with respect to God." Oliphint, *Reasons*, 275. That is unbiblical, since "Scripture seems to represent God as determining the choices of human creatures, and yet holding them fully responsible for their choices, good and bad (cf. Ge 50:20; Isa 10:5-15; Lk 22:22; Ac 2:23, 4:27-28; 13:48; Php 2:12-13; 1 Ki 8:58, 61; Ex 4:21, 7:3, 10:20, 10:27). In other words, it doesn't seem that Scripture shares the distinctive assumption of the FWD." Erlandson, "A New Perspective," n.10. Indeed, in Rom 9:19-21 Paul appeals to the difference between God as the potter and us as the clay to counter the problem of evil. John Frame points out, "This answer to the problem of evil turns entirely on God's sovereignty. It is as far as could be imagined from a free will defense." Frame, "The Problem," 164. Related to this is another issue: "If an omniscient God foreknows what I shall do — and surely, it seems, He must — then I cannot act other than I do and, consequently, I do not act freely [in the libertarian sense]. Hence, the insistence that God is omniscient seems logically incompatible with the free will defense against the problem of evil." Runzo, "Omniscience," 131. Other problems also exist with the idea of libertarian freedom and the free will defense from a biblical standpoint, but we need not address them here. See Keller, *Walking*, 90-93; Feinberg, "And the Atheist," 149-50; Frame, *The Doctrine*, 135-45.

"Moral evil is not something God created when he created other things. It is not a substance at all. God created substances, including the world and the people in it. God intended that we could act, for he made us able to act. But he neither made our actions nor does he perform them. Hence, we cannot say that God intended there to be moral evil because we have it in our world. God intended to create and did create agents who can act; he did not make their acts (good or evil)."[56] In other words, God respects people's integrity *as human beings*. He does not control people as if they were puppets or program them as if they were robots. People are able to think their own thoughts and make real choices.

On the other hand, the Bible's writers "do not shy away from making Yahweh himself in some mysterious way (the mysteriousness of which safeguards him from being himself charged with evil) the 'ultimate' cause of many evils. . . . God does not stand behind evil action in precisely the same way that he stands behind good action. . . . A certain distance is preserved between God and his people when they sin. . . . In short, although we may lack the categories needed for full exposition of the problem, *nevertheless we must insist that divine ultimacy stands behind good and evil asymmetrically*."[57]

This interdependent divine-human interrelationship "is a relationship of unequals; it is an asymmetrical relationship. God is God and we're not."[58] This means there is a difference in metaphysical level and status between God as creator and us as creatures. One consequence of this is that, because of the "fall" of mankind into sin and its resultant effects on us and on the world, we humans, not God, are ultimately responsible for moral and natural evil; "God is not guilty, for He does not do the evil."[59] This God-human relationship also is a paradox that defies complete definition or understanding. Nevertheless, given the existence of an omnipotent, omniscient, omnipresent God who has a plan for the world, is sovereign, and is actualizing his plan, and given creatures who have the ability to make real choices and take real actions for which they are responsible, the relationship between God and his creatures as described above *could not be otherwise*.

The different "metaphysical levels" between God and us might be analogized to the difference between a playwright and a character in a play. In *Macbeth*, Macbeth killed Duncan. "Shakespeare wrote the murder into

---

56. Feinberg, *No One*, 788; see also Adams, *The Grand*, 59 ("He has decreed the existence of sin in such a way that men themselves freely (i.e., uncoerced and in accord with their own natures) become the authors of their sin"); Koukl, "A Good," n.p.

57. Carson, *Divine*, 28, 36–37, emph. in orig.; see *Westminster*, 3.1; 5.4.

58. Fretheim, *God and World*, 16.

59. Feinberg, *The Many Faces*, 148.

his play. But the murder took place in the world of the play.... We sense the rightness of Macbeth paying for his crime. But we would certainly consider it very unjust if Shakespeare were tried and put to death for killing Duncan. ... Indeed, there is reason for us to praise Shakespeare for raising up this character, Macbeth, to show us the consequences of sin."[60] Because of the different levels of reality between God and us, God's prerogatives as "playwright" (e.g., creator, sustainer, lawgiver, judge, savior) are far greater than ours. While this analogy is not exact (we, after all, are real while Macbeth is not), this metaphysical difference in levels between God and us entails different roles between God and us.

The asymmetric relationship that God has between good and evil means that "God stands behind evil in such a way that not even evil takes place outside the bounds of his sovereignty, yet the evil is not morally chargeable to him: it is always chargeable to secondary agents, to secondary causes. On the other hand, God stands behind good in such a way that it not only takes place within the bounds of his sovereignty, but it is always chargeable to him, and only derivatively to secondary agents."[61] In other words, God is not responsible for evil in such a way that He is the author of the *evilness* of the evil or the *sinfulness* of sin.[62] The fundamental metaphysical difference in *levels* between God and us and, therefore, the fundamentally different *roles* God and we play in the drama of existence, means that, as Keith Yandell states, "What God can allow compatible with his goodness is not what we can allow compatible with ours."[63]

James 1 describes how sin arises. Jas 1:2, 12 commend people who encounter and persevere in various "trials." Jas 1:13–15 then states, *"Let no one say when he is tempted, 'I am being tempted by God'; for God cannot be tempted by evil, and He Himself does not tempt anyone. But each one is tempted when he is carried away and enticed by his own lust. Then when lust has conceived, it gives birth to sin; and when sin is accomplished, it brings forth death."* The words "trial" and "tempt" are cognates, i.e., the noun and verb forms of the same Greek root word (*peirasmos* [trial] and *peirazō* [tempt]).

---

60. Frame, "The Problem," 162–63.

61. Carson, *How Long,* 213.

62. Dennis Johnson illustrates this from the book of Revelation, "Although the destructive judgments revealed in the trumpet cycle come from the heavenly altar by the purpose of God [Rev 8:1–19], the blame for the earth's destruction falls not on the holy Creator but on those who seduce human beings into resisting him and his Christ, sowing seeds of avarice, suspicion, competition, and hostility that violate the world and its inhabitants [Rev 8:20–21]". Johnson, *Triumph,* 154n.13; see also Gen 4:1–7; Isa 10:5–16; Hab 1:1–11; Hag 1:5–11; Acts 2:22–24.

63. Yandell, "Gratuitous," 30.

The context provides the distinction: God places us in circumstances to test or try us—including circumstances where we may be tempted to sin and circumstances where he knows we will, in fact, sin—*yet he does not induce us to sin*. Rather, the temptation to sin comes from within the person or from a secondary source such as Satan, and the willing to sin comes from within the person.[64]

We see this when we consider how sin and evil entered the world. God created the world without sin or evil in a state that was *"very good"* (Gen 1:31). God created human beings *"in the image of God"* (Gen 1:26-27). He gave them the ability to reason and have emotions, desires, intentions, the ability to choose, and the capacity for bodily movement, all of which we may use for good (or evil). He blessed the man and woman (Gen 1:28), spoke to them, had fellowship with them (Gen 1:28-30; 2:16-17, 19; 3:8-9), and placed them in an ideal environment (Gen 2:8-15). God specifically told Adam not to eat from the tree of the knowledge of good and evil and even warned him of the consequences if he did (Gen 2:16-17). Sin entered the world when Adam and Eve disobeyed God and rebelled against him by eating the fruit (Gen 3:1-6). Gen 3:6 recounts how sin sprang from Adam's and Eve's desire: *"When the woman saw that the tree was good for food, and that it was a delight to the eyes, and that the tree was desirable to make one wise, she took some of its fruit and ate; and she also gave some to her husband with her, and he ate."* This is known as "the Fall" of mankind.[65]

Since Adam and Eve represented and had been placed in charge of the entire creation, the Fall affected not only them but the rest of humanity and the created order (Gen 3:14-19; Rom 5:12-19; 8:20-22). "Suffering and death in general is a natural consequence and just judgment of God on our sin."[66] In short, the original design for creation has been broken and is now abnormal. Despite the Fall, people still have the capacities for reason, choice, etc. with which God created us, although now we are predisposed and inclined to sin and rebel against God (see Rom 3:9-18).

God permits and ordains sin, not for the evilness or sinfulness of the sin itself, but for "wise, holy, and most excellent ends and purposes."[67] In this regard, Randy Alcorn states that God "intended from the beginning to permit evil, then to turn evil on its head, to take what evil angels and people

---

64. See Feinberg, *No One*, 789.

65. The Bible clearly implies that Satan "fell" before the sin of Adam and Eve, since Satan is the one who tempted Adam and Eve and lied to them about the nature and consequences of eating the fruit of the knowledge of good and evil (compare Gen 2:16-17 and Gen 3:1-4).

66. Keller, *Walking*, 115.

67. Edwards, *Freedom*, §IX: 76; see also Piper, "Are There," 107-31.

intended for evil and use it for good.... It is possible to plan for something you know is coming without forcing that thing to happen. God didn't *force* Adam and Eve to do evil, but he did create them with freedom and permitted Satan's presence in the garden, fully knowing they would choose evil and knowing that what he would do in his redemptive plan would serve a greater good."[68]

Indeed, people may have one motive for what they do (e.g., to bring about evil), but God may have another motive for ordaining the very same event (e.g., to bring about good). God is able to work in and through his creatures without forcing them to act against their own will or desires (even when his own desire or motive is different from theirs) and without himself sinning (even when his creatures do, in fact, sin) (see Prov 16:2). The selling of Joseph into slavery (Gen 45:4–8; 50:20; Ps 105:17), the defeat of Judah by Israel (2 Chron 28:1–15), the invasion of Israel by Assyria (2 Kgs 19:20–31; Isa 10:5–16), the destruction of Judah by Babylon (Ezek 11:5–12; Hab 1:5–11), the betrayal of Jesus by Judas (Matt 26:20–24; John 6:64), the conspiracy by Caiaphas, the chief priests, and the Pharisees to kill Jesus (John 11:47–53), and the crucifixion of Jesus by Herod, Pilate, the Gentiles, and the people of Israel (Isa 53:3–10; Acts 2:22–23; 4:27–28) are examples of this.

Because God exhaustively knows the entire future—including its end and all the short-term and long-term, direct and indirect, effects of every word, deed, and other events, he is uniquely qualified to know when to ordain or permit evil and suffering and when not to. Consequently, he alone can be good in allowing evil and suffering that a good human being (who does not have God's exhaustive knowledge) would try to prevent.

Although sin and evil are part of God's overall plan, he stands against sin and evil

Perhaps of greatest importance is that, although the existence of sin and evil are part of God's plan, God stands *against* sin and evil. This stems from his nature as holy, just, righteous, and good. Hab 1:13 says that God is *"too pure to approve evil, and You cannot look on wickedness with favor."* We tend to think that sin is a relatively trivial matter. That trivialization of sin reflects our own sinful nature. From God's point of view, however, sin is absolutely horrendous.[69] We see this in John 11:1–44 concerning the death of Lazarus, whom Jesus raised from the tomb. Death, of course, entered the world as a

---

68. Alcorn, *If God*, 226–27.
69. Feinberg, *The Many Faces*, 331.

result of sin (Gen 2:17; Rom 5:12–14). First Cor 15:26 calls death *"the last enemy."* When Jesus approached Lazarus's tomb, John 11:38 says that he was *"deeply moved"* (or *"groaning in Himself,"* NKJV). Timothy Keller points out that "these translations are too weak. The Greek word used by the gospel writer John means 'to bellow with anger.' It is a startling term."[70] It indicates that Jesus is furious at sin and the suffering and death that sin has brought into the world. But that is not the end of the story. Jesus does not simply rail against sin, evil, and death; instead, he is God's instrument to eliminate those things. D. A. Carson explains that God "stands over against it [sin; evil; moral wickedness], so much so that the *logos* becomes the lamb of God who takes away the world's sin, and the wrath of God is manifest against it ([John] 1.29; 3.36)."[71] Ronald Rittgers points out the importance of both sides of God's relationship to suffering and evil: "A God who has no causal relationship to suffering is no God at all, certainly not the God of the Bible, who both suffers with humanity—supremely on the cross—and yet is in some sense also sovereign over suffering. Both beliefs were (and are) essential to the traditional Christian assertion that suffering ultimately has some meaning and that the triune God is able to provide deliverance from it."[72]

This is probably the greatest mystery regarding evil, suffering, and death—that God chose to come into the world and personally be subject to evil, suffering, and death in the person of Jesus Christ. Not only is it a mystery but it was a radical plan to himself bear evil in order to turn evil on its head, create a new people to stand against evil, and ultimately end evil without destroying the very people who commit evil and who are so intimately connected with it. Yet God in Christ "takes on the rebellion that is not his, and he makes it his, so that those whose rebellion it is will not suffer eternally because of it, but will be counted as righteous before him (2 Cor. 5:21)."[73] That rebellion amounts to humanity's putting itself in God's place; but salvation is God sacrificing himself for humanity and putting himself where we deserve to be. In short, as John Stott summarizes, "Man claims prerogatives which belong to God alone; God accepts penalties which belong to man alone."[74]

The depth of our sin and what it cost God to forgive us (i.e., *"His only begotten Son,"* John 3:16) is revealed by Jesus on the cross. Jesus said that

---

70. Keller, *Walking*, 136; see Zodhiates, *The Complete*, *embrimaomai*, 574 ("to roar, storm with anger").

71. Carson, *Divine*, 160–61.

72. Rittgers, *The Reformation*, 261.

73. Oliphint, *Reasons*, 340.

74. Stott, *The Cross*, 160.

physical death and destruction does not compare with the infinitely worse death and destruction of hell (Matt 10:28). The essence of hell is being separated from and forsaken by God. When Jesus cried from the cross, *"My God, My God, why have you forsaken me?"* (Matt 27:46), he was experiencing hell itself. By definition, hell lasts forever (Matt 25:46). Jesus did not bear just one eternity in hell, but millions of eternities in hell—the hells deserved by us, the people for whom he died. Yet when he died, after approximately three hours on the cross, Jesus said that it—his payment for our sins—was "finished" (John 19:30). This means that millions of eternities in hell were all compressed onto Jesus in the time that he was on the cross. That is beyond our ability to comprehend, but it is the reality that Jesus experienced and endured for us; that is what it took to redeem us from the penalty for our sin. And he did it all voluntarily, because he loves us. In short, while atheists who raise the problem of evil may talk about the amount and intensity of pain and suffering, the suffering that Christ endured—on our behalf—is unfathomable; the worst suffering ever endured by any creature, whether human or animal, is infinitesimal compared to the suffering endured by Christ.

In light of the cross, Randy Alcorn reminds us, "One thing we must never say about God—that he doesn't understand what it means to be abandoned utterly, suffer terribly, and die miserably. . . . Some people can't believe God would create a world in which people would suffer so much. Isn't it more remarkable that God would create a world in which no one would suffer more than he?"[75] Non-Christian Albert Camus recognized the unique answer to the "problem of evil" in what Christ accomplished on the cross:

> Christ came to solve two major problems, evil and death, which are precisely the problems that preoccupy the rebel. His solution consisted, first, in experiencing them. The man-god suffers, too—with patience. Evil and death can no longer be entirely

---

75. Alcorn, *If God*, 214–15. The crucifixion of Christ also perfectly illustrates that compatibilism has to be true if God is both sovereign and good and people are justly responsible for their actions. D. A. Carson explains, "If the initiative had been entirely with the conspirators, and God simply came in at the last minute to wrest triumph from the jaws of impending defeat, then the cross was not his plan, his purpose, the very reason why he sent his Son into the world—and that is unthinkable. If on the other hand God was so orchestrating events that all the human agents were nonresponsible puppets, then it is foolish to talk of conspiracy, or even of sin—in which case there is no sin for Christ to remove by his death, so why should he have to die? God was sovereignly at work in the death of Jesus; human beings were evil in putting Jesus to death, even as they accomplished the Father's will; and God himself was entirely good." Carson, *How Long*, 212.

imputed to Him since He suffers and dies. The night on Golgotha is so important in the history of man only because, in its shadow, the divinity abandoned its traditional privileges and drank to the last drop, despair included, the agony of death.... Only the sacrifice of an innocent god could justify the endless and universal torture of innocence. Only the most abject suffering by God could assuage man's agony.[76]

To put it another way, "If God is the co-sufferer of each and every victim, then quite clearly the justice of his ways with men and women cannot be in dispute: what is meted out to them is no less than what God himself has to endure."[77] Since Christ bore the ultimate evil for us and used it for our forgiveness, salvation, and eternal life, can we not trust him in the remaining evils that we experience?

In fact, Christ's people now have the means to diminish the evil within themselves and act as redemptive agents to diminish evil and promote justice, mercy, and goodness in the world. That ability to diminish evil and promote justice, mercy, and goodness stems from the nature of the gospel and Christian conversion. The gospel involves a personal encounter with what Christ did for us on the cross. Sebastian Moore states that the gospel "presents us with the vision of Jesus, the man without evil in him, destroyed simply because he *is* without evil. It invites us, under the pressure of a new force called the Holy Spirit, to discover ourselves in that classic murder ... to experience our evil as never before, at last unmasked, to experience our decent death-wish as murder, and *in* that experience to feel for the first time the love that overpowers evil."[78] Christian conversion then includes adoption into the family of God (John 1:12; Rom 8:14–17, 23; 9:4; Gal 3:26; 4:5–7; Eph 1:5; 2:19; 1 John 3:1), receipt of a new heart (Ezek 36:26; 2 Cor 3:3), the mind of Christ (1 Cor 2:16), and the Spirit from Christ (Ezek 36:26; John 14:17) who works in us and through us (Phil 2:12–13) to make us more like Christ himself (Rom 8:29; Eph 4:11–16). This is the authentically Christian response to the "problem of evil" and the only way to eradicate evil and thus solve the "problem" itself; "human beings are able to overcome sin only if they first receive from God to undergo a decisive transformation of self: without this prevenient grace [i.e., divine grace operating on the human will prior to its turning to God] creaturely beings cannot even begin their conquest of evil."[79]

76. Camus, *The Rebel*, 32, 34.
77. Surin, *Theology*, 90.
78. Moore, *The Crucified*, 14.
79. Surin, *Theology*, 122.

That Christ's radical plan made a difference in people's lives was demonstrated historically: In AD 165, a smallpox plague, lasting approximately 15 years, killed and estimated one-quarter to one-third of the Roman Empire. Diana Severance reports, "The noted Roman physician Galen, who described the disease in detail, was in Rome during the first outbreak and fled the city for the country. While Galen fled, Christians remained in the city and cared for the ailing and dying. Mercy and pity was not a virtue among the pagans, but the Christians knew God as a God of mercy. They were to be merciful and love one another, and they showed mercy in caring for others during the plague."[80] From AD 249–262 another pandemic swept over the Roman Empire. Dionysius, the Bishop of Carthage, described the response of the Christians, "The most of our brethren were unsparing in their exceeding love and brotherly kindness. They held fast to each other and visited the sick fearlessly, and ministered to them continually, serving them in Christ. And they died with them most joyfully, taking the affliction of others, and drawing the sickness from their neighbors to themselves and willingly receiving their pains. And many who cared for the sick and gave strength to others died themselves having transferred to themselves their death."[81] Timothy Keller observes, "Writers such as Cyprian, Ambrose, and later Augustine made the case that Christians *suffered and died better*—and this was empirical, visible evidence that Christianity was 'the supreme philosophy.'"[82]

Christ's incarnation and crucifixion are not the end of the story of God's dealing with the problem of sin and evil. Christ will return to the earth; at that time the dead will be raised and he will judge all evil and evildoers (Rev 20:11–15) and will inaugurate a new heaven and a new earth in which there will no longer be any natural evil (Rom 8:21; 2 Pet 3:10) or any moral evil, pain, suffering, death, or curse (2 Pet 3:13; Rev 21:1, 4; 22:3). Therefore, the issues of evil and suffering need to be viewed in the in the larger context of the total history of humanity which includes eternity, not just in the temporal context of this life on this earth. William Ferraiolo points out, "The most hideous embodied life that we can imagine is tantamount to no more than a pin prick by comparison with a postmortem eternity. No matter the severity or intensity of one's terrestrial suffering, one's subsequent eternal experience must, of mathematical necessity, dwarf the dissatisfaction accumulated from cradle to grave."[83] In light of this perspective, Jesus stated, *"Do not fear those who kill the body but are unable to kill the soul; but rather fear Him who*

---

80. Severance, "Christian Mercy," Pandemic.
81. Dionysius, quoted in Eusebius, *Church History*, 7.22.
82. Keller, *Walking*, 42.
83. Ferraiolo, "Eternal," Eternal Selves.

is able to destroy both soul and body in hell" (Matt 10:28). John Hick adds, "the 'good eschaton' will not be a reward or compensation proportioned to each individual's trials, but an infinite good that would render worth while any finite suffering endured in the course of attaining to it."[84]

More than that, the resurrection and the new heaven and new earth mean that, not only will evil and evildoers be judged and justice done, but evil itself will be undone. In the new heaven and new earth, people will have glorious, new, resurrection bodies—new bodies of an incalculably more glorious nature than our current bodies and will be living on a new earth of unimaginable beauty, richness, and wonder (1 Cor 15:20-22, 35-54; Rev 21:10—22:6). In fact, 1 Cor 15:54 says that, at Christ's return, when all is renewed, *"then will come about the saying that is written, 'Death is swallowed up in victory.'"* The language of "swallowing" suggests that death (and the sin and evil that occasioned it) will in some way be taken up into the new heaven and new earth and transformed, like food is swallowed and transformed to nourish the body. This indicates that all of the evil, sin, and suffering we experience are being used as part of an amazing process to make existence greater, more glorious, and more wonderful than it otherwise possibly could be—and greater, more glorious, and more wonderful than it would have been if the evil, sin, and suffering never had existed at all. Thus, "human suffering will be transfigured by God at the consummation of history, a consummation that has already been inaugurated by the event of the cross."[85]

As with Christian conversion, the prospect of Judgment Day and the new heaven and new earth have practical importance in being able to deal with evil, injustice, and suffering now. Miroslav Volf, a firsthand observer of the violence in his native Croatia, says, "The practice of nonviolence requires a belief in divine vengeance,"[86] and "The certainty of God's just judgment at the end of history is the presupposition for the renunciation of violence in the middle of it."[87] The prospect of Judgment Day thus enables us to live with confidence and hope now. We can have confidence that all wrongs will be made right, all injustices will be redressed, and that we can live as agents of peace and justice now—instead of seeking vengeance and revenge—because we know that *"Vengeance is Mine, I will repay,"* says the Lord" (Rom 12:19).

---

84. Hick, *Evil*, 341.
85. Surin, *Theology*, 135.
86. Volf, *Exclusion*, 304.
87. Volf, *Exclusion*, 302.

The promise of God's just judgment and a new world proved to be a powerful, living hope that gave Christians the ability to endure terrible torture and suffering with grace and even joy: Christians in the Roman Empire faced torture and death with poise and grace, some even singing as they entered the arena to be torn apart by wild animals.[88] Howard Thurman adds that Christianity and its hope of Judgment Day and the new heaven and new earth served "to deepen the capacity of endurance and the absorption of suffering [of American slaves]. . . . What greater tribute could be paid to religious faith in general and to their religious faith in particular than this: It taught a people how to ride high in life, to look squarely in the face of those facts that argue most dramatically against all hope and to use those facts as raw material out of which they fashioned a hope that the environment, with all its cruelty, could not crush."[89] J. Christiaan Beker, who himself had been a slave of the Nazis, concludes,

> A biblical theology of hope views the present power of death in terms of its empty future and in the knowledge of its, not God's, sure defeat. It can tolerate, therefore, the agonizing presence of the power of death as "on the way out," and be confident that evil will not have the final say over God's creation. And this confidence enables Christians to devise strategies of hope under the guidance of the Spirit, strategies which not only confront the idolatrous scheme of our world, but also seek to roll back the onslaught of the power of death in our midst.[90]

In short, the gospel enables believers to answer Hume's questions:

> "Is [God] willing to prevent evil, but not able? then is he impotent." "No," answer the faithful, "he will come again in glory to judge the living and the dead." "Is he able, but not willing? then is he malevolent." "On the contrary, he is merciful *towards* the malevolent, and willing that all come to repentance." "Is he both able and willing? whence then is evil?" "Evil is everywhere, and nowhere more than on the cross, where God himself became its victim. He, more than anyone, bore the evil of his own justice and mercy. Yet it was on Calvary that evil was vanquished. We would have been vanquished along with it, if not for the time

---

88. See Novak, *Christians*, 111–14; Raymond, "They Went," n.p.; Keller, *Walking*, 314.

89. Thurman, *A Strange*, 71.

90. Beker, *Suffering*, 121–22.

God has given for us (and you too?) to be numbered among the victors."[91]

One can look at God's ordaining that sin and evil occur as analogous to the sun's relationship to darkness and cold

Jonathan Edwards points out that there is a great difference between God's permitting, ordaining, and/or not hindering sin versus his being the proper actor, author, or positive, effective agent of the sin. He compares this to the sun and its relationship between light and darkness, warmth and cold. The sun is the direct agent of light and warmth when it is shining. However, when the sun sets, darkness and cold prevail. Edwards states,

> The motion of the sun is the occasion of the latter kind of events; but it is not the proper cause, efficient, or producer of them; though they are necessarily consequent on that motion, under such circumstances: no more is any action of the Divine Being the cause of the evil of men's Wills. If the sun were the proper *cause* of cold and darkness, . . . it might be justly inferred, that the sun itself is dark and cold, and that his beams are black and frosty. But from its being the cause no otherwise than by its departure, no such thing can be inferred.[92]

He concludes,

> It would be strange arguing, indeed, because men never commit sin, but only when God leaves them *to themselves,* and necessarily sin when he does so, that therefore their sin is not *from themselves,* but from God; and so, that God must be a sinful being: as strange as it would be to argue, because it is always dark when the sun is gone, and never dark when the sun is present, that therefore all darkness is from the sun, and that his disk and beams must needs be black.[93]

---

91. Work, "Advent's Answer," 110.
92. Edwards, *Freedom,* §IX: 77, emph. in orig.
93. Edwards, *Freedom,* §IX: 77, emph. in orig.

Because God can look at an event through both a "narrow lens" and a "wide-angle lens" at the same time, he may decree something by his secret (or "decretive") will which his revealed (or "preceptive") will forbids

Deut 29:29 says, *"The secret things belong to the Lord our God, but the things revealed belong to us and to our sons forever, that we may observe all the words of this law."* While some passages state that God *"desires all men to be saved"* (1 Tim 2:4; see also Ezek 18:23; 2 Pet 3:9), other passages affirm that *not* all people will be saved but God unconditionally elects only *some* (Matt 11:27; John 1:12–13; 6:37–39, 44, 65; 10:25–29; Acts 13:48; Eph 1:4–5, 11; 2:8–9). I. Howard Marshall points out, "The fact that God wishes or wills that all people should be saved does not necessarily imply that all will respond to the gospel and be saved. *We must certainly distinguish between what God would like to see happen and what he actually does will to happen, and both of these things can be spoken of as God's will.*"[94] John Piper adds, "Affirming the will of God to save all, while also affirming the unconditional election of some, implies that there are at least "two wills" in God, or two ways of willing. It implies that God decrees one state of affairs while also willing and teaching that a different state of affairs should come to pass."[95]

Piper explains one aspect of this:

> God has the capacity to look at the world through two lenses. He can look through a narrow lens or through a wide-angle lens. When God looks at a painful or wicked event through his narrow lens, he sees the tragedy or the sin for what it is in itself and he is angered and grieved. "I do not delight in the death of anyone, says the Lord God" (Ezek. 18:32). But when God looks at a painful or wicked event through his wide-angle lens, he sees the tragedy or the sin in relation to everything leading up to it and everything flowing from it. He sees it in all the connections and effects that form a pattern or mosaic stretching into eternity. This mosaic, with all its (good and evil) parts he does delight in (Ps. 115:3).[96]

There is an important corollary that, because God can see the same thing through both the "narrow lens" and the "wide-angle lens," he may forbid and punish the evil *as evil* that people do even though he had ordained the event for his own good reasons. As we have seen, humans may have one

---

94. Marshall, "Universal," 56, emph. added.
95. Piper, "Are There," 109.
96. Piper, "Are There," 126.

motive for doing a particular act, yet God may have an entirely different motive for ordaining that very same act; humans may will and enjoy the act as sin, whereas God may ordain the act, not as sin but for a completely different and good reason. Thus, Jonathan Edwards states that there is no inconsistency in God's hating a thing "as it is in itself, and considered simply as evil, and yet that it may be his Will it should come to pass, considering all consequences. . . . His willing to order things so that evil should come to pass, for the sake of the contrary good, is no argument that he does not hate evil, as evil: and if so, then it is no reason why he may not reasonably forbid evil as evil, and punish it as such."[97] Examples of this include God's using Assyria to punish Israel for its sin but then punishing Assyria for its arrogance (Isa 10:5–19); raising up Babylon to destroy Israel but then holding Babylon guilty for its godlessness (Hab 1:5–11); and ordaining the betrayal and crucifixion of Christ but then pronouncing woe on the man who betrayed him (Matt 26:24; Mark 14:21; Luke 22:22).

A second important corollary is that God's secret or unrevealed decrees and the existence of sin and evil in the world do not in any way counteract God's revealed will concerning how we should act. God's "two wills" therefore counteract the idea of fatalism. Randy Alcorn states, "If God permits racism, slavery, and child sex trafficking, then why should we battle them? Here's why: the Bible speaks much about God's sovereignty, yet constantly calls upon people to take action, and to speak up for and help the poor and needy (see, for example, Proverbs 31:8–9)—this is the polar opposite of fatalism."[98] In sum, for his own good reasons which in large part he has *not revealed* to us God has permitted and ordained that sin and evil will exist in this world until Christ returns to earth, but at the same time he *has revealed* to us *"what is good"* and what he requires of us: *"to do justice, to love kindness, and to walk humbly with your God"* (e.g., Mic 6:8; see also, e.g., Deut 10:12–13; Matt 5:38–48; 22:36–40; 25:31–46; Luke 6:27–38; Eph 4:25—5:21; Jas 1:27).

POSSIBLE REASONS WHY GOD HAS ORDAINED THE EXISTENCE OF SIN AND EVIL

Although the Bible does not give us definitive answers concerning why God ordained the existence of sin and evil in general or specific instances of sin

---

97. Edwards, *Freedom*, §IX: 78–79; see also Piper, "Are There," 107–31; Edwards, *Remarks*, ch. 3: 525–43.

98. Alcorn, *If God*, 263.

and evil, there are enough statements and examples in the Bible to give us reasonably clear indications of why he has done so.

Because God is the greatest good that could possibly be, sin and evil are necessary in order that all aspects of God's nature and character are properly revealed

"God is utterly unique. He is the only being in the universe worthy of worship."[99] He is the source of all perfections: love, goodness, truth, holiness, righteousness, justice, mercy, grace, etc. Consequently, his glory is greater than anything (e.g., Isa 43:6-7; Hab 2:14; John 7:18; 1 Cor 10:31; 1 Pet 4:11; Rev 21:23). The "problem of evil" itself (along with many theodicies) is based on the implicit premise that humanity—our well-being and happiness—is central; that God created the world to bring about the best state possible for humanity. That assumption is incorrect. God did not create this world primarily for our benefit. Rather, the Bible states that *"by Him all things were created, both in the heavens and on earth, visible and invisible, . . . all things have been created through Him and for Him"* (Col 1:16). Ultimately, everything that God has ordained—including sin and evil—is part of a great plan, designed before the foundation of the world, to manifest the glory of God, the glory of Christ, and the glory of the grace of God in Christ (e.g., Ps 148:1-13; John 13:31-32; 17:1-5, 22-24; Rom 8:28-30; Eph 1:3-6; Phil 2:5-11; Heb 2:9-10). Charles Hodge states,

> The knowledge of God is eternal life. It is for creatures the highest good. And the promotion of that knowledge, the manifestation of the manifold perfections of the infinite God, is the highest end of all his works. . . . The glory of God being the great end of all things, we are not obliged to assume that this is the best possible world for the production of happiness, or even for securing the greatest degree of holiness among rational creatures. It is wisely adapted for the end for which it was designed, namely, the manifestation of the manifold perfections of God.[100]

A number of passages give examples of God's ordaining sin and evil in order to demonstrate the different facets of his character:

99. Piper, *Let the Nations*, 51.

100. Hodge, *Systematic*, 435-36; see also Erlandson, "A New Perspective," A Biblical Perspective ("God has ordained evil in order to display to all creation, and in particular to humanity, His glory in a way otherwise impossible. Namely, He has ordained man's fall and the resulting evils to demonstrate His righteousness, justice, grace, and mercy as fully as possible.").

- *Jesus answered, "It was not that this man sinned, or his parents, but that the works of God might be displayed in him." (John 9:3)*
- *Jesus said, "For judgment I came into this world, that those who do not see may see, and those who see may become blind." (John 9:39)*
- *For the Scripture says to Pharaoh, "For this very purpose I raised you up, to demonstrate My power in you, and that My name might be proclaimed throughout the whole earth." (Rom 9:17)*
- *What if God, although willing to demonstrate His wrath and to make His power known, endured with much patience vessels of wrath prepared for destruction? And He did so to make known the riches of His glory upon vessels of mercy, which He prepared beforehand for glory. (Rom 9:22–23)*
- *But the Scripture imprisoned everything under sin, so that the promise by faith in Jesus Christ might be given to those who believe. (Gal 3:22)*
- *He predestined us to adoption as sons and daughters through Jesus Christ to Himself, according to the good pleasure of His will, to the praise of the glory of His grace. (Eph 1:5–6a)*
- *In Him we also have obtained an inheritance, having been predestined according to the purpose of Him who works all things in accordance with the plan of His will, to the end that we who were the first to hope in the Christ would be to the praise of His glory. (Eph 1:11–12)*
- *You have heard of the endurance of Job and have seen the outcome of the Lord's dealings, that the Lord is full of compassion and is merciful. (Jas 5:11)*

In commenting on the Romans verses, Hodge states, "The punishment of the wicked is not an arbitrary act, having no object but to make them miserable; it is designed to manifest the displeasure of God against sin, and to make known his true character. On the other hand, the salvation of the righteous is designed to display the riches of his grace."[101]

Jonathan Edwards discusses *why* the existence of sin and evil are necessary for all aspects of God's full nature to be manifest. He observes that, because God's glory is of infinite value, all aspects of that glory should be revealed:

> Thus it is necessary, that God's awful majesty, his authority and dreadful greatness, justice, and holiness, should be manifested. But this could not be, unless sin and punishment had been

---

101. Hodge, *Commentary*, 319.

decreed. . . . If it were not right that God should decree and permit and punish sin, there could be no manifestation of God's holiness in hatred of sin. . . . There would be no manifestation of God's grace or true goodness, if there was no sin to be pardoned, no misery to be saved from. . . . And as it is necessary that there should be evil, because the display of the glory of God could not but be imperfect and incomplete without it, so evil is necessary.[102]

Although it may seem counter-factual that the existence of evil ultimately should augment our fullness and happiness, this actually is the case. The reason is that, "the creature's happiness consists in the knowledge of God, and sense of his love."[103] The existence of evil is necessary to reveal the fullness of God's character and glory. Consequently, "if the knowledge of him be imperfect, the happiness of the creature must be proportionably imperfect."[104]

It also should be remembered that the drama of existence—including the role of sin and evil, suffering and death—is being enacted on a stage far greater than what we can perceive or even imagine. God's glory and nature are demonstrated not just to people here on earth but throughout the universe, including the redeemed in heaven and the angels (e.g., 2 Kgs 6:15–17; Ps 19:1; Luke 15:10; 1 Cor 4:9; Eph 3:8–10; 1 Tim 3:16; Heb 12:1; Rev 15:3–4; 19:1–6). And, as discussed earlier, these matters all have eternal, not merely temporal, implications.

Finally, we earlier discussed the importance of the incarnation and the atonement for sin that Christ accomplished on the cross. The centrality of this is discussed throughout the NT:

---

102. Edwards, *Remarks*, ch. 3: 528; see also Piper, "Is God," 2.2 Why Does God Ordain; Erlandson, "A New Perspective," A Biblical Perspective ("Righteousness and justice are more fully displayed when not only is good rewarded but evil punished. Mercy and grace are more perfectly manifested when the recipients are utterly unworthy. . . . Grace and mercy are also more wondrously displayed in a world in which man's fall resulted in spiritual *death*, not partial impairment. A spiritually *sick* person might claim a hand in restoring himself to God's favor. Only a once-dead person who has been restored to divine favor will see the *extent* of Gods mercy."); Edwards, *The End*, 94–121; Hodge, *Systematic*, 435 ("Sin, therefore, according to the Scriptures, is permitted, that the justice of God may be known in its punishment, and his grace in its forgiveness. And the universe, without the knowledge of these attributes, would be like the earth without the light of the sun."); Piper, *Desiring*, 17–50; Piper, *Let the Nations*, 39–54)

103. Edwards, *Remarks*, ch. 3: 528.

104. Edwards, *Remarks*, ch. 3: 528.

- *Those whom He foreknew, He also predestined to become conformed to the image of His Son, so that He would be the firstborn among many brethren. (Rom 8:29)*

- *I pray that the eyes of your heart may be enlightened, so that you will know what is the hope of His calling, what are the riches of the glory of His inheritance in the saints, and what is the boundless greatness of His power toward us who believe. These are in accordance with the working of the strength of His might which He brought about in Christ, when He raised Him from the dead and seated Him at His right hand in the heavenly places, far above all rule and authority and power and dominion, and every name that is named, not only in this age but also in the one to come. And He put all things in subjection under His feet, and made Him head over all things to the church, which is His body, the fullness of Him who fills all in all. (Eph 1:18–23)*

- *Being found in appearance as a man, He humbled Himself by becoming obedient to the point of death, even death on a cross. For this reason also, God highly exalted Him, and bestowed on Him the name which is above every name, so that at the name of Jesus every knee will bow, of those who are in heaven and on earth and under the earth, and that every tongue will confess that Jesus Christ is Lord, to the glory of God the Father. (Phil 2:8–11)*

- *He is also head of the body, the church; and He is the beginning, the firstborn from the dead, so that He Himself will come to have first place in everything. (Col 1:18)*

W. Gary Crampton points out a probably little-thought of implication of this, namely, that God is ultimately glorified through the glorification of his Son. However, if Adam had passed the test in Eden and not sinned by eating the forbidden fruit, his positive righteousness would have been confirmed by God. In that case

> Adam's righteousness, then, would have been imputed to all of his descendants (that is, the entire human race). And all mankind would have gratefully looked to him, not Christ, as Savior. For all eternity, God would then share His glory with His creature: Adam. Ironically, the obedience of Adam would have led to idolatry. Therefore, that alternative would be logically impossible. Only the actual world, in which the fall of man occurred, is logically possible and redounds to the glory of God alone. Had Adam obeyed, Jesus Christ would have been denied His role as "the first-born among many brothers" and the Lord

of His church. And the Father would not receive the glory for His work through the Son.[105]

God cannot eliminate evil without at the same time eliminating human beings and the world as we know it

In his goodness and wisdom God chose to create a world populated by human beings. There are several characteristics that define what it means to be human. These characteristics make humans different from superhuman or subhuman beings. Although they vary from individual to individual, humans have the ability to reason, emotions, a will, desires, intentions, and the capacity for bodily movement. Further, human beings are finite creatures, which includes being physically, mentally, and morally finite, as opposed to possessing the non-physical nature of spiritual beings or God's omnipresence, omniscience, and moral perfection. God cannot eliminate moral evil because to do so would contradict his intention to create human beings and the world as he has.

The following reasons indicate why God's eliminating all moral evil necessarily would entail eliminating human beings and the world as we know it. An inherent part of this world is the fact that human beings are dependent upon each other to an enormous degree. Richard Swinburne points out that, since God has the power to benefit or harm people, for his created agents (human beings) to be in his likeness and share in his creative work, "they must have that power too.... A world in which agents can benefit each other but not do each other harm is one where they have only very limited responsibility for each other," as opposed to the great responsibility for each other which God intended and designed into creation and into human beings.[106] God would have to constantly constrain people's reason, emotions, will, desires or the objects of desire, intentions, and bodily movements, and/or interfere with the operation of natural laws, to prevent sin and evil from occurring.[107] Indeed, to bring even one person to the point of always and only freely choosing to do good would require significantly rearranging the lives of a host of others.[108] In short, there would no longer be a world as we know it or human beings as we know them.

A stable and predictable natural order is necessary for deliberation, planning, prediction, social interaction, and action of virtually every kind.

105. Crampton, "A Biblical," 5–6.
106. Swinburne, *The Existence*, 189.
107. Feinberg, *No One*, 789–95.
108. Feinberg, *No One*, 790.

Peter van Inwagen observes that, for God to miraculously or otherwise prevent cases of natural or moral evil would result in a world that is massively irregular. "And, of course, there is no sharp cut-off point between a world that is massively irregular and a world that is not. . . . There is, therefore, no minimum number of cases of intense suffering that God could allow without forfeiting the good of a world that is not massively irregular."[109] Again, therefore, to interfere with or change the natural laws and processes of the world would necessitate a different sort of world and thereby different sorts of creatures than human beings to populate that world.

The point is not that God uses evil for good (as in Rom 8:28) but that the existence of human beings in the nature in which they have been created and in a world like this are "a value of the first order," i.e., a good in-and-of-itself, superior to all other values.[110] Human beings are an antecedent good that is worth having despite the sin and evil we cause.

All the evil that God allows and ordains ultimately serves and brings about the greater good of creation itself

Paul said, *"We know that God causes all things to work together for good to those who love God, to those who are called according to his purpose"* (Rom 8:28). *One* of the reasons why God ordains evil is that *sometimes* evil brings about a greater good for individuals—either the sufferers or others—*in this present age*. God may intend to accomplish a host of things in many different people with respect to any particular act of evil. There are an almost infinite number of examples of this. Here are just a few:

- "The amputation of a limb is an evil; but if necessary to save life, it is a good. Wars are dreadful evils, yet the world is indebted to wars for the preservation of civil and religious liberty, for which they are a small price. . . . Thus, if sin be the necessary means of the greatest good, it ceases to be an evil, on the whole, and it is perfectly consistent with the benevolence of God to permit its occurrence."[111]
- Joseph was sold into slavery by his brothers but later told them, *"You meant evil against me, but God meant it for good in order to bring about this present result, to preserve many people alive"* (Gen 50:20). As the story of Joseph unfolds, we see that God was using the evil of selling

---

109. Van Inwagen, "The Problem," 173n.11.

110. See Presbyterian, "The Nature," 287 for a Christian affirmation of this and Mueller, "Carl Menger Explains," *passim* for a non-theistic affirmation of this.

111. Hodge, *Systematic*, 432–33.

Joseph into slavery to accomplish different things in Joseph, in his brothers, in his extended family, in the nation of Egypt, in the lives of thousands of people throughout the Middle East who otherwise would have starved in a famine; this ultimately led to the creation of the nation of Israel and the coming of the Messiah. Almost none of this could have been known or predicted by anyone who looked only at the evil of selling Joseph into slavery itself.

- In the Bible, God uses evil to test his servants (Job; Jas 1:3; 1 Pet 1:7); to discipline them (1 Cor 11:31–32; Heb 12:4–11); to preserve their lives (Gen 50:20); to teach them patience and perseverance, develop character, and instill hope (Rom 5:3–5; Jas 1:2–4); to redirect their attention to what is most important (Psalm 37); to deepen their faith in Christ (Phil 3:7–11); to enable them to comfort others (2 Cor 1:3–7); to enable them to bear powerful witness to the truth (Acts 7); to give them greater joy when suffering is replaced by glory (1 Pet 4:13); to judge the wicked in history (Deut 28:15–68) and in the life to come (Matt 25:41–46); to bring reward to persecuted believers (Matt 5:10–12); and to display the work of God (Exod 9:16; John 9:3; Rom 9:17).

- Timothy Keller and John Feinberg list ten categories of how God may use suffering and affliction in our lives: (1) To transform our attitudes of ourselves, humble us, and remove our pride and boasting; (2) To cause us to see that we have valued too highly certain good things in our lives; (3) To strengthen and deepen our relationship with God, ultimately leading to our exaltation (see 2 Cor 4:7–18); (4) To make us more compassionate toward the suffering of others (see 2 Cor 1:3–5) and thereby demonstrate, to believers and unbelievers alike, the body of Christ and even lead to a ministry that is possible in one's suffering and to the suffering; (5) To provide an opportunity for God to manifest his power (see John 9:1–3); (6) To allow God to demonstrate through us true faith to Satan and others; as he did through Job; (7) To promote our sanctification; (8) To prepare us for further trials; (9) To refine us and our works in preparation for our judgment (see 1 Pet 1:7); (10) To use our affliction as a means to take us to be with Himself.[112]

- God mercifully *withholds* his judgment and the vengeance and repayment that will be exacted upon the unrighteous. This may cause frustration, and even suffering and death for the innocent who wait for God's *"judging and avenging our blood"* (Rev 6:10). As Telford Work points out, "The result of God's extraordinary mercy in withholding

---

112. See Keller, *Walking*, 190–92; Feinberg, *The Many Faces*, 340–46.

judgment is, of course, *the problem of evil*. Why does God wait while people wound and annihilate other people? Who could have thought he does it out of love? But God replies: 'Should I not pity Nineveh, that great city, in which there are more than a hundred and twenty thousand persons who do not know their right hand from their left, and also much cattle?' (Jon. 4:11)."[113]

- With respect to such virtues as courage, compassion, forgiveness, self-sacrifice, etc., various evils need to exist, because "evils give men the opportunity to perform those acts which show men at their best. A world without evils would be a world in which men could show no forgiveness, no compassion, no self-sacrifice. And men without that opportunity are deprived of the opportunity to show themselves at their noblest."[114] John Hick likens this to a "vale of soul-making." While we all seek pleasure, we do not seek for ourselves or our children "unalloyed pleasure at the expense of their growth in such even greater values as moral integrity, unselfishness, compassion, courage, humour, reverence for the truth, and perhaps above all the capacity for love.... Rather, this world must be a place of soul-making."[115] He then quotes the poet John Keats who coined the phrase "vale of soul-making" and said, "Do you not see how necessary a World of pains and troubles is to school an Intelligence and make it a Soul?[116]

- Some people reject God as a result of affliction and suffering. However, "Just as many people *find* God through affliction and suffering. They find that adversity moves them toward God rather than away."[117] Elie Wiesel, himself a survivor of Nazi extermination camps, captures the different responses people may have to similar afflictions: "'And Auschwitz? What do you make of Auschwitz?' . . . Gregor was angry. 'After what happened to us, how can you believe in God?' With an understanding smile on his lips the Rebbe answered, 'How can you *not* believe in God after what has happened?'"[118]

---

113. Work, "Advent's Answer," 107, emph. in orig. (the online version of this article says "theodicy" instead of "the problem of evil"); see also Rom 2:4; 1 Tim 2:4; 2 Pet 3:9; Rev 2:21.

114. Swinburne, *The Existence*, 214–15.

115. Hick, *Evil*, 253, 256, 258, 259.

116. Hick, *Evil*, 259n.1.

117. Keller, *Walking*, 5.

118. Wiesel, *The Gates*, 192.

The great good that God is working even through evil is beginning now and applies at the individual level. Thus, God is with us in our suffering now (e.g., Deut 31:6; Ps 23:4; John 14:16–20; Rom 8:35–39; 2 Cor 12:7–10; Phil 4:12–13; Heb 13:5). He knows what we are going through and enables us to withstand and even be refined by our suffering (e.g., Ps 119:71; Matt 5:10–12; Acts 5:40–42; 1 Cor 10:13; 2 Cor 1:3–4; 4:16–17; Jas 1:2–4). Christ so identifies with his people that he senses our sufferings as his own (Acts 9:4–5). In fact, God takes our grief and mourning and turns it into joy (Ps 30:11; Jer 31:13; John 16:20). But growth and transformation through the fire of affliction are not automatic. We must recognize him, turn to him not away from him, believe in him, know him, call on him, trust in him, and embrace him as we experience hardship and suffering in order to see our affliction as part of his plan for us and be transformed and matured by him through it.

The Bible does *not promise* that *every* sin and evil will result in some greater good or "happy ending" *in this life*. Suffering, often unjust suffering, happens to all kinds of people. Bad things, often horrible things, happen to people who have done nothing to deserve it. The problem with only looking to this life for the goodness, justice, and recompense we long for is that our perspective is too limited—because our lives do not end when we die. Instead, the Bible promises us new, resurrected bodies living on a new, redeemed earth, all guaranteed by the resurrection of Christ (1 Cor 15:20–26, 50–58). Ironically, all of this is brought about by the greatest sin ever committed: the betrayal and crucifixion of the only perfect, holy, sinless person who ever lived—Jesus Christ; yet it was only by his submitting to this gross sin and evil that Christ was able to bear our sins and the punishment for those sins that we deserved in order to destroy the power of sin and evil, reconcile mankind to God, and transform our lives.

All of the suffering of this world cannot compare to the great, everlasting glory that God will bring about in the consummation (Rom 8:18–21; 2 Cor 4:16–18; Rev 21:1–4). "When we live peacefully on the New Earth, where joy will permeate the very air we breathe, we will look back at this present world and affirm not by faith but by sight that all the evil and suffering was worth it—and that Christ's incarnation and redemption have made the universe eternally better."[119] Indeed, for the redeemed, the eternal and therefore infinite experience of the new heaven and new earth not only will provide "a new perspective on the evaluation of life in the body" but will "dwarf the entirety of one's earthly sorrows—however great they may have

---

119. Alcorn, *If God*, 195; see also Willard, *God and*, n.p.

seemed during the embodied lifetime."[120] In the consummation, God's justice, grace, mercy, and righteousness will be plain to everyone; no one will accuse him of wrongdoing. Rather, *"all the nations will come and worship before You, For Your righteous acts have been revealed"* (Rev 15:4).

We began this section with Rom 8:28, and that verse contains a key word which we need to bear in mind. That word is "together." Rom 8:28 is saying that "all things—even bad ones—will ultimately *together* be overruled by God in such a way that the intended evil will, in the end, only accomplish the opposite of its designs—a greater good and glory than would otherwise have come to pass."[121] Now, only God has the perspective to see how that is being accomplished; but one day we will see it, too.

THE EXISTENCE OF HELL

According to the Bible, all suffering, evil, and death ultimately stem from humanity's rejecting God, their fall into sin, and their continued pursuit of sin (see, e.g., Gen 2:16–17; 3:1–19; Rom 5:12). However, there will come a day of judgment. The OT speaks of the *"day of the Lord,"* which typically meant judgment involving the concurrent destruction of the wicked and salvation of the righteous (e.g., Isa 13:1—14:23; Joel 1:13—3:21; Amos 5:18—9:15; Obad 15–17; Zeph 1:7—3:20). The NT makes clear that the day of judgment will take place in connection with the second coming of Christ and will entail the judgment of all people, believers and unbelievers alike (e.g., Matt 7:21–23; 16:27; 25:31–46; John 5:25–29; Acts 17:31; Rom 2:5–16; 2 Cor 5:10; 2 Thess 1:6–10; Rev 20:11–15; 22:12). This will also entail the destruction or cleansing of the present world and the restoration of creation, i.e., the inauguration of the new heaven and new earth (see Acts 3:19–21; Rom 8:17–25; 2 Pet 3:3–13; Rev 21:1–2, 10).

The Bible says that the punishment for sin against God is, first, consignment of those who have not repented of their sins and turned in faith and obedience to God to a place called Hades (see Luke 16:19–31), and then, ultimately, to a place called Gehenna or the *"lake of fire"* or *"the second death,"* commonly known as hell (e.g., Rev 19:20; 20:6, 10, 14–15). It is also described as *"outer darkness"* (Matt 8:12; 22:13; 25:30). Jesus warned, *"Do not fear those who kill the body but are unable to kill the soul; but rather fear Him who is able to destroy both soul and body in hell"* (Matt 10:28). Hell will last forever (e.g., Matt 25:46; Mark 9:43–48; Rev 20:10). Some object to this idea. They think that for God to do this is unjust and that everlasting

---

120. Ferraiolo, "Eternal," Time Heals All Wounds.
121. Keller, *Walking*, 301–2.

punishment is excessive. There are at least two responses to such objections: (1) justice: and (2) respect for human dignity and choice.[122]

With respect to justice, we humans tend to minimize the significance and seriousness of sin. That simply reveals our own "fallen" and corrupt nature. To a large extent, our view of sin is a problem of our perspective. For example, children may think that disobedience to their parents is insignificant, and their parents' discipline is excessive; whereas, the parents know how serious the matter may be and where, if it continues, it likely will lead.[123] Unlike us, and unlike disobedient children, God is perfectly holy. He sees clearly and completely our sin and all of its consequences for the sinner, for those hurt by one's sins, for others, and for the world itself. Indeed, our sin—moral evil—affects not simply the persons committing the moral evil but has affected all of humanity and the created order itself (see Gen 3:14–19; Rom 5:12–19; 8:20–22). The effects of sin spiral far beyond our ability to perceive them. What we think of as finite sins in reality have infinite or everlasting effects.

God sees the utterly horrid nature of sin. All sin ultimately is against God and affects him personally (see Acts 9:4–5).[124] Hence, he cannot abide in the presence of sin (Hab 1:13). One principle of justice is that the punishment should fit the crime. Nicola Yacoub Ghabril gives the following example: "If a student at school insults his fellow pupil, he is punished lightly, whereas if he insults his teacher he would be expelled from school. In legislative terms, if someone reviles his equal it is considered an offence, but if he insults the judge his punishment would be greater. However, if he insults the king his sentence would be greater still. But if he should sin against God, who is unsurpassed in greatness and holiness, how much more would be his punishment!"[125] God is infinite and all sin ultimately is against him; he also sees the infinite, rippling effects of sin on people and the world. Given the infinite and infinitely holy nature of the One we sin against, and the infinite, everlasting effects of our sin, it is reasonable to conclude that the everlasting nature of hell is not excessive retribution for the great evil of people's rejecting God and destroying humanity and the world through sin.

With respect to honoring human dignity and choice, Rom 1:19–20 tells us that all people know from the natural world that God exists and know his essential nature. Rom 2:15 goes on to say that God's law (the moral

---

122. For good defenses of the traditional view of hell see Peterson, *Hell*, passim; Feinberg, *The Many Faces*, 3rd ed., 395–444; see also the resources at Feinberg, *The Many Faces*, 3rd ed., 531–32n.44.

123. See Feinberg, *The Many Faces*, 3rd ed., 434–35; Feinberg, *The Many Faces*, 331.

124. See Appendix 1n.7 and associated text.

125. Ghabril, *Themes*, 20.

law) is written in our hearts (see also Rom 1:32); hence, everyone knows the difference between right and wrong. Despite this inborn knowledge of God and the moral law, people *"suppress the truth in unrighteousness"* (Rom 1:18), and *"even though they knew God, they did not honor him as God or give thanks"* (Rom 1:21); instead, they *"exchanged the truth of God for a lie, and worshiped and served the creature rather than the Creator"* (Rom 1:25). Rom 1:24, 26, and 28 go on to say that people want to follow their own sinful passions and desires and even *"give hearty approval"* to those who do likewise (Rom 1:32). As a result, God *"gave them over"* and let them do as they themselves wish to do (Rom 1:24, 26, 28). Eph 4:19 adds that sinful people *"have given themselves over"* to their sinful passions and desires. Consequently, as Paul says, *"There is none righteous, not even one; . . . There is none who seeks for God; . . . There is none who does good, there is not even one"* (Rom 3:10–12). Given God's natural revelation of himself and his moral law, we are *"without excuse"* (Rom 1:20).

Despite all of this, God did not give up on humanity. Instead, he continued to give people more and more revelation of himself by sending prophets, giving us his written Word, communicating to people through visions and dreams (e.g., Gen 20:3–7; Job 33:13–18), miracles, answered prayers, angels (e.g., Matt 1:20; 2:13; 28:5), and ultimately coming himself to the world in the person of Jesus Christ. Feinberg summarizes that the upshot is, "not only do all people at all times have some revelation of God, but more, up to and including a message about salvation of their souls, is available, if they genuinely seek God."[126] Yet, did the vast bulk of people seek, submit to, and follow God, even when he came to us in person? No. They crucified him.

So what is hell? Hell is God's giving us over to what we have been striving for all of our lives—to be in charge of our own lives and get away from him. In short, people are receiving in the afterlife what they have always desired in this life: to be free from God.[127] There is a corollary to this, namely, that hell is a "natural" consequence of our life-choices. A life of self-centeredness shrinks the soul, whereas a life of God-centeredness leads a person to joy, wholeness, and richness of community. These two trajectories are apparent in this life. They evidently continue in the after-life. Timothy Keller concludes, "If, as the Bible teaches, our souls will go on forever, then just imagine where these two kinds of souls will be in a billion years. Hell is simply one's freely chosen path going on forever. We wanted to get away

---

126. Feinberg, *The Many Faces*, 3rd ed., 438.

127. Keller, "The Importance," sec. 3; see also Lewis, *The Problem*, 118–23, 127–28; Feinberg, *The Many Faces*, 3rd ed., 432–33.

from God, and God, in his infinite justice, sends us where we wanted to go."[128] In short, the doctrine of hell is not contrary to and does not detract from either God's justice or his goodness.

GOD'S SOVEREIGNTY, HUMANITY'S RESPONSIBILITY, AND THE EXISTENCE OF SIN AND EVIL: CONCLUSION

People legitimately raise serious questions in the face of evil, particularly when evil they have not directly caused happens to them or to their loved ones and friends.[129] God has good and sufficient reasons for everything he has ordained and allows—including all the sin and evil—but he has not revealed all of those reasons to us and often does not reveal why any specific evil has occurred. Deut 29:29 and the sufferings of Job demonstrate this. One thing that makes it impossible for us to know why God has ordained and allowed any particular act of evil to occur is that he may have different reasons and different purposes for what appear to us to be similar or identical acts of evil. Feinberg illustrates this with the example of a father who refuses to let his child stay up for a party: "One time he may refuse because the child has a cold, another time some guest may not want the child there, and another time he may refuse because the next morning the family must go somewhere and he wants his son have a good night's sleep."[130] So with God and his decisions to ordain or not prevent the existence of evil.

While people rightly are troubled by the existence and pervasiveness of sin and evil in the world, so is God. There is a certain disingenuousness to the "problem of evil." We tend to blame God for the existence of evil instead of working to eradicate it, despite the fact that "God has placed in our own hands the means to assuage many of the evils we deplore."[131] On the other hand, God will justly judge the perpetrators of sin and evil who, in fact, already stand condemned and under God's judgment (Gen 18:25; Num 14:18; Ps 7:8–16; John 3:18; 16:11; Acts 10:42; Rom 2:12–16). All the accounts will be balanced, and justice and righteousness will prevail. As we saw earlier, only that gives us the ability to be people of confidence and hope, who can

128. Keller, "The Importance," sec.3.

129. Feinberg observes that there is no *one* "problem of evil." The phrase stands for different problems that confront different theological systems. Those problems include the theological issues we have dealt with in this book, but the "problem of evil" also includes what Feinberg calls the "religious problem of evil," namely, the emotional and spiritual crisis that may occur to us when bad things happen to us, our loved ones, and our friends. See Feinberg, *The Many Faces*, 14, 315.

130. Feinberg, *The Many Faces*, 308.

131. Boyd, *Why Doesn't God*, 107.

pursue peace and justice, not hatred and vengeance now, because we know God will right all wrongs and bring about perfect justice in the end and for all eternity.

But God has done more than just assure us that he will justly judge humanity for the sins, wrongs, and evils they have committed: God himself came to earth in the person of Jesus Christ and was subject to sin and evil; he bore our sin and paid the price for our sin so that all those who turn to him will receive life instead of eternal death at the judgment. In light of all of this, Russian Christian novelist Fyodor Dostoevsky concluded,

> I believe like a child that suffering will be healed and made up for. I believe that all the humiliating absurdity of human contradictions will vanish like a mirage, like the despicable fabrication of the impotent and infinitely small Euclidean mind of man. I believe that at the world's end, at the moment of eternal harmony, something so precious will come to pass that it will suffice for all hearts, for the comforting of all resentments, for the atonement of all the crimes of humanity, of all the blood that has been shed. I believe that it will not only be possible to forgive but to justify all that has happened.[132]

---

132. Dostoevsky, *The Brothers*, 217.

Appendix 1
The Gospel

GOD IS HOLY, JUST, righteous, and good (Gen 18:25; Exod 34:6–7; Lev 11:44; Job 34:10–12; Ps 5:4; 136:1; 145:17; Hab 1:13; Rom 1:18; Jas 1:13). Although the first human beings (Adam and Eve) were created without sin, they chose to follow Satan and disobey God and therefore became sinful (Gen 3:1–19). As a result, every human being since Adam and Eve has been born in a state of moral corruption known as indwelling sin; this indwelling sin is a "law" or power that is actively working inside every person (Rom 7:5, 8–11, 14–24; Gal 5:17; Heb 3:12–13). It leads to universal actualized sins as people go through their lives (Gen 8:21; Ps 51:5; 143:1–2; Jer 17:9; Mark 7:20–23; Rom 3:9–18, 23; 5:12–14; 7:14–24). The Bible correctly tells us the result of this: *"the wages of sin is death"* (Rom 6:23; see also Gen 2:17; Ezek 18:4, 20; Rom 5:12).

Every person knows in his or her heart that we have a fundamental problem deep within us that we cannot eradicate. Many people tend to downplay the seriousness of this by saying something like "to err is human." However, we must consider what we are like in relation to God. God's holiness is foundational. Sin is incompatible with his holiness. Closely related to God's holiness is his wrath. God's wrath "is in fact his holy reaction to evil. . . . God's holiness exposes sin; his wrath opposes it."[1] Hence, God cannot tolerate sin.

There is an important corollary to this, namely, that "God is not indifferent to our immoral thoughts and behaviour. On the contrary, his holy nature is deeply offended by such things. As a perfect God, he cannot ignore anything evil. The smallest lie is an offense to the One who is truth. The tiniest feeling of animosity towards another person is repulsive to the One who is love. Due to his holy and perfect nature, God cannot turn a blind eye to perverse human behaviour as if it does not matter."[2] Consequently,

---

1. Stott, *The Cross*, 103, 106; see Hab 1:13; Rom 1:18.
2. Alexander, *From Eden*, 130.

"if God is to be true to his own righteous nature, all wrongdoing must be punished. In addition, if God is to condemn and punish Satan, then he must be consistent in condemning and punishing . . . every other creature that has rebelled against his divine authority."[3]

This raises the issue that was once raised by Sultan Muhammad Khan, the issue that goes to the heart of every religion:

> The more I thought, the more evident it became to me that salvation is the vital breath of religion and its necessary foundation. Without it a religion is not a religion. Furthermore, I considered that all men agree that man, as his name indicates, is a bundle of forgetfulness, disobedience, and transgressions. His life never remains so pure as to be absolutely free from the stain of sin. Sin has become man's second nature. It is a true saying that "to err is human". The question is how can one escape accountability and punishment? How is one to be saved? . . . It is my duty to investigate this important matter honestly and without prejudice.[4]

The answer to Sultan Khan's question reveals the fact that, although there are many religions in the world, there are only two *kinds* of religion: Christianity and everything else. Every religion except Christianity is based on the principle that, ultimately, each person must save him- or herself by "trying harder," doing enough "good deeds," making enough sacrifices, or denying oneself enough things. They think, "If my good deeds outweigh my bad deeds, I'm in!" However, that approach to salvation is doomed to failure for at least five reasons:

- First, because God himself is morally holy and perfect, that is the standard to which God holds us (Matt 5:48). However, "once a person sins, it is impossible to ever be perfect."[5]

- Second, even our good deeds are tainted with sin and typically arise from mixed motives. Indeed, if we are doing good deeds in order to escape God's punishment and hell, that alone makes our good deeds *not* "good." The reason is that if our motive is to escape hell by doing "good deeds," then those deeds are, by definition, selfish and self-centered, e.g., when we help the poor, we are really primarily helping *ourselves*

---

3. Alexander, *From Eden*, 131; see Rom 2:16; 2 Cor 5:10; Heb 9:27; Rev 20:10–15. Although most people deny their connection with Satan, Jesus called Satan *"the ruler of this world"* (John 12:31). Jesus told the Pharisees, *"You are of your father the devil"* (John 8:44). Elsewhere Satan is called *"the god of this world [age]"* (2 Cor 4:4) who holds unbelievers "captive" (2 Tim 2:26) and in his power (1 John 5:19; see also Eph 2:2; Col 1:13).

4. Khan, *A Testimony*, 11.

5. Sproul, *Saved*, 94; see also at 53.

avoid hell. Thus, no amount of good deeds, since they themselves are tainted with sin, can atone for other sins.

- Third, it is impossible to ever know whether one has "done enough" good deeds or made enough sacrifices to satisfy God. All people know, in our "heart of hearts," that we should be more loving, caring, generous, and kind than we are. We all know that we should not be as self-centered and selfish as we are. We all know that we do not and cannot even meet our own standards, let alone God's.

- Fourth, no amount of good deeds changes the sinful nature and sinful propensities of the heart. Thus, good deeds do not transform corrupt, sinful people into righteous, sinless people at their core; they remain sinful people. If God let sinful people into heaven and the new earth in which people will live forever, heaven and the new earth would be forever corrupted. God could not be there, since "sin cannot approach God, and God cannot tolerate sin."[6] Indeed, given humanity's innate corruption and sinful propensities, heaven would be turned into a hell.

- Fifth, ultimately all sin is against God directly. When Saul was persecuting the church, Jesus appeared to him on the road to Damascus and said, *"Saul, Saul, why are you persecuting Me?"* (Acts 9:4); he did not just say, "Why are you persecuting my people?" Because God's law comes from him and is a reflection of his holy nature, to sin by transgressing his law is to offend him personally. Further, to sin against other people is to sin against God because people are made in the image of God (Gen 1:26–27; 9:6; Jas 3:9–10); sin amounts to dishonoring and defiling God's image and thereby reveals what the sinner really thinks about God himself.[7] God is infinite: infinitely holy; infinitely lovely; infinitely good. Therefore, our obligation to him is infinite (Deut 6:5; Matt 22:37; Mark 12:30; Luke 10:27). Consequently, our sin against him amounts to an infinite evil. Even at the human level, sin is like dropping a rock into a pool of water; the rock creates ripples from its point of entry to the surrounding waters. In the same way sin permanently corrupts and changes the sinner, other people, and the world in ways perhaps unknown to the sinner, which may have effects that last for generations. Any "good deeds" or other things we try to do to atone for our sin and earn our salvation, by their very nature, are *temporal and imperfect*. They do not transform the sinner into a holy

---

6. Stott, *The Cross*, 106.

7. Jesus epitomized this when he forgave people of their sins. He did not consult those whom the sinner had wronged or offended. In forgiving the sinner, Jesus acted as he was the chief party wronged or offended by the sin. See Lewis, *Mere Christianity*, 55.

person and they cannot eliminate the effects of the sin which has *permanently* corrupted the sinner's soul and has affected other people and the world. In short, there is no such thing as a finite offense against an infinite God. Consequently, no temporal, finite, and imperfect deeds of ours can ever hope to atone for the infinity of our sin.

Since we cannot save ourselves, "some may say the problem is not severe because God in His kindness will overlook it. God could do this if He were willing to negotiate His own righteousness or sacrifice His own justice."[8] Even an earthly judge who didn't enforce the law but simply let the guilty go free without punishment would be universally recognized as unjust. That is why God cannot just say, "In My mercy and compassion, I forgive you sinful people." To do that would be both unjust and would result in sinful people forever inhabiting and corrupting heaven and the new earth. On the other hand, as discussed above, human beings are not able to save themselves. Because all humans are corrupt at their core and sin against God in thought, word, and deed, no amount of "good deeds," rule keeping, or other actions could ever hope to atone for our sin. Thus, if left to themselves, all humans have earned and deserve only God's judgment. This results in a profound dilemma: "Man as a sinner owes God for his sin what he is unable to pay, and cannot be saved without paying"[9]

However, God is loving and does not desire that anyone would perish (Ezek 18:23; 33:11; 2 Pet 3:9; 1 John 4:8). This is where Christianity is different from every other religion. Christianity alone recognizes and takes seriously the "fallenness" of human beings, the gravity of sin, the holiness and perfection of God, the incompatibility of God and sin coexisting together, the fact that all humans have earned and deserve judgment for their sins, and the inability of people by their own efforts to save themselves. Jesus is unlike the founders of all other religions. They simply told people what the people had to believe and do (e.g., follow the five pillars of Islam or the eight-fold path of Buddhism). Jesus said that he *is* the way of salvation (John 14:6). He came to do for us what we never could do for ourselves. The difference of Christianity is Jesus; the difference of Christianity is the cross.

That is why the fact that Jesus was fully man and also was fully God not only is important but is absolutely necessary for salvation. God cannot forgive us for our sins unless those sins are fully paid for; to do otherwise would be to condone the sin and the violation of his own law. Therefore, as Gleason Archer states, "It was only as a man that God in Christ could furnish a satisfaction sufficient to atone for the sins of mankind; for only

---

8. Sproul, *Saved*, 94.
9. Anselm, *Cur Deus*, I:25.

a man, a true human being, could properly represent the human race. But our Redeemer also had to be God, for only God could furnish a sacrifice of infinite value, to compensate for the penalty of eternal hell that our sin demands, according to the righteous claims of divine justice."[10] Anselm of Canterbury puts it like this:

> Because man *cannot* satisfy his debt to God, none but God *can* make this satisfaction. But none but a man *ought* to do this, other wise man does not make the satisfaction. If it be necessary, therefore, as it appears, that the heavenly kingdom be made up of men, and this cannot be effected unless the aforesaid satisfaction be made, which none but God can make and none but man ought to make, it is necessary for the God-man to make it. . . . Therefore, in order that the God-man may perform this, it is necessary that the same being should be perfect God and perfect man, in order to make this atonement. . . . Since, then, it is necessary that the God-man preserve the completeness of each nature, it is no less necessary that these two natures be united entire in one person, just as a body and a reasonable soul exist together in every human being; for otherwise it is impossible that the same being should be very God and very man.[11]

Only Jesus Christ meets the qualifications.

So, what is the gospel? The word "gospel" is a Greek word (*euaggelion*) which means "good news."[12] The Greek word "gospel" was "news of a great historical event, such as a victory in war or the ascension of a new king, that changed the listeners' condition and required a response from the listener. So the gospel is news of what God has done to reach us. It is not advice about what we must do to reach God."[13] The gospel is the good news that God has done for us what we never could do for ourselves. God became a man in the person of Jesus Christ. Jesus lived the life we should have lived *as a man*; he perfectly obeyed God the Father in everything; he was *"tempted in all things as we are, yet without sin"* (Heb 4:15). That qualified him to be our representative, to take upon himself our sin and pay the penalty that otherwise we would have to pay but never could (Rom 8:1–4; 2 Cor 5:21; Gal 3:13; Col 2:13–14; 1 Tim 2:5–6; 1 Pet 2:24). At the same time, Jesus Christ was God. Thus, on the cross God did not cause sin, pain, evil, and death to

---

10. Archer, *Encyclopedia*, 323.

11. Anselm, *Cur Deus*, II:6–7.

12. Danker, *A Greek-English, euaggelion*, 402; Green and McKnight, *Dictionary*, 282.

13. Keller, "The Gospel," 1.

be inflicted on someone else; instead, he took it all onto himself. "Why did Jesus *have* to die in order to forgive us? There was a debt to be paid—God himself paid it. There was a penalty to be borne—God himself bore it."[14]

Jesus' rising from the dead and ascending back to the Father validated who Jesus is and demonstrated that the Father accepted Christ's sacrifice of himself on the cross for us. Consequently, who Jesus is and what he has done is the heart of the gospel. It is repeatedly proclaimed throughout the NT, e.g., 1 Cor 15:1-5: *"Now I make known to you, brethren, the gospel which I preached to you, which also you received, in which also you stand, by which also you are saved, if you hold fast to the word which I preached to you, unless you believed in vain. For I delivered to you as of first importance what I also received, that Christ died for our sins according to the Scriptures, and that He was buried, and that he was raised on the third day according to the Scriptures, and that He appeared to Cephas, then to the twelve"* (see also John 20:30-31; Acts 10:36-43; 16:30-31; Rom 1:1-4, 16-17; 3:23-28; 10:8-13; 1 Cor 2:2; 1 Pet 3:18).

Because the gospel—and people's salvation—is based on what Christ has done, salvation cannot be "earned" by doing "good deeds." Rather, salvation is *given* by God to people as a *gift* of his *grace*; it is *received* by people solely by *faith* in Christ. As Eph 2:8-9 says, *"For by grace you have been saved through faith; and that not of yourselves, it is the gift of God; not as a result of works, so that no one may boast."* To be saved means to repent of our sins, accept by faith what Christ has done for us, and turn to Christ as the Lord of our life (Matt 11:28; Mark 1:14-15; John 1:12; 3:16; 17:3; Acts 26:20; 1 John 1:8-9). The *Westminster Confession of Faith* (1647) summarizes: "The principal acts of saving faith are accepting, receiving, and resting upon Christ alone for justification, sanctification, and eternal life."[15] In Christ, we are as free from the guilt and penalty of sin as if we had paid the full price for our sin ourselves (Rom 6:3-7; Gal 2:20). In fact, when we turn to Christ in faith, he not only takes our sin onto himself and pays the price for our sin that we should have paid, but he also imputes to us his righteousness so that we can stand before God (Isa 53:5-6, 10-11; Rom 10:4; 2 Cor 5:21; Heb 2:17-18; 1 Pet 2:4; 3:18).

When we believe the gospel and turn to Christ as our Lord, all aspects of our lives are affected: (1) All those who are united to Christ by faith have assurance of their salvation. If salvation depended even in part on our own efforts, we could never have the assurance that we had "done enough" to merit salvation. However, because God-in-Christ did for us what we could

---

14. Keller, *The Reason*, 193.
15. *Westminster*, XIV:2.

not do, Christians can and do have assurance that they are and forever will remain saved (John 3:36; 6:37, 47; 11:25; 1 John 5:11–12). (2) Being saved and united with Christ changes the legal status of Christians. "The cross liberates from the power of sin, propitiates God's wrath, washes away the guilt and stain of sin, reconciles believers to God, and achieves cosmic victory over deadly spiritual foes."[16] (3) Being saved and united with Christ changes Christians on the inside. When one comes to Christ, he or she receives a new heart (Ezek 36:26; 2 Cor 3:3), the mind of Christ (1 Cor 2:16), and the Spirit from Christ (Ezek 36:26; John 14:17). (4) Being saved and united with Christ gives Christians an intimate, personal relationship with God through Christ. Christians can *"draw near with confidence to the throne of grace"* (Heb 4:16; see also Heb 7:19) because Christ is "in" believers (e.g., Gal 2:20; Eph 3:17; Col 1:27; 1 John 3:24) and believers are "in Christ" (e.g., Rom 8:1; 1 Cor 1:30; 2 Cor 1:21; 5:17; 1 Pet 5:14). (5) Being saved and united with Christ creates a new humanity (John 3:3; Rom 6:4; 2 Cor 5:17; Gal 6:15); believers are adopted into God's family as his children (John 1:12; Rom 8:14–17, 23; 9:4; Gal 3:26; 4:5–7; Eph 1:5; 2:19; 1 John 3:1) and become deeply related to each other as brothers and sisters (e.g., Matt 12:50; Acts 1:16; Rom 14:10; 1 Tim 5:1–2). (6) One day, Christ will return and renew the entire world and all of creation (Rom 8:18–23; 2 Pet 3:3–13; Rev 21:1–11). That, in essence, is the gospel.

All of this has ethical implications for our lives. Being saved and united with Christ gives Christians a new motive and means of living compared to that of every other religion and worldview. "Religion operates on the principle 'I obey—therefore I am accepted by God.' But the operating principle of the gospel is 'I am accepted by God through what Christ has done—therefore I obey.'"[17] The situation is similar to falling in love and marrying someone: When you marry your beloved, you do not say, "Now I can do whatever I want." Instead, "You anticipate whatever pleases and delights them. There's no coercion or sense of obligation, yet your behavior has been radically changed by the mind and heart of the person you love."[18] That is why Rom 6:1–2 says, *"What shall we say then? Are we to continue in sin so that grace may increase? May it never be! How shall we who died to sin still live in it?"* While we cannot work our way to heaven but are saved only by God's grace through faith in Christ (John 3:16–18; 6:28–29; Rom 2:16–17; 10:8–13; Gal 3:1–14; Eph 2:8–9), we are saved for a *purpose*: *"For we are His*

---

16. Demarest, *The Cross*, 196.
17. Keller, *The Reason*, 179–80.
18. Keller, *The Reason*, 183.

workmanship, created in Christ Jesus for good works, which God prepared beforehand so that we would walk in them." (Eph 2:10)[19]

Additionally, "Christ's example of suffering on our behalf releases a new moral power that transforms our attitudes, motives, and conduct."[20] The source of guidance and power to live righteously is not primarily external (conformity to rules and rituals) but is internal—it is Jesus, through his word, mind, and Spirit, who now lives in and through his people; he has implanted *"the law of Christ"* (Gal 6:2) in our hearts (Jer 31:33; Heb 8:10), which includes the teachings of Jesus and the NT writers (see, e.g., John 14:24–26; 17:8; 1 Cor 14:37; 1 Thess 2:13; 2 Thess 2:15; 3:14; Rev 1:11). Because Christ is in us and we have a new heart, new mind, and new Spirit, his values and priorities become our values and priorities. By the internal means given to the believer by Christ, Christ's people are inevitably and progressively being sanctified and changed on the inside *"to become conformed to the image of His Son [i.e., Jesus Christ]"* (Rom 8:29). Regarding the commands to love God and our neighbor, 1 John 4:19 says, *"We love, because He first loved us"* (see also Eph 5:2). "If anyone ever asks, 'How does the fact that God loves you result in your loving others?' the answer is: The new birth creates that connection. The new birth is the act of the Holy Spirit connecting our dead, selfish hearts with God's living, loving heart so that his life becomes our life and his love becomes our love."[21]

The gospel affects how we live and what we do in every area of our lives. This is illustrated in Gal 2:11–14. In Acts 10 Peter had been shown that God does not show partiality between Jews and Gentiles. Peter, a Jew, had been eating with Gentiles but later withdrew himself and stopped eating with them. The apostle Paul confronted Peter publicly, called him a hypocrite, and said that Peter was not being *"straightforward about the truth of the gospel"* (Gal 2:14). The NIV translates this as being *"in line with the truth of the gospel."* In other words, Peter was denying the very gospel he had preached by the way he was living, by denying Gentiles complete acceptance *in his private life* (i.e., in who he ate with) because of the fact that they were Gentiles. The issue for us may not be who we eat with, but the same

---

19. The works we do after we receive Christ by faith "are an index of the spiritual condition of a person's heart. . . . The judgment is not a balancing of good works over bad works. Rather, works are seen as unmistakable evidence of the loyalty of the heart; they express belief or unbelief, faithfulness or unfaithfulness. The judgment will reveal whether or not people's loyalties have been with God and the Lamb or with God's enemies." Ngundu, "Revelation," 1576; see, e.g., Matt 24:45–51; 25:31–46; John 3:19–21; 1 Tim 6:18–19.

20. Demarest, *The Cross*, 196.

21. Piper, "The New Birth," Introduction.

type of issue occurs any time a church or individual Christian denies people membership, positions of leadership, fellowship, or full equality because of tribal, ethnic, socio-economic, or other similar reasons. In other words, the practical implications of the gospel are radical and transformative; they affect our attitudes towards people, our relationships, and all areas of our lives. Daniel Shayesteh concludes by pointing out, "We understand that the so-called Christian world has extensively failed to surrender itself to Jesus Christ. Therefore, it is the *disbelief* in Jesus Christ that has spread immorality among those who apparently live under the name of Christianity. For the Gospel of Jesus Christ, there is only one type of Christian in the world, only those who are saved from the ruler of immorality. Muslims [and others], therefore, must not take the immorality of so-called Christian societies as a sign of the Christian faith having shortcomings."[22]

---

22. Shayesteh, *The Difference,* 204, emph. added.

Appendix 2
Biblical Examples of the Doctrine of Concurrence

The following biblical examples show how both God and secondary causes are involved in the same phenomena, including events involving sin and evil:

Event	Attributed to God	Attributed to Secondary Causes
Creation of animals	Gen 1:25	Gen 1:24
Abram's defeat of four kings	Gen 14:20	Gen 14:14–16
Sarah's conception & birth of Isaac	Gen 21:1	Gen 21:2, 5
Joseph's brothers selling him into slavery	Gen 45:7–8; 50:20	Gen 37:25–28; 45:4–5
Joseph going to Egypt	Ps 105:17	Gen 37:28
Joseph's prospering while a slave	Gen 39:3, 23	Gen 39:3, 23
The return of money to Joseph's brothers	Gen 42:27–28	Gen 42:25
Israel's exodus from Egypt	Exod 3:7–8	Exod 3:10; Deut 6:18–19
The hardening of Pharaoh's heart	Exod 4:21; 7:3; 9:12; 10:1, 20, 27	Exod 7:14, 22–23; 8:15; 9:34
The golden calf & Israel's worship of idols	Exod 32:1–8; Acts 7:39–41	Acts 7:41–42
Israel's consecration & sanctification	Lev 20:8	Lev 20:7–8
Defeat of Sihon	Deut 2:30–31, 33, 36	Deut 2:32–36
Defeat of Bashan	Deut 3:2–3	Deut 3:1, 3–6
Ability of people to make wealth	Deut 8:18	Deut 8:18
Victories of Joshua	Deut 3:21–22	Deut 3:28

Appendix 2

Israel's conquest of the promised land	Exod 23:23, 29–30; Deut 4:37–38; 7:1–2, 22–24; 9:3a	Exod 23:24, 31; Deut 7:2, 24; 9:3b
Defeat of Jericho	Josh 6:2	Josh 6:3–5
Defeat of Ai	Josh 8:1	Josh 8:2–22
Defeat of Makkedah	Josh 10:19b	Josh 10:19a, 20–21
Defeat of other kings	Josh 11:8a	Josh 11:8b–9
Gideon's defeat of Midian	Judg 7:7, 9, 14–15	Judg 7:16–22
Samson's marriage to a Philistine woman	Judg 14:4	Judg 14:1–3
Samson's killing 1000 Philistines	Judg 15:18	Judg 15:14–16
Defeat of Benjamin by Israel	Judg 20:28	Judg 20:29–48
Eli's sons do not listen to him	1 Sam 2:25	1 Sam 2:22–25
Saul defeats the Amalekites	1 Sam 15:2	1 Sam 15:3–6
Abigail's interceding for Nabal	1 Sam 25:32	1 Sam 25:14–31
Hushai's advice is accepted	2 Sam 17:14	2 Sam 17:5–14
David defeats his enemies	2 Sam 22:18–20, 40–42, 48–49	2 Sam 22:38–39, 43
David sins by numbering the people	2 Sam 24:1	2 Sam 24:10, 17; 1 Chron 21:1–4
The death of Joab	1 Kgs 2:32–33	1 Kgs 2:31, 34
The division of Israel and Judah	1 Kgs 12:22–24	1 Kgs 12:16–20
Ahab goes to war & defeats Aram	1 Kgs 20:13, 28	1 Kgs 20:14–21, 29–30
Ahab goes to war & is killed	1 Kgs 22:19–23	1 Kgs 22:29–37
Return of Rabshakeh to his own land and his death	2 Kgs 19:6–7	2 Kgs 19:7
Recovery of Hezekiah	2 Kgs 20:5–6	2 Kgs 20:7
The death of Saul	1 Chron 10:14	1 Chron 10:4
Invasion of Judah by Philistines & Arabs	2 Chron 21:12–16a	2 Chron 21:16b–17
The defeat of Judah & death of Amaziah	2 Chron 25:14–16	2 Chron 25:17–28
Preparation of the temple for restored worship	2 Chron 29:36	2 Chron 29:5–35
The defeat of Judah & death of Josiah	2 Chron 35:20–21	2 Kgs 23:29; 2 Chron 35:22–24
God speaks through his prophets	2 Chron 15–16	2 Chron 15–16

Destruction of Judah by Babylon	2 Chron 36:15–17; Jer 21:8–10; Ezek 5:7–11, 13	2 Kgs 25:8–21; 2 Chron 36:17–19; Jer 21:8–10; Ezek 5:12
Decree that the Jews could return to Jerusalem and rebuild the temple	Jer 16:15; 29:10–14; 2 Chron 36:22; Ezra 1:1; 6:14	2 Chron 36:22–23; Ezra 1:1; 6:14
Ezra granted favor	Ezra 7:6, 9–10, 27–28	Ezra 7:6, 9–10, 27–28
Nehemiah granted favor	Neh 2:8	Neh 2:7–9
The plans of the Jews' enemies are frustrated	Neh 4:15	Neh 4:11–14
Rebuilding the walls of Jerusalem	Neh 6:16	Neh 3:1–32; 4:6, 21–22; 6:3, 15
The trials of Job	Job 1:12, 21–22; 2:6; 42:11	Job 1:13–19; 2:7
Creation of people	Job 10:8; 31:15; Ps 139:13–16	Gen 4:1; 5:3; Job 14:1; Ps 51:5
Defeat of David's enemies	Ps 18:17–19, 43a, 47–48	Ps 18:37
Growth of plants	Ps 104:14a–b	Ps 104:14c
Building a house or any venture	Ps 127:1a	Ps 127:1b
Guarding a city	Ps 127:1c	Ps 127:1d
People's plans, speech, and actions	Prov 16:1b, 9b	Prov 16:1a, 9a
People's decisions	Prov 16:33b	Prov 16:33a
The invasion of Judah by Assyria	Isa 7:17–20; 8:5–8	Isa 7:17–20; 8:5–8
The destruction of Israel	Isa 9:8–21	Isa 9:8–21
The destruction of Babylon	Isa 13:1–5	Isa 13:1–5
The destruction of Egypt	Isa 19:1, 2a, 4a	Isa 19:2b–3, 4b
Success of Cyrus	Isa 45:1–7	Isa 45:1–7
Death of the men of Anathoth	Jer 11:22a, 23	Jer 11:22b
Baruch & Jeremiah hide from the king	Jer 36:26	Jer 36:19
Gog's invasion of Israel	Ezek 38:1–6, 16	Ezek 38:7–16
Destruction of Edom	Obad 8–9	Obad 6–7
Casting Jonah into the sea	Jonah 2:3	Jonah 1:15
Drought in the land	Hag 1:9, 11	Hag 1:5–6, 10
Rebuilding the temple in Jerusalem	Hag 1:14	Hag 1:14

Appendix 2

The writing & testimony of the Bible	Matt 19:4–5; John 5:37–38; 2 Tim 3:16; 2 Pet 1:20–21	Gen 2:24; Luke 24:27; John 5:46–47; Acts 26:22
People coming to Christ for salvation	John 6:37, 44, 65; Acts 13:38	John 6:37, 44, 65; Acts 13:38
The betrayal of Jesus	Luke 22:22a	Luke 22:21, 22b; John 13:21–27
The crucifixion of Jesus	Isa 53:10; Acts 2:23; 4:28	Mark 14:43—15:39; Acts 2:23; 4:27
Salvation of believers	John 1:12–13; Eph 2:8–9	John 3:36; Rom 10:12–17
The righteous acts of believers	John 3:21; Eph 2:10; Phil 2:13	John 3:21; Eph 2:10; Phil 2:12
Salvation of people in Corinth	Acts 18:10b	Acts 18:9–10a
Saving Paul & sailors from a shipwreck	Acts 27:22–25, 34	Acts 27:30–32, 38–44
Preaching the gospel	1 Cor 2:4	1 Cor 2:4
The persecution of Christians	1 Cor 4:7–11; Rev 6:9–11	1 Cor 4:7–11; Rev 6:9–11
Paul's "thorn in the flesh"	2 Cor 12:7–9	2 Cor 12:7
The preservation of the saints	1 Thess 5:23–24	1 Thess 5:12–22
People who follow the "man of lawlessness"	2 Thess 2:11	2 Thess 2:9–10, 12
Where people go & everything they do	Jas 4:13–15	Jas 4:13–15
The actions of the "harlot," "ten kings," and "beast" of Revelation	Rev 17:17	Rev 17:1–16

Appendix 3
Who Created God?

IN HIS BOOKS *THE Blind Watchmaker* (1986) and *The God Delusion* (2006), Richard Dawkins raises the questions, "Who designed the designer?" and "Who created God?" Dawkins stated, "Organized complexity is the thing we are having difficulty in explaining. . . . Any God capable of intelligently designing something as complex as the DNA/protein replicating machine must have been at least as complex and organized as that machine itself."[1] Elsewhere, he made a similar argument in the context of the explanation for the design and fine-tuning of the universe itself, "*Any creative intelligence, of sufficient complexity to design anything, comes into existence only as the end product of an extended process of gradual evolution.* Creative intelligences, being evolved, necessarily arrive late in the universe, and therefore cannot be responsible for designing it."[2]

Dawkins may think such questions are very clever, but they are not; they do not place his naturalistic evolutionary position on any different ground from the theistic position he is attacking. Dallas Willard explains, "To say that order emerged from disorder is not to explain anything, but, like invocation of the big-bang, is to draw a line at where explanations are to stop. That fact is what marks both order-from-disorder and bang-from-nothing as myths in the standard sense. The job of myths is to stop the 'why' line; and that is all that these myths of naturalistic cosmology do. So God is in as good a position as order from non-order or explosions of nothing."[3] Thomas Nagel similarly pointed out, "All explanations come to an end somewhere. . . . The God hypothesis does not explain the existence of God, and naturalistic physicalism does not explain the laws of physics."[4]

---

1. Dawkins, *The Blind*, 141; see also at 316 (creationists "assume the existence of the main thing we want to explain, namely organized complexity").
2. Dawkins, *The God Delusion*, 31, emph. in orig.; see also 114, 147.
3. Willard, "Reflections," n.p., emph. in orig.
4. Nagel, "The Fear," 26.

Additionally, C. S. Lewis explained that, as a beginning point, it is more reasonable to look to an explanation outside the natural order, rather than within, to explain the natural order itself, "An egg which came from no bird is no more 'natural' than a bird which had existed from all eternity. And since the egg-bird-egg sequence leads us to no plausible beginning, is it not reasonable to look for the real origin somewhere outside sequence altogether? You have to go outside the sequence of engines, into the world of men, to find the real originator of the Rocket [early steam locomotive]. Is it not equally reasonable to look outside Nature for the real Originator of the natural order?"[5]

Further, Dawkins' questions are irrelevant, if not nonsensical, to any theist, because the "God" Dawkins is positing is not the God, or even anything like the God, believed in by any theist. Indeed, Dawkins is begging the very question of the existence of God because he is assuming *a priori* that everything is matter, everything came into existence by evolution, and, specifically, "*any creative intelligence, of sufficient complexity to design anything, comes into existence only as the end product of an extended process of gradual evolution.*" In short, Dawkins' very questions posit a "created God" who, by definition, *is not God at all.*

God is Spirit (John 4:24); therefore, he is not composed of parts. Consequently, he is not "supremely complex" like a complicated machine or other created thing. Even atheist philosopher Thomas Nagel points out Dawkins' fundamental error, "But God, whatever he may be, is not a complex physical inhabitant of the natural world. The explanation of his existence as a chance concatenation of atoms is not a possibility for which we must find an alternative, because that is not what anybody means by God."[6] Nagel goes on to observe, "If the God hypothesis makes sense at all, it offers a different kind of explanation from those of physical science: purpose or intention of a mind without a body, capable nevertheless of creating and forming the entire physical world. The point of the hypothesis is to claim that not all explanation is physical, and that there is a mental, purposive, or intentional explanation more fundamental than the basic laws of physics, because it explains even them."[7]

The questions also are illogical because the answer is that no one designed or created God since, by definition, God is a necessary, uncreated,

---

5. Lewis, "Two Lectures," 211.

6. Nagel, "The Fear," 26; see also Plantinga, "The Dawkins," for a general critique of Dawkins' argument.

7. Nagel, "The Fear," 26.

eternal being who is the cause of everything else.[8] As the creator of everything (Gen 1:1), God is non-contingent; he has no cause and is not dependent on anything other than himself. In other words, "If something came into existence at a certain point in time—that is, if it had a beginning—then there needs to be a cause, an explanation, for why it came to be. But if something exists outside of time—like God—then it does not need an explanation for its beginning, because it does not have one. In the same way, if something doesn't have to exist, then we need an explanation for why it does exist. But if something *does* have to exist—if it is a necessary being, like God—then it does not need a further explanation."[9] Thus, "it is a category fallacy [i.e., the error of assigning to something a quality or action that can properly be assigned to things only of another category, for example, treating abstract concepts as though they had a physical location] to ask for a cause for God since this is really asking for a cause for an uncaused being."[10]

Dawkins believes that everything is brought into being by evolution, i.e., nothing exists necessarily on its own, but everything is contingent on something else. J. L. Mackie articulated the significance of this,

> The world as a whole, being a collection of such [contingent] things, is therefore itself contingent. The series of things and events, with their causes, with causes of those causes, and so on, may stretch back infinitely in time; but, if so, then however far back we go, or if we consider the series as a whole, what we have is still contingent and therefore requires a sufficient reason outside this series. That is, there must be a sufficient reason *for* the world which is *other than* the world. This will have to be a necessary being, which contains its own sufficient reason for existence. Briefly, things must have a sufficient reason for their existence, and this must be found ultimately in a necessary being.[11]

There is no basis for claiming that the universe itself is "necessary."[12] We have already seen, from Scripture and science, that the universe *did not have*

---

8. See Wallace, "Who Created."
9. Fradd, "Who Created."
10. Moreland, *Scaling*, 38.
11. Mackie, *The Miracle*, 82, emph. in orig.; see also Budziszewski, *What We*, 84.
12. Although sometimes one cannot reason from the nature of the parts to the nature of the whole (e.g., if each drink on the table is tasty, a drink composed of all of them may not necessarily be tasty), one *can* argue the contingent nature of the whole universe, just as one can argue that if every brick in a wall is red, we may legitimately infer that the wall as a whole is red. For someone to claim that, even though every part of the universe is contingent the universe as a whole is not, would be to smuggle in

to exist and had a beginning. What is at issue is why the universe exists at all, or "why is there something rather than nothing?"

The only logical and valid answer, and the only answer which provides a *sufficient reason* for the existence of the universe, is the necessary, uncreated, eternal being of God. To put it another way, belief in God is properly basic. What Dawkins' questions are attempting to do is to place belief in God in the wrong "family of beliefs." Some beliefs, particularly scientific beliefs, e.g., the earth orbits around the sun or water consists of one part oxygen and two parts hydrogen, are "evidence-essential": if we posited a belief like this without adequate evidence, people would be justified in doubting our assertion. On the other hand, another kinds or families of beliefs are properly basic. The rationality or reasonableness of properly basic beliefs does not require external, supporting evidence. Examples of this second set or family of beliefs includes the belief that people have minds; that we and others exist; that people are human, not robots, that human beings have intrinsic value; and that truth, good, bad, right, and wrong exist. As Nash puts it, "Belief in God and belief in other minds are in the same epistemological boat."[13]

The properly basic belief in God is indicated in Rom 1:19–20, *"For what can be known about God is plain to them, because God has shown it to them. For his invisible attributes, namely, his eternal power and divine nature, have been clearly perceived, ever since the creation of the world, in the things that have been made. So they are without excuse."* This is *not* to say that "God exists because the Bible says so, and the Bible is true because the Bible is true." Rather, as we have already seen, we must presuppose the existence of God and the truth of the Bible *in order to reason at all*. Ultimate truth—that which is fundamental and necessary—cannot be justified by something independent of itself: It is self-existent and necessary. While that is true, it also should be recalled that other evidence for God's existence, which confirms God's existence as stated in Rom 1:19–20, has been amply provided in this book, including fulfilled prophecy, the resurrection of Jesus Christ, and the impossibility of the contrary.

Anselm of Canterbury (1033–1109) explained God's existence by the doctrine of aseity, namely, "the idea that God's existence is dependent upon himself, within his own nature, and not on anything else."[14] John Howell summarizes,

---

"the assumption that the world is a necessary being." Nash, *Faith,* 132; see also Geisler, *Christian Apologetics,* 254–55. No one, not even Dawkins, is claiming that.

13. Nash, *Faith,* 74.
14. Howell, "Should We," 40.

> God cannot be explained by something outside of himself (for then he would owe his existence to that thing and thus be inferior to it), so that his existence must be explained by himself.... Anselm provides an analogy: consider a rock near a campfire. If one were to ask for an explanation of the rock's being warm, it would be ridiculous to answer that the explanation comes from within the rock itself (obviously for fire has made the rock warm). But if one were to ask the same question about the fire, such an answer would not seem ridiculous—it simply is the nature of fire to be warm, and it simply is the nature of God to exist.[15]

In fact, John Frame points out the absurdity and impossibility of denying the existence of a necessary being, "What happens when you deny the existence of a necessarily existent being? ANY necessarily existent being? What would the world be like without the number six? It is impossible to say, because there is no possible world without the number six. So if there is no number six, everything is askew. Meaning and rationality are lost. Same, I think, if you deny God."[16]

Dawkins' questions are an absurdity because he is implying that answering them would create an infinite regress of explanations (i.e., if you say "X created God," then the question is "Who created X," and so on), which means that there could never be an explanation of anything. However, the validity of an answer to one question (i.e., Q: "How did the universe come into being?" A: "God created the universe") is not negated by the fact that that answer may itself invite an explanation; that is a separate issue (and, as we have seen, Dawkins' implied infinite regress is not a valid causal explanation of God, since God, by definition, is uncreated and properly basic).

Finally, with respect to Dawkins' claim that what we are trying to explain is "organized complexity," Paul Nelson uses the example of a dam across a river consisting of branches and debris. The dam may have formed naturally by the action of the water; humans may have made it, or it may have been made by beavers. If, upon all of the evidence, one concludes that the dam was made by beavers, it would be absurd to say, "That does not prove anything: you are explaining one organized complexity, the dam, by another organized complexity, the beavers; but unless you can tell us who made the beavers, you might as well say that the dam was always there."[17]

---

15. Howell, "Should We," 40–41.
16. Frame, "Frame's Final," Logic.
17. Nelson, "The Hopeless," 16.

Dawkins' principle (you cannot explain something by design unless you can explain who created the designer) would "prevent us from inferring design in cases where no one, not even Dawkins, questions the legitimacy of such inferences."[18] For example, if archaeologists discovered pottery shards and arrowheads and concluded that they were designed and made by human beings as opposed to having created themselves as the result of the mixing of wind, rain, and sand and the erosion of rocks, their conclusion is valid even if they have no idea who the human beings were or where they came from. Ultimately, the real question that needs to be asked is: What is the best explanation for the creation of the universe and of life, with their specified complexity, information, and apparent design—an intelligent mind or mindless matter?

18. Meyer, *Signature*, 390.

Bibliography

Abdulahugli, Hasan. "Factors Leading to Conversion among Central Asian Muslims." In *From the Straight Path to the Narrow Way*, ed. David Greenlee, 157–66. Waynesboro, GA: Authentic, 2005.

Adams, Jay. *The Grand Demonstration*. Santa Barbara, CA: Eastgate, 1991. Online: https://archive.org/details/granddemonstratioooadam.

Adler, Mortimer. *How to Think About God*. New York: Collier, 1980. Online: https://archive.org/details/isbn_9780553271324/mode/2up.

After Death. 2023. Online: https://www.angel.com/movies/after-death.

Ajijola, Alhaj A. D. *The Myth of the Cross*. Mafmdeen [online publisher], 1972. Online: https://archive.org/details/mythofcrossooooajij.

Albright, William. *The Archaeology of Palestine*, rev. ed. Baltimore: Penguin, 1954. Online: https://archive.org/details/archaeologyofpaloooowill_f6k8/mode/2up?view=theater.

———. "Retrospect and Prospect in New Testament Archaeology." In *The Teacher's Yoke: Studies in Memory of Henry Trantham*, ed. E. Jerry Vardaman and James Garrett, Jr., 27–41. Waco, TX: Baylor University Press, 1964. Online: https://archive.org/details/teachersyokestudooooejet/mode/2up?view=theater.

Alcorn, Randy. *If God Is Good*. Colorado Springs, CO: Multnomah, 2009.

Alexander, T. D. *From Eden to the New Jerusalem: Exploring God's plan for life on earth*. Nottingham, England: InterVarsity, 2008.

Aling, Charles. "Joseph in Egypt – Part II. *Associates for Biblical Research*. 2010. Online: https://www.biblearchaeology.org/patriarchal-era-list/3724-joseph-in-egypt-part-ii.

Alston, William. "Divine Action: Shadow or Substance?" In *The God Who Acts*, ed Thomas Tracy, 41–62. University Park, PA: The Pennsylvania State University Press, 1994. Online: https://archive.org/details/godwhoactsphilosoooounse.

———. "The Inductive Argument from Evil and the Human Cognitive Condition." In *The Evidential Argument From Evil*, ed. Daniel Howard-Snyder, 97–125. Bloomington, IN: Indiana University Press, 1996. Online: https://archive.org/details/evidentialargumeooounse.

Alter, Robert. *Genesis*. New York: W. W. Norton, 1996. Online: https://archive.org/details/genesisooounse_h9l6.

Ali, Yusuf. *The Meaning of the Noble Qurʾan*, 2006. Online: https://www.holybooks.com/wp-content/uploads/2010/05/english-quran-with-commentariesyusuf-ali.pdf.

Arnold, Patrick. "Book review of *The Moral Landscape: How Science Can Determine Human Values*." *Westminster Theological Journal* 73 (2011) 393–96.

Anselm of Canterbury. *Cur Deus Homo*. Translated by Sidney Norton Deane. Chicago: Open Court, 1903. Online: http://www.ccel.org/ccel/anselm/basic_works.i.html.

Archer, Gleason. *Encyclopedia of Bible Difficulties*. Grand Rapids: Zondervan, 1982. Online: https://archive.org/details/encyclopediaofbiooarch.

Arthur, Wallace. *The Origin of Animal Body Plans: A Study in Evolutionary Developmental Biology*. Cambridge, UK: Cambridge University Press, 1997. Online: https://archive.org/details/originofanimalboooooarth.

Asad, Muhammad. *The Message of the Quran*. Gibraltar: Dar Al-Andalus, 1980. Online: https://islamicbulletin.org/en/ebooks/quran/quran_asad.pdf.

Associates for Biblical Research. *Evidence for the Exodus and Conquest*. Akron, PA: Associates for Biblical Research, 2019.

Axe, Douglas. *Undeniable: How Biology Confirms Our Suspicion That Life Is Designed*. New York: HarperOne, 2016.

Ayala, Francisco. "Philosophical Issues." In *Evolution*, edited by Theodosius Dobzhansky, Francisco Ayala, G. Ledyard Stebbins, and James Valentine, 474–516. San Francisco: W. H. Freeman, 1977. Online: https://archive.org/details/evolutionooluti/mode/2up?view=theater.

Ayala, Francisco, and James Valentine. *Evolving: The Theory and Processes of Organic Evolution*. Menlo Park, CA: Benjamin/Cummings, 1979. Online: https://archive.org/details/evolvingtheoryprooooayal.

Ayoub, Mahmoud. "Towards an Islamic Christology, II: The Death of Jesus, Reality or Delusion." *The Muslim World* 70 (1980): 91–121. Online: https://www.scribd.com/document/253228919/The-Muslim-World-Volume-70-Issue-2-1980-Doi-10-1111-2fj-1478-1913-1980-Tb03405-x-Mahmoud-m-Ayoub-Towards-an-Islamic-Christology-II-The-Death-o.

Babylonian Talmud: Tractate Sanhedrin, Folio 43a. c.70–200. Online: http://www.come-and-hear.com/sanhedrin/sanhedrin_43.html.

Bachrach, Judy. *Glimpsing Heaven: The Stories and Science of Life After Death*. Washington, DC: National Geographic, 2014.

Baggini, Julian. "Yes, life without God can be bleak. Atheism is about facing up to that." *The Guardian* (9 March 2012). Online: https://www.theguardian.com/commentisfree/2012/mar/09/life-without-god-bleak-atheism.

Bahnsen, Greg. *Always Ready: Directions for Defending the Faith*, ed. Robert Booth. Nacogdoches, TX: Covenant Media Foundation, 1996. Online: https://archive.org/details/alwaysreadydirecooobahn.

———. "The Problem of Evil." 1991. Online: https://www.monergism.com/topics/philosophy-religion/02-problem-evil.

Baker, Deane-Peter. "Dawkins' Moral Argument in *The God Delusion*: A Critical Assessment." *Journal of Theology for Southern Africa* 135 (2009) 75–84.

Ball, Steven. "A Christian Physicist Examines the Big Bang Theory." 2003. Online: https://www.letu.edu/academics/arts-and-sciences/files/big-bang.pdf.

"Baptism." *Jewish Encyclopedia*. 1906. Online: http://www.jewishencyclopedia.com/articles/2456-baptism.

Barker, Glenn, William Lane, and J. Ramsay Michaels. *The New Testament Speaks*. San Francisco: Harper & Row, 1969. Online: https://archive.org/details/newtestamentspeaoobark.

Barlow, Nora, ed., *The Autobiography of Charles Darwin*. New York: Harcourt, Brace, 1958. Online: https://archive.org/details/autobiographyofcoooonora/mode/2up?view=theater.

Barnes, Luke. "The Fine-Tuning of the Universe for Intelligent Life." 2012. Online: https://arxiv.org/pdf/1112.4647.pdf.

Barnett, Paul. *Behind the Scenes of the New Testament*. Downers Grove, IL: InterVarsity, 1990.

Barnett, Tim. "Four Problems with Evolutionary Morality," *Stand to Reason* (9 January 2017). Online: https://www.str.org/w/four-problems-with-evolutionary-morality#fnref:8.

Barrett, Justin. *Why Would Anyone Believe in God?* Walnut Creek, CA: AltaMira, 2004. Online: https://archive.org/details/whywouldanyonebeooobarr.

Bates, Gary, and Lita Sanders. "Are there out-of-sequence fossils that are problematic for evolution?" *Creation Ministries International*. 2014. Online: https://creation.com/fossils-out-of-order.

Batten, Don. "Living fossils: a powerful argument for creation." *Creation* 33 (2011) 20–23. Online: https://creation.com/werner-living-fossils.

Bauckham, Richard. *God Crucified: Monotheism and Christology in the New Testament*. Grand Rapids: Eerdmans, 1999.

———. *Jesus and the Eyewitnesses: The Gospels as Eyewitness Testimony*. Grand Rapids: Eerdmans, 2006. Second edition online: https://archive.org/details/richard-bauckham-jesus-and-the-eyewitnesses-the-gospels-as-eyewitness-testimony-eerdmans-2017.

———. "The Sonship of the Historical Jesus in Christology." *Scottish Journal of Theology* 31 (1978) 245–60.

Baynes, T. S. "Darwin on Expression." *Edinburgh Review* 137 (1873) 492–528. Online: http://darwin-online.org.uk/converted/pdf/1873_Review_Expression_EdinRev_A1625.pdf.

Behe, Michael. *Darwin's Black Box: The Biochemical Challenge to Evolution*. New York: Simon and Schuster, 1996. Online: https://archive.org/details/B-001-000-168/mode/2up.

———. *The Edge of Evolution: The Search for the Limits of Darwinism*. New York: The Free Press, 2007. Online: https://lionandlambapologetics.org/wp-content/uploads/2022/06/The-Edge-of-Evolution_-The-Search-for-the-Limits-of-Darwinism-Behe.pdf.

Behe, Michael, and David Snoke. "Simulating evolution by gene duplication of protein features that require multiple amino acid residues." *Protein Science* 13 (2004) 2651–64. Online: https://www.ncbi.nlm.nih.gov/pmc/articles/PMC2286568/.

Beilby, James. "Is evolutionary naturalism self-defeating?" *International Journal for Philosophy of Religion* 42, no. 2 (1997) 69–78.

Beker, J. Christiaan. *Suffering and Hope*. Grand Rapids: Eerdmans, 1987.

Bergman, Jerry. "Does gene duplication provide the engine for evolution?" *Journal of Creation* 20 (2006) 99–104. Online: https://creation.com/does-gene-duplication-provide-the-engine-for-evolution.

———. "Some Biological Problems of Natural Selection Theory. *Creation Research Society Quarterly* 29 (1992) 146–58. Online: https://www.creationresearch.org/crsq-1992-volume-29-number-3_some-biological-problems-of-natural-selection-theory.

Berkhof, Louis. *Systematic Theology*, 4th ed. Grand Rapids: Eerdmans, 1949. Online: http://downloads.biblicaltraining.org/Systematic%20Theology%20by%20Louis%20Berkhof.pdf [the page numbers in the text are from the online version].

Bickersteth, Edward. *The Trinity*. Grand Rapids: Kregel, 1957 (reprint). Online: https://archive.org/details/TheTrinityByEHBickersteth.

"Big Bang." *Wikipedia*. 2024. Online: https://en.wikipedia.org/wiki/Big_Bang.

Birch, L. C. and P. R. Erlich. "Evolutionary History and Population Biology." *Nature* 214 (1967) 349–52. Abstract online: https://www.nature.com/articles/214349a0.

Blomberg, Craig. *The Historical Reliability of the Gospels*, 2nd ed. Downers Grove, IL: InterVarsity Academic, 2007. First edition online: https://archive.org/details/historicalreliaboooblom_08go.

———. *The Historical Reliability of the New Testament*. Nashville: B&H Academic, 2016.

———. "Matthew." In *Commentary on the New Testament Use of the Old Testament*, edited by G. K. Beale and D. A. Carson, 1–109. Grand Rapids: Baker Academic, 2007.

Bode, Edward. *The First Easter Morning*. Analecta Biblica 45. Rome: Biblical Institute, 1970. Online: https://archive.org/details/firsteastermorniooobode.

Bohlin, Raymond. "The Quiet passing of Punctuated Equilibrium, Finally!" *Evolution News* (22 July 2013). Online: https://evolutionnews.org/2013/07/the_quiet_passi/.

Boslough, John. *Stephen Hawking's Universe*. New York: William Morrow, 1985. Online: https://archive.org/details/stephenhawkingsuoobosl_0.

Boyd, R. Maurice. *Why Doesn't God Do Things Perfectly?* Nashville: Abingdon, 1999. Online: https://archive.org/details/whydoesntgoddothoooboyd.

Braaten, Carl. *History and Hermeneutics*, vol. 2 in *New Directions in Theology Today*, edited by William Hordern. Philadelphia: Westminster, 1966. Online: https://archive.org/details/historyhermeneutooo2braa.

Brady, Ronald. "Natural Selection and the Criteria by which a Theory is Judged," *Systematic Zoology* 28 (1979) 600–621. Online: https://www.natureinstitute.org/ronald-h-brady/natural-selection.

Breining, Greg. "Are Darwin's Finches One Species or Many?" *Discover*. 2015. Online: https://www.discovermagazine.com/planet-earth/are-darwins-finches-one-species-or-many.

Briggs, Andy. "What is the Big Bang?" *EarthSky*. 2020. Online: https://earthsky.org/space/definition-what-is-the-big-bang/.

Broad, C. D. *Religion, Philosophy and Psychical Research*. New York: Harcourt, Brace, 1953.

Brooke, John Hedley. "The Wilberforce-Huxley Debate: Why Did It Happen?," *Science & Christian Belief* 13, no. 2 (2001) 127–41. Online: https://www.cis.org.uk/serve.php?filename=scb-13-2-hedley-brooke.pdf.

Bruce, F. F. *The Canon of Scripture*. Downers Grove, IL: InterVarsity, 1988. Online: https://archive.org/details/canonofscriptureoooobruc.

———. *The New Testament Documents: Are They Reliable?*, 5th ed. Downers Grove, IL: InterVarsity, 1960. Online: https://www.cob-net.org/compare/nt-documents-reliable-bruce.pdf.

Budziszewski, J. *What We Can't Not Know: A Guide*. Dallas: Spence, 2003. Online: https://archive.org/details/whatwecantnotknooooobudz_z9u8.

Buell, John, and Virginia Hearn, eds. *Darwinism: Science or Philosophy*. Richardson, TX: Foundation for Thought and Ethics, 1997. Online: https://archive.org/details/darwinismscienceoooounse/mode/2up.

al-Bukhari, Muhammad. *Sahih al-Bukhari*. Not dated. Online: http://sunnah.com/bukhari.

Burge, Gary. "John." In *Evangelical Commentary on the Bible*, edited by Walter Elwell, 840–80. Grand Rapids: Baker, 1989.

Burpo, Todd. *Heaven is for Real*. Nashville: Thomas Nelson, 2011. Online: https://archive.org/details/heavenisforrealloo/mode/2up?view=theater.

Butt, Kyle. "Believing What Jesus Believed." *Apologetics Press*. 2022. Online: https://apologeticspress.org/believing-what-jesus-believed-1223/.

"Cambrian explosion." *Wikipedia*. 2024. Online: https://en.wikipedia.org/wiki/Cambrian_explosion.

Campbell, Keith. "Naturalism." In *Encyclopedia of Philosophy*, vol. 6, 2nd ed., edited by Donald Borchert, 492–95. Farmington Hills, MI: Thomson Gale, 2006. Online: https://archive.org/details/encyclopedia-of-philosophy_202010/Volume%206/mode/2up?view=theater.

Camus, Albert. *The Rebel*. New York: Alfred A. Knopf, 1967. Online: https://cyberdandy.org/wp-content/uploads/2021/07/Albert-Camus-The-Rebel_-An-Essay-on-Man-in-Revolt-Vintage-International-1992.pdf.

Carroll, Sean. *The Big Picture*. New York: Dutton, 2016. Summary and analysis online: https://archive.org/details/summaryofbigpictooooinst/mode/2up?view=theater.

———. "The Origins of Form." *Natural History* (2008–2024): 1–5. Online: https://www.naturalhistorymag.com/features/061488/the-origins-of-form.

Carson, D. A. *Divine Sovereignty and Human Responsibility*. Eugene, OR: Wipf and Stock, 1994. Online: https://archive.org/details/divinesovereigntooooocars.

———. *The Gospel of John* (PNTC). Grand Rapids: Eerdmans, 1991.

———. *How Long, O Lord?* Grand Rapids: Baker, 1990. Online: https://archive.org/details/howlongolordreflooooocars_t4e2.

Carson, D. A., and Douglas Moo. *An Introduction to the New Testament*, 2nd ed. Grand Rapids: Zondervan, 2005. Online: https://archive.org/details/introductiontoneooooocars_r6q4.

Carter, Paul. "What Did Jesus Believe About the Bible?" *The Gospel Coalition*. 2017. Online: https://ca.thegospelcoalition.org/columns/ad-fontes/jesus-believe-bible/.

"Celsus on the 'resurrection.'" *Flavius Claudius Julianus*. 2023. Online: https://flaviusclaudiusjulianus.com/celsus-on-the-resurrection/.

Chamblin, J. Knox. "Matthew." In *Evangelical Commentary on the Bible*, edited by Walter Elwell, 719–60. Grand Rapids: Baker, 1989.

Chapman, Allan. *Slaying the Dragons: Destroying Myths in the History of Science and Faith*. Oxford, England: Lion Hudson, 2013. Online: https://archive.org/details/slayingdragonsdeoooochap.

"Chicago Statement on Biblical Inerrancy." *International Council on Biblical Inerrancy*. 1978. Online: https://library.dts.edu/Pages/TL/Special/ICBI_1.pdf.

Churchland, Patricia. "Epistemology in the Age of Neuroscience," *Journal of Philosophy* 84 (1987) 544–53. Online: https://www.researchgate.net/publication/243764802_Epistemology_in_an_Age_of_Neuroscience.

Cleaver, Gerald. "Multiverse: Philosophical and Theological Perspectives," *Ex Auditu* 32 (2016) 69–93.

Clement of Rome. *First Epistle of Clement to the Corinthians*. c.95. Online: http://www.ccel.org/ccel/lightfoot/fathers.ii.i.html.

"Codon." *National Human Genome Research Institute*. 2024. Online: https://www.genome.gov/genetics-glossary/Codon.

Cohen, I. L. *Darwin was Wrong–A Study in Probabilities*. Greenvale, NY: New Research, 1984. Online: https://archive.org/details/darwinwaswrongstoooocohe.

Cole, Victor Babajide. "Mark." In *Africa Bible Commentary*, edited by Tokunboh Adeyemo, 1171–1202. Nairobi: Word Alive, 2006.

Colson. Charles. *Born Again*. Old Tappan, NJ: Chosen, 1976. Online: https://archive.org/details/bornagainooooocols_k3p3.

———. "An UnHoly Hoax? The Authenticity of Christ." *Breakpoint Commentary* (29 March 2002). Online: http://www.epm.org/resources/2002/Mar/29/unholy-hoax-authenticity-christ/.

Corduan, Winfried. "Why I Believe the Bible Alone is the Word of God." In *Why I am a Christian: Leading Thinkers Explain Why They Believe*, edited by Norman Geisler and Paul Hoffman, 182–201. Grand Rapids: Baker, 2001. Online: https://archive.org/details/whyiamchristianlooounse.

Cornelius. "Allah: Truthful or Deceiver?" *Answering Islam*. Not dated. Online: http://www.answering-islam.org/authors/cornelius/makr.html.

Craig, William Lane. "Creation ex nihilo: Theology and Science." Not dated. Online: https://www.reasonablefaith.org/images/uploads/Creation_ex_nihilo_Theology_and_Science.pdf.

———. "The Indispensability of Theological Meta-Ethical Foundations for Morality." *Foundations* 5 (1997) 9–12. Online: https://www.reasonablefaith.org/writings/scholarly-writings/the-existence-of-god/the-indispensability-of-theological-meta-ethical-foundations-for-morality.

———. "Navigating Sam Harris' *The Moral Landscape*." *Reasonable Faith*. 2022. Online: https://www.reasonablefaith.org/writings/popular-writings/existence-nature-of-god/navigating-sam-harris-the-moral-landscape.

———. *The Son Rises: The Historical Evidence for the Resurrection of Jesus*. Chicago: Moody, 1981. Online: https://www.reasonablefaith.org/writings/popular-writings/existence-nature-of-god/navigating-sam-harris-the-moral-landscape.

———. "The Ultimate Question of Origins: God and the Beginning of the Universe." *Astrophysics and Space Science* 269 (1999) 721–38. Online: http://www.leaderu.com/offices/billcraig/docs/ultimatequestion.html#text11.

Craig, William Lane, and Walter Sinnott-Armstrong. *God? A Debate Between a Christian and an Atheist*. Oxford: Oxford University Press, 2004. Online: https://archive.org/details/goddebatebetweenoooocrai.

Craighead, Houston. "C. S. Lewis' Teleological Argument," *Encounter* 57 (1996) 171–85.

Crampton, W. Gary. "A Biblical Theodicy." *The Trinity Review* 167 (1999) 1–6. Online: https://www.trinityfoundation.org/PDF/The%20Trinity%20Review%2000167%20ABiblicalTheodicy.pdf.

Crick, Francis. *The Astonishing Hypothesis: The Scientific Search for the Soul*. New York: Scribner, 1994. Online: https://archive.org/details/astonishinghypotoocric_0.

Cromie, William. "How Darwin's finches got their beaks." *The Harvard Gazette*. 2006. Online: https://news.harvard.edu/gazette/story/2006/07/how-darwins-finches-got-their-beaks/.

Crossan, John. *Jesus: A Revolutionary Biography.* New York: HarperSanFrancisco, 1994. Online: https://archive.org/details/jesus-a-biography-john-dominic-crossan_202302.

Cullmann, Oscar. *The Earliest Christian Confessions.* Translated by J. K. S. Reid. London: Lutterworth, 1949. Online: https://archive.org/details/earliestchristia0000osca.

Cvijovic, Ivana, Benjamin Good, and Michael Desai. "The Effect of Strong Purifying Selection on Genetic Diversity." *Genetics* 208 (2018) 1235–78. Online: https://academic.oup.com/genetics/article/209/4/1235/5930988.

Danielou, Jean. *From Shadows to Reality: Studies in the Biblical Typology of the Fathers.* Westminster, MD: Newman, 1960. Online: https://archive.org/details/fromshadowstorea0000dani/page/n5/mode/2up.

Danker, Frederick, ed. *A Greek-English Lexicon of the New Testament and Other Early Christian Literature.* Chicago: The University of Chicago Press, 2000. Online: https://archive.org/details/a-greek-english-lexicon-of-the-new-testament-and-other-early-christian-literatur/page/675/mode/2up.

Darling, David. "Forum: On creating something from nothing," *New Scientist* 151 (14 September 1996) 49. Online: https://www.newscientist.com/article/mg15120475-000-forum-on-creating-something-from-nothing/.

Darwin, Charles. *On the Origin of Species by Means of Natural Selection.* New York: P. F. Collier & Son, 1859 (reprint 1909). Online: https://archive.org/details/originofspecies00darwuoft/mode/2up?view=theater.

———. *The Origin of Species by Means of Natural Selection,* 6th ed. New York: A. L. Burt, 1872. Online: https://archive.org/details/cu31924090296199/mode/2up.

Darwin, Francis ed. *The Life and Letters of Charles Darwin,* vol. 2. London: John Murray, 1887. Online: http://darwin-online.org.uk/content/frameset?viewtype=text&itemID=F1452.2&pageseq=1.

Davies, Paul. "The Appearance of Design in Physics and Cosmology." In *God and Design,* edited by Neil Manson , 147–54. London: Routledge, 2003.

———. "A Brief History of the Multiverse," *New York Times* (12 April 2003). Online: https://www.nytimes.com/2003/04/12/opinion/a-brief-history-of-the-multiverse.html.

———. *The Mind of God.* New York: Touchstone, 1992. Online: https://archive.org/details/mindofgodscience0000davi_w2l3.

———. "Space-Time Singularities in Cosmology and Black Hole Evaporation." In *The Study of Time III,* edited by J. T. Fraser, N. Lawrence, and D. Park, 74–93. New York: Springer Science+Business Media, LLC, 1978. Online: https://archive.org/details/studyoftimeiiipro0000inte/mode/2up.

———. "Taking Science On Faith," *Edge* (31 December 2006). Online: https://www.edge.org/conversation/paul_davies-taking-science-on-faith.

Davis, Ted. "Science and the Bible." *BioLogos.* 2019. Online: https://biologos.org/series/science-and-the-bible.

Davidson, Eric. "Evolutionary bioscience as regulatory systems biology." *Developmental Biology* 357 (2011) 35–40. Online: https://www.ncbi.nlm.nih.gov/pmc/articles/PMC3135751/.

Dawkins, Richard. *The Blind Watchmaker.* New York: W. W. Norton, 1986. Online: https://archive.org/details/B-001-001-263/mode/2up.

———. *A Devil's Chaplain.* New York: Houghton Mifflin, 2003. Online: https://archive.org/details/devilschaplainre0000dawk.

———. *The God Delusion*. Boston: Houghton Mifflin, 2006. Online: https://archive.org/details/isbn_9780552773317.

———. "Obscurantism to the Rescue," *The Quarterly Review of Biology* 72 (1997) 397–99. Online: https://www.scribd.com/document/731854415/Dawkins-Richard-Obscurantism-to-the-Rescue-1997.

———. *River Out of Eden: A Darwinian View of Life*. New York: Basic, 1995.

Abi Dawud. *Sunan Abi Dawud*. Not dated. Online: http://sunnah.com/abudawud.

Deedat, Ahmed. *Crucifixion or Cruci-Fiction?* Jeddah: Abul-Qasim, 1984. Online: https://archive.org/details/CrucifixionOrCruci-fictiondeedat.pdf.

Demarest, Bruce. *The Cross and Salvation*. Wheaton, IL: Crossway, 1997.

Dembski, William. *The Design Inference*. New York: Cambridge University Press, 1998. Online: https://archive.org/details/designinferenceeoooodemb.

———. "Foreword." In Benjamin Wiker, *Moral Darwinism: How We Became Hedonists*, 9–13. Downers Grove, IL: InterVarsity, 2002. Online: https://archive.org/details/moraldarwinismhooooowike.

———. "An ID Prediction for CRISPR Gene Editing" (27 July 2021). Online: https://billdembski.com/intelligent-design/id-prediction-for-crispr-gene-editing/.

———. "Science and Design." *First Things* (October 1998): Online: https://www.firstthings.com/article/1998/10/science-and-design.

Dennett, Daniel. *Darwin's Dangerous Idea*. New York: Simon & Schuster, 1995.

———. *Darwin's Dangerous Idea: Evolution and the Meanings of Life*. New York: Simon and Schuster, 2014.

Dennett, Daniel, and Alvin Plantinga. *Science and Religion: Are they Compatible?* New York: Oxford University Press, 2011. Online: https://archive.org/details/sciencereligionaooooodenn.

Denton, Michael. *Evolution: A Theory in Crisis*. Bethesda, MD: Adler & Adler, 1986. Online: https://dokumen.pub/qdownload/evolution-a-theory-in-crisis-new-developments-in-science-are-challenging-orthodoxy-darwinism-0917561058.html.

———. *Evolution: Still a Theory in Crisis*. Seattle: Discovery Institute, 2016. Online: https://dokumen.pub/qdownload/evolution-still-a-theory-in-crisis-2015960652-9781936599325-9781936599332-9781936599349.html. Audio version online: https://archive.org/details/esticr.

Derrida, Jacques. "On Forgiveness: A Roundtable Discussion with Jacques Derrida," moderated by Richard Kearney. Not dated. Online: https://eclass.uoa.gr/modules/document/file.php/PPP668/%CE%97%20%CF%83%CF%85%CE%B3%CF%87%CF%8E%CF%81%CE%B7%CF%83%CE%B7/Derrida%2C%20J.%2C%20On%20Forgiveness.%20A%20Roundtable%20Discussion%20with%20Jacques%20Derrida%2C%20pp.%2052-72.pdf.

Dever, William. *What Did the Biblical Writers Know and When Did They Know It?* Grand Rapids: Eerdmans, 2001.

Didache. c.70–110. Online: http://www.ccel.org/ccel/richardson/fathers.viii.i.html.

Dirks, Jerald. *The Cross & the Crescent*. Riyadh: International Islamic, 2008. Online: https://islamicbulletin.org/en/ebooks/the_cross_and_the_crescent.pdf.

"Discovery of ancient textile fragment sheds light on priestly garments." *Israel Hayom*. 2024. Online: https://www.israelhayom.com/2024/07/18/discovery-of-ancient-textile-fragment-sheds-light-on-priestly-garments/.

Dobzhansky, Theodosius. 1977. "Evolution of mankind." In *Evolution*, edited by Theodosius Dobzhansky, Francisco Ayala, G. Ledyard Stebbins, and James Valentine, 438–63. San Francisco: W. H. Freeman. Online: https://archive.org/details/evolutionooluti/mode/2up?view=theater.

Dodd, C. H. "The Appearances of the Risen Christ: An Essay in Form-Criticism of the Gospels." In *More New Testament Studies*, 103–33. Grand Rapids: Eerdmans, 1968. Online: https://archive.org/details/morenewtestamentoooododd/page/n5/mode/2up.

Dose, Klaus. "The Origin of Life: More Questions than Answers." *Interdisciplinary Science Reviews* 13 (1988) 348–56. Abstract online: https://www.tandfonline.com/doi/abs/10.1179/isr.1988.13.4.348.

Dostoevsky, Fyodor. *The Brothers Karamazov*. Translated by Constance Garnett. New York: New American Library, 1957. Online: https://archive.org/details/in.ernet.dli.2015.70970.

Doyle, Shaun. "Precambrian rabbits—death knell for evolution?" *Journal of Creation* 28 (2015) 10–12. Online: https://dlo.creation.com/articles/p094/c09436/j28_1_10-12.pdf.

Draper, Paul. "Pain and Pleasure: An Evidential Problem for Theists." In *The Evidential Argument from Evil*, edited by Daniel Howard-Snyder, 12–29. Bloomington, IN: Indiana University Press, 1996. Online: https://archive.org/details/evidentialargumeooooounse.

Dulle, Jason. "The Size of the Stone Covering Jesus' Tomb." *Thinking to Believe*. 2011. Online: https://thinkingtobelieve.com/2011/03/24/the-size-of-the-stone-covering-jesus%E2%80%99-tomb-2/.

———. "You Can't Know Atheism is True Unless God Exists." Not dated. Online: https://www.onenesspentecostal.com/knowrequiresgod.htm.

Dunn, James D. G. *Jesus Remembered*. Grand Rapids: Eerdmans, 2003.

Dunning, Craig. "Palestinian Muslims Converting to Christianity: Effective Evangelistic Methods in the West Bank." Ph.D. diss. University of Pretoria, 2013. Online: https://www.academia.edu/5769303/Palestinian_Muslims_converting_to_Christianity_effective_evangelistic_methods_in_the_West_Bank.

Eden, Murray. "Inadequacies of Neo-Darwinian Evolution as a Scientific Theory." In *Mathematical Challenges to the Neo-Darwinian Interpretation of Evolution*, edited by Paul Moorhead and Martin Kaplan, 5–19. New York: Wistar Institute of Anatomy and Biology, 1967.

Eddy, Paul, and Gregory Boyd. *The Jesus Legend*. Grand Rapids: Baker Academic, 2007.

Editors of Guideposts Magazine. *His Mysterious Ways*. Dallas: Word, 1988. Online: https://archive.org/details/hismysteriouswayooounse_d2x6.

Edwards, Jonathan. *The Works of Jonathan Edwards*, vol. 1, *A Careful and Strict Inquiry into the Prevailing Notions of the Freedom of Will; Dissertation on the End for which God Created the World; The Great Christian Doctrine of Original Sin Defended; A History of the Work of Redemption*. Carlisle, PA: The Banner of Truth, 1984 (reprint). Online: http://www.ccel.org/ccel/edwards/works1.html.

———. *The Works of Jonathan Edwards*, vol. 2, *Remarks on Important Theological Controversies*. Carlisle, PA: The Banner of Truth, 1986 (reprint). Online: http://www.ccel.org/ccel/edwards/works2.toc.html.

Edwards, William, Wesley Gabel, and Floyd Hosmer. "On the Physical Death of Jesus Christ." *Journal of the American Medical Association* 255 (21 March 1986)

1455–63. Online: https://www.researchgate.net/publication/19648788_On_the_Physical_Death_of_Jesus_Christ.

Egnor, Michael. "Neuroscience and Dualism." In *Minding the Brain: Models of the Mind, Information, and Empirical Science*, edited by Angus Menuge, Brian Krouse, and Robert Marks, 237–64. Seattle: Discovery Institute, 2023. Online: https://robertmarks.org/REPRINTS/2023-MTB.pdf.

Einstein, Albert. *Ideas and Opinions*. New York: Crown, 1982. Online: https://archive.org/details/dli.scoerat.5587ideasandopinionsbyalberteinstein/mode/2up.

———. "Remarks on Bertrand Russell's Theory of Knowledge." In *The Library of Living Philosophers*, vol. 5, *The Philosophy of Bertrand Russell*, edited by Paul A. Schilpp, trans. Paul A. Schilpp, 279–91. Evanston, IL: Northwestern University Press, 1944. Online: https://www.scribd.com/document/500922490/Einstein-Remarks-on-Bertrand-Russell.

Eldredge, Niles, and Stephen Jay Gould. "Punctuated Equilibria: An Alternative to Phyletic Gradualism." In *Models in Paleobiology*, edited by Thomas Schopf, 82–115. San Francisco: Freeman, Cooper, and Co, 1972. Online: https://archive.org/details/B-001-004-118.

Ellis, George. "Does the Multiverse Really Exist?" *Scientific American*. 2011. Online: https://www.scientificamerican.com/article/does-the-multiverse-really-exist/.

Emerick, Yahiya. *The Complete Idiot's Guide to Understanding Islam*, 2nd ed. New York: Alpha, 2004. Earlier edition online: http://www.islamicbulletin.org/free_downloads/new_muslim/complete_idiot_guide_islam.pdf.

Eric, Walter. *Why Trust the Bible*. Nairobi: Life Challenge Assistance, 2011.

Erlandson, Doug. "A New Perspective on the Problem of Evil." *Antithesis Magazine* 2, no. 2 (1991) no pages. Online: http://www.reformed.org/webfiles/antithesis/index.html?mainframe=/webfiles/antithesis/v2n2/ant_v2n2_evil.html.

Eusebius Pamphilius. *Church History*. 325. Online: https://ccel.org/ccel/schaff/npnf201/npnf201.iii.i.html.

"Evolution of sexual reproduction." *Wikipedia*. 2024. Online: https://en.wikipedia.org/wiki/Evolution_of_sexual_reproduction.

Falde, Nathan. "Inscription Finally Confirms Biblical Record of Hezekiah's Tunnel." *Ancient Origins*. 2022. Online: https://www.ancient-origins.net/news-history-archaeology/hezekiahs-tunnel-inscription-0017684.

Feinberg, John. "And the Atheist Shall Lie Down with the Calvinist: Atheism, Calvinism, and the Free Will Defense." *Trinity Journal* 1 (1980) 142–52. Online: https://www.scribd.com/document/468920631/And-the-Atheist-Shall-Lie-Down-with-the-Calvinist-Atheism-Calvinism-and-the-Free-Will-Defense-John-S-Feinberg.

———. *The Many Faces of Evil*, rev. ed. Grand Rapids: Zondervan, 1994.

———. *The Many Faces of Evil*, 3rd ed. Wheaton, IL: Crossway, 2004.

———. *No One Like Him*. Wheaton, IL: Crossway, 2001.

Fennell, R. C. "A moral challenge to pantheism." *Creedalandlovingit*. 2017. Online: https://creedalandlovingit.wordpress.com/2017/11/04/a-moral-challenge-to-pantheism/.

Ferm, Vergilius, ed. *An Encyclopedia of Religion*. Paterson, NJ: Littlefield, Adams and Co., 1964. Online: https://archive.org/details/encyclopediaofreoooverg_f3n7/mode/2up?view=theater.

Ferraiolo, William. "Eternal Selves and the Problem of Evil." *Quodlibet* 7:2 (April-June 2005).

"Fingerprints of Creation." *Earth Science Associates*. 2010. Online: http://www.halos.com/.
Flew, Antony. "Negative Statement: Antony G. N. Flew." In *Did Jesus Rise from the Dead: The Resurrection Debate*, edited by Terry Miethe, 3–13. San Francisco: Harper & Row, 1987. Online: https://archive.org/details/didjesusrisefromoohabe.
Foote, Mike. "Sampling, taxonomic description, and our evolving knowledge of morphological diversity." *Paleobiology* 23 (1997) 181–206. Abstract online: https://www.cambridge.org/core/journals/paleobiology/article/abs/sampling-taxonomic-description-and-our-evolving-knowledge-of-morphological-diversity/5D44EF179954D44ED12A77D18D7DAA22.
Foster, David. *The Philosophical Scientists*. New York: Dorset: 1985. Online: https://archive.org/details/philosophicalscioooofost.
Fradd, Matt. "Who Created God?" *Catholic Answers*. 2013. Online: https://www.catholic.com/magazine/online-edition/who-created-god.
Frame, John. *Cornelius Van Til: An Analysis of His Thought*. Phillipsburg, NJ: P&R, 1995. Online: https://archive.org/details/corneliusvantilaooofram.
———. *The Doctrine of God*. Phillipsburg, NJ: P&R, 2002.
———. "Frame's Final Response." 1996–2022. Online: https://reformed.org/apologetics/frames-final-response-by-john-frame/.
———. "The Problem of Evil." In *Suffering and the Goodness of God*, edited by Christopher Morgan and Robert Peterson, 141–64. Wheaton, IL: Crossway, 2008.
Fretheim, Terrence. *God and World in the Old Testament: A Relational Theory of Creation*. Nashville: Abingdon, 2005.
Frisbee, Lonnie, and Roger Sachs. *Not by Might, Nor by Power: The Great Commission*. Santa Maria, CA: Freedom, 2016.
———. *Not by Might, Nor by Power: The Jesus Revolution*, 2nd ed. Santa Maria, CA: Freedom, 2017.
———. *Not by Might, Nor by Power: Set Free*. Santa Maria, CA: Freedom, 2019.
Gale, Richard. "Some Difficulties in the Theistic Treatments of Evil." In *The Evidential Argument from Evil*, edited by Daniel Howard-Snyder, 206–18. Bloomington, IN: Indiana University Press, 1996. Online: https://archive.org/details/evidentialargumeoooounse.
Gardner, Rex. *Healing Miracles: A Doctor Investigates*. London: Darton, Longman & Todd, 1986.
Garrison, David. *A Wind in the House of Islam*. Monument, CO: WIGTake Resources, 2014. Online: https://archive.org/details/windinhouseofislooogarr.
Garte, Sy. *The Works of His Hands*. Grand Rapids: Kregel, 2019.
Gay, Craig. *The Way of the (Modern) World: Or, Why It's Tempting To Live As If God Doesn't Exist*. Grand Rapids: Eerdmans, 1998.
Geisler, Norman. *Christian Apologetics*. Grand Rapids: Baker, 1976. Online: https://archive.org/details/christianapologeooogeis.
Geisler, Norman, and William Nix. *A General Introduction to the Bible*, rev. ed. Chicago: Moody, 1986. Online: http://www.scribd.com/doc/133575464/A-General-Introduction-to-the-BIBLE#scribd.
Gentry, Robert. *Creation's Tiny Mystery*. Knoxville, TN: Earth Science Assocs., 1986. Online: https://archive.org/details/creationstinymysooogent.
"Geologic time scale." *Wikipedia*. 2024. Online: https://en.wikipedia.org/wiki/Geologic_time_scale.

Ghabril, Nicola Yacoub. *Themes for the Diligent*. Rikon, Switzerland: The Good Way, 2003. Online: http://www.the-good-way.com/eng/books.

Gibbs, H. Lisle, and Peter Grant. "Oscillating selection on Darwin's finches." *Nature* 327 (1987) 511–13. Abstract online: https://www.nature.com/articles/327511a0.

Gilbert, Greg. *Why Trust the Bible?* Wheaton, IL: Crossway, 2015. Online: https://archive.org/details/whytrustbibleooogilb.

Gilbert, Scott, John Opitz, and Rudolf Raff. "Resynthesizing Evolutionary and Developmental Biology." *Developmental Biology* 173 (1996) 357–72. Online: https://www.sciencedirect.com/science/article/pii/S0012160696900329?via%3Dihub.

Gilchrist, John. *Christ in Islam and Christianity*. Rikon, Switzerland: The Good Way, 2010. Online: http://www.the-good-way.com/eng/books.

———. *Facing the Muslim Challenge*. Claremont, South Africa: Life Challenge Africa, 2002. Online: https://www.answering-islam.org/Gilchrist/Challenge/index.html.

Gilley, Sheridan, and Ann Loades. "Thomas Henry Huxley: The War Between Science and Religion," *Journal of Religion* 61, no. 3 (1981) 285–308.

Gish, Duane. *Evolution: The Fossils Still Say NO!* El Cajon, CA: Institute for Creation Research, 1995. Online: https://archive.org/details/evolutionchallenoooogish/mode/2up?view=theater.

Gould, Stephen Jay. "Evolution's Erratic Pace." *Natural History* 86 (May 1977) 12–16. Abstract online: https://www.scirp.org/reference/referencespapers?referenceid=133602.

———. "The Five Kingdoms." *Natural History* 85 (June-July 1976) 30–37.

———. "Is a new and general theory of evolution emerging?" *Paleobiology* 6 (1980) 119–30. Abstract online: https://ui.adsabs.harvard.edu/abs/1980Pbio....6..119G/abstract.

———. "The Return of Hopeful Monsters." *Natural History* 86 (June-July 1977) 22–30. Abstract online: https://philpapers.org/rec/GOUTRO-2.

———. "Soapy Sam's Logic." *Natural History* 95 (April 1986) 16–26.

———. *The Structure of Evolutionary Theory*. Cambridge, MA: Belknap, 2002. Online: https://archive.org/details/jaygouldthestructureofevolutionarytheory.

———. *An Urchin in the Storm*. New York: W. W. Norton, 1987.

Gould, Stephen Jay, and Niles Eldredge. "Punctuated equilibria: the tempo and mode of evolution reconsidered," *Paleobiology* 3 (1977) 115–51. Online: http://mechanism.ucsd.edu/teaching/philbio/readings/gould.eldridge.punceq.1977.pdf.

Grant, Michael. *Jesus: An Historian's Review of the Gospels*. New York: Charles Scribner's Sons, 1977.

Grant, Myrna. *Vanya*. Carol Stream, IL: Creation House, 1974. Online: https://archive.org/details/vanyaooogran.

Grassé, Pierre-Paul. *Evolution of Living Organisms*. New York: Academic, 1977.

"The Great Isaiah Scroll." *The Digital Dead Sea Scrolls*. 2019. Online: http://dss.collections.imj.org.il/isaiah.

Green, David, and Robert Goldberger. *Molecular Insights into the Living Process*. New York: Academic, 1967. Online: https://archive.org/details/isbn_9780122978500/page/n5/mode/2up?view=theater.

Green, Joel, and Scot McKnight, eds. *Dictionary of Jesus and the Gospels*. Downers Grove: InterVarsity, 1992.

Greenham, Ant(hony). "A Study of Palestinian Muslim Conversions to Christ." *St. Francis Magazine* 6:1 (February 2010) 116–75.

Greeson, Kevin. *The Camel*. Arkadelphia, AR: WIGTake Resources, 2007.
Grene, Marjorie. "The Faith of Darwinism." In *The Knower and the Known*, 185–201. New York: Basic, 1966. Online: https://archive.org/details/knowerknown00gren.
Grossman, Lisa. "Death of the eternal cosmos." *New Scientist* (14 January 2012). Online as "Why physicists can't avoid a creation event" (11 January 2012): https://iweb.langara.ca/rjohns/files/2017/09/Physics_creation.pdf.
Guliuzza, Randy. "Major Evolutionary Blunders: Evolutionary Predictions Fail the Reality Test." *Acts & Facts*. 2015. Online: https://www.icr.org/article/major-blunders-evolutionary-predictions.
Gura, Trisha. "Bones, molecules…or both?" *Nature* 406 (2000) 230–33. Online: https://www.nature.com/articles/35018729.
Habermas, Gary. *Ancient Evidence for the Life of Jesus*. Nashville: Thomas Nelson, 1984. Online: https://archive.org/details/ancientevidencefoooohabe.
———. "Evidential Near-Death Experiences." In *Minding the Brain: Models of the Mind, Information, and Empirical Science*, edited by Angus Menuge, Brian Krouse, and Robert Marks, 323–56. Seattle: Discovery Institute, 2023. Online: https://robertmarks.org/REPRINTS/2023-MTB.pdf.
———. "Rebuttal: Gary R. Habermas." In *Did Jesus Rise from the Dead: The Resurrection Debate*, edited by Terry Miethe, 39–47. San Francisco: Harper & Row, 1987. Online: https://archive.org/details/didjesusrisefromoohabe.
———. "Why I Believe the New Testament is Historically Reliable." In *Why I am a Christian: Leading Thinkers Explain Why They Believe*, edited by Norman Geisler and Paul Hoffman, 147–60. Grand Rapids: Baker, 2001. Online: https://archive.org/details/whyiamchristianloooounse.
Habermas, Gary, and Michael Licona. *The Case for the Resurrection of Jesus*. Grand Rapids: Kregel, 2004. Online: https://archive.org/details/caseforresurrectoooohabe.
Hagopian, David, ed. *The Genesis Debate: three views on the days of creation*. Mission Viejo, CA: Crux, 2001. Online: https://archive.org/details/g3n3sisdebatethrooounse.
Haldane, J. B. S. "When I am Dead." In *Possible Worlds and Other Papers*, 214–21. New York: Harper & Brothers, 1928. Online: https://archive.org/details/possibleworldsotoohald.
———. "Some Consequences of Materialism." In *The Inequality of Man and Other Essays*, 161–75. London: Chatto & Windus, 1932. Online: https://archive.org/details/in.ernet.dli.2015.59251.
———. "I Repent an Error," *The Literary Guide* (April 1954) 7, 29.
Haleem, M. A. S. Abdel. *The Qur'an*. New York: Oxford University Press, 2005. Online: https://archive.org/details/TheQuranANewTranslation/mode/2up
Halverson, William. *A Concise Introduction to Philosophy*, 3rd ed. New York: Random House, 1976. Online: https://archive.org/details/conciseintroductoooohalv/mode/2up?view=theater.
Hancock, Zachary B., Emma S. Lehmberg, and Gideon S. Bradburd. "Neo-darwinism still haunts evolutionary theory: A modern perspective on Charlesworth, Lande, and Slatkin," *Evolution* 75, no. 6 (2021) 1244–55. Online: https://www.ncbi.nlm.nih.gov/pmc/articles/PMC8979413/.
Hardy, Alister. *The Living Stream: Evolution and Man*. Cleveland: Meridian, 1965. Online: https://archive.org/details/livingstreamoooounse/page/n5/mode/2up.
Harris, Sam. *The Moral Landscape: How Science Can Determine Human Values*. New York: Free, 2010.

Hart, David Bentley. *The Experience of God: Being, Consciousness, Bliss.* New Haven: Yale University Press, 2013.

Hartzler, H. Harold. "Foreword." In *Science Speaks*, rev. online ed., by Peter Stoner, 4–5. Chicago: Moody, 2005. Online: https://archive.org/details/sciencespeakspeterw.stoner/mode/2up?view=theater.

Hatala, Kevin, Brigitte Demes, and Brian Richmond. "Laetoli footprints reveal bipedal gait biomechanics different from those of modern humans and chimpanzees." *Proceedings of the Royal Society* (17 August 2016) 1–9. Online: https://royalsocietypublishing.org/doi/epdf/10.1098/rspb.2016.0235.

Hawking, Stephen. *A Brief History of Time.* New York: Bantam, 1988.

———. *Brief Answers to the Big Questions.* New York: Bantam, 2018.

Hawking, Stephen, and Leonard Mlodinow. *The Grand Design.* New York: Bantam, 2010.

"Hebrew Bible." *Wikipedia.* 2024. Online: https://en.wikipedia.org/wiki/Hebrew_Bible.

Heidegger, Martin. *An Introduction to Metaphysics.* New Haven: Yale University Press, 1959. Online: https://archive.org/details/metaphysicsintrooooheid.

Hesse, Hermann. *Siddhartha.* Project Gutenberg eBook, 2001. Online: https://www.gutenberg.org/files/2500/2500-h/2500-h.htm.

Hick, John. *Evil and the God of Love,* rev. ed. New York: HarperSanFrancisco, 1977. Online: https://archive.org/details/evilgodofloveoooohick_q301/mode/2up?view=theater&q=%22evil+is+only+apparent%22.

Ho, M. W., and P. T. Saunders. "Beyond neo-Darwinism—An Epigenetic Approach to Evolution." *Journal of Theoretical Biology* 78 (1979) 573–91. Online: https://www.researchgate.net/publication/22628078_Beyond_neo-Darwinism-an_epigenetic_approach_to_evolution.

Hodge, Charles. *Commentary on the Epistle to the Romans,* rev. ed. Grand Rapids: Eerdmans, 1886 (reprint). Online: https://books.google.com/books?id=BX8fAAAAYAAJ.

———. *Systematic Theology,* vol. 1. Grand Rapids: Eerdmans, 1981. Online: https://archive.org/details/systematic-theology-vol-1/mode/2up.

———. *What is Darwinism?* London: T. Nelson and Sons, 1874. Online: https://archive.org/details/b24877323/mode/2up?view=theater.

Howell, Elizabeth. "What is the Big Bang Theory?" *Space.com.* 2021. Online: https://www.space.com/25126-big-bang-theory.html.

Howell, John. "Should We Fear That We Are Deluded? Some Comments on Dawkins' *The God Delusion.*" *Southwestern Journal of Theology* 54 (2011) 29–44. Online: https://swbtsv7.s3.amazonaws.com/media/Theology_Journal/54.1/54.1_Howell.pdf.

Hoyle, Fred. "The Big Bang in Astronomy." *New Scientist* 92 (19 November 1981) 521–24. Abstract online: https://ui.adsabs.harvard.edu/abs/1981NewSc..92..521H/abstract.

———. "The Universe: Past and Present Reflections." *Engineering & Science* (November 1981) 8–12. Online: https://calteches.library.caltech.edu/527/2/Hoyle.pdf.

Hoyle, Fred, and Chandra Wickramasinghe. *Evolution from Space.* London: J. M. Dent & Sons, 1981.

Hume, David. *Dialogues Concerning Natural Religion,* 2nd ed. London, 1779. Online: https://archive.org/stream/dialoguesreligiooohumeuoft?ref=ol#mode/2up.

———. *An Enquiry concerning Human Understanding*. New York: Oxford University Press, 1748. Online: https://fitelson.org/confirmation/hume_enquiry.pdf.

Hunt, Dave. *Confessions of a Heretic*. Plainfield, NJ: Logos, 1972. Online: https://archive.org/details/confessionsofheroooohunt.

Hunt, Tam. "Reconsidering the logical structure of the theory of natural selection," *Communicative & Integrative Biology* 7 (December 2014): 1–5. Online: https://www.ncbi.nlm.nih.gov/pmc/articles/PMC4594354/.

Huntemann, Georg. *The Other Bonhoeffer*. Grand Rapids: Baker, 1993. Online: https://archive.org/details/otherbonhoeffereoooohunt.

Hunter, A. M. *Jesus: Lord and Saviour*. London: SCM, 1976. Online: https://archive.org/details/jesuslordsaviouroooohunt.

Huxley, Thomas Henry. Letter to Frederick Dyster (9 September 1860). In the *Huxley Papers* 15:106. Online: https://mathcs.clarku.edu/huxley/letters/60.html.

———. *Science and Christian Tradition*. New York: D. Appleton, 1895. Online: https://archive.org/details/sciencechristian1895huxl/mode/2up.

Ibrahim, Naajeh, Sheikh 'Aasim 'Abdul Maajid, and Sheikh 'Esaam-ud-Deen Darbaalah. *In Pursuit of Allah's Pleasure*. Translated by A. Ibrahim and Al-Arabi Ben Razzaq. Not dated. Online: https://archive.org/details/InPursuitOfAllahsPleasureBook/mode/2up.

Ignatius. *Epistle to the Ephesians*. c.110. Online: http://www.ccel.org/ccel/schaff/anf01.v.ii.html.

———. *Epistle to the Magnesians*. c.110. Online: http://www.ccel.org/ccel/schaff/anf01.v.iii.html.

———. *Epistle to the Romans*. c.110. Online: http://www.ccel.org/ccel/schaff/anf01.v.v.html.

———. *Epistle to the Smyrnaeans*. c.110. Online: https://www.newadvent.org/fathers/0109.htm.

IANDS (International Association of Near-Death Studies, Inc). 2022. Online: https://iands.org/.

Irenaeus. *Against Heresies*. c.185. Online: http://www.ccel.org/ccel/schaff/anf01.ix.html.

Irons, Lee, with Meredith Kline. "The Framework View." In *The Genesis Debate: three views on the days of creation*, edited by David Hagopian, 217–57. Mission Viejo, CA: Crux, 2001. Online: https://archive.org/details/g3n3sisdebatethroooounse.

"Is there Much Evidence for the Bible's Reliability?" *Evidence for God's Unchanging Word*. Not Dated. Online: https://www.unchangingword.com/manuscript-evidence/.

Jepson, J. W. *Don't Blame It All on Adam*. Minneapolis: Bethany House, 1984. Online: https://archive.org/details/isbn_0871234378.

Jeremias, Joachim. *The Eucharistic Words of Jesus*. Translated by Norman Perrin. London: SCM, 1966. Online: https://archive.org/details/eucharisticwordsoooojere_01v9.

Johanson, Donald, and Maitland Edey. *Lucy: The Beginnings of Humankind*. New York: Simon and Schuster, 1981. Online: https://archive.org/details/lucybeginningsofoooojoha_r1n0.

Johnson, Dennis. *Triumph of the Lamb: A Commentary on Revelation*. Phillipsburg, NJ: P&R, 2001.

Johnson, Phillip. "Daniel Dennett's Dangerous Idea." *Origins & Design* (Winter 1996): 27–30. Online: http://www.arn.org/docs/johnson/dennett.htm.

———. *Darwin on Trial*. Washington, DC: Regnery Gateway, 1991.

———. *Reason in the Balance.* Downers Grove, IL: InterVarsity, 1995. Online: https://archive.org/details/reasoninbalancecoooojohn.

Josephus. *Against Apion.* In *The Works of Josephus,* new updated ed. Translated by William Whiston, 773–812. Peabody, MA: Hendrickson (1987 reprint). Online (another edition): http://www.ccel.org/ccel/josephus/works/files/works.html.

———. *The Antiquities of the Jews.* In *The Works of Josephus Complete and Unabridged.,* 27–542. Translated by William Whiston. Peabody, MA: Hendrickson (1987 reprint). Online (another edition): http://www.ccel.org/ccel/josephus/works/files/works.html.

Justin Martyr. *Dialogue with Trypho.* In *The Ante-Nicene Fathers,* vol. 1, edited by Alexander Roberts and James Donaldson, revised by A. Cleveland Coxe, 194–270. New York: Christian Literature. Reprint, Peabody, MA: Hendrickson, 1994. Online (another edition): http://www.ccel.org/ccel/schaff/anfo1.viii.iv.html.

———. *First Apology.* c.155. Online: http://www.ccel.org/ccel/schaff/anfo1.viii.ii.html.

Kaiser, Walter. *The Old Testament Documents: Are They Reliable and Relevant?* Downers Grove, IL: InterVarsity, 2001. Online: https://archive.org/details/oldtestamentdocuoookais.

Kapolyo, Joe. "Matthew." In *Africa Bible Commentary,* edited by Tokunboh Adeyemo, 1105–70. Nairobi: Word Alive, 2006.

Keller, Timothy. "The Gospel—Key to Change." Not dated. Online: https://www.cru.org/content/dam/cru/legacy/2013/01/Gospel_KeytoChange_TimKeller.pdf.

———. "The Importance of Hell." *Redeemer Report.* 2009. Online: http://www.redeemer.com/redeemer-report/article/the_importance_of_hell.

———. *Making Sense of God.* New York: Penguin, 2016.

———. *The Reason for God.* New York: Dutton, 2008.

———. *Walking with God through Pain and Suffering.* New York: Riverhead, 2013.

Kennedy, Titus. *Unearthing the Bible.* Eugene, OR: Harvest House, 2020.

Kenyon, Frederic. *The Bible and Archaeology.* London: George G. Harrap & Co. Ltd., 1949. Online: https://archive.org/details/biblearchaeologyoookeny/mode/2up?view=theater.

"Ketef Hinnom scrolls." *Wikipedia.* 2024. Online: https://en.wikipedia.org/wiki/Ketef_Hinnom_scrolls.

Kew, Ben. "'Corpses of Children': The Intellectual Dishonesty of Sam Harris." *El American* (18 August 2022). Online: https://elamerican.com/corpses-of-children-the-intellectual-dishonesty-of-sam-harris/.

Keynes, Randal. *Darwin, His Daughter, and Human Evolution.* New York: Riverhead, 2002.

Khan, Sultan Muhammad. *A Testimony to the Truth of the Holy Writings.* Nairobi: English Press Limited, 1992. Online: http://www.answering-islam.org/Testimonies/khan.html.

King-Farlow, John. "Monism, Naturalism and Nominalism: Can an Atheist's World View be Logically Expressed?" *Laval théologique et philosophique* 29 (1973) 123–142. Online: https://www.erudit.org/en/journals/ltp/1973-v29-n2-ltp0988/1020348ar.pdf.

Kitchen, Kenneth. *The Bible in its World: The Bible & Archaeology Today.* Downers Grove, IL: InterVarsity, 1977. Online: https://archive.org/details/bibleinitsworld booookitc.

———. *On the Reliability of the Old Testament*. Grand Rapids: Eerdmans, 2003. Online: https://archive.org/details/on-the-reliability-of-the-old-testament-kitchen-kenneth-anderson.

Koestler, Arthur. *Janus: A Summing Up*. New York: Random House, 1978. Online: https://archive.org/details/janussummingupooookoes.

Koons, Robert. "Science and theism: concord, not conflict." In *The Rationality of Theism*, edited by Paul Copan and Paul Moser, 72–90. London: Routledge, 2003. Online: https://www.difa3iat.com/wp-content/uploads/2016/09/www.difa3iat.com_-5.pdf.

Koukl, Gregory. "Evil as Evidence for God." *Stand to Reason*. 2013. Online: http://www.str.org/articles/evil-as-evidence-for-god#ANCHOR2.

———. "A Good Reason for Evil." *Stand to Reason*. 2012. Online: http://www.str.org/articles/a-good-reason-for-evil#.VonkD-QauVQ.

———. *Tactics*. Grand Rapids: Zondervan, 2009. Online: https://archive.org/details/tacticsstudyguidooookouk.

Krahmalkov, Charles. "Exodus Itinerary Confirmed by Egyptian Evidence." *Biblical Archaeology Review* 20, no. 5 (1994) 54–62, 79. Online: https://library.biblicalarchaeology.org/article/exodus-itinerary-confirmed-by-egyptian-evidence/.

Külling, Samuel. *Zur Datierung der "Genesis-P-Stück" : Namentlich Des Kapitels Genesis XVII*. Kampen: J. H. Kok, 1964.

Kurtz, Paul. "Does Humanism Have an Ethic of Responsibility?" In *Humanist Ethics: Dialogue on Basics*, edited by Morris Stoner, 11–25. Buffalo, NY: Prometheus, 1980. Online: https://archive.org/details/humanistethicdiooobuff.

———. "Reply by Paul Kurtz to Markovic." In *Humanist Ethics: Dialogue on Basics*, edited by Morris Stoner, 33–35. Buffalo, NY: Prometheus, 1980. Online: https://archive.org/details/humanistethicdiooobuff.

Lack, David. *Evolutionary Theory and Christian Belief: The Unresolved Conflict*. London: Methuen, 1957.

Ladd, George Eldon. 1975. *I Believe in the Resurrection of Jesus*. Grand Rapids: Eerdmans. Online: https://archive.org/details/ibelieveinresurooooladd.

Laskaris, Ernie. "The New Atheist Sledgehammer: Like Epistemological Air Boxing." *Themelios* 43 (2018) 434–47. Online: https://www.thegospelcoalition.org/themelios/article/the-new-atheist-sledgehammer-like-epistemological-air-boxing/.

Lawson, James. *Deeper Experiences of Famous Christians*. Anderson, IN: Warner, 1911. Online: https://archive.org/details/deeperexperienceoolaws. Audio version online: https://archive.org/details/deeperexperiences_2404_librivox.

Lawton, Graham. "Why Darwin was wrong about the tree of life." *New Scientist* (21 January 2009). Online: https://www.newscientist.com/article/mg20126921-600-why-darwin-was-wrong-about-the-tree-of-life/.

Leff, Arthur. "Unspeakable Ethics, Unnatural Law." *Duke Law Journal* 28, no. 6 (1979) 1229–49. Online: https://scholarship.law.duke.edu/cgi/viewcontent.cgi?article=2724&context=dlj.

Lewis, C. S. *The Abolition of Man*. New York: MacMillan, 1947. Online: https://archive.org/details/abolitionofmanoocsle.

———. "Answers to Questions on Christianity." In *God in the Dock,* edited by Walter Hooper, 48–62. Grand Rapids: Eerdmans, 1970. Online: https://archive.org/details/collectedworksofoocsle/mode/2up.

———. "Christian Apologetics." In *God in the Dock,* edited by Walter Hooper, 89–103. Grand Rapids: Eerdmans, 1970. Online: https://archive.org/details/collectedworksofoocsle/mode/2up.

———. "De Futilitate." In *Christian Reflections,* edited by Walter Hooper, 57–71. Grand Rapids: Eerdmans, 1967. Online: https://archive.org/details/collectedworksofoocsle/mode/2up.

———. "Evil and God." In *God in the Dock,* edited by Walter Hooper, 129–46. Grand Rapids: Eerdmans, 1970. Online: https://archive.org/details/collectedworksofoocsle/mode/2up.

———. "Is Theology Poetry?" In *The Weight of Glory and Other Essays,* rev. ed., edited by Walter Hooper, 74–92. New York: Macmillan, 1980. Essay online: http://www.samizdat.qc.ca/arts/lit/Theology=Poetry_CSL.pdf.

———. "The Laws of Nature." In *God in the Dock,* edited by Walter Hooper, 76–79. Grand Rapids: Eerdmans, 1970. Online: https://archive.org/details/collectedworksofoocsle/mode/2up.

———. *Mere Christianity.* New York: Touchstone, 1980. Earlier edition online: https://archive.org/details/merechristianityooounse_q8b8.

———. *Miracles.* New York: Harper San Francisco, 2001. Earlier edition online: https://archive.org/details/in.ernet.dli.2015.260876.

———. "Modern Theology and Biblical Criticism." In *Christian Reflections,* edited by Walter Hooper, 152–66. Grand Rapids: Eerdmans, 1967. Online: https://archive.org/details/collectedworksofoocsle/mode/2up.

———. "The Poison of Subjectivism." In *Christian Reflections,* edited by Walter Hooper, 72–81. Grand Rapids: Eerdmans, 1967. Online: https://archive.org/details/collectedworksofoocsle/mode/2up.

———. *The Problem of Pain.* New York: MacMillan, 1947. Online: https://archive.org/details/in.ernet.dli.2015.264598/mode/2up?view=theater.

———. *Reflections on the Psalms.* New York: Harcourt, Brace, Jovanovich, 1958. Online: https://archive.org/details/belovedworksofcsoooolewi/mode/2up?view=theater.

———. "Religion Without Dogma?" In *God in the Dock,* edited by Walter Hooper, 21–24. Grand Rapids: Eerdmans, 1970. Online: https://archive.org/details/collectedworksofoocsle/mode/2up.

———. "Two Lectures." In *God in the Dock,* edited by Walter Hooper, 208–11. Grand Rapids: Eerdmans, 1970. Online: https://archive.org/details/collectedworksofoocsle/mode/2up.

———. "We have No 'Right to Happiness.'" In *God in the Dock,* edited by Walter Hooper, 317–22. Grand Rapids: Eerdmans, 1970. Online: https://archive.org/details/collectedworksofoocsle/mode/2up.

———. "What are We to Make of Jesus Christ?" In *God in the Dock,* edited by Walter Hooper, 156–60. Grand Rapids: Eerdmans, 1970. Online: https://archive.org/details/collectedworksofoocsle/mode/2up.

Lewontin, Richard. "Billions and Billions of Demons" *New York Review of Books* (9 January 1997) 28–32.

Licona, Michael. *The Resurrection of Jesus: A New Historigraphical Approach.* Downers Grove: IVP Academic, 2010.

Lindley, David. *The End of Physics: The Myth of a Unified Theory*. New York: Basic, 1993. Online: https://archive.org/details/endofphysicsmythoolind.

Lindsley, Arthur. "Christ and the Bible." *C. S. Lewis Institute*. 2007. Online: https://www.cslewisinstitute.org/resources/christ-and-the-bible/.

Lipson, H. S. "A Physicist Looks at Evolution." *Strategic Studies* 4 (1981) 64–67.

Livingston, G. Herbert. 1974. *The Pentateuch in its Cultural Environment*. Grand Rapids: Baker. Online: https://archive.org/details/isbn_0801056306.

Lloyd-Jones, Martyn. *Joy Unspeakable*. Wheaton, IL: Harold Shaw, 1984. Online: https://archive.org/details/joyunspeakablepooooolloy.

Long, Jeffery. "Near-Death Experience Evidence for Their Reality." *Missouri Medicine* 111 (2014) 372–80. Online: https://www.ncbi.nlm.nih.gov/pmc/articles/PMC 6172100/.

Lönnig, Wolf-Ekkehard. "Darwin's Finches": Galápagos Islands as an Evolutionary Model" *Evolution News*. 2020: Online: https://evolutionnews.org/tag/galapagos-finches-series/.

———. "Galápagos Finches — A Paradigm of the Limits of Natural Selection?" *Evolution News*. 2020. Online: https://evolutionnews.org/2020/11/galapagos-finches-a-paradigm-of-the-limits-of-natural-selection/.

Løvtrup, Søren. *Darwinism: The Refutation of a Myth*. London: Croom Helm, 1987.

Lucas, J. R. *The Freedom of the Will*. Oxford: Clarendon, 1970. Online: https://archive.org/details/freedomofwilloooojrlu/mode/2up?view=theater.

———. "Wilberforce and Huxley: A Legendary Encounter," *Historical Journal* 22 (1979) 313–30.

Lucian of Samosata. *The Passing of Peregrinus*. c.165–75. Online: http://www.earlychristianwritings.com/text/peregrinus.html.

Luskin, Casey. "A Primer on the Tree of Life (Part 2): Conflicts in the Molecular Evidence." *Evolution News*. 2009. Online: https://evolutionnews.org/2009/05/a_primer_on_the_tree_of_life_p_1/#backfn2.

Lynch, Michael, and John Conery. "The evolutionary demography of duplicate genes." *Journal of Structural and Functional Genomics* 3 (2003) 35–44. Online: https://www.researchgate.net/publication/10681486_The_Evolutionary_Demography_of_Duplicate_Genes.

Macbeth, Norman. *Darwin Retried: an appeal to reason*. Ipswich, MA: Gambit, 1971. Online: https://archive.org/details/darwinretriedappoooomacb.

MacDonald, Hope. *When Angels Appear*. Grand Rapids: Zondervan, 1982. Online: https://archive.org/details/whenangelsappearoomacd.

Machen, J. Gresham. *Christianity and Liberalism*. Grand Rapids: Eerdmans, 1923. Online: https://archive.org/details/christianitylibeoooomach_i2l5. Audio version online: https://archive.org/details/christianityandliberalism_2107_librivox.

Mackie, J. L. *The Miracle of Theism: Arguments for and against the existence of God*. Oxford: Clarendon, 1982. Online: https://archive.org/details/TheMiracleOfTheismArgumentsForAndAgainstTheExistenceOfGodJLMackie/mode/2up?view=theater.

MacNutt, Francis. *Healing*. New York: Bantam, 1974. Online: https://archive.org/details/isbn_0553225723.

Maier, Paul. "The Empty Tomb as History." *Christianity Today* 19 (28 March 1975) 4–6.

———. *First Easter*. New York: Harper & Row, 1973. Online: https://archive.org/details/firsteastertrueuoomaie.

Ibn Majah, Yazid. *Sunan Ibn Majah.* Not dated. Online: http://sunnah.com/ibnmajah.
Major, Lee Elliot. "Big enough to bury Darwin." *The Guardian* (23 August 2001). Online: https://www.theguardian.com/education/2001/aug/23/highereducation.peopleinscience.
Malthus, Thomas. *An Essay on the Principle of Population.* London: John Murray, 1798. Online: http://www.esp.org/books/malthus/population/malthus.pdf.
Manser, A. R. "The Concept of Evolution." *Philosophy* 40 (1965) 18–34.
Manson, Neil, ed. *God and Design: The Teleological Argument and Modern Science.* London: Routledge, 2003.
Mara Bar-Serapion. *Letter.* Not dated. Online: http://www.earlychristianwritings.com/text/mara.html.
Markovic, Mihailo. "Comment by Mihailo Markovic on Kurtz." In *Humanist Ethics: Dialogue on Basics,* edited by Morris Stoner, 31–33. Buffalo, NY: Prometheus, 1980. Online: https://archive.org/details/humanistethicsdioobuff.
Marshall, I. Howard. "Universal Grace and Atonement in the Pastoral Epistles." In *The Grace of God, the Will of Man,* edited by Clark Pinnock, 51–69. Grand Rapids, MI: Academie, 1989. Online: https://archive.org/details/graceofgodwillofoooounse.
The Martyrdom of Polycarp. c.160. Online: http://www.ccel.org/ccel/schaff/anfo1.iv.iv.html.
al-Masih, Abd. *A Question that Demands an Answer.* Rikon, Switzerland: The Good Way, 1993. Online: http://path-of-peace.org/AQuestionThatDemandsAnAnswer.htm.
"Masoretic Text." *Wikipedia.* 2024. Online: http://en.wikipedia.org/wiki/Masoretic_Text.
"Materialism." *Wikipedia.* 2024. Online: https://en.wikipedia.org/wiki/Materialism.
Matthews, Kenneth. *Genesis 1—11:26* (NAC 1A). Nashville: Broadman & Holman, 1996.
Matthews, L. Harrison. "Introduction." In *On the Origin of Species* by Charles Darwin, v-xiii. London: J. M. Dent & Sons, 1972.
Maudlin, Tim. "Distilling Metaphysics From Quantum Physics." In *The Oxford Handbook of Metaphysics,* edited by Michael Loux and Dean Zimmerman, 461–90. New York: Oxford University Press, 2005. Online: https://archive.org/details/oxfordhandbookofoooounse_n804.
A'la Mawdudi, Sayyid Abul. *Towards Understanding the Qur'an.* Markfield, Leicestershire, England: The Islamic Foundation, Not dated. Online: http://www.tafheem.net/tafheem.html.
McCauley, Brian. "Animal Phyla." 2022. Online: https://brianmccauley.net/bio-6a/bio-6a-lab/animal-phyla.
McDonald, John. "The Molecular Basis of Adaptation: A Critical Review of Relevant Ideas and Observations." *Annual Review of Ecology and Systematics* 14 (1983) 77–102. Online: https://www.researchgate.net/publication/234150452_The_Molecular_Basis_of_Adaptation_A_Critical_Review_of_Relevant_Ideas_and_Observations.
McDowell, Josh. *Evidence That Demands A Verdict.* San Bernardino, CA: Here's Life, 1979. Online: https://archive.org/details/evidencethatdemao1mcdo.
———. *The Resurrection Factor.* San Bernardino, CA: Here's Life, 1981. Online: https://archive.org/details/resurrectionfactoomcdo.

McDowell, Josh, and Don Stewart. *Answers to Tough Questions*. San Bernardino, CA: Here's Life, 1980. Online: https://archive.org/details/answerstotoughquoomcdo.
———. *Reasons Skeptics Should Consider Christianity*. Wheaton, IL: Tyndale House, 1986. Online: https://s3.amazonaws.com/jmm.us/Books-Downloadable/Reasons+Skeptics+Should+Consider+Christianity.pdf.
McMullin, Ernan. "Plantinga's Defense of Special Creation." *Christian Scholar's Review* 31 (September 1991) 55–70. Online: https://www3.nd.edu/~afreddos/courses/43150/mcmullin2.htm.
Meacham (leBeit Yoreh), Tirzah. "Legal-Religious Status of the Jewish Female." *Jewish Women: A Comprehensive Historical Encyclopedia*. Jewish Women's Archive, 2021. Online: http://jwa.org/encyclopedia/article/legal-religious-status-of-jewish-female.
Medawar, Peter. *The Limits of Science*. New York: Harper & Row, 1984. Online: https://archive.org/details/limitsofscienceoooomeda.
Menn, Jonathan. *Christianity and Islam: The Essentials*. 2020. Online: https://www.eclea.net/courses.html#islam.
———. *Biblical Theology*. 2021. Online: https://www.eclea.net/courses.html#theology.
Menuge, Angus. "Declining Physicalism and Resurgent Alternatives." In *Minding the Brain: Models of the Mind, Information, and Empirical Science,* edited by Angus Menuge, Brian Krouse, and Robert Marks, 25–44. Seattle: Discovery Institute, 2023. Online: https://robertmarks.org/REPRINTS/2023-MTB.pdf.
Menuge, Angus, Brian Krouse, and Robert Marks, eds. *Minding the Brain: Models of the Mind, Information, and Empirical Science*. Seattle: Discovery Institute, 2023. Online: https://robertmarks.org/REPRINTS/2023-MTB.pdf.
Merriam-Webster Dictionary. 2024. Online: https://www.merriam-webster.com/.
Metzger, Bruce. "Bible." In *The Oxford Companion to the Bible,* edited by Bruce Metzger and Michael Coogan, 78–80. New York: Oxford University Press, 1993. Online: https://archive.org/details/isbn_9780965072595.
Meyer, Stephen. *Darwin's Doubt*. New York: HarperOne, 2013. Online: https://archive.org/details/darwins-doubt. Audio version online: https://archive.org/details/ddbscm.
———. "The Origin of Biological Information and the Higher Taxonomic Categories." *Proceedings of the Biological Society of Washington* 117 (2004) 213–39. Online: https://www.discovery.org/a/2177/.
———. *Return of the God Hypothesis*. New York: HarperOne, 2021.
———. *Scientific Evidence for a Creator*. Center for Science and Culture, 2021. Online: https://www.discovery.org/m/securepdfs/2021/12/Meyer-SciEvidforCreatorsm2.pdf.
———. *Signature in the Cell: DNA and the Evidence for Intelligent Design*. New York: HarperOne, 2009. Online: https://archive.org/details/SignatureInTheCellDNAAndTheEvidenceForIntelligentDesignStephenC.Meyer. Audio version online: https://archive.org/details/sitcid.
Miethe, Terry, ed. *Did Jesus Rise from the Dead: The Resurrection Debate*. San Francisco: Harper & Row, 1987. Online: https://archive.org/details/didjesusrisefromoohabe.
"Miller-Urey experiment." *Wikipedia*. 2024. Online: https://en.wikipedia.org/wiki/Miller%E2%80%93Urey_experiment.
"Monism." *Wikipedia*. 2024. Online: https://en.wikipedia.org/wiki/Monism#Buddhism.

Monod, Jacques. *Chance and Necessity*. Translated by Austryn Wainhouse. New York: Alfred A. Knopf, 1971. Online: https://archive.org/details/chancenecessity00jacq.

Moo, Douglas. "Jesus and the Authority of the Mosaic Law." *Journal for the Study of the New Testament* 20 (1984) 3–49. Online: https://static1.squarespace.com/static/537a4700e4b0cc86709d564c/t/538e0b52e4b08cd19602c185/1401817938919/jesusandauthority.pdf.

Moody, Jr., Raymond. *Life After Life*. New York: Bantam, 1976. Online: https://archive.org/details/raymondmoodylifeafterlife_201907/mode/2up.

Moore, Sebastian. *The Crucified Jesus Is No Stranger*. New York: Seabury, 1981. Online: https://archive.org/details/crucifiedjesusiso000moor.

Moreland, J. P. "Neuroscience and the Metaphysics of Consciousness and the Soul." In *Minding the Brain: Models of the Mind, Information, and Empirical Science*, edited by Angus Menuge, Brian Krouse, and Robert Marks, 45–71. Seattle: Discovery Institute, 2023. Online: https://robertmarks.org/REPRINTS/2023-MTB.pdf.

———. *Scaling the Secular City: A Defense of Christianity*. Grand Rapids: Baker, 1987. Online: https://archive.org/details/scalingsecularcio000more.

———. "What is Scientific Naturalism?" *Boundless*. 2004. Online: https://www.boundless.org/faith/what-is-scientific-naturalism/.

Morris, Henry. *Men of Science—Men of God*. El Cajon, CA: Master Books, 1988. Online: https://archive.org/details/menofsciencemeno00morr/mode/2up?view=theater.

Moskowitz, Clara. "Fact or Fiction?: Energy Can Neither Be Created Nor Destroyed." *Scientific American*. 2022. Online: https://www.scientificamerican.com/article/energy-can-neither-be-created-nor-destroyed/.

Moule, C. F. D., and Don Cupitt. "The Resurrection: A Disagreement." *Theology* 75 (1972) 507–19. Online: https://archive.org/details/doncupittselectio006cupi/mode/2up?view=theater.

Moyise, Steve. *Jesus and Scripture*. Grand Rapids: Baker Academic, 2010.

Müller, Julius. *The Theory of Myths, in its Application to the Gospel History, Examined and Confuted*. London: John Chapman, 1844.

Mueller, Antony. "Carl Menger Explains Value." *Mises Wire*. 2021. Online: https://mises.org/mises-wire/carl-menger-explains-value.

Mumford, Lewis. *Technics and Civilization*. Chicago: University of Chicago Press, 1934. Online: https://archive.org/details/dli.scoerat.5244lewismumfordtechnicsandcivilization.

Muslim, Imam. *Sahih Muslim*. Not dated. Online: http://sunnah.com/muslim.

"NABT Position Statement on Teaching Evolution." *National Association of Biology Teachers*. 2019. Online: https://nabt.org/Position-Statements-NABT-Position-Statement-on-Teaching-Evolution.

Nagel, Thomas. "The Fear of Religion." *The New Republic* (23 October 2006) 25–29. Online: https://keithburgess-jackson.com/wp-content/uploads/2007/04/nagel-the-fear-of-religion-2006-volume-235.pdf.

———. *Mind & Cosmos: Why the Materialist Neo-Darwinian Conception of Nature is Almost Certainly False*. Oxford: Oxford University Press, 2012. Online: https://archive.org/details/mindcoswhymato000nage/mode/2up?view=theater.

———. *The View From Nowhere*. New York: Oxford University Press, 1989.

Naja, Ben. "A Jesus Movement Among Muslims: Research from Eastern Africa." *International Journal of Frontier Missiology* 30:1 (Spring 2013) 27–29. Online: http://www.ijfm.org/PDFs_IJFM/30_1_PDFs/IJFM_30_1-Naja.pdf.

---. "Sixteen Features of Belief and Practice in Two Movements Among Muslims in Eastern Africa: What Does the data Say?" *International Journal of Frontier Missiology* 30:4 (Winter 2013) 155–60. Online: http://www.ijfm.org/PDFs_ IJFM/30_4_PDFs/IJFM_30_4-Naja.pdf.

Nash, Ronald. *Faith and Reason*. Grand Rapids: Zondervan, 1988. Online: https://archive.org/details/faith-and-reason-searching-for-a-rational-faith-pdfdrive/mode/2up.

Nathan, N. M. L. "Naturalism and Self-Defeat: Plantinga's Version." *Religious Studies* 33 (1997) 135–42. Abstract online: https://www.cambridge.org/core/journals/religious-studies/article/abs/naturalism-and-selfdefeat-plantingas-version/5B6B8F6973E9B028B303EBCDA9CE6585.

"Naturalism (philosophy)." *Wikipedia*. 2024. Online: https://en.wikipedia.org/wiki/Naturalism_(philosophy).

NDERF (Near-Death Experience Research Foundation). 2022. Online: https://www.nderf.org/.

Neill, Stephen. *The Interpretation of the New Testament 1861–1961*. London: Oxford University Press, 1964. Online: https://archive.org/details/interpretationofooooneil.

Nelson, Paul. "The Hopeless Watchmaker." *Origins Research* (1988) 10–12, 16.

New American Standard Bible, rev. ed. Grand Rapids: Zondervan, 1995. Online: https://www.biblegateway.com.

New International Version. 1978. Grand Rapids: Zondervan. Online: https://www.biblegateway.com.

New King James Version. 1982. Nashville: Thomas Nelson. Online: https://www.biblegateway.com.

Newman, Stuart. "The Developmental-Genetic Toolkit and the Molecular Homology Analogy Paradox." *Biological Theory* 1 (2006) 12–16. Online: https://www.researchgate.net/publication/247712843_The_Developmental-Genetic_Toolkit_and_the_Molecular_HomologyAnalogy_Paradox.

Ngundu, Onesimus. "Revelation." In *Africa Bible Commentary*, edited by Tokunboh Adeyemo, 1543–79. Nairobi: Word Alive, 2006.

Nietzsche, Friedrich. *Twilight of the Idols and The Antichrist*. Translated by Thomas Common. Mineola, NY: Dover, 2004. Online (another edition): https://archive.org/details/nietzschetheantichristeccehomotwilightoftheidolsandotherwritingsby_164_j.

Noebel, David. *Understanding the Times*. Manitou Springs, CO: Summit, 1991. Online: https://archive.org/details/understandingtimoooonoeb/mode/2up.

Novak, Ralph. *Christians and the Roman Empire: Background Texts*. Harrisburg, PA: Trinity, 2001.

NYU Grossman School of Medicine and NYU Langone. "Lucid Dying: Patients Recall Death Experiences During CPR." *PRN Newswire*. 2022. Online: https://www.prnewswire.com/news-releases/lucid-dying-patients-recall-death-experiences-during-cpr-301669519.html.

Oard, Michael. "Are fossils ever found in the wrong place?" *Creation* 32 (2010) 14–15. Online: https://creation.com/fossils-wrong-place.

---. "Evolution Pushed Further into the Past." *Creation ex nihilo Technical Journal* 10 (1996) 171–72. Online: https://dlo.creation.com/articles/p028/c02808/j10_2_171-172.pdf.

———. "Origin of vertebrates confirmed in the Early Cambrian." *Journal of Creation* 18 (2004) 10–11. Online: https://creation.com/images/pdfs/tj/j18_1/j18_1_10-11.pdf.

Ohno, Susumu. *Evolution by Gene Duplication*. New York: Springer Science+Business Media,LLC.,1970.Online:https://archive.org/details/evolutionbygenedooooohno/mode/2up?view=theater&q=%22early+Homo+was+already+provided%22.

Oliphint, K. Scott. *Reasons (for Faith)*. Phillipsburg, NJ: P&R, 2006. Online: https://archive.org/details/reasonsforfaithpooooolip.

Orgel, L. E., and F. H. C. Crick. "Selfish DNA: the ultimate parasite." *Nature* 284 (1980) 604–7. Abstract online: https://www.nature.com/articles/284604a0.

Origen. *Against Celsus*. 248. Online: http://www.ccel.org/ccel/schaff/anf04.vi.ix.html.

Oxford University. "Humans 'predisposed' to believe in gods and the afterlife." *Phys.org*. 2011. Online: https://phys.org/news/2011-05-humans-predisposed-gods-afterlife.html.

Packer, James. "Response to the Debate." In *Did Jesus Rise from the Dead: The Resurrection Debate*, edited by Terry Miethe, 143–50. San Francisco: Harper & Row, 1987. Online: https://archive.org/details/didjesusrisefromoohabe.

Page, Don. "Does God So Love the Multiverse?" 2008. Online: https://arxiv.org/pdf/0801.0246.pdf.

Pannenberg, Wolfhart. *Jesus—God and Man*. Philadelphia: Westminster, 1968. Online: https://archive.org/details/jesusgodmanooopann.

Patterns of Evidence: The Exodus. 2014. Online: https://patternsofevidence.com/exodus-film/.

Patterson, Colin. *Evolution*, 2nd ed. Ithaca, NY: Cornell University Press, 1999.

———. "Speech at the American Museum of Natural History." 1981. Online: https://origins.swau.edu/temp/classes/patterson.pdf.

Paulsen, Steve, and Francis Collins. "The believer." *Salon*. 2006. Online: https://www.salon.com/2006/08/07/collins_6/.

Payne, J. Barton. *Encyclopedia of Biblical Prophecy*. Grand Rapids, MI: Baker, 1980 (reprint). Online: https://archive.org/details/encyclopediaofbioooopayn_t6r4.

Pearcey, Nancy. "The Influence of Evolution on Philosophy and Ethics." In *Science at the Crossroads: Observation or Speculation?* ed. National Creation Conference, 166–71. Richfield, MN: Onesimus, 1985.

———. "Why Evolutionary Theory Cannot Survive Itself." *Evolution News* (8 March 2015). Online: https://evolutionnews.org/2015/03/why_evolutionar/.

"Peer Review in Creation Research." *Answers in Genesis* (13 October 2020). Online: https://answersingenesis.org/creation-vs-evolution/peer-review/.

Perry, Michael. *Toward a Theory of Human Rights*. New York: Cambridge University Press, 2007. Online: https://archive.org/details/towardtheoryofhuoooperr.

Persaud, Trevor. "Christ of the Klingons," *Christianity Today* 54, no. 12 (2010) 46–49. Online: https://www.christianitytoday.com/ct/2010/december/31.46.html.

Peters, Robert Henry. "Tautology in Evolution and Ecology," *The American Naturalist* 110 (1976) 1–12. Abstract online: https://www.journals.uchicago.edu/doi/abs/10.1086/283045.

Peterson, Michael. *Evil and the Christian God*. Grand Rapids: Baker, 1982. Online: https://archive.org/details/evilchristiangodoooopete.

Peterson, Robert. *Hell on Trial: The Case for Eternal Punishment*. Phillipsburg, NJ: P&R, 1995. Online: https://archive.org/details/hellontrialcasefoooopete.

Piper, John. "Are There Two Wills In God?" In *Still Sovereign,* edited by Thomas R. Schreiner and Bruce A. Ware, 107–31. Grand Rapids, MI: Baker, 2000. Online: http://www.desiringgod.org/ResourceLibrary/Articles/ByDate/1995/1580_Are_ There_Two_Wills_in_God/.

———. *Desiring God.* Colorado Springs, CO: Multnomah, 2003. Revised edition online: http://www.desiringgod.org/books/desiring-god.

———. "Is God Less Glorious Because He Ordained that Evil Be?" 1998. Online: http://www.desiringgod.org/ResourceLibrary/ConferenceMessages/ByDate/1998/1476_Is_God_Less_Glorious_Because_He_Ordained_that_Evil_Be/.

———. *Let the Nations be Glad!,* 3rd ed. Grand Rapids: Baker Academic, 2010.

———. "The New Birth Produces Love." 2008. Online: https://www.desiringgod.org/messages/the-new-birth-produces-love.

Plantinga, Alvin. "Appendix: Two Dozen (or so) Theistic Arguments." 2006. Online: https://appearedtoblogly.files.wordpress.com/2011/05/plantinga-alvin-22two-dozen-or-so-theistic-arguments221.pdf.

———. "A Christian Life Partly Lived." In *Philosophers Who Believe,* edited by Kelly James Clark, 45–82. Downers Grove, IL: InterVarsity, 1993. Online: https://archive.org/details/philosopherswhobooounse.

———. "The Dawkins Confusion: Naturalism *'ad absurdum'*. *Books & Culture* (March/April 2007). Online: https://www.booksandculture.com/articles/2007/marapr/1.21.html.

———. "Dennett's Dangerous Idea, Part 2." *Books & Culture* (May-June 1996) 35. Online: https://www.booksandculture.com/articles/1996/mayjun/6b316b.html.

———. "Epistemic Probability and Evil." In *The Evidential Argument from Evil,* edited by Daniel Howard-Snyder, 69–96. Bloomington, IN: Indiana University Press, 1996. Online: https://archive.org/details/evidentialargumeooounse.

———. "Evolution vs. Naturalism." *Books & Culture* (July/August 2008). Online: https://www.booksandculture.com/articles/2008/julaug/11.37.html.

———. *God, Freedom, and Evil.* Grand Rapids: Eerdmans, 1974. Online: https://archive.org/details/alvin-plantinga-god-freedom-and-evil-wm.-b.-eerdmans-publishing-company-1977.

———. "Introduction." In *Naturalism Defeated?* edited by James Beilby, 1–12. Ithaca, NY: Cornell University Press, 2002. Online: https://archive.org/details/naturalismdefeatoounse.

———. "Methodological Naturalism?" *Origins & Design* (Winter 1997) 18–27. Online: https://www.asa3.org/ASA/PSCF/1997/PSCF9-97Plantinga.html.ori.

———. "Naturalism Defeated." Unpublished paper. 1994. Online: https://www.google.com/url?sa=i&url=http%3A%2F%2Fstatic1.1.sqspcdn.com%2Fstatic%2Ff%2F38692%2F383655%2F1263300179793%2FNaturalism%2BDefeated.pdf%3Ftoken%3DskqA3gfcDvUI1SxovlJA43%252FXQEs%253D&psig=AOvVaw2UsruRU3iixx_Z85A857KP&ust=1718292962295000&source=images&cd=vfe&opi=89978449&ved=0CAUQn5wMahcKEwiY8IWfstaGAxUAAAAAHQAAAAAQBA.

———. *Warrant and Proper Function.* New York: Oxford University Press, 1993. Online: https://archive.org/details/warrantandproperfunctionplantinga.

———. *Warranted Christian Belief.* New York: Oxford University Press, 2000. Online: https://archive.org/details/warrantedchristiooooplan.

———. *Where the Conflict Really Lies.* New York: Oxford University Press, 2011. Online: https://archive.org/details/whereconflictreaooooplan.

Polanyi, Michael. *Personal Knowledge: Towards a Post-Critical Philosophy*. New York: Harper Torchbooks, 1964.

Polycarp. *Epistle to the Philippians*. c.110. Online: http://www.ccel.org/ccel/schaff/anf01.iv.ii.html.

Popper, Karl. *Conjectures and Refutations*. New York: Harper & Row, 1965. Online: https://archive.org/details/karl-popper-conjectures-and-refutations-the-growth-of-scientific-knowledge/mode/2up.

———. "Is Determinism Self-refuting?" *Mind* 92 (1983) 103–4.

———. "Scientific Reduction and the Essential Incompleteness of All Science." In *Studies in the Philosophy of Biology*, edited by Francisco Jose Ayala and Theodosius Dobzhansky, 259–84. Berkeley: University of California Press, 1974. Abstract of article online: https://www.semanticscholar.org/paper/Scientific-Reduction-and-the-Essential-of-All-Popper/ee3ad79ef1054100fdc71f7ec7f59022ef1808ae.

———. *Unended Quest: An Intellectual Autobiography*. LaSalle, IL: Open Court, 1976. Online: https://archive.org/details/popper-karl-unended-quest-an-intellectual-autobiography/mode/2up.

Potter, Ellis. "Buddhism for Beginners." 2012. Online: https://www.unionpublishing.org/resource/buddhism-for-beginners/.

Poythress, Vern. "Why Scientists Must Believe in God: Divine Attributes of Scientific Law." *Journal of the Evangelical Theological Society* 46 (2003) 111–23. Online: https://www.ldolphin.org/JETS.pdf.

Presbyterian Church (USA). "The Nature and Value of Human Life": 285–304. 1981. Online: https://www.pcusa.org/site_media/media/uploads/_resolutions/the-nature-and-value-of-human-life.pdf.

Price, Randall. *Searching for the Original Bible*. Eugene, OR: Harvest House, 2007. Online: https://archive.org/details/searchingfororigooopric.

"Probable Reasoning Has no Rational Basis." Not dated. Online: https://www.scribd.com/document/471709568/Hume-on-empirical-reasoning#.

Provine, William. "Scientists, Face It! Science And Religion Are Incompatible." *The Scientist*. 1988. Online: https://www.the-scientist.com/opinion-old/scientists-face-it-science-and-religion-are-incompatible-62695.

Provine, William, and Phillip Johnson. "Debate: Darwinism: Science or Naturalistic Philosophy?" *Origins Research* 16 (Fall/Winter 1994) 5–14. Video debate online: https://josephsmithfoundation.org/darwinism-science-or-naturalistic-philosophy/.

Purtill, Richard. *Reason to Believe*. Grand Rapids: Eerdmans, 1974. Online: https://archive.org/details/reasontobelieveooopurt/mode/2up?view=theater.

Ramm, Bernard. 1985. *An Evangelical Christology*. Nashville, TN: Thomas Nelson. Online: https://archive.org/details/evangelicalchrisooramm.

Rashdall, Hastings. *The Theory of Good and Evil*, vol. 2, 2nd ed. London: Oxford University Press, 1924. Online: https://archive.org/details/theoryofgoodevilooo2rash/mode/2up?view=theater.

Rasmussen, Joshua, and Filipe Leon. *Is God the Best Explanation of Things? A Dialogue*. London: Palgrave Macmillan, 2019.

Raup, David. "Conflicts between Darwin and Paleontology." *Field Museum of Natural History Bulletin* 50 (1979) 22–29. Online: https://ia800700.us.archive.org/19/items/cbarchive_36375_conflictsbetweendarwinandpaleo1930/conflictsbetweendarwinandpaleo1930.pdf.

Raymond, J. D. "'They Went to Their Deaths Singing:' The Martyrs and the Joyful Death." *Gaudium*. 2022. Online: https://www.gaudiummag.com/p/they-went-to-their-deaths-singing.

Reasons to Believe. *Why the Bible Can be Trusted*. Not dated. Online: https://mcusercontent.com/8906841e0b76067a1c57df68d/files/7cf8e606-563b-8d85-b509-51619057b825/WhytheBible_EBook_2022_V04.pdf.

Rees, Martin. *Just Six Numbers*. New York: Basic, 2000.

Reichenbach, Bruce. *Evil and a Good God*. New York: Fordham University Press, 1982.

"Religious interpretations of the big bang theory." *Wikipedia*. 2024. Online: https://en.wikipedia.org/wiki/Religious_interpretations_of_the_Big_Bang_theory.

Reppert, Victor. "The Argument from Reason." 1998. Online: https://infidels.org/library/modern/the-argument-from-reason/.

———. *C. S. Lewis's Dangerous Idea*. Downers Grove, IL: InterVarsity, 2003. Online: https://archive.org/details/cslewissdangerouoooorepp.

———. "QCI Interview: Dr. Victor Reppert on the 'Argument from Reason.'" Not dated. Online: https://www.google.com/url?sa=t&source=web&rct=j&opi=8997 8449&url=http://static1.1.sqspcdn.com/static/f/38692/384808/1262870390447/ QCI%2BInterview%2B-%2BDr.%2BVictor%2BReppert%2Bon%2Bthe%2BArgu ment%2Bfrom%2BReason.pdf%3Ftoken%3DSkfKgoCyoUSfxQJbpHPnam4ezC Q%253D&ved=2ahUKEwj_tpjWudaGAxWH4ckDHbO4B_MQFnoECA4QAQ &usg=AOvVaw3aW92JOGQG8Gmre1NiZyih.

———. "Several Formulations of the Argument from Reason." *Philosophia Christi* 5 (2003) 9–33.

Rifkin, Jeremy. *Algeny*. New York: Penguin, 1984. Online: https://archive.org/details/algenyoorifk.

Ripken, Nik. *The Insanity of God*. Nashville: B&H, 2013. Online: https://archive.org/details/insanityofgodtruooooripk.

Rittgers, Ronald. *The Reformation of Suffering*. Oxford: Oxford University Press, 2012.

Robbins, J. Wesley. "Is Naturalism Irrational?" *Faith and Philosophy* 11, no. 2 (1994) 255–59. Online: https://place.asburyseminary.edu/cgi/viewcontent.cgi?article=14 78&context=faithandphilosophy.

Roberts, Peter. "Review: Just Six numbers." *Vision*. 2001. Online: https://www.vision.org/review-just-six-numbers-1139.

Robinson, John A. T. *Redating the New Testament*. Philadelphia: Westminster, 1976. Online: https://archive.org/details/redatingnewtestaooooorobi_s8t2.

Rohl, David. *Exodus: Myth or History?* Minneapolis: Thinking Man Media, 2015.

"Rolling Stone, The." *Eutychus*. 2009. Online: http://eutychusnerd.blogspot.com/2009/04/rolling-stone.html.

Rowe, William. *Philosophy of Religion: An Introduction*, 4th ed. Belmont, CA: Wadsworth, Cengage Learning, 2007.

———. "The Problem of Evil and Some varieties of Atheism." In *The Evidential Argument from Evil*, edited by Daniel Howard-Snyder, 1–11. Bloomington, IN: Indiana University Press, 1996. Online: https://archive.org/details/evidentialargumeoooounse.

Runzo, Joseph. "Omniscience and Freedom for Evil." *International Journal for Philosophy of Religion* 12 (1981) 131–47.

Ruse, Michael. *Darwinism as Religion*. New York: Oxford University Press, 2017. Online: https://archive.org/details/darwinismasreligoooooruse/mode/2up.

———. "Is Darwinism a Religion?" *HuffPost* (20 September 2011). Online: https://www.huffpost.com/entry/is-darwinism-a-religion_b_904828.

———. "Is Darwinism a Religion?" *Toronto Journal of Theology* 32 (2016): 369–89. Abstract online: https://utpjournals.press/doi/abs/10.3138/tjt.4133?role=tab&journalCode=tjt.

Ruse, Michael, and Edward O. Wilson. "Moral Philosophy as Applied Science," *Philosophy* 61, no. 236 (1986) 173–92.

———. "The Evolution of Ethics." In *Religion and the Natural Sciences*, edited by James Huchingson, 308–11. New York: Harcourt Brace College Publishers, 2005. Online: https://archive.org/details/religionnaturalsoooounse_a1p5.

Russell, Bertrand. *The Problems of Philosophy*, rev. ed. London: Williams and Norgate, 1912. Online: https://archive.org/details/in.ernet.dli.2015.262666/mode/2up?view=theater.

Russell, E. S. *The Diversity of Animals: An Evolutionary Study*. Leiden: Brill, 1962. Online: https://archive.org/details/diversityofanimaooooruss.

Sagan, Carl. *Cosmos*. New York: Ballantine, 1980. Online: https://archive.org/details/cosmos_201910.

Salisbury, Frank. "Natural Selection and the Complexity of the Gene." *Nature* 224 (1969) 342–43.

Sartre, Jean-Paul. "Existentialism Is a Humanism." 1946. Online: https://www.marxists.org/reference/archive/sartre/works/exist/sartre.htm.

Schafersman, Steven. "Naturalism is Today and Essential Part of Science." 1996. Online: https://web.archive.org/web/20190705061915/http://www.stephenjaygould.org/ctrl/schafersman_nat.html.

Schaeffer, Francis. *He Is There and He Is Not Silent*. In *The Complete Works of Francis Schaeffer: A Christian Worldview*, vol. 1, *A Christian View of Philosophy and Culture*, 273–352. Westchester, IL: Crossway, 1982. Online: https://archive.org/details/completeworksoffooooscha_u5h1.

Schoville, Keith. "The Reliability of the Scriptural Documents." In *Christianity Challenges the University*, edited by Peter Wilkes, 63–77. Downers Grove, IL: InterVarsity, 1981. Online: https://archive.org/details/christianitychalooounse/page/n1/mode/2up?view=theater.

Schutte, Augustine. "The Refutation of Determinism," *Philosophy* 59 (1984): 481–90.

Schützenberger, Marcel-Paul. "Algorithms and the Neo-Darwinian Theory of Evolution." In *Mathematical Challenges to the Neo-Darwinian Interpretation of Evolution*, edited by Paul Moorhead and Martin Kaplan, 73–80. New York: Wistar Institute of Anatomy and Biology, 1967.

———. "Interview: Marcel-Paul Schützenberger: The Miracles of Darwinism." *Origins & Design* (Spring 1996) 10–15.

Schwartz, Jeffrey, and Bruno Maresca. "Do Molecular Clocks Run at All? A Critique of Molecular Systematics." *Biological Theory* 1 (2006) 357–371. Online: https://www.researchgate.net/publication/254008229_Do_Molecular_Clocks_Run_at_All_A_Critique_of_Molecular_Systematics.

The Science Council. "Our definition of science." 2024. Online: https://sciencecouncil.org/about-science/our-definition-of-science/.

"Scientism." *Wikipedia*. 2024. Online: https://en.wikipedia.org/wiki/Scientism.

Scott, Eugenie. "The 'Science and Religion Movement' An Opportunity for Improved Public Understanding of Science?" In *Science and Religion: Are They Compatible?*, edited by Paul Kurtz, 111–16. Amherst, NY: Prometheus, 2003. Online: https://archive.org/details/sciencereligionaookurt.

Septuagint (LXX). Online: http://www.ellopos.net/elpenor/greek-texts/septuagint/default.asp (Greek/English).

"Septuagint." *Wikipedia*. 2024. Online: http://en.wikipedia.org/wiki/Septuagint.

Severance, Diana. "Christian Mercy in a Time of Plague." *Credo*. 2020. Online: https://credomag.com/2020/04/christian-mercy-in-a-time-of-plague/.

Shakespeare, William. *Hamlet*. Not dated. Online: https://shakespeare.folger.edu/downloads/pdf/hamlet_PDF_FolgerShakespeare.pdf.

Shamoun, Sam. "Allah – The Greatest Deceiver of them All." *Answering Islam*. Not dated. Online: http://www.answering-islam.org/Shamoun/allah_best_deceiver.htm.

———. "The Quranic Witness to Biblical Authority." *Answering Islam*. Not dated. Online: http://www.answering-islam.org/Shamoun/aboutbible.htm.

Shapiro, James. "In the Details . . . What?" *National Review* (16 September 1996) 62–65. Online: https://shapiro.bsd.uchicago.edu/Shapiro.1996.Nat%27lReview.pdf.

Shayesteh, Daniel. *The Difference is The Son*. Castle Hill, NSW, Australia: Shayesteh, 2004.

Shehadi, Fadlou. *Ghazali's Unique Unknowable God*. Leiden: Brill, 1964. Online: http://www.ghazali.org/books/fad-guuG.pdf.

Sherry, Patrick. "Problem of Evil." *Encyclopedia Britannica*. 2021. Online: https://www.britannica.com/topic/problem-of-evil.

Sherwin-White, A. N. *Roman Society and Roman Law in the New Testament*. Grand Rapids: Baker, 1992 (reprint). Online: https://archive.org/details/romansocietyromaooooosher_s4u3.

Siegel, Ethan. "Surprise: the Big Bang isn't the beginning of the universe anymore." *BigThink.com*. (13 October 2021). Online: https://bigthink.com/starts-with-a-bang/big-bang-beginning-universe/.

"Siloam inscription." *Wikipedia*. 2024. Online: https://en.wikipedia.org/wiki/Siloam_inscription.

Simmons III, Richard. "The Eternal Wager." 2016. Online: https://richardsimmons3.com/the-eternal-wager/.

Simon, Herbert. "A Mechanism for Social Selection and Successful Altruism." *Science* 250 (1990) 1665–68. Abstract online: https://www.jstor.org/stable/2878538?seq=1#metadata_info_tab_contents.

Simpson, George Gaylord. "The History of Life." In *Evolution After Darwin: volume 1–The Evolution of Life*, edited by Sol Tax, 117–80. Chicago: University of Chicago Press, 1960. Online: https://archive.org/details/evolutionafterdoo1taxs.

———. *The Meaning of Evolution*, rev. ed. New Haven: Yale University Press, 1967. Online: https://archive.org/details/meaningofevolutioooogeor_n4g7.

Sire, James. 2004. *The Universe Next Door,* 4th ed. Downers Grove, IL: InterVarsity.

Skinner, B. F. *Beyond Freedom and Dignity*. New York: Bantam/Vintage, 1971. Online: https://archive.org/details/beyondfreedomdigooobfsk/mode/2up?view=theater&q=%22Survival+is+the+only+value+according+to+which+%22.

Smith, Huston. *The Religions of Man*. New York: Mentor, 1958. Online: https://archive.org/details/religionsofmanoohust/mode/2up?view=theater.

Smith, Wilbur. *The Incomparable Book*. Minneapolis: Beacon, 1961. Online: https://archive.org/details/incomparablebookooooowilb/mode/2up?view=theater.

Snelling, Andrew. "Radiohalos—Mysterious Bullet Holes in Rocks." *Answers in Genesis*. 2012. Online: https://answersingenesis.org/age-of-the-earth/mysterious-bullet-holes-in-rocks/.

Sookhdeo, Patrick. *Understanding Islamic Terrorism*. Pewsey, Wiltshire, UK: Isaac, 2004. Online: https://archive.org/details/understandingisloooosook_u1t6.

"Some Islamic Doctrines." *Faith Freedom*. 2018. Online: http://www.faithfreedom.org/some-islamic-doctrines-2/.

Sproul, R. C. *Essential Truths of the Christian Faith*. Wheaton, IL: Tyndale, 1992. Online: https://archive.org/details/essentialtruthsoooooospro.

———. *Saved from What?* Wheaton, IL: Crossway, 2002. Online: https://archive.org/details/savedfromwhatoooospro_n6f1.

Stanley, Brian. In "The Discussion," 1 of 14. Not dated. Online: http://www.st-edmunds.cam.uk/cis/brooke/lecture6.html [that link apparently is no longer valid].

Stanley, Steven. *Macroevolution: Pattern and Process*. San Francisco: W. H. Freeman, 1979. Online: https://archive.org/details/macroevolutionpaoooostan.

Stansfield, William. *The Science of Evolution*. New York: MacMillan, 1977. Online: https://archive.org/details/scienceofevolutiooooounse.

Stein, Robert. "Was the Tomb really Empty?" *Journal of the Evangelical Theological Society* 20 (1977) 23–29. Online: https://etsjets.org/wp-content/uploads/2010/09/files_JETS-PDFs_20_20-1_20-1-pp023-029_JETS.pdf.

Stevens, L., and P. L. Dorn. "Population genetics of Triatominae." In *American Trypanosomiasis Chagas Disease: One Hundred Years of Research*, 2nd ed., edited by Jenny Telleria and Michel Tibayrenc, 169–208. Amsterdam: Elsevier, 2017. Online: https://archive.org/details/isbn_9780123848765.

Stoner, Peter. *Science Speaks*, rev. online ed. Chicago: Moody, 2005. Online: https://archive.org/details/sciencespeakspeterw.stoner/mode/2up?view=theater.

Stott, John. *Basic Christianity*. Nottingham, U.K.: Inter-Varsity, 2008. Online: https://www.scribd.com/document/317881851/9780830834136.

———. *The Cross of Christ*. Downers Grove, IL: InterVarsity, 1986. Online: https://archive.org/details/crossofchristoooostot/mode/2up.

Stove, David. *Darwinian Fairytales*. Aldershot, England: Avebury, 1995. Online: https://archive.org/details/darwinianfairytaoooostov/mode/2up?view=theater.

Straehler, Reinhold. "Coming to Faith in Christ: Case Studies of Muslims in Kenya." Doctoral diss. University of South Africa. 2009. Online: http://uir.unisa.ac.za/handle/10500/3527.

Strauss, David Friedrich. *A New Life of Jesus*, vol. 1. London: Williams and Norgate, 1865. Online: https://archive.org/details/anewlifejesuso6stragoog.

Stripling, Scott, et al. "'You are Cursed by the God YWH:' an early Hebrew inscription from Mt. Ebal." *Heritage Science* 11 (2023) 1–24. Online: https://link.springer.com/epdf/10.1186/s40494-023-00920-9?sharing_token=ZH_X7apyCLdgXbGLWJD7KG_BpE1tBhCbnbw3BuzI2ROILk6dtBVvXew7J6yS1PSgVXtWhHhzfoyYkIoXMFcgFRj5oPY-Et4_hlZnzvm4ghDS8dAaRkdNlPrboW9gnPgNAUPkdHwJqwTdTmezZb1zu6G-EIralvFyXEeeN17-SUI=.

Stroud, Barry. "The Charm of Naturalism." In *Naturalism in Question*, edited by Mario De Caro and David Macarthur, 21–35. Cambridge: Harvard University Press, 2004.

Study Qur'an. Not dated. Online: http://www.studyquran.co.uk/. The specific page cited in text is: http://www.studyquran.co.uk/14_MIIM.htm.

As-Suhaym, Muhammad bin Abdullah. *Islam: Its Foundations and Concepts*. Riyadh: Darussalam, 2006. Online: https://www.google.com/books/edition/Islam_Its_Foundations_and_Concepts/jtWXEAAAQBAJ?hl=en&gbpv=1.

Sukenik, Naama, et al. "Early evidence of an archaeological dyed textile using scale-insects: The Cave of Skulls, Israel." *Journal of Archaeological Science: Reports* 57 (2024) 104673. Online: https://www.sciencedirect.com/science/article/abs/pii/S2352409X24003018.

Sundiata, Abbas. *Look Behind the Façade*. Xulon [online publisher], 2006.

Surin, Kenneth. *Theology and the Problem of Evil*. Oxford: Basil Blackwell, 1986.

Swinburne, Richard. *The Existence of God*. New York: Oxford University Press, 1979. Online: https://archive.org/details/richard-swinburne-the-existence-of-god.

———. *Is There A God?*, rev. ed. New York: Oxford University Press, 2010. Online: https://archive.org/details/richard-swinburne-is-there-a-god.

Tacitus. *Annals*. c.115. Online: http://www.earlychristianwritings.com/text/annals.html.

Tate, Karl. "Alternatives to the Big Bang Theory (infographic)." *Space.com* (8 March 2022). Online: https://www.space.com/24781-big-bang-theory-alternatives-infographic.html.

Taylor, Charles. "Ethics and Ontology." *The Journal of Philosophy* 100 (2003): 305–20.

Taylor, Gordon Rattray. *The Great Evolution Mystery*. New York: Harper & Row, 1983.

Taylor, Ian. *In the Minds of Men: Darwin and the New World Order*. Toronto: TFE, 1984.

Taylor, Richard. *Ethics, Faith, and Reason*. Englewood Cliffs, NJ: Prentice-Hall, 1985.

———. *Metaphysics*, 2nd ed. Englewood Cliffs, NJ: Prentice-Hall, 1974. Fourth edition online: https://archive.org/details/metaphysicsootayl.

ten Boom, Corrie, and John and Elizabeth Sherrill. *The Hiding Place*. Carmel, NY: Guideposts, 1971. Online: https://archive.org/details/corrietenboomherooootenb/mode/2up.

Tertullian. *Prescription Against Heretics*. c.200. Online: http://www.ccel.org/ccel/schaff/anf03.v.iii.html.

Thaxton, Charles, Walter Bradley, and Roger Olsen. *The Mystery of Life's Origin*. Dallas: Lewis and Stanley, 1984. Online: https://archive.org/details/mysteryoflifesoroooothax.

Thomson, Keith. "Marginalia: The meaning of evolution." *American Scientist* 70 (1982): 529–31.

Thompson, William. "A Critique of Evolution." *Journal of the American Scientific Affiliation* 12 (1960) 2–10. Online: https://www.asa3.org/ASA/PSCF/1960/JASA3-60Complete.pdf.

Thorvaldsen, Steinar, and Ola Hössjer. "Using statistical methods to model the fine-tuning of molecular machines and systems." *Journal of Theoretical Biology* 501 (2020) 1–14. Online: https://www.sciencedirect.com/science/article/pii/S0022519320302071?ref=pdf_download&fr=RR-2&rr=8954692b790786da.

Thurman, Howard. *A Strange Freedom: The Best of Howard Thurman on Religious Experience and Public Life*. Boston: Beacon, 1998. Online: https://archive.org/details/strangefreedombeoooothur.

Tinder, Glenn. "Can We Be Good Without God?" *The Atlantic Monthly* (December 1989) 69–85. Online: https://cdn.theatlantic.com/media/archives/1989/12/264-6/132674469.pdf.

at-Tirmidhi, Muhammad. *Jami' at-Tirmidhi*. Not dated. Online: http://sunnah.com/tirmidhi.

"Toledot Yeshu." *Wikipedia*. 2024. Online: https://en.wikipedia.org/wiki/Toledot_Yeshu.

Toledot Yeshu. Not dated. Online: https://www.essene.com/History&Essenes/toled.htm?ref=legiochristi.com.

Tour, James. "We're Still Clueless About the Origin of Life." In *The Mystery of Life's Origin: The Continuing Controversy*, 323–58. Seattle: Discovery Institute, 2020. Article online: https://www.discovery.org/a/were-still-clueless-about-the-origin-of-life/.

Trau, Jane Mary. "Fallacies in the Argument from Gratuitous Suffering." *The New Scholasticism* 60 (1986) 485–89.

Trivers, Robert. "Foreword." In Richard Dawkins, *The Selfish Gene*, xix–xx. Oxford: Oxford University Press, 1989. Online: https://archive.org/details/isbn_9780195690668.

Tyler, David. "Darwinism's theological agenda." *The Biblical Creation Society*. 1997. Online: https://www.biblicalcreation.org.uk/scientific_issues/bcs083.html.

Ulam, Stanislaw. "How to Formulate Mathematically Problems of Rate of Evolution?" In *Mathematical Challenges to the Neo-Darwinian Interpretation of Evolution*, edited by Paul Moorhead and Martin Kaplan, 21–35. New York: Wistar Institute of Anatomy and Biology, 1967.

Van de Weghe, Rob. *Prepared to Answer*. Port Hadlock, WA: Windmill Ministries, 2007. Online: https://www.scribd.com/document/58502410/Prepared-to-Answer.

Van Inwagen, Peter. "The Problem of Evil, the Problem of Air, and the Problem of Silence." In *The Evidential Argument from Evil*, edited by Daniel Howard-Snyder, 151–74. Bloomington, IN: Indiana University Press, 1996. Online: https://archive.org/details/evidentialargumeoooounse.

Van Til, Cornelius. *The Defense of the Faith*, 3rd ed. Phillipsburg, NJ: P&R, 1979. Online: https://archive.org/details/defenseoffaithoooocorn.

Vilenkin, Alexander. *Many Worlds in One: The Search for Other Universes*. New York: Hill and Wang, 2006.

Vohra, Ashok. "Metaphysical Unity, Phenomenological Diversity and the Approach to the Other: Hindu Perspective on Xenophobia and the Hope for Human Flourishing." In *The Religious Other*, edited by Alon Goshen-Gottstein, 93–108. Lanham, MD: Rowman & Littlefield, 2014.

Volf, Miroslav. *Exclusion and Embrace*. Nashville: Abington, 1996. Online: https://archive.org/details/exclusionembraceoooovolf_x6c6.

von Campenhausen, Hans. *The Formation of the Christian Bible*. Philadelphia: Fortress, 1972. Online: https://archive.org/details/formationofchrisoooocamp.

von Sydow, Momme. "Charles Darwin: A Christian Undermining Christianity?" In *Science and Beliefs: From Natural Philosophy to Natural Science, 1700–1900*, edited by David Knight and Matthew Eddy, 141–56. Aldershot, England: Ashgate, 2005. Article online: https://www.researchgate.net/publication/265114252_Charles_Darwin_A_Christian_Undermining_Christianity.

von Weizsäcker, C. F. *The Relevance of Science: Creation and Cosmogony*. New York: Harper and Row, 1964. Online: https://archive.org/details/relevanceofscienoooweiz.

Wallace, Alfred Russel. *Contributions to the Theory of Natural Selection.* London: MacMillan and Co., 1870. Online: https://archive.org/details/contributionstotoowall/mode/2up?view=theater.

Wallace, J. Warner. "Who Created God?" *Cold-Case Christianity.* 2017. Online: https://coldcasechristianity.com/writings/who-created-god/.

Waltke, Bruce. *Genesis: A Commentary.* Grand Rapids: Zondervan, 2001.

Walton, John. *The Lost World of Genesis One.* Downers Grove, IL: IVP Academic, 2009.

Wayne, Luke. "The Ethical Incoherence of Pantheism." *Christian Apologetics and Research Ministry.* 2017. Online: https://carm.org/hinduism/the-ethical-incoherence-of-pantheism/.

Weber, Hans-Ruedi. *The Cross: Tradition and Interpretation.* Translated by Elke Jessett. Grand Rapids: Eerdmans, 1979. Online: https://archive.org/details/makercraftsmanstoooodale.

Wells, Jonathan. "Misrepresenting the Galapagos Finches." *Explore Evolution.* 2009. Online: https://exploreevolution.com/2009/02/23/misrepresenting_the_galapagos_1/.

Wenham, David. "A Historical View of John's Gospel." *Themelios* 23, n. 2 (1998) 5–21. Online: https://www.thegospelcoalition.org/themelios/article/a-historical-view-of-johns-gospel/.

Wenham, Gordon. "Christ's View of Scripture." In *Inerrancy,* edited by Norman Geisler, 3–36. Grand Rapids: Zondervan, 1980. Online: https://archive.org/details/inerrancyooooounse.

Westminster Confession of Faith. 1647. Online: https://www.monergism.com/thethreshold/sdg/westminster/The-Westminster-Confession-of-Faith(1).pdf.

Whitehead, Alfred North. *Science and the Modern World.* New York: The Free Press, 1967. Online: https://archive.org/details/sciencemodernworooooalfr_p8s2.

Wieland, Carl. "Goodbye, peppered moths: A classic evolutionary story comes unstuck." *Creation* 21 (1999) 56. Online: https://creation.com/goodbye-peppered-moths.

Wiesel, Elie. *The Gates of the Forest.* New York: Avon, 1966. Online: https://archive.org/details/gatesofforestoooelie.

Wiker, Benjamin. *Moral Darwinism: How We Became Hedonists.* Downers Grove, IL: InterVarsity, 2002. Online: https://archive.org/details/moraldarwinismhooooowike.

Wilberforce, Samuel. "Review of *On the Origin of Species,* by Charles Darwin," *Quarterly Review* 108 (1860) 225–64. Online: https://darwin-online.org.uk/content/framest?itemID=A19&viewtype=text&pageseq=1.

Wilckens, Ulrich. *Resurrection.* Translated by A. M. Stewart. Atlanta: John Knox, 1978. Online: https://archive.org/details/resurrectionbiblooowilc.

Williams, Peter. *Can We trust the Gospels?* Wheaton, IL: Crossway, 2018. Online: https://s3.amazonaws.com/media.thegospelcoalition.org/private/Can+We+Trust+The+Gospels.pdf?utm_campaign=Can%20We%20trust%20the%20Gospels%3F&utm_medium=email&_hsmi=295370532&_hsenc=p2ANqtz--Rmcn4Ay7zX1F97jMV54v1mnRh9m_BnqtV7JBTmYUgfSff_TRUooAQKnRFZ3yaYNor9mpmrlZhlN8GSVDc_ZAVtnNXeQ&utm_content=295370532&utm_source=hs_automation.

Williamson, H. G. M. "Book Review of K.A. Kitchen, *On the Reliability of the Old Testament.*" *Bulletin of the Anglo-Israel Archaeological Society* 24 (2006) 115–19.

Willard, Dallas. "God and the Problem of Evil." 2002. Online: http://www.leaderu.com/philosophy/willard_godandevil.html.

———. "Knowledge and Naturalism." Not dated. Online: https://dwillard.org/articles/knowledge-and-naturalism.

———. "Reflections on Dawkins' The Blind Watchmaker." Not dated. Online: https://dwillard.org/articles/reflections-on-dawkins-the-blind-watchmaker.

Wilson, A. N. "Religion of hatred: Why we should no longer be cowed by the chattering classes ruling Britain who sneer at Christianity." *Daily Mail* (10 April 2009). Online: https://www.dailymail.co.uk/news/article-1169145/Religion-hatred-Why-longer-cowed-secular-zealots.html.

Wilson, Robert. *A Scientific Investigation of the Old Testament*. New York: Harper & Brothers, 1929. Online: http://babel.hathitrust.org/cgi/pt?id=uc1.$b283799;view=1up;seq=1.

Windle, Bryan. "Top Ten Discoveries Related to Moses and the Exodus." *Bible Archaeology Report*. 2021. Online: https://biblearchaeologyreport.com/2021/09/24/top-ten-discoveries-related-to-moses-and-the-exodus/.

"Witness." *Encyclopaedia Judaica*. The Gale Group. 1998–2024. Online: http://www.jewishvirtuallibrary.org/jsource/judaica/ejud_0002_0021_0_21003.html.

Wolchover, Natalie. "How Did Life Begin? Dividing Droplets Could Hold the Answer." *Wired*. 2017. Online: https://www.wired.com/2017/01/life-begin-dividing-droplets-hold-answer/.

Wolf, Fred Alan. *Parallel Universes*. New York: Simon and Schuster, 1988. Online: https://archive.org/details/paralleluniverseoofred.

Wolterstorff, Nicholas. *Justice: Rights and Wrongs*. Princeton: Princeton University Press, 2008.

Wood, Nathan. *The Trinity in the Universe*. Grand Rapids: Kregel, 1978. Online: https://archive.org/details/trinityinuniversooooowood.

Woodberry, J. Dudley, and Russell Shubin. "Muslims tell . . . 'Why I Chose Jesus.'" *Mission Frontiers* (March 2001). Online: https://www.missionfrontiers.org/issue/article/muslims-tell...-why-i-chose-jesus.

Woodmorappe, John. "Anomalously Occurring Fossils." *Creation Research Society Quarterly* 18 (1982). Online: https://creationwiki.org/Anomalously_Occurring_Fossils.

Work, Telford. "Advent's Answer to the Problem of Evil." *International Journal of Systematic Theology* 2 (2000) 100–111. Online: https://telfordwork.net/articles/advent.html.

Wright, N. T. "Grave Matters." *Christianity Today* (6 April 1998) 51–53.

———. *Jesus and the Victory of God*. Minneapolis: Fortress, 1996.

———. *The Resurrection of the Son of God*. Minneapolis: Fortress, 2003. Online: https://archive.org/details/resurrectionofso0002wrig.

———. *Who Was Jesus?* Grand Rapids: Eerdmans, 1993.

Wright, Robert. *The Moral Animal*. New York: Pantheon, 1994.

Wurmbrand, Richard. *In God's Underground*. London: Hodder and Stoughton, 1968. Online: https://archive.org/details/ingodsundergrounooowurm_k0z4.

Wykstra, Stephen. "Rowe's Noseeum Arguments from Evil." In *The Evidential Argument from Evil*, edited by Daniel Howard-Snyder, 126–50. Bloomington, IN: Indiana University Press, 1996. Online: https://archive.org/details/evidentialargumeooounse.

Wysong, R. L. *The Creation-Evolution Controversy.* Midland, MI: Inquiry, 1976. Online: https://archive.org/details/creationevolutiooooowyso.

Xinping, Zhou. "The Significance of Christianity for the Modernization of Chinese Society." *Crux* 33 (1997) 31–39.

Yamauchi, Edwin. "Easter: Myth, Hallucination, or History?" 1974. Online: https://www.leaderu.com/everystudent/easter/articles/yama.html.

Yandell, Keith. "Gratuitous Evil and Divine Existence." *Religious Studies* 25 (1989) 15–30.

Young, Robert. *Darwin's Metaphor: Nature's Place in Victorian Culture.* Cambridge: Cambridge University Press, 1985. Online: http://www.psychoanalysis-and-therapy.com/human_nature/darwinmet/dar.html.

Zodhiates, Spiros. *The Complete Word Study Dictionary: New Testament*, rev. ed. Chattanooga, TN: AMG, 1993. Online: https://archive.org/details/completewordstudooooozodh.

Subject and Name Index

TABLES

Geologic ages, 133–34n.50
Names/Titles/Attributes applied to God and Jesus, 47–48
Prophecies re. Jesus as Messiah, 54–55
Prophecies re. Jesus' death and burial, 55–57
Biblical Examples of the Doctrine of Concurrence, 278–81

A

a posteriori, 164n.194
a priori, 74, 75, 106, 111, 114, 163n.192, 166, 179n.70, 206, 209, 225, 283
The Abolition of Man (Lewis), xxiii
Abraham, 4, 6, 21, 28, 54, 57, 62, 94, 185n.108, 229, 278
Abrahamic Covenant, 57
abstract, universal, absolutes, xii, xiv, xxii–xxiii, 110–23, 111nn.5–6, 116n.32, 169, 171–73, 176, 182, 184, 184n.98, 185–86, 217, 226, 230, 284
Adam and Eve, 28, 30n.141, 36n.13, 157n.161, 216, 231n.26, 239n.52, 243, 243n.65, 244, 257, 269
Adler, Mortimer, 191n.131
Adonis, 85
Aggasiz, Louis, 127
agnostic/agnosticism, 105n.16, 192n.139
Ahab, 23, 279
Ahaz, 23
Ajijola, Alhaj A. D., 32

Albright, William F., 6, 25
Alcorn, Randy, 243, 246, 253
Ali, Yusuf, 44, 89n.68
Allah, 15, 180–82, 186, 215–18, 215n.262
Alleged Discrepancies of the Bible (Haley), 27n.133
Alston, William, 232
Ambrose, 248
Amenhotep II, 6n.13
American Scientific Affiliation, 59n.10
Ancient Near East, 21–23, 24n.115, 57, 165n.197
angel(s), 29, 36n.13, 40, 43–44, 50, 51, 67n.12, 204, 209, 243, 256, 265
Annals (Tacitus), 70
Annas, 19
Anselm of Canterbury, 273, 285, 286
anthropic principle (see fine-tuning)
Apocrypha (and apocryphal gospels), 3n.2, 10n.42, 91
Archer, Gleason, 272
Aristotle, 104
Arthur, Wallace, 149
artificial selection, 143–44
Asad, Muhammad, 89, 89n.68, 90
Associates for Biblical Research, 16–17n.77
Assyria/Assyrian, 23–24, 244, 253, 280
atheism/atheists, xix, xxi, 27n.133, 62, 74, 105, 106n.16, 108, 111, 111n.8, 113, 114n.18, 168n.4, 171, 173, 173n.32, 174–75, 178n.66, 179, 195, 200, 202, 205, 207n.220, 212, 217, 223–24nn.2–3, 225–37, 225n.7, 246, 283

Attis, 85
Augustine/Augustinian, 124, 248
Axe, Douglas, 153
Ayala, Francisco, 111n.5, 158n.166, 165
Ayala, Francisco, and James Valentine, 129, 158–59n.166
Ayoub, Mahmoud, 36n.13

B

Babylon/Babylonian, 7, 7n.21, 8, 19, 23, 25, 244, 253, 280
Babylonian Talmud, 12, 68
Bachrach, Judy, 211–13
Baggini, Julian, 173n.32
Bahnsen, Greg, 113, 228
Baker, Deane-Peter, 177
Balaam, 23, 23n.112
Balder, 85
baptism, 40, 88
Barker, Glenn, Lane, William, and J. Ramsey Michaels, 10
Barnabas, 50
Barnes, Luke, 196, 196n.164
Barnett, Paul, 19, 88
Barrett, Justin, 121
Baruch, 23, 280
Bates, Gary, and Lita Sanders, 134
Bauckham, Richard, 9, 18, 45, 52
Bavinck, Herman, 238
Baynes, T. S., 162n.187
"beg the question," 74, 86n.53, 110–11, 117–18, 123, 132, 169, 179n.70, 201, 204, 206, 209, 230, 235, 282n.1, 283
Behe, Michael, 144, 147–48, 149n.122, 150–51, 153–54, 164, 164n.197, 166, 166n.202, 186, 199
Behe, Michael, and David Snoke, 150
Beker, J. Christian, 250
Bergman, Jerry, 151
Berkhof, Louis, 238
Bethlehem, 49, 54, 58, 58n.6
Bible, xi, xiii, xv, xvii–xix, xxi–xxii, xxiv, 3–7, 3n.1, 5n.9, 7n.21, 9, 11, 14–30, 30n.142, 31n.3, 32, 50, 52n.43, 53, 58–62, 64, 74, 84, 94n.82, 97–99, 105, 137, 157, 157n.161, 164–65n.197, 184, 204–6, 217–18, 219n.278, 224n.4, 226, 228, 230, 231, 236–39, 239n.53, 240, 241, 243n.65, 245, 253–54, 260, 262–63, 265, 269, 281, 285
  and archaeology, 6, 6n.13, 7n.21, 16–17, 16–17n.77, 21–27, 21nn.99–100, 26–27n.133, 31, 157n.161
  canon, 3n.2, 8–11, 8n.26, 8n.28
  development of, 4, 6–11, 7n.21
  manuscripts of, 11–16, 14n.67, 21
  Masoretic text, 11–12
  NT (see also Gospels), 3–5, 3n.2, 8–11, 9n.34, 10n.42, 13–15, 18–19, 25–26, 28–29, 31, 44–49, 47n.36, 50, 52, 54–57, 61, 61n.1, 64, 67, 81, 82, 85, 86n.56, 88, 91–92, 98, 205, 217, 256, 263, 274, 276
  OT (Hebrew Bible) (see also Septuagint; Torah), 3–4, 3n.2, 6–8, 6n.25, 8n.28, 11–16, 20–21, 23, 25, 28–29, 30n.141, 31, 45–49, 47n.36, 53–60, 59n.10, 61n.1, 69, 71, 75, 86, 88, 98, 205, 217, 263
  reliability/accuracy of, 6–7, 6n.11, 14–30, 19n.89, 24n.115, 26–27n.133, 57–60, 59n.10, 92–93n.78, 97–99, 157, 157n.161
  and science, 26–28, 157, 157n.161, 164–65n.197, 219n.278
  translation of, 8n.25, 11–16
  uniqueness of, 3–6, 230
  as Word of God, 4–5, 5n.9, 57–60, 59n.10, 97–99
biblical creation (see also creation; creationism/creationists), 136, 144n.100, 154, 156, 163n.191, 164–65n.197, 192n.137, 192n.139, 198n.173, 278, 280, 285
The Biblical Basis for Modern Science (Morris), 27n.133
Biblical Eschatology (Menn), xix

Subject and Name Index

Biblical Theology (Menn), xxiii
Bickersteth, Edward, 47n.36
Bielby, James, 122n.56
big bang, 188, 191–92, 192n.137, 193, 199, 282
The Big Book of Bible Difficulties (Geisler and Howe), 27n.133
Bin Laden, Osama, 173
Bird, W. R., 125n.3
birds, 134, 137, 138–39, 142–43, 147, 154, 283
The Blind Watchmaker (Dawkins), 282
Blomberg, Craig, 6n.11, 17, 41, 43, 98n.95, 208
Bode, Edward, 77, 79
Borde, Arvind, 197
Boyle, Robert, 104
Brahman, 112, 183, 214–15
Brave New World (Huxley), 174n.42
Broad, C. D., 206
Bruce, F. F., 3n.2, 8n.28, 26
Buckland, William, 104
Buddha, 51
Buddhism/Buddhist, xxi, 112, 185, 272
Budziszewski, J., 184
burial practices, 72, 93, 96

C

C. S. Lewis's Dangerous Idea (Reppert), 114n.20
Caiaphas, 19, 244
Cain and Abel, 28
Calvin, John, 104
"Cambrian Explosion" (see under fossil record)
Campbell, Keith, 205
Camus, Albert, 246
Cana, 19
Canaan/Canaanite, 7, 22
Capernaum, 19
Carson, D. A., 38, 41, 245, 246n.75
cells (see also DNA; genes and genetic code), 117, 120, 127, 138n.64, 139–49, 149n.122, 150, 152–54, 186–89, 189n.127, 190
Celsus, 68

Chamblin, J. Knox, 41, 43
Chapman, Allan, 103, 162n.187
"Chicago Statement on Biblical Inerrancy," 5
Christ (see Jesus Christ)
Christianity (see also under science), xi, xiii–xv, xvii, xix, xxi–xxiv, 3, 5, 15, 50, 60–61, 62n.2, 67–69, 72–73, 80, 82, 86n.53, 87–89, 92–94, 99, 103–4, 108–9, 113, 122–23, 137, 156–157, 157n.161, 162, 162n.187, 166, 180, 184–86, 184n.98, 190, 192n.139, 217–18, 231, 248, 250, 270, 272, 277
Christianity and Islam: The Essentials (Menn), xxiii, 52n.43
Christian/Christians, xii, xvii–xix, 3, 5–7, 8n.26, 10–11, 13–16, 36, 50, 52, 52n.43, 62n.2, 64, 66n.9, 67, 69–70, 73, 77–79, 79n.21, 80, 82–89, 92, 95, 97–99, 103–4, 114, 122, 125, 157, 162, 166, 169, 171, 180, 185, 185n.108, 196n.165, 198n.173, 202, 202n.201, 204, 206–8, 217, 224, 226–27, 227n.10, 228–29, 231, 239, 245, 247–48, 250, 259n.110, 267, 275, 277, 281
Christian conversion, xvii, 84–85, 98, 157n.161, 192n.139, 206–7, 247–49
church/churches, xii–xiv, xxi, 9–11, 9n.34, 14, 31, 38, 46, 79–81, 80n.27, 84–85, 87–88, 92, 207, 257–58, 271, 277
Churchland, Patricia, 121n.51
Cleaver, Gerald, 202, 202n.201
1 Clement, 10
Clement of Rome, 14, 82
Code of Hammurabi, 21n.99
Codex Alexandrinus, 14, 14n.66
Codex Sinaiticus, 14, 14n.66
Codex Vaticanus, 14, 14n.66
Cohen, I. L., 148
Cold-Case Christianity (Wallace), 27n.133
Cole, Victor Babajide, 47n.37
Collins, Francis, 164n.197, 198

Colson, Charles, xvii–xviii, 83n.43
compatibilism, 240n.55, 246n.75
concurrence, doctrine of, xix, 238–44, 278–81
Copernicus, Nicholas/Copernican, 104, 158
Cornelius, 50
cosmos (see also multiverse; universe), 4, 108, 112–13, 156, 165n.197, 178, 192, 200, 202, 202n.197
Council of Carthage (AD 419), 11
Council of Hippo (AD 393), 11
Craig, William Lane, 66n.9, 81, 91, 173, 179, 213, 217, 227
Craighead, Houston, 119
Crampton, W. Gary, 227n.10, 257
creation (see also biblical creation), 108, 144, 146, 148, 154, 156, 164, 164–65n.197, 165, 167, 180, 187, 191–92, 198, 203, 213, 215, 224, 231n.26, 236, 239, 243, 250, 254n.100, 258–60, 263, 275, 287
creationism/creationists (see also biblical creation), 133, 144n.100, 157n.161, 159, 163n.192, 164–65n.197, 166, 282n.1
Creator, xi–xiii, 5, 36n.10, 48, 113, 119, 156, 164–66, 171n.22, 193, 199, 203–4, 213, 214, 217v18, 236–37, 239, 241, 242, 242n.62, 265, 284
Crossan, John Dominic, 73
crucifixion/death of Jesus, xviii, 9, 18, 26, 31, 37, 40, 46, 53, 55–57, 61n.1, 63–73, 66n.11, 67, 67nn.11–12, 68n.18, 72, 74, 79n.20, 80–82, 84, 86–90, 92, 97, 211n.242, 213n.253, 244–47, 246n.75, 248, 253, 257, 262, 265, 272–74, 281
  evidence of historical fact of, 26, 63–73
  burial in a tomb, 66, 69–70, 66n.11, 77
  confirmation by hostile and non-Christian sources, 26, 68–70
  earliness of Christian creeds, 64–65
  failure of alternative explanations, 70–73
    swoon theory, 71–73
    substitution theory, 71
  medical evidence of death, 65, 71–73
  multiple witnesses, 63–64
  prevalence of self-damaging material, 67–68, 67n.12
  reaction of the disciples, 66–67
  what the cross accomplished, 57–58, 61–62, 62n.2, 245–51, 256–57, 272–77
Cuvier, Georges, 157n.161
Cyprian, 248

D

Daniel, 29, 42,
Darbaalah, 'Esaam-ud-Deen, 182
Darling, David, 194
Darwin, Charles, 103, 105, 105–6n.16, 119, 124–29, 136, 137, 141, 141n.82, 143, 145, 152, 154–56, 159, 159–60n.173, 160, 162n.187, 166, 169v70, 175–76
Darwin's Black Box: The Biochemical Challenge to Evolution (Behe), 147–48
Darwin's finches, 143, 143n.90, 144
Darwinism (see evolution)
Darwinism as Religion (Ruse), 162n.187
David, 7, 14, 23, 49, 54, 279, 280
Davidson, Eric, 152
Davies, L. Merson, 157n.161
Davies, Paul, 114n.18, 191, 196, 202, 202n.197, 217, 223, 230
Dawkins, Richard, xix, 36n.10, 108, 133, 146, 151, 173, 176, 177n.60, 200, 205, 209–10, 225n.7, 282–87, 282n.1, 283n.6, 285n.12
Dead Sea Scrolls, 6, 11, 12, 89
death (see also under life), 4, 44, 79n.20, 82–83, 85, 89–90, 94n.82, 98, 150, 197, 210–13,

Subject and Name Index

234, 236–37, 242–46, 248, 249, 250, 252, 256, 256n.102, 260, 263, 267, 269, 273, 279, 280
Decalogue (see Ten Commandments)
Deedat, Ahmed, 72
Demarest, Bruce, 61n.1
Dembski, William, 108, 108n.7, 199
Demeter, 85
demons, 29, 35n.9, 41, 181
Dennett, Daniel, 108, 161, 167
Denton, Michael, 143–44, 151, 191, 211
Derrida, Jacques, 185n.108
design (see intelligent (purposeful) design)
determinism, 115, 117, 122, 174, 178, 203
Devil (see Satan)
Dewar, Douglas, 157n.161
Dialogue with Trypho (Justin Martyr), 77
Dialogues Concerning Natural Religion (Hume), 223
Diaspora, 9
Didache, 9
dinosaur(s), 133–35
Dionysius, 248
Dionysus, 85
Dirks, Jerald, 10n.42, 14
disciples of Jesus, 33, 38–41, 50, 56, 63, 66–67, 67n.12, 71, 73, 76–79, 79n.20, 80–83, 83n.43, 84–86, 88, 91–96, 92–93n.78, 205
DNA (see also cells; genes and genetic code), 139–41, 139n.73, 145, 148, 151–52, 155, 163, 188–89, 189n.127, 190, 282
Dobzhansky, Theodosius, 167
Documentary hypothesis, 7n.21
Dodd, C. H., 81
Dostoevsky, Fyodor, 225, 267
Dualism, 227n.10
Dulle, Jason, 72
Dunn, James, 78, 83n.44, 87, 96

E

East-West Schism of 1054, 9n.34

Eddington, Arthur, 105
Edwards, Jonathan, 251, 253, 255
Egnor, Michael, 211n.242
Egypt/Egyptian, 6, 6n.13, 17, 21–23, 57n.4, 260, 278, 280
Einstein, Albert, 120n.49, 125, 168, 170, 173, 197n.167
Elijah, 29
Elisha, 29
Ellis, George, 191, 201
Emerick, Yahiya, 15, 71, 217
Encyclopedia of Bible Difficulties (Archer), 27n.133
An Enquiry Concerning Human Understanding (Hume), 110
Ephesus, xiii
Epicurus, 210
epistemology, 121–22, 169, 217, 285
Epistle to the Philippians (Polycarp), 82
Equipping Church Leaders East Africa (www.eclea.net), xviii
Eric, Walter, 16
Erlandson, Doug, 224n.4, 228, 254n.100, 256n.102
An Essay on the Principle of Population (Malthus), 136
ethics (see moral/morality)
Evidence That Demands A Verdict (McDowell), xix, 27n.133
evil (see also good and bad/evil; pain/suffering; "problem of evil"), xxiii, 4, 36n.13, 83, 172–73, 178–79, 180–81, 183, 216, 248, 223–267, 223–24nn.2–4, 225n.7, 227n.10, 231n.26, 232n.31, 235n.39, 235n.41, 240n.55, 246n.75, 254n.100, 256n.102
evolution (a/k/a Darwinism; macroevolution) (see also Darwin's finches; DNA; fossil record; genes and genetic code; information; language/languages; life, origin of; microevolution; mutations; natural selection; naturalism; neo-Darwinism; punctuated equilibrium), 105–9, 108n.7, 124–66, 125n.3,

(evolution continued)
  126n.10, 127n.10, 142nn.84–85,
  143n.90, 162n.187, 164–65n.197,
  166n.202, 172, 176–78, 213,
  228n.14, 282–84
 development of new organs, forms,
  functions, and organisms,
  141–58
  the eye, 141, 141n.82, 145–46
  sexual reproduction, 146
 effect of natural selection on
  mutations, 149–51, 154–55
 inconsistencies and anomalies,
  132–36
 irreducible complexity, 147–49,
  149n.22
 microbiological/genetic evidence,
  137–41, 138nn.64–65, 139n.73,
  147–54, 149n.122, 163
 non-evolving organisms, 133, 138
 non-organic (see universe,
  existence and origin of)
 of mind/reason, 109, 112, 114–23,
  116n.32, 120n.45, 120n.49,
  121n.51, 167–71, 168n.4,
  170n.17
 social/philosophical aspects and
  effects, 7n.21, 108, 112, 162–63,
  162–63n.187, 166, 166n.202,
  172, 176–78, 186n.109
 "taxa-defining novelties," 132–33
 theistic, 164–65n.197
 theory of naturalistic evolution is
  not a proper scientific theory,
  158–63, 158–59n.166, 162n.184,
  162–63n.187, 202
existentialism/existentialists, 109, 225
exodus, 6, 6n.13, 17, 21–22, 21n.100,
  28, 278

F

Faraday, Michael, 104
Faro, Ingrid, xix
Feinberg, John, 233, 240n.55, 260,
  265, 266, 266n.129
Ferraiolo, William, 248

fine-tuning, 163, 198–202, 198n.175,
  200n.190, 201n.192, 204, 215,
  218, 282
first law of thermodynamics, 196, 197
Flew, Antony, 62
fossil record, xxiii, 124, 126–37,
  126n.7, 127nn.10–11, 130n.26,
  160–61, 161n.183, 163
 "Cambrian Explosion," 127–29
  127nn.10–11, 131, 165
 (lack of) transitional forms,
  126–33, 130n.26, 136, 138
 "wrong order" of fossils, 133–36,
  135n.52
Foster, David, 188
Frame, John, 233, 240n.55, 286
free will, 172, 240n.55
"free will defense," 240n.55
Freud, Sigmund, 109, 158
fruit flies (*drosophila melanogaster*),
  139, 140, 142–45, 150

G

Gabriel, 40–41
Galapagos Islands, 143
Galen, 248
Galilee, 19, 55, 92n.78
Galilei, Galileo, 104
Gardner, Rex, 208
Garrison, David, 206
Garte, Sy, 195, 196n.164, 202n.200
Gassendi, Pierre, 104
Gay, Craig, 104
Geisler, Norman, 29–30n.141, 113,
  190n.131
genes and genetic code (see also cells;
  DNA), 115, 124, 132, 139–46,
  139n.73, 141n.82, 144n.100,
  149–56, 149n.122, 165, 170,
  176–77, 177n.60, 186n.109,
  188–90, 233
Gentry, Robert, 135, 136, 157n.161,
  165n.197
Geshem, 25
Ghabril, Nicola Yacoub, 264
Al-Ghazali, Abu Hamid Muhammad
  ibn, 216

Gilbert, Greg, 5, 10, 27, 99
Gilbert, Scott, John Opitz, and Rudolf
    Raff, 154n.151
Gilchrist, John, 16, 38
Gish, Duane, 165n.197
*Glimpsing Heaven: The Stories and
    Science of Life After Death*
    (Bachrach), 211
God (see also Kingdom of God;
    Trinity), xi–xiv, xvii–xix, xxi–
    xxii, 4–5, 8, 17, 25, 29, 30n.141,
    33–40, 36n.10, 40n.22, 42–46,
    46n.35, 49–52, 52n.43, 57n.4,
    58–59, 62, 70, 74, 74n.2, 92, 97,
    99, 104–5, 105–6n.16, 109, 112–
    13, 116n.32, 122, 137, 155–57,
    157n.161, 159n.173, 160n.177,
    162n.187, 164, 164–65n.197,
    171, 171n.22, 175, 179–80,
    179n.70, 184–86, 190, 192n.137,
    195, 198–204, 202n.200, 217–19,
    223n.2, 223–67, 223–24nn.2–4,
    231n.26, 232n.31, 235n.41,
    246n.75, 254n.100, 269–77,
    276n.19, 282–87
  attributes of, xi–xiii, 4–5, 32,
    47–48, 47n.37, 116n.32, 122,
    184, 198n.173, 213–14, 217–19,
    223–25, 224n.3, 229, 235n.41,
    237–38, 242, 244, 254–58,
    254n.100, 256n.102, 246n.75,
    256n.102, 264, 269–70
  intervention in the world, 20,
    28–32, 40n.22, 57, 57n.4, 82,
    106n.16, 160n.173, 164n.197,
    190–91n.131, 197n.170,
    198n.173, 204–10, 204n.208,
    218–19, 237–44, 240n.55,
    246n.75, 258–59, 278–81
  names/titles of, 42n.16, 48–49
  will/plan of, 3–4, 229–37, 232n.31,
    238n.50, 240n.55, 241, 243–45,
    246n.75, 248, 252–63, 266
  Yahweh (YHWH), 7, 21, 25, 41,
    44–45, 50, 241
The God Delusion (Dawkins), 282
Goldberger, Robert, 187

good and bad/evil, xi, xxiv, 168n.4,
    172, 178, 178n.66, 179, 179n.70,
    180, 182–83, 186, 216, 225,
    225.7, 227, 227n.10, 240n.55,
    241–43, 243n.65, 252, 285
Gospel, The, xi, xiii, xix, xxii, xxiv, 14,
    50, 58, 71, 98n.95, 99, 208, 245,
    247, 250, 252, 269–77, 281
Gospels (Matthew, Mark, Luke, John),
    5, 6n.11, 9, 9n.38, 10, 10n.42, 14,
    18–19, 19n.89, 28, 40n.21, 42, 52,
    61n.1, 64, 67, 71, 76n.8, 79n.21,
    88, 91, 98n.95, 99
Gould, Stephen Jay, 129, 130, 132,
    136, 161, 172
Gould, Stephen, and Niles Eldredge,
    124, 130–32
Grant, Michael, 77, 78
Grassé, Pierre-Paul, 126, 130, 133,
    139, 145, 161
Gray, Asa, 159
Green, David, 187
Grene, Marjorie, 142n.85
Guth, Alan, 197

H

Habermas, Gary, 31, 80, 213n.253
Habermas, Gary, and Michael Licona,
    5, 62, 84n.45
Hadith, 180, 182, 216
Haldane, J. B. S., 115, 115n.26
Haleem, M. A. S. Abdel, 89n.68
Halverson, William, 108, 174
Hamlet, 210
Harris, Sam, 173–74, 174n.42, 176
Hart, David Bentley, 177
Hartzler, H. Harold, 59n.10
Hawking, Stephen, 114, 168–69,
    192–96, 198–200, 203, 210
Hawking, Stephen, and Leonard
    Mlodinow, 192
Hawking, Stephen, Roger Penrose,
    and George Ellis, 191
Hayes, William C., 21
heaven/heavens (including new
    heaven and new earth), 28–29,
    32, 36, 40, 42–44, 47–48, 71, 99,

(heaven/heavens continued)
113, 183, 191, 204, 208, 210, 225, 237, 238, 242n.62, 248–50, 254, 256–57, 262–63, 271–73, 275
Hebrew Bible (see Bible, OT)
Hegel, Georg W. F., xxi, 7n.21, 109
Heidegger, Martin, 190
hell, 29, 35, 43, 58, 99, 246, 249, 263–66, 264n.122, 270–71, 273
Herod/Herodians, 19, 244
Herodotus, 90
Hesse, Hermann, 183
Hezekiah, 23–24, 279
Hick, John, 237, 249, 261
Hinduism, xxi, 112
The Historical Christ and the Jesus of Faith (Evans), 27n.133
historical (higher) criticism, 7n.21
The Historical Reliability of the Gospels (Blomberg), 26n.133
The Historical Reliability of the New Testament (Blomberg), 27n.133
Hitler, Adolf, 177
Ho, M. W., and P. T. Saunders, 142
Hodge, Charles, 106n.16, 254, 255, 256n.102
Holy Spirit, 5, 33, 36, 40, 45–46, 49, 52n.43, 54, 56, 85, 185–86, 206–7, 217, 247, 250, 275–76, 283
Howell, John, 285
Hoyle, Fred, 141, 161, 187, 187n.116, 190, 190n.129, 200
Hoyle, Fred, and Chandra Wickramasinghe, 127n.10, 171
human beings (nature of), xvii, xxii–xxiii, 4, 31–32n.3, 36, 75, 108, 114–15, 116n.32, 122, 138n.65, 139–40, 139n.73, 147, 164–65n.197, 167, 168n.4, 170–71, 170n.17, 177n.60, 168n.4, 170n.17, 180, 184–86, 185n.108, 204–5, 210–11, 217–18, 219n.277, 233–34, 236–37, 239–44, 239n.52, 240n.55, 246n.75, 247, 258–59, 264, 269, 271–72, 278–81
human rights, 172, 179n.70, 184, 184n.98, 185

Hume, David, 110, 209–10, 223, 229, 233, 237, 250
Huntemann, Georg, 7n.21
Hunter, A. M., 65, 80
Huxley, Thomas Henry, 105, 105n.16, 166

I

Ibrahim, Naajeh, Sheikh 'Aasim 'Abdul Maajid, and Sheikh 'Esaam-ud-Deen Darbaalah, 182
Ignatius, 14, 81, 88
Image of God (including Image of His Son), xii, 122, 165n.197, 171, 218, 243, 257, 271, 276
induction (see inference/induction)
inference/induction, 104, 110–11, 111nn.5–6, 112, 112n.10, 116–17, 120n.45, 120n.49, 121n.51, 122, 158, 164, 164n.194, 164n.197, 165, 171, 189, 200, 206, 219, 223–24n.2, 228–30, 232, 235, 251, 284n.12, 287
information (genetic; specified; evidence of design) (see also intelligent (purposeful) design), 118–19, 126n.10, 142, 148–49, 151–52, 158, 163–64, 164n.197, 165, 188, 190, 199–200, 287
instinct(s), 78, 147, 160, 175–76
intelligent (purposeful) design (see also information), 105, 108, 121, 137, 144n.100, 148–49, 154–55, 157–58, 163–66, 163n.192, 164n.194, 164n.197, 173, 186, 190, 195, 198–203, 218–19, 230, 282–83, 287
International Association for Near-Death Studies, Inc., 212
International Council on Biblical Inerrancy, 5
irreducible complexity, 147–49, 149n.122
Isaac, 21, 21n.99, 28, 54, 62, 278
Isaiah, 23, 49
Isis, 85

Islam, xxi, xxiii, 20, 50, 180, 182, 186, 215–17, 272
Israel (the land/nation; for the person, see Jacob), 4, 6–8, 17, 20–24, 40, 43, 45, 47, 49, 57n.4, 67, 68, 244, 253, 260, 278–80
Israelites/Hebrews, 21–22, 46

J

Jacob (a/k/a Israel, the person), 21, 21n.99, 28, 54, 62
James, 67, 80, 84–85, 92
Jehu, 23
Jeremiah, 23, 280
Jeroboam I, 23
Jerusalem, 19, 24–26, 49, 55, 58, 78–79, 80n.27, 82, 85, 88, 280
Jesus and the Eyewitnesses (Bauckham), 27n.133
Jesus Christ (see also crucifixion; Messiah; miracles; prophecy; resurrection), xiii–xiv, xvii–xix, xxi–xxiv, 4, 8–10, 17–20, 40n.21, 61, 88, 205, 267, 270n.3, 272–74, 276, 276n.19, 281
  as fully God and fully man, xviii, 29–32, 36, 42, 46n.35, 50–52, 52n.43, 59–61, 239n.52, 98–99, 205, 257, 272–73
  as a man, xxii, 29, 31, 31–32n.3
  as God, xviii, xxii, 5, 31–52, 35n.9, 36n.10, 40n.22, 47nn.36–37, 271n.7
    called "God" and "Lord," 44–46
    prophecies as applied to Jesus, 53–60, 58n.6, 59n.10, 61
    received worship as God, 35, 41, 50–51, 68, 70, 73, 87–88, 92–93n.78, 97
  sinless life, 36–37, 36n.13, unique relationship with the Father, 37–39, 40n.22, 44
  "Son of God," 39–41, 40n.22, 44
  "Son of Man," 42–44
  the "trilemma," 35–36, 36n.10
  worshipped as God, 50–51

  his life, 10, 31–32, 36–37, 53, 61, 61n.1, 67, 69, 72–73, 84, 91, 273
  his view of the Bible, 6n.12, 8, 28–30, 29–30nn.141–42, 98–99, 184
  second coming of, 88, 248–50, 253, 263, 275
Jews/Jewish, 3, 6–8, 8n.26, 8n.28, 9, 11–12, 15, 16, 34–35, 37–38, 40, 44, 50–52, 55, 63–70, 77–80, 83–88, 86n.56, 89–90, 92–97, 99, 177, 276, 280
Jezebel, 23
Joash, 23
Job, 255, 260, 266, 280
John, 19, 26, 37–38, 42, 64, 79, 245
John the Baptist, 29
Johnson, Dennis, 242n.62
Johnson, Phillip, 108, 109, 122, 156, 164n.197, 196
Jonah, 29, 280
Joseph (husband of Mary), 75n.4
Joseph (son of Jacob), 21, 21n.99, 244, 259–60, 278
Joseph of Arimathea, 66, 66n.9, 76, 80n.27, 93, 96
Josephus, 8, 8n.28, 15, 19, 69, 73, 77, 84
Journal of the American Medical Association, 65, 72
Judah (the land/nation), 23, 25, 49, 244, 279, 280
Judah (the person), 54
Judaism, xxi, xxiii, 12, 50–51, 68, 76, 78, 85–86, 88
Judas Iscariot, 37, 244
Judas the Galilean, 89
Judea, 68, 79
Judeo-Christian faith/worldview, 103–4, 217
Judgment (of God)/Judgment Day, 43, 58, 224n.3, 242n.62, 243, 248–50, 255, 260–61, 263, 266–67, 272, 276n.19
Julius Caesar, xxii
justice (including injustice), 70, 174–76, 182, 185, 225, 227, 247, 249–50, 253–54, 254n.100,

Subject and Name Index

(justice continued)
    255, 256n.102, 262–64, 266–67,
    272–73
Justice: Rights and Wrongs
    (Wolterstorff), 184n.98
Justin Martyr, 77, 88

K

Kaiser, Walter, 20
Kant, Immanuel, 7n.21, 109
Kapolyo, Joe, 41
Keats, John, 261
Keeping Faith in an Age of Reason
    (Lisle), 27n.133
Keller, Timothy, 10, 87, 174n.42, 233,
    245, 248, 260, 265
Kennedy, Titus, 6n.13, 16, 21, 21n.99
Kenyon, Frederic, 26
Kepler, Johannes, 104
Ketef Hinnom scrolls, 7
Khan, Muhammad, 270
Kingdom of God, xvii, 40–43, 46, 48,
    273
Kitchen, Kenneth A., 17, 25
Koestler, Arthur, 143, 147
Koons, Robert, 104
Koukl, Greg, 178
Krahmalkov, Charles, 22, 23
Külling, Samuel, 7n.21
Kurtz, Paul, 175

L

Lack, David, 121
Ladd, George Eldon, 95
language/languages, 4, 19, 22, 28, 42,
    49, 249
    as evidence against evolution, 147,
        170–71, 195
Latin Vulgate, 14
laws of nature/science (see under
    science)
Lawton, Graham, 139, 140
Leff, Arthur, 179n.70
Lemaître, Georges, 105
Lewis, C. S., xvii, xxi, xxiii, 9n.38, 18,
    33, 35, 36n.10, 74n.4, 85, 86n.53,
    112nn.9–10, 114, 114n.20,
    115–17, 119n.43, 175–76, 180,
    185, 194n.157, 227, 227n.10,
    228, 283
Lewontin, Richard, 106, 160n.177,
    189, 201
Licona, Michael, 83–84
life, xiii–xiv, xviii, xxi, 21, 26, 35,
    38–39, 41, 48, 51–52, 62, 65, 83,
    85, 105–7, 125, 127, 129, 131,
    153, 166, 172–73, 174n.42, 178,
    183–84, 186, 205, 207–8, 234,
    236–37, 248, 250, 259, 262, 270,
    274, 276
    after death, 29, 99, 210–13,
        213n.253, 260, 265–67
    eternal, 34, 38, 43, 46, 52, 86, 247,
        254, 274
    origin of, xxiii, 34, 107, 125,
        127n.10, 132, 139–41, 146,
        155–56, 163–65, 164–65n.197,
        186–90, 187n.116, 189n.127,
        190n.129, 198–200, 202, 213,
        218, 230, 287
Lindley, David, 195
Lindsley, Arthur, 29, 30n.142
Linnaeus, Charles, 157n.161
Lipson, H. S., 162–63
logic/laws of logic (see also "beg the
    question"), xviii, xxii–xxiii, 111–
    14, 111nn.5–6, 112nn.9–10, 115,
    117, 119–20, 122–23, 164n.194,
    169, 188, 208–10, 229–30, 284,
    284n.12
Long, Jeffrey, 212–13
Lord's Supper, 88
Lot, 28
Løvtrup, Søren, 126n.7, 130n.26, 144,
    159, 161n.182
Lucas, J. R., 115
Lucian of Samosata, 70
Luke, 91
Lyell, Charles, 159n.173

M

M-theory, 125, 192 193n.145, 202,
    202n.201

Subject and Name Index

Macbeth, 241–42
Machen, J. Gresham, 74n.2, 103
Mackie, J. L., 223n.2, 284
MacNutt, Francis, 208
Maier, Paul, 77, 80n.27, 93, 95–96
malaria, 153–54, 154n.149
Malthus, Thomas, 125
Manasseh, 23
Mara Bar-Serapion, 70
Margenau, Henry, 200
Markovic, Mihailo, 175
Marshall, I. Howard, 252
Marx, Karl (including Marxism and Marxist), 109, 158, 225
Mary (mother of Jesus), 36n.13, 40, 45, 63, 75n.4
Mary Magdalene, 67n.12, 76
Al-Masih, Abd, 36n.13
materialism (see naturalism)
Matthews, Kenneth, 6, 142n.84
Maunder, Edward, 157n.161
Maury, Matthew, 157n.161
A'la Mawdudi, Sayyid, 36n.13, 71
Maxwell, James Clerk, 105, 157n.161
Mayr, Ernst, 138, 155–56
McDowell, Josh, xix, 66n.11
McDowell, Josh, and Don Stewart, 12, 29
Medawar, Peter, 155–56, 191
Men of Science—Men of God (Morris), 157n.161
Menahem, 23
Mendel, Gregor, 105, 124
Menn, Jonathan, xi–xiv, xviii, 52n.43
Mere Christianity (Lewis), xvii, 227
Merneptah, 22
Messiah, xviii, 20, 31, 41, 43–44, 51, 53–55, 61n.1, 67, 69, 81, 85–86, 89, 92, 260
metaphysics/metaphysical, xxiiin.4, 107, 108n.7, 109, 120, 161, 161n.182, 162n.187, 165n.197, 167, 175, 190, 194–96, 201–2, 214, 241–42
Meyer, Stephen, 104, 131, 153, 164n.197, 187, 196–97n.167, 199, 200–1, 201n.192
Michelangelo, 170

microbiology (see evolution, microbiological evidence)
microevolution, 130n.26, 142–44, 142n.84, 143n.90, 144n.100, 154, 154n.149, 154n.151, 155, 165n.197
Miethe, Terry, 79
Mill, John Stuart, 109
Miller-Urey experiment, 189n.127
mind, xi, xiii–xiv, xvii, xxiii, 35n.9, 48, 90, 92, 94, 113, 116n.32, 119, 122, 123n.59, 157, 167, 169–71, 184, 186, 190, 203, 205, 207, 210–11, 211n.242, 214, 225, 233, 247, 267, 275–76, 283, 285, 287
origin of (see under evolution and under naturalism)
Mind & Cosmos: Why the Materialist Neo-Darwinian Conception of Nature is Almost Certainly False (Nagel), 168n.4
Minding the Brain (Menuge), 168n.4
miracles (see also resurrection), 29, 55, 69, 74–75, 74n.2, 74n.4, 89, 98n.95, 131, 158, 160n.173, 193, 203, 204–10, 207n.220, 212, 218, 230, 259, 265
miracles of Jesus, 35n.9, 75, 204–5
Miracles (Lewis), 114
Moiseyev, Ivan, 207n.220
monism/monistic (see also pantheism), xxi, xxiii, 172, 180, 183–84, 186, 214–15
monotheism (see theism/theists)
Moore, Sebastian, 247
Moral Darwinism: How We Became Hedonists (Wiker), 172n.25
moral/morality (including immorality) (see also good and bad/evil; moral law; right and wrong), xi–xii, xiv, xxii–xxiv, 35–36, 37, 77, 108, 108n.7, 162n.187, 168n.4, 170, 172–86, 172n.25, 173n.32, 174n.42, 177n.60, 178n.66, 179n.70, 185n.108, 186n.109, 213, 217, 223n.2, 224n.3, 225–27, 227n.10, 228–30, 231n.26, 233, 235n.39,

(moral/morality continued)
  236, 240n.55, 241, 245, 248, 258–59, 261, 264, 269–70, 276–77
moral law (a/k/a God's law; natural law), 180–82, 184–85, 185n.108, 264–65, 271
More Evidence that Demands a Verdict (McDowell), 27n.133
Moreland, J. P., 123n.59, 228n.14
Morris, Henry, 157n.161
Moses, 6, 6n.12, 21, 21n.100, 22, 28, 33, 44, 57n.4
Moule, C. F. D., 86
Mount Sinai, 33, 57n.4
Moyise, Steve, 28
Mozart, Wolfgang Amadeus, 170
Muhammad, 78, 181–82
Müller, Julius, 90–91
multiverse (see also cosmos; universe), 192, 193n.145, 222, 196, 196nn.164–65, 197, 200–1, 201n.192, 202, 202nn.200–1
Mumford, Lewis, 219n.277
Muslim/Muslims, 10n.42, 14–16, 32, 36n.13, 44, 51, 71–72, 78, 89n.68, 99, 181, 182, 186, 206–8, 217, 277
mutations, 124, 126, 130n.26, 131–33, 141n.82, 142–44, 144n.100, 145–56, 164, 164n.197, 188
Myanmar, 59n.8
myth(s)/mythical, 9n.38, 17–18, 75, 85, 86n.53, 89–92, 93n.78, 204, 282

N

Nagel, Thomas, 168n.4, 171, 282–83
Nash, Ronald, 116, 209, 285
National Association of Biology Teachers, 105
natural law (see moral law)
natural selection (see also artificial selection), 105–6n.16, 117, 121, 121n.51, 124, 126–27, 132, 141, 141n.82, 142–55, 144n.100, 159–64, 159–60n.173, 168–70, 170n.17, 176, 188

naturalism/naturalistic (a/k/a materialism; physicalism) (see also evolution), xix, xxi, xxiii, xxiiin.4, 72, 83, 105–6, 105n.16, 106–9, 111n.8, 124–25, 136–37, 139–40, 144, 146, 150–63, 157n.161, 160n.177, 164–5n.197, 165–66, 196n.167, 228n.14, 282
  cannot account for abstract universals, 110–14, 111nn.5–6, 111n.8, 114n.18
  cannot account for consciousness and mind, xxiii, 114, 123n.59, 167–71, 168n.4, 170n.17
  cannot account for the existence of the universe, 190–204, 190–91n.131, 196nn.164–65, 197n.170, 198n.175, 200n.190, 202n.197, 202n.200
  cannot account for morality and human rights, 172–80, 172n.25, 173n.32, 174n.42, 177n.60, 178n.66, 179n.70, 186, 186n.109, 227
  cannot account for the origin of life, 186–90, 187n.116, 189n.127, 190n.129
  cannot account for post-death experiences, 210–13, 211n.242, 213n.253
  cannot account for the regularity/uniformity of nature, 110–11, 111n.6, 113–14, 125, 171, 217
  cannot account for the reliability of mind or reason, xxii–xxiv, 111n.5, 112n.9, 114–23, 116n.32, 120n.45, 120n.49, 121n.51, 167–71, 168n.4, 170n.17, 228
    argument from reason, 114–19, 116n.32
    evolutionary argument against naturalism, 119–22, 119n.43, 120n.45, 120n.49, 121n.51, 122n.56
  cannot account for supernatural experiences, 204–10, 207n.220
  is a non-scientific, metaphysical philosophy/worldview,

106–9, 122, 160n.177, 156, 158–66, 160n.177, 161n.182, 162–63n.187, 171–72, 193, 195, 201–2, 213, 218–19
  is self-referentially incoherent (self-refuting), 110–23, 112n.9, 178n.66
nature (see also science, laws of nature/science), xi, xxiii, 103, 105n.16, 107, 111–18, 124, 126, 131, 137, 146, 157, 169, 172–73, 178–79, 190, 195–96, 196–97n.167, 200, 202–3, 217, 225n.7, 238–39, 283
Naziism/Nazis, 179, 250, 261
Near-Death Experience Research Foundation, 212
Near East Archaeological Society, 16, 17n.77
Nehemiah, 25, 280
Nelson, Paul, 286
neo-Darwinism, 108, 124–26, 125n.3, 136, 142, 147, 151–53, 155, 160, 164n.197
Nero, 70
New American Standard Bible, 3n.1, 7
New Testament (NT) (see under Bible, NT)
Newnham, Michael, xix
Newton, Isaac, 104, 170, 218–19
Nicodemus, 40n.21, 96
Nietzsche, Friedrich, 109, 180
Nixon, Richard, xvii
Noah, 28
Nüsslein-Volhard, Christiane, and Eric Wieschaus, 150

O

Odin, 85
Ohno, Susumu, 170
Old Testament (OT; Hebrew Bible) (see under Bible, OT)
Oliphint, K. Scott, 231, 231n.26, 239n.52
On the Origin of Species by Means of Natural Selection (Darwin), 103, 105, 105n.16, 124, 126, 128, 141, 141n.82, 160, 166
ontology, xxiiin.4, 123n.59, 217
Origen, 82
The Origin of Species Revisited (Bird), 125n.3
Osiris, 85
Owen, Richard, 157, 157n.161, 158

P

Packer, J. I., xiii
paganism/pagans, 26, 85v86, 86n.53, 89, 96, 191n.131, 248
Page, Don, 196n.165
pain/suffering, 31n.3, 37, 56, 70, 73, 75, 82–84, 183, 205, 211, 225, 225n.7, 229, 231–33, 235, 235n.41, 236, 243–50, 252, 256, 259–63, 266–67, 273, 276
paleontolgy/paleontologists, xviii, 126, 129–30, 132, 134, 138, 157n.161, 161
Palestine/Palestinian, 6, 9–10, 23, 70, 76n.8
Papias, 14
pantheism/pantheistic (see also monism), xxiii, 35, 112–13, 180, 183–84, 186, 214–15, 217, 239
  pantheistic philosophy, xxi, 112, 183, 214
  pantheistic religions, xxi, 112, 183, 214
Parmenides, xxi
Parnia, Sam, 211
The Passing of Peregrinus (Lucian of Samosata), 70
Pasteur, Louis, 157n.161
Patterns of Evidence: The Exodus, 21n.100
Patterson, Colin, 138, 161n.183
Paul, xiii, xvii–xviii, xxii, 19, 50, 62, 65–66, 80, 81–85, 84n.45, 88, 91–95, 95n.87, 229, 239, 240n.55, 259, 265, 276, 281
Pearcey, Nancy, 169, 176–78
Penrose, Roger, 191
Pentateuch (see Torah)

peppered moths (*biston betularia*), 142 142nn.84–85, 143–44
persecution, 15, 56, 80n.27, 82–83, 83n.43, 84, 92, 98, 207, 250, 260, 271, 281
Persephone, 85
Peter (a/k/a/ Cephas; Simon Peter), 37, 41, 46, 50, 62–63, 79–82, 91–92, 274, 276
Peters, Robert Henry, 162
Peterson, Michael, 236
Pharisees, 33, 83, 244, 270n.3
Philip, 39
physicalism (see naturalism)
Pictet de la Rive, Francois Jules, 127
Pilate, Pontius, 37, 65–66, 69, 70–71, 73, 96, 244
Piper, John, 252
Plantinga, Alvin, 104, 109, 119, 119n.43, 120, 120n.45, 121, 122n.56, 171, 201, 204n.208, 227, 232n.31, 240n.55
Plotinus, xxi
Polanyi, Michael, 168, 168n.4
Polycarp, 14, 81, 82
polonium and uranium halos, 135–36, 157n.161
Popper, Karl, 75, 158–59, 161, 189
prediction, 20, 40, 61, 75, 80–81, 113, 128, 130n.26, 131, 133, 136–39, 146, 154, 159–60, 162, 166, 171, 192, 195–96, 204, 234, 258, 260
presupposition(s), xxiii, 74n.4, 86n.53, 118–19, 123, 125, 156–58, 163n.192, 164n.194, 178n.66, 202, 224, 224n.4, 226, 228, 249, 285
Price, Randall, 13
probability analysis, 20, 24n.115, 58–60, 58n.6, 59n.10, 121, 187–88, 187n.116, 198–202, 230
"problem of evil," xix, 223–67, 223–24nn.2–3, 235n.39, 240n.55, 261n.113, 266n.129
  the existence of hell, 263–66, 264n.122
  a good, omnipotent God is necessary to talk coherently about good and evil, 225–28
  invalidity of atheistic arguments from the existence of evil, 228–37
    gratuitous evil, 229, 231–33, 235, 235n.39
    intensity of evil, 229, 233, 235n.41, 246, 248
    natural evils, 229, 233–34, 236, 241, 248
    quantity of evil, 229, 235–36, 235–36n.41
  possible reasons why God ordained the existence of sin and evil, 253–63
  relationship between a good God and the existence of sin and evil, 237–53
prophecy, xviii, 4, 5n.9, 20, 29, 31, 53, 57n.4, 61, 61n.1, 69, 88
  fulfilled, xxii, 20, 48–49, 53–60, 69, 230, 285
prophets, 3n.2, 15, 23, 28–29, 32, 40, 40n.22, 50, 59, 62, 69, 217, 265, 279
Protestant Reformation, 8n.34, 104
Provine, William, 172, 210
punctuated equilibrium, 124, 131–32, 136
Purtill, Richard, 117

Q

quantum mechanics, 125, 192, 194–95, 196–97n.167, 203–4, 204n.208
Qur'an, 20, 36n.13, 44, 70, 89, 89n.68
  Q. 2:120, 182n.83
  Q. 2:191, 182
  Q. 2:217, 182n.83
  Q. 3:28, 182, 182n.83
  Q. 3:54, 181
  Q. 3:118, 182, 182n.83
  Q. 4:88, 181
  Q. 4:89, 182
  Q. 4:142, 181

Subject and Name Index

Q. 4:144, 182
Q. 4:157, 70, 89
Q. 5:51, 182
Q. 5:54, 182
Q. 7:16, 181
Q. 7:99, 181
Q. 8:30, 181
Q. 8:43–44, 181
Q. 9, 216
Q. 9:5, 182
Q. 9:23, 182
Q. 9:29, 182
Q. 9:115, 181
Q. 9:123, 182
Q. 9:193, 182
Q. 11:34, 181
Q. 11:113, 182n.83
Q. 13:42, 181
Q. 14:4, 181
Q. 15:39, 181
Q. 16:93, 181
Q. 19:19, 36n.13
Q. 27:50, 181
Q. 43:36–37, 181
Q. 48:29, 182
Q. 58:22, 182n.83
Q. 61:8, 182n.83
Q. 66:9, 182, 182n.83
Q. 68:45, 181
Q. 86:15–16, 181
Quatrefages, Jean Louis Armand de, 160

R

Ramm, Bernard, 44
Ramsay, William, 157n.161
Rashdall, Hasting, 120
Raup, David, 128, 160
rationality/reason, ability to (includes irrationality) (see also under evolution and under naturalism), xi, xvii–xviii, xxii–xxiv, 74, 104–5, 111n.6, 111n.8, 112, 114–23, 125, 156, 158, 165, 168, 168n.4, 169, 171, 189, 191, 195, 208, 214, 226, 228, 233, 238, 243, 254, 283–86, 284n.12, 285–86

Reasons to Believe, 20
reductio ad absurdum, 171
Rees, Martin, 198, 198n.175, 199–200, 202
Reichenbach, Bruce, 231, 234
The Religions of Man (Smith), 53
Reppert, Victor, 107, 114n.20, 123
resurrection, 74, 85–86, 86n.53, 94n.82, 249, 262
   Jewish conception of, 79, 86, 86n.56, 94, 96
   of Jesus Christ, xviii, xxii–xxiii, 5, 18, 41, 60–62, 62n.2, 71–72, 74–99, 98n.95, 230, 262, 274
   evidence of historical fact of Jesus' resurrection, 67n.12, 74–99, 204–5
   early Christian creeds, 64, 80–81, 84, 88, 91
   failure of alternative explanations, 89–97
   body was stolen or moved, 77, 95–97
   hallucinations or visions, 94–95, 94n.82, 95n.87
   legend theory, 89–92
   psychological explanations, 92–93, 92–93n.78
   resurrection as "spiritual," 93–94
   formation and existence of the church, 85–89
   Baptism, 88
   Lord's Supper, 88
   early writing of NT, 88–89
   Sunday worship, 87–88
   lives of early Christians were changed, 81–85, 83nn.43–44
   multiple appearances and witnesses, 76, 79n.21, 80–82, 81n.33, 83nn.43–44, 84–85, 91, 92–93n.78, 95, 98, 204–5
   non-Christian sources, 31, 69
   proclamation in Jerusalem, 78–80, 79n.20, 80n.27
   sudden conversion of James, 84–85

340 Subject and Name Index

(resurrection continued)
    sudden conversion of Paul, 83–84, 84n.45
    tomb was empty, 76–78, 76n.8
    lack of veneration of the grave, 78
    significance of the Jews, 77–78
    significance of the women, 76–77

The Resurrection of the Son of God (Wright), 27n.133

Return of the God Hypothesis (Meyer), 104, 164n.197

Rifkin, Jeremy, 146

right and wrong, xxi, 168n.4, 178n.66, 179, 182, 186, 226–27, 227n.10, 230, 265, 285

Rittgers, Ronald, 245

Robinson, John A. T., 9

Roman Catholic Church, 3n.2, 9n.34, 104

Roman Empire, 15, 66n.11, 81, 97, 248, 250

Romania, xvii

Romans, 25, 26, 63, 65–69, 71, 73, 77, 79–80, 86, 248

Romulus, 86

Ross, Hugh, 164n.197

Rousseau, Jean-Jacques, 109

Rowe, William, 210, 223n.2, 235

Ruse, Michael, 162, 162n.187

Ruse, Michael, and Edward O. Wilson, 176, 186n.109

Russell, Bertrand, 111

Russell, E. S., 130

S

Sabbath, 33, 42, 44, 69, 87, 97

Sagan, Carl, 108

Salisbury, Frank, 154

salvation (save), 5, 33, 40, 43, 45, 240, 245, 247, 252, 255–56, 263, 265, 270–72, 274–75, 277, 282

Sanballat, 25

Sandage, Allan, 192n.139

Sanhedrin, 63, 66, 66n.9

Sartre, Jean-Paul, 109, 225

Satan (the Devil), 29, 35, 36n.13, 41, 180–81, 216, 240, 243, 243n.65, 244, 260, 269–70, 270n.3

savior, 20, 33, 46, 47, 67, 242, 257

"scarlet worm," 22

Schaeffer, Francis, 215n.262, 217

Schoville, Keith, 4, 16, 25

Schützenberger, Marcel, 155, 156

science, xxii, 74, 105–6, 106n.16, 108–9, 111n.5, 114n.18, 119–21, 123n.59, 124–25, 125n.3, 126, 147, 149, 154, 156–66, 158n.166, 162–63n.187, 171n.22, 172–74, 174n.42, 180, 187n.116, 189–91, 192n.139, 195–96, 196n.165, 198, 201–2, 202n.197, 202n.200, 203–4, 210, 213, 218–19, 218–19n.277, 228n.14, 234, 283–85

    and Christianity, 16, 26–27, 103–6, 109, 122–23, 125, 137, 156–58, 157n.161, 162–66, 162–63n.187, 163n.192, 164–65n.197, 168n.4, 171, 171n.22, 202n.201, 219n.278, 284–85

    laws of nature/science (see also first law of thermodynamics; second law of thermodynamics), xxii, 74n.4, 109, 111, 111n.6, 113–14, 114n.8, 117, 151, 169, 171n.22, 178, 191–97, 193n.145, 194n.157, 197n.170, 199–200, 202, 202n.197, 203–4, 209, 217–19, 233–34, 239, 258–59, 282–83

scientific method, 113, 158–59, 158–59n.166, 196, 202n.200, 213, 218–19n.277

scientists, xxiiin.4, 103, 105–6, 114n.18, 121, 125, 133, 133n.50, 135, 143, 150–51, 157–58, 157n.161, 160, 163, 166, 174, 191–92, 197n.167, 201–2, 202nn.200–1, 211, 213, 218–19, 219n.278, 228

Scientific Facts in the Bible (Comfort), 27n.133

A Scientific Investigation of the Old Testament (Wilson), 26n.133

Subject and Name Index

scientific materialism (see naturalism)
Searching for the Original Bible
  (Price), 26n.133
second law of thermodynamics, 20,
  196–97, 197n.170
Sedgwick, Adam, 127
Septuagint, 3n.2, 8, 8n.25, 13
Severance, Diana, 248
Shakespeare, William, 168, 241–42
Shamoun, Sam, 13, 181
Shayesteh, Daniel, 216
Shehadi, Fadlou, 248
Shepherd of Hermas, 10
Sherry, Patrick, 223n.2
Sherwin-White, A. N., 90–91
Siddhartha (Hesse), 183
Simpson, George Gaylord, 129
Simpson, James, 157n.161
sin(s) (see also sinner(s)), 4, 33–34,
  36, 36n.13, 37, 42, 45, 48, 51,
  56, 58, 61–62, 65, 90, 162n.187,
  181–84, 223, 224n.3, 225–26,
  233, 237–38, 240–49, 241n.56,
  243n.65, 246n.75, 251–56,
  256n.102, 258–59, 262–64,
  266–67, 269–75, 271n.7, 278
  the "fall" into sin, 231, 233, 241,
    243, 243n.65, 254, 256–57,
    263–64, 272
"singularity," 191–92, 194, 202, 215
sinner(s) (see also sin(s)), xi, xiii, 173,
  240, 264, 271–72, 271n.7
Sire, James, xxi, xxin.3, 183
Skinner, B. F., 176, 178
Smith, Huston, 51
Smith, Wilber, 20
Sodom, 28
soul, xi, xiii–xiv, 36, 92, 94, 122,
  123n.59, 160n.173, 183–84, 210,
  248–49, 261, 263, 265, 272–73
Spinoza, Baruch, xxi
spirit/spirits, xxiin.4, 29, 32n.3, 35n.9,
  36n.13, 45, 56, 81–82, 93–94,
  113, 237
spiritual, 82, 93–94, 95n.87, 107, 111,
  164n.197, 177, 256n.102, 258,
  266n.129, 275, 276n.19
Stanley, Steven, 130

Stansfield, William, 187, 187n.116,
  191, 197
Stein, Robert, 76n.8
Stephen, 45
Stoner, Peter W., 58–59, 59n.10
Stott, John, xxi, 36–37, 245
Stove, David, 125–26, 177n.60
Strauss, David, 73
As-Suhaym, Muhammad bin
  Abdullaah, 14–15
Sunday, 66, 67n.12, 76, 87, 97
Sundiata, Abbas, 15, 36
supernatural/supernaturalism, 74,
  74n.2, 105–7, 105–6n.16, 111,
  119, 163, 172, 187, 191n.131,
  202n.200, 204–10, 207n.220,
  212–14, 228, 230
superstition/superstitious, 4, 12, 74,
  99, 175, 207
survival and "survival of the fittest,"
  117, 121, 144, 146–47, 154n.151,
  161, 161n.182, 162n.184,
  169–71, 176–78, 210
Swinburne, Richard, 218, 234, 258
Sydow, Momme von, 162–63n.187
Synod of Carthage (AD 397), 11

T

Tacitus, 70, 73, 79
Talmud (see *Babylonian Talmud*)
Tammuz, 85
tautology, 162, 162n.184
Taylor, Charles, 178
Taylor, Richard, 118–19, 119n.43,
  179, 226
Ten Commandments (Decalogue), 33,
  57n.4, 184
Testimonium Flavianum (Josephus),
  69
Texas, 59, 59n.8
Thaxton, Charles, Walter Bradley, and
  Roger Olsen, 189n.127
theism/theists (includes monotheism)
  (see also atheism; monism;
  pantheism), xxi, xxiii, 50, 52,
  83, 99, 103–5, 108–9, 113–14,
  114n.18, 122, 122n.56, 123, 162,

(theism/theists continued)
    164–65n.197, 171, 178n.66, 180,
    186, 200, 204, 223n.2, 224n.3,
    226–27, 229, 232n.31, 233,
    282–83
theodicy, 223–24, 224n.3, 225, 232,
    254, 261n.113
Thomas, 39, 45, 67n.12
Thompson, J. A., 21
Thompson, William, 132, 160
Thomson, Keith, 161
Thorvaldsen, Steinar, and Ola Hössjer,
    163, 196n.165, 199
Thurman, Howard, 250
Tinder, Glenn, 180
Tobiah, 25
Toledot Yeshu, 69
tomb, 57, 66, 66n.11, 67n.12, 71–72,
    76, 76n.8, 77–79, 81–82, 93–98,
    244–45
Torah (Pentateuch), 3n.2, 6–7, 7n.21,
    8n.25, 14, 17n.80, 28
Trinity, 52n.43, 217–18
Trivers, Robert, 121n.51
truth/truthfulness, xi–xiv, xvii–xix,
    xxi–xxiv, 5, 28, 35, 36n.10,
    36n.13, 37, 39, 45, 58, 60–61,
    63–64, 69, 75, 77, 80, 86n.53, 90,
    97, 99, 103, 111, 111n.5, 114–16,
    116n.32, 117–21, 121n.51,
    122n.56, 126, 156, 158–59, 166,
    169, 182, 184–85, 201, 206, 217,
    218, 219n.277, 224n.3, 225, 228,
    230, 232, 254, 260–61, 265, 269,
    276, 285

U

Ulam, Stanislaw, 155–56
Unearthing the Bible (Kennedy),
    27n.133
universe (see also cosmos;
    multiverse), xi, xiv, 59, 108,
    112n.9, 113–15, 122, 164–
    65n.197, 167, 172–73, 173n.32,
    183, 227, 230, 233, 256, 256n.102

as a closed system, 107–8, 111, 115,
    117, 169, 196, 196–97n.167, 203,
    228
existence and origin of, xxiii, 105,
    115, 123–25, 164–65n.197,
    186–204, 187n.116, 190n.129,
    190–91n.131, 192n.137,
    192n.139, 197n.170, 198n.173,
    202n.197, 213–15, 217–19, 230,
    232, 284–85, 284n.12, 286–87
The Universe Next Door (Sire), xxin.3

V

Van de Weghe, Rob, 5n.9
van Inwagen, Peter, 259
Van Til, Cornelius, 217
Vilenkin, Alexander, 197
virtue and virtues, xii, 178, 248, 261
Volf, Miroslav, 249
von Weizsäcker, C. F., 104, 109,
    111n.5

W

Waddington, C. H., 155–56
Wallace, Alfred Russel, 170, 170n.17
Waltke, Bruce, 7, 17n.80
Walton, John, 165n.197
Weber, Hans-Ruedi, 73
Wells, Jonathan, 143n.90
Werner, Carl, 133–34
Westminster Confession of Faith,
    231n.26, 274
What is Darwinism (Hodge), 106n.16
White, R. Fowler, xi, xv, xviii–xix
Whitehead, Alfred North, 103
Why I am a Christian (Geisler and
    Hoffman), 27n.133
Wieland, Carl, 142
Wiesel, Elie, 261
Wiker, Benjamin, 108, 172, 172n.25,
    173, 179–80
Wilckens, Ulrich, 62n.2, 89
Willard, Dallas, 282
Williams, Peter, 19n.89, 79n.21
Williamson, H. G. M., 23
Wilson, A. N., 111n.8

Wilson, Robert, 12, 23, 24n.115, 26n.133
woman/women, xviii, 45, 63, 67n.12, 76–77, 81, 207, 212, 243, 247, 279
Wood, Nathan, 218
Work, Telford, 260
World War II, xvii, 175, 177, 179, 207
worldview(s), xii, xxi, xxin.3, xxii–xxiii, 3, 87, 94, 97–98, 105, 107, 108–9, 114, 114n.18, 156–58, 160, 162–63, 176, 178n.66, 202, 213, 224, 226–27, 275
Wright, N. T., 40, 81n.33, 85, 95, 98, 121n.51
Wright, Robert, 121n.51
Wurmbrand, Richard, xvii
Wykstra, Stephen, 232
Wysong, R. L., 145

X

Xinping, Zhou, 185, 185n.108

Y

Yahweh (YHWH) (see under God, Yahweh)
Yamauchi, Edwin, 76
Yandell, Keith, 235n.39, 242

Z

Zambia, 59n.8
Zink, Robert, 143
Zodhiates, Spiros, 46n.35
Zur Datierung der "Genesis-P-Stücke" (Külling), 7n.21

Scripture Index

GENESIS

Genesis	6, 21n.99, 27n.133, 165n.197
1	157n.161, 165n.197
1:1—2:3	165n.197
1:1	48, 137, 191, 204, 284
1:3	5n.7
1:11–12	137
1:20–21	137
1:24–25	137
1:24	278
1:25	278
1:26–29	5n.7
1:26–28	157n.161
1:26–27	243, 271
1:26	122
1:28–30	243
1:28	243
1:31	233, 243
2:8–15	243
2:16–17	243, 243n.65, 263
2:17	245, 269
2:19	243
2:21	157n.161
2:24	281
3:1–19	263, 269
3:1–6	243
3:1–4	243n.65
3:6	243
3:8–9	243
3:13–14	5n.7
3:14–19	243, 233
3:17–19	233
4:1–7	242n.62
4:1	280
4:3–10	184
4:26	45
5:3	280
6:5–6	184
6:13	5n.7
8:21	269
9:6	271
11:31—12:5	21
13:15	54
14	6
14:14–16	278
14:20	278
15	57
15:1–18	57
15:8	57
15:13–14	57n.4
15:17	56–57
17:9	5n.7
18:25	47, 184, 225, 229, 266, 269
20:3–7	265
20:17–18	237
21:1	278
21:2	278
21:5	278
21:12	54
22:17–18	57
28:15–22	20
37:25–28	278
37:28	278
39—50	21
39:3	278
39:23	278
42:25	278
42:27–28	278
45:4–8	244

(Genesis continued)

45:4–5	278
45:5–8	238
45:7–8	278
49:10	54
50:20	240n.55, 244, 259, 260, 278

EXODUS

Exodus	17, 19, 22
1:15	21
3:7–8	278
3:10	278
3:11–12	20
3:13–14	47
3:14	5n.7
4:11	237
4:21	240n.55, 278
7:3	240n.55, 278
7:14	278
7:22–23	278
8:15	278
9:12	278
9:16	260
9:34	278
10:1	278
10:20	240n.55, 278
10:27	240n.55, 278
13:21	57n.4
17:14	4n.6
19:18	57n.4
20:1–17	33, 184
20:1–5	50
20:1	4n.6
20:3–5	50
23:23	279
23:24	279
23:31	279
23:29–30	279
24:4	4n.6
24:7	4n.6
26:1	22
32:1–8	278
34:6–7	184, 225, 269
34:7	48
34:14	50
34:27	4n.6

LEVITICUS

11:44	184, 225, 269
14:6	22
17:11	26
20:7–8	278
20:8	278
24:14	44
24:16	44
24:23	44

NUMBERS

6:24–26	7
14:18	266
22–24	23
22:12	5n.7
24:17	54
33:45b–50	22

DEUTERONOMY

Deuteronomy	19, 22, 25
2:30–31	278
2:32–36	278
2:33	278
2:36	278
3:1	278
3:2–3	278
3:3–6	278
3:21–22	278
3:28	278
4:2	11
4:19	50
4:37–38	279
5:6–21	184
5:6–9	50
5:7–9	50
6:5	271
6:18–19	278
7:1–2	279
7:2	279
7:22–24	279
7:24	279
8:18	278
8:19	50
9:3a	279
9:3b	279
10:12–13	253

Scripture Index

12:32	11
18:18	54
18:20–22	53
21:22–23	67, 68n.18
28:15–68	260
29:29	232, 252, 266
30:19	17n.80
31:6	262
31:19	17n.80
31:26	17n.80
31:28	17n.80
32:4	48
32:39	48

JOSHUA

3:7	20
3:10	20
6:2	279
6:3–5	279
8:1	279
8:2–22	279
8	7
8:31	5n.8
10:19a	279
10:19b	279
10:20–21	279
11:8a	279
11:8b–9	279
24	22

JUDGES

Judges	8n.28
4–5	22
7:7	279
7:9	279
7:14–15	279
7:16–22	279
14:1–3	279
14:4	279
15:14–16	279
15:18	279
20:28	279
20:29–48	279

RUTH

Ruth	8n.28

1 SAMUEL

Samuel	3n.2
2:2	47
2:6	48
2:7	237
2:22–25	279
2:25	279
10:1–7	20
12:3–5	17n.80
15:2	279
15:3–6	279
17:37	20
25:14–31	279
25:32	279

2 SAMUEL

Samuel	3n.2
7:12–16	54
7:12	75
12:15	237
17:5–14	279
17:14	279
22:18–20	279
22:32	48
22:38–39	279
22:40–42	279
22:43	279
22:48–49	279
24:1	279
24:10	279
24:17	279

1 KINGS

Kings	3n.2
1:50–53	24n.117
2:31	279
2:32–33	279
2:34	279
3:11	5n.7
8:58	240n.55
8:61	240n.55
9:6–7	50

(1 Kings continued)

9:28	24
12:16–20	279
12:22–24	279
18:24	45
20:13	279
20:14–21	279
20:28	279
20:29–30	279
22:19–23	279
22:28	53
22:29–37	279

2 KINGS

Kings	3n.2
3:21	5n.8
6:15–17	256
18:9–12	24
19:6–7	279
19:7	279
19:20–31	244
20:5–6	279
20:7	279
20:20	24
23:29	279
25:8–21	280
25:29–30	25

1 CHRONICLES

Chronicles	3n.2, 7, 8
10:4	279
10:14	279
17:11–14	54
21:1–4	279
28:9	48
29:11–12	237

2 CHRONICLES

Chronicles	3n.2, 7, 8
15–16	279
20:6	237
21:12–16a	279
21:16b–17	279
25:4	5n.8
25:14–16	279
25:17–28	279
28:1–15	244
29:5–35	279
29:36	279
31:3	5n.8
32:2–4	24
35:20–21	279
35:22–24	279
36:15–17	280
36:15	32
36:17–19	280
36:22–23	280
36:22	280

EZRA

Ezra	3n.2
1:1	280
3:2–4	5n.8
6:14	280
6:22	237
7:6	280
7:9–10	280
7:27–28	280

NEHEMIAH

Nehemiah	3n.2
2:7–9	280
2:8	280
2:10	25
2:12	237
2:19	25
3:1–32	280
4:6	280
4:11–14	280
4:15	280
4:21–22	280
6:3	280
6:15	280
6:16	280
7:5	237
9:6	48, 237
9:13–14	4n.6

JOB

Job	233, 260

1:12	280	22:18	56
1:13–19	280	23:1	48
1:21–22	280	23:4	262
2:6	280	27:1	47
2:7	280	30:11	262
9:8	41	31:5	56
10:8	280	33:10–11	237
12:9–10	237	33:13–15	48
12:13–25	237	34:8	47
14:1	280	34:20	56
21:22	48	36:9	48
28:25	26	37	260
31:15	280	38:11	56
33:13–18	265	41:9	55
34:10–12	184, 225, 269	45:6–7	47
34:14–15	48	45:6	48
38:19–20	26	50:4–6	47
39	237	50:16	5n.7
42:11	280	51:5	269, 280
		53:1	xxii

PSALMS

		55:12–14	55
		57:5	47
Psalms	14, 17	57:11	47
1	7	62:12	48
2:6	54	68:18	55
2:7	54, 55, 75	69:4	55
3:5	48	69:8	55
5:4	184, 269	69:9	54
7:8–16	266	69:20	56
7:9	48	69:21	56
8:8	157n.161	74:12	49
14:1	xxii	77:19	41
16:8	48	78	17
16:10	55, 75	78:2	55
18:17–19	280	80:1	48
18:37	280	80:18	45
18:43a	280	89:26	48
18:47–48	280	90:2	49
19	184	93:2	49
19:1	256	95:3	47
22:1	56	96:13	47
22:6	58	102:25–27	48
22:7–8	56	102:25–26	48
22:7	56	103:19	237
22:14	56	104:14a–b	280
22:15	56	104:14c	280
22:16	56	105	17
22:17	56	105:17	244, 278

(Psalms continued)		6:10	49
105:25	237	7:14	49, 54
108:5	47	7:17–20	280
110:1	54, 55	8:5–8	280
110:4	54	8:13–14	49
115:3	252	8:14	55
118:22	48, 55	9:1	55
119:71	262	9:8–21	280
127:1a	280	10:5–19	253
127:1b	280	10:5–16	242n.62, 244
127:1c	280	10:5–15	240n.55
127:1d	280	11:1	54
130:7–8	47	11:2	54
132:11	54, 75	11:4	54
135:6	238	11:10	54
136:1	184, 225, 269	12:4	45
139:1–4	48	13:1—14:23	263
139:13–16	280	13:1–5	280
139:23	48	19:1	280
143:1–2	269	19:2a	280
145:17	184, 225, 269	19:2b–3	280
147:18	237	19:4a	280
148:1–13	254	19:4b	280
		28:16	55
PROVERBS		32:3–4	55
		33:22	54
16:1a	280	35:5–6	55
16:1b	280	40:3	47, 49, 54
16:2	244	40:11	48
16:9a	280	40:21–26	237
16:9b	280	40:23–25	237
16:33a	280	40:28	48
16:33b	280	41:4	42, 47
30:6	11	41:19–20	237
31:8–9	253	42:1	54
		42:8	50
ECCLESIASTES		42:9	20
		43:3	47
1:6	26	43:6–7	254
		43:11	46, 47
ISAIAH		43:13	47, 49
		43:15	47
Isaiah	12	44:6	40n.22, 42, 47
1:18	122	44:24–27	48
6	49	44:24	237
6:1–13	49	44:28	237
6:5	49	45:1–7	280
6:8–13	49	45:22–23	48, 50

45:23–24	47	26:5	32
44:28	237	28:9	53
46:9–11	237	29:10–14	280
46:10–11	238	31:13	262
46:10	58, 113, 217	31:33	276
48:5	53	31:35	113, 237
48:12	40n.22, 42, 47	32:19	48
49:6	55	33:22	26
49:7	55	36:19	280
50:6	56	36:26	280
53:3–12	236n.41	42:20	5n.7
53:3–10	244		
53:3	55		
53:5–6	56, 274		
53:5	48, 56		
53:7	56, 58		
53:8	56		
53:9	57		
53:10–12	56		
53:10–11	274		
53:10	281		
53:12	56		
54:5	48		
55:7	48		
56:7	49		
60:3	55		
60:20	47		
61:1–13	49		
61:1–2	54		
62:5	48		
63:16	49		

LAMENTATIONS

Lamentations	8n.28

EZEKIEL

2:7	4n.6
5:7–11	280
5:12	280
5:13	280
11:5–12	244
18:4	269
18:20	269
18:23	252, 272
18:32	252
24:15–18	237
33:11	272
33:33	53
36:26	247, 275
38:1–6	280
38:7–16	280
38:16	280

JEREMIAH

Jeremiah	8n.28
1:4	4n.6
1:9	4n.6
2:13	48
3:1	5n.7
11:22a	280
11:22b	280
11:23	280
16:15	280
17:9	269
17:10	48
21:8–10	280
23:5	54
23:6	54

DANIEL

Daniel	25
4:35	237
5	25
5:29	25
7:9	42
7:13–14	42, 43
7:13	42
9:9	48
9:13	5n.8

HOSEA

2:16	48
6:2	55

JOEL

1:13—3:21	263
2:32	45, 47

AMOS

4:13	237
5:18—9:15	263
8:9	56

OBADIAH

6–7	280
8–9	280
15–17	263

JONAH

1:15	280
2:3	280
4:9	5n.7
4:11	261

MICAH

5:2	49, 54, 58
6:8	253
7:8	47

NAHUM

1:15	20

HABAKKUK

1:1–11	242n.62
1:5–11	244, 253
1:13	113, 225, 244, 264, 269, 269n.1
2:14	254

ZEPHANIAH

1:7—3:20	263
3:9	45
3:15	47

HAGGAI

1:5–11	242n.62
1:5–6	280
1:9	280
1:10	280
1:11	280
1:14	237, 280

ZECHARIAH

2:9	53
2:11	53
4:9	53
6:15	53
9:9	54, 55, 58
11:12	55, 58
11:13	55, 58
12:10	48, 49, 56
13:6	55, 58
13:7	56
13:9	45

MALACHI

Malachi	7
3:1	54, 55, 58

MATTHEW

Matthew	19, 64, 91
1:1	54
1:2	54
1:6	54
1:18–20	75n.4
1:18	54
1:20,	265
1:21	33, 47, 48
1:22–23	49
1:23	45, 54
1:24–25	54
2:1	54
2:4–8	54

Scripture Index

2:6	49	9:4	35n.9
2:11	50	9:6	42
2:13	265	9:27	54
3:1–6	88n.63	9:32–35	55
3:1–3	54	9:32–33	29
3:3	49	9:36	31n.3
3:11	33	10:1	35n.9
3:12	34	10:4	55
3:16–17	54	10:15	28
3:17	40, 54	10:28	29, 99, 246, 249, 263
4:1–11	28	10:32–33	37
4:2	31n.3	11:4–6	55
4:1–10	32n.3	11:7–10	29
4:3	41	11:10	29, 54
4:4–10	5n.8	11:23–24	28, 39
4:7	41	11:27	32, 34, 37, 252
4:10	50	11:28	274
4:11	31n.3	12:1–8	32, 33
4:12–13	55	12:8	42
4:17	55	12:17–21	54
5:10–12	260, 262	12:25–28	29
5:17–19	28	12:38–40	61, 75
5:17	29	12:39–40	29
5:18	28	12:40	29, 33
5:19	11	12:41	29
5:21–48	34	12:50	37, 275
5:38–48	253	13:14	29
5:48	184, 270	13:34	55
6:9	38	13:41–42	43
7:12	184	13:41	29
7:21–23	34, 263	13:49	29
7:21	37	13:55–56	84
7:22–23	45	14:13–21	35n.9
7:24–26	34	14:22–33	35n.9
8:1–17	35n.9	14:28–31	35n.9
8:4	6n.12, 28	14:33	41, 50
8:10	32n.3	15:3	28
8:12	58, 263	15:4	5n.7
8:23–27	35n.9	15:6	28
8:24	31n.3	15:22	54
8:27	31n.3	16:1–4	61, 75
8:28–34	35n.9	16:13–17	43
8:28–32	29	16:16	54
8:29	41	16:17	37
9:2–8	33	16:21–23	81
9:2–3	44	16:21	33, 61
9:2	34	16:27	29, 34, 43, 48, 263
9:3	34	17:1–2	206

(Matthew continued)		25:30	58, 263
17:5	40	25:31–46	29, 34, 43, 99, 253,
17:22–23	61, 98		263, 276n.19
18:10	29, 37	25:31	29
18:19	37	25:34	37
19:4–6	28, 29n.141	25:41–46	260
19:4–5	281	25:41	29
19:7–8	6n.12, 28	25:46	246, 263
20:23	37	26:15	55
19:27–28	43	26:20–24	244
20:28	61	26:24	5n.8, 29
20:30–31	54	26:31	5n.8, 29, 56
21:5	54	26:37–38	32n.3
21:6–11	55	26:38	32n.3
21:9	54	26:39	37
21:11	54	26:42	37, 253
21:12–13	32n.3	26:47–50	55
21:12	55	26:53	29, 37
21:13	5n.8, 49	26:56	29, 63
21:15	54	26:63–66	44
21:18	31n.3	26:63–65	43
21:33–46	40	26:65	44
21:42–43	55	26:67	31n.3, 56
22:13	58, 263	26:69–74	56
22:16	19	26:69	63
22:23–30	28	27:3	55
22:29–32	29, 99	27:4	37
22:29	28	27:5	55
22:30	29	27:6–10	55
22:31–32	28	27:12	56
22:32	28	27:26–31	31n.3
22:36–40	184, 253	27:26	56, 66
22:37	xvii, 271	27:31	56
22:41–46	54	27:32	31n.3, 63
22:43–45	28, 54	27:34	56
22:43	28	27:35	63
23:34–35	28, 32	27:37	54
23:35	8n.29	27:38	56
24:15–16	29	27:39–40	63
24:15	28	27:39	56
24:25	20	27:41	63
24:30–31	43	27:45	56, 58
24:31	29	27:46	56, 58, 246
24:35	34	27:48	31n.3
24:36	29	27:50	31n.3
24:37–39	28	27:51	57
24:42–44	43	27:54	37, 63
24:45–51	276n.19	27:55–56	56, 63, 64

Reference	Page(s)
27:57–66	31n.3
27:57–60	56, 76
27:57–58	66
27:59–60	66
27:60–66	66
27:60	72
27:61	76
27:62–66	96
27:62–63	98
28:1–7	76
28:4	75, 204
28:5	265
28:6	55
28:8	76
28:9	50, 94
28:11–15	77
28:16–17	50
28:17	75, 92n.78, 205
28:18–20	71
28:18	34, 48
28:19	40

MARK

Reference	Page(s)
Mark	19, 63, 64, 91
1:2–4	47
1:2	29
1:4	88n.63
1:8	33
1:10–11	54
1:11	40
1:13	32n.3
1:14–15	274
1:23–28	35n.9
1:23–26	29
1:24	32
1:34	35n.9
1:39	35n.9
1:41	31n.3
1:44	6n.12, 28
2:1–12	35n.9, 42
2:3–12	33
2:5	34, 48
2:6–7	44
2:7	31n.3, 34
2:8	35n.9, 48
2:10	42
2:18–19	48
2:23–28	33
2:28	33, 42
3:5	32n.3
3:6	19
3:11–12	29
3:21	84, 92
3:31	84, 92
4:35–41	35n.9
4:38	31n.3
4:41	75, 204
5:1–13	29
5:7	41
6:3	84
6:6	32n.3
6:7	35n.9
6:34	31n.3
6:45–51	35n.9
7:6	5n.8
7:10	6n.12, 28
7:13	28
7:20–23	269
7:26–30	29
7:33–35	55
8:1–9	35n.9
8:2	31n.3
8:31	33, 98
8:38	29, 43
9:7	40, 54
9:9–11	86n.56
9:9	98
9:10	54
9:12–13	29
9:13	29
9:30–32	81
9:31	61, 98
9:37	34
9:43–48	263
10:3–5	6n.12, 28
10:6	28
10:17–19	35n.9
10:18	47n.37
10:21	31n.3
10:32–34	61, 98
10:33–34	56
10:47–48	54
11:12	31n.3
11:15–17	32n.3
12:1–12	40

(Mark continued)

12:13	19
12:24–27	29, 99
12:26	6n.12, 28
12:28–34	184
12:30	271
13:26	43
14:21	5n.8, 29, 253
14:27	5n.8, 29, 56
12:28–34	184
14:33–34	32n.3
14:43—15:39	281
14:50	56
14:54	63
14:58	75
14:61–64	44
14:61–63	43
14:62	34, 38
14:65	31n.3
15:7	19
15:15	66
15:16–20	31n.3
15:21	31n.3, 63
15:24	63
15:27–28	56
15:31	63
15:36	31n.3
15:37	31n.3
15:39	31n.3, 63
15:40	56
15:42–47	31n.3
15:42–45	66
15:45–46	76
15:46	66
15:47	76
16:1–9	76
16:3–4	66
16:6	55
16:10–11	76, 92n.78
16:10	66
16:11	67n.12, 75, 205
16:13	67n.12, 75, 92n.78, 205
16:15–18	71
16:19	55, 71

LUKE

Luke	19, 63, 64, 91
1:1–4	17n.80
1:17	54
1:26–35	54
1:32–33	34
1:32	40
1:33	54
1:34	40
1:35	32, 41
1:42–43	45
2:4–7	54
2:11	33, 47, 54
2:23	5n.8
2:40	31n.3
2:49	37
2:52	31n.3
3:1–3	19
3:3	88n.63
3:2–4	4n.6
3:4	29
3:16	33
3:22	40
3:23	54
3:31	54
3:32	54
3:33	54
3:34	54
4:1–13	28, 32n.3
4:2	31n.3
4:3	41
4:8	50
4:9	41
4:18–21	29
4:18	54
4:21	29, 54
4:25–27	29
4:31–36	35n.9
4:33–35	29
4:38–40	35n.9
4:41	35n.9, 41
5	37
5:8	37
5:14	6n.12, 28
5:17–26	33
5:20–21	44
5:21	31n.3
5:22	35n.9

Scripture Index

5:24	42	19:35-37	55
6:1-5	33	18:38-39	54
6:5	33, 42	19:41	32n.3
6:27-38	253	19:45-46	32n.3
6:31	184	19:46	5n.8
7:11-17	35n.9	20:9-19	40
7:13	31n.3	20:34-38	29, 99
7:16	54	20:36	29
7:24-27	29	20:37-38	28
7:27	29	20:37	6n.12, 28
8:22-25	35n.9	22:19-23	55
8:24	31n.3	22:21	281
8:28	41	22:22	238, 240n.55, 253
8:40-56	35n.9	22:22a	281
9:1	29, 35n.9	22:22b	281
9:22-26	43	22:29-30	43
9:22	61	22:29	37
9:35	40, 54	22:31-32	29
9:37-42	29	22:37	29, 56
9:58	42	22:44	31-32n.3
10:12	28	22:63-65	56
10:17-20	29	22:63-64	31n.3
10:17-19	35n.9	22:66-71	43, 44
10:18	29	22:69-70	34
10:21	32n.3	22:70	54
10:22	34, 37, 39	23:4	37
10:25-28	184	23:11	31n.3
10:27	271	23:14	37
11:2	38	23:19	19
11:29-30	75	23:22	32
11:49-51	32	23:24-25	66
11:49	5n.7	23:25	19
11:50	28	23:26	31n.3
11:51	8n.29, 28	23:27	63
12:89	43	23:33	56
13:55	76	23:34	37, 56
15:10	29, 256	23:35	56, 63
16:17	28	23:39	68n.18
16:19-31	29, 94, 99, 263	23:40-41	32
16:22-31	28	23:41	37
16:22	29	23:42-43	29, 99
16:29-31	6n.12, 28	23:46	31n.3, 56
16:31	29	23:47	32, 37, 63
17:26-37	28	23:49	56, 63, 64
17:28-32	28	23:50-56	31n.3
18:19	47n.37	23:50-53	76
18:31-33	29, 98	23:50-52	66
19:9-10	43	23:53	66

Scripture Index

(Luke continued)

24	66
24:1–8	76
24:6–7	98
24:9–12	76
24:10–11	67n.12, 75, 92n.78, 205
24:13–49	71
24:13–27	29
24:17	66
24:18–26	81
24:20–21	67
24:21	55
24:25–27	4n.5, 29
24:25	28
24:27	6n.12, 28, 281
24:36–43	81, 94
24:36–41	75, 205
24:36–37	75, 92n.78
24:41	92n.78
24:44–47	4n.5
24:44–45	29
24:44	6n.12, 28
24:46	5n.8, 55
24:49	33, 37
24:50–53	71
24:51–52	50

JOHN

John	19, 26, 38, 64, 91, 245
1:1–14	50
1:1–2	32, 54
1:1	45, 47
1:1b	38
1:3	48
1:4–5	47
1:4	34
1:9	47
1:10	48
1:11	55
1:12–13	252, 281
1:12	247, 274, 275
1:13	xvii
1:14–15	32
1:14	31n.3, 45, 47
1:18	32, 47
1:23	49, 54
1:25–27	88n.63
1:29	33, 245
1:30	32, 54
1:32	54
1:33	33
1:34	54
1:49–51	43
1:49	47, 54
1:51	29
2:1–11	35n.9, 80
2:11	75, 204
2:13–16	32n.3
2:13	19
2:15–17	54
2:16	37
2:18–21	61, 75
2:18–22	33, 61, 98
2:23	75, 204
2:24–25	48
3:2	75, 204
3:3	275
3:10	28, 40n.21
3:13	32, 42
3:14	6n.12, 28
3:16–21	40n.21
3:16–18	40, 275
3:16	29, 34, 99, 245, 274
3:17	33
3:18	266
3:19–21	276n.19
3:19	47
3:21	32, 281
3:23	19
3:31	34
3:36	245, 275, 281
4:6	31n.3
4:10	48
4:14	34, 48
4:19	54
4:24	283
4:29	31n.3
4:42	47
4:46–53	35n.9
4:47	19
4:49	19
4:51	19
5:1–2	26
5:2	19
5:5–9	55

5:16–18	32	7:40	54
5:17–23	34	7:42	54
5:17–18	33, 44	7:48	55
5:17	37	8	37
5:18	38, 44	8:1–11	33, 36
5:19–29	43	8:12	47
5:19	32, 34, 36	8:19	34, 37, 52
5:22–23	50	8:23	32
5:22	34, 47, 48	8:24	47
5:23	34	8:26–28	34
5:24–29	29, 99	8:28–29	28
5:24	34	8:28	32, 36, 47
5:25–29	34, 263	8:29	32
5:25	40	8:38–59	38
5:26	34	8:38	37
5:27–29	34	8:40	31n.3
5:30	32, 36, 54	8:42	32
5:37–38	281	8:44	29, 270n.3
5:39	4n.5, 29	8:46	32, 36, 37
5:40	34	8:49	38
5:43	37	8:53	44
5:45–47	28	8:54	38
5:45–46	6n.12	8:56–58	28
5:46–47	28, 281	8:58	32, 47, 54
6:14	54	8:59	44
6:16–21	35n.9	9:1–3	260
6:27	43	9:3	255, 260
6:28–29	275	9:5	47
6:32	6n.12, 28, 37	9:6–11	55
6:37–39	252	9:35–39	43
6:37	275, 281	9:35–38	50
6:38	32, 36	9:39	255
6:40	37, 43	10:11	47, 48
6:44	252, 281	10:16	48
6:46	32, 34	10:17–18	61
6:47	275	10:18	38
6:49	28	10:24–33	32
6:53–54	43	10:25–29	252
6:62	42	10:25	38
6:64	244	10:28	38, 48
6:65	252, 281	10:29	38, 39
7:1–5	84, 92	10:30–33	44
7:5	55	10:30	34, 38
7:18	254	10:33–36	28
7:19	6n.12, 28	10:33	39
7:22–23	6n.12, 28	10:34–38	34
7:33	32	10:34–35	28
7:37–38	48	10:35	28

(John continued)

10:36	40	14:17	247, 275
10:37	38	14:20	38
10:39	44	14:21	38
11:1–44	244	14:23	38
11:1–16	35n.9	14:24–26	276
11:4	40	14:26	29
11:5	31n.3	14:29	20
11:18	19	15:1	38
11:23–24	86n.56	15:8	38
11:25–26	29, 99	15:10	38
11:25	34, 41, 48	15:15	38
11:27	41	15:23	35, 38
11:33	32n.3	15:24	38
11:35	32n.3	15:25	29, 55
11:36	31n.3	15:26	29, 33
11:38	32n.3, 245	16:5	32
11:43–47	55	16:7	33
11:47–53	244	16:11	266
12:12–16	81	16:13–15	29
12:13	47	16:13	20
12:14	5n.8	16:20	262
12:27	32n.3	16:27–28	32
12:31	270n.3	16:30	48
12:40	49	17:1–5	254
12:41	49	17:1–3	34
12:44–50	28	17:3	274
12:44	35	17:5	32, 54
12:45	35	17:8	276
12:48–50	34	17:11	47
12:49	32, 36	17:12	29
13:3	32, 34	17:17	28
13:10–11	35n.9	17:21–23	34
13:11	32n.3	17:22–24	254
13:18	28, 29	17:24	32, 54
13:19	20	17:25	32
13:21–27	281	18:5–6	47
13:21	32n.3	18:13	19
13:23	31n.3	18:33–38	54
13:31–32	254	19:1–3	31n.3
14:2	38	19:7	44
14:6–14	39	19:13	19, 26
14:6–11	34	19:16	66
14:6	xvii, 217, 272	19:17	19
14:7	38	19:18	63
14:9	35	19:20	19
14:10	32, 36	19:23–24	56
14:16–20	262	19:23	63
		19:25–27	63, 64, 84

19:25	63	2:1–4	207
19:28–30	31n.3	2:17	5n.7
19:28–29	56	2:21	45
19:28	56	2:22–24	242n.62
19:30–42	31n.3	2:22–23	244
19:30	246	2:23–24	238
19:31–34	65	2:23	240n.55, 281
19:33	56	2:25	48
19:34–37	56	2:27	75
19:34	31n.3, 56	2:30–36	34
19:35	64	2:30–31	75
19:37	48, 49	2:31	55
19:38–42	66, 76	2:34–35	55
19:38	66	2:36	47, 50
19:41–42	66	2:42	29
19:42	19	3:14	47
20:1	76	3:18	4n.5
20:2–18	76	3:19–21	263
20:11—21:24	71	3:26	33
20:15–17	94	4:1–31	82
20:17	38	4:11	49
20:19–29	81	4:12	33
20:19	66	4:19–20	17n.80
20:22	33	4:20	79
20:24–29	94	4:27–28	237, 238, 240n.55, 244
20:24–25	67n.12, 75, 92n.78, 205	4:27	281
		4:28	281
20:25–27	56	4:31	207
20:28	45, 47, 50	5:17–42	82
20:30–31	274	5:28	31n.3
20:31	29	5:30	68n.18
20:37–38	28	5:37	89
21:9–14	81, 94	5:40–42	262
21:17	48	5:45–46	6n.12
21:24–25	17n.80	6:7—7:60	82
		6:32	6n.12
ACTS		7	260
		7:19	6n.12
Acts	14, 64, 91	7:22–23	6n.12
1:5	33, 207	7:39–41	278
1:8	33	7:41–42	278
1:9–11	71	7:42	5n.8
1:9	55	7:54—8:3	83
1:14	85	7:59–60	45, 50
1:16	275	8:20–21	242n.62
1:20	5n.8	8:32–35	56
2–7	79	9:1–22	84
2:1–21	33	9:1–2	83

(Acts continued)

9:4–5	262, 264
9:4	271
9:14	45
10	276
10:25–26	50
10:36–43	274
10:36	45
10:39	68n.18
10:42	34, 266
10:43	4n.5
10:44–47	207
13:22–23	54
13:27	238
13:30–33	54
13:33	55, 75
13:38	281
13:47–48	55
13:48	xvii, 240n.55, 252
14:11–18	50
15:13–21	85
16:30–31	274
16:31	45
16:34	45
17:2–4	xvii
17:28	238
17:31	34, 263
18:9–10a	281
18:10b	281
19:1–6	207
20:7	87
20:28	46, 50
21:11	5n.7
22:3	83
22:4–5	83
25:19	31n.3
26:4–5	83
26:9–11	83
26:18	48
26:20	274
26:22–23	4n.5
26:22	281
26:23	55
27:22–25	281
27:30–32	281
27:34	281
27:38–44	281
28:28	55

ROMANS

Romans	91, 255
1:1–4	274
1:3	31n.3
1:4	61, 75, 98
1:7	38
1:16–17	274
1:17	5n.8
1:18—2:16	184
1:18–23	50
1:18	xxii, 184, 265, 269, 269n.1
1:19–20	xxii, 264, 285
1:20	265
1:21–22	xxii
1:21	265
1:24	265
1:25	265
1:26	265
1:28	265
1:32	265
2:4	261n.113
2:5–16	263
2:12–16	266
2:15	264
2:16–17	275
2:16	34, 224n.3, 270n.3
2:24	5n.8
3:4	5n.8, 229
3:9–18	243, 269
3:10–12	265
3:10	5n.8
3:23–28	274
3:23	269
4:24–25	61
4:25	56
5:1	33
5:3–5	260
5:6–11	33
5:8–11	61
5:8	31n.3
5:12–19	243, 264
5:12–14	184, 245, 269
5:12	263, 269
5:15	31n.3
6:1–2	275
6:3–7	274
6:3–5	88
6:4	275

6:23	34, 269	2:2	274
7:5	269	2:4	281
7:8–11	269	2:7–8	46
7:14–24	269	2:9	5n.8
8:1–4	273	2:10–13	29
8:1	275	2:12–13	4n.6
8:14–17	247, 275	2:16	122, 247, 275
8:15	38	3:19	5n.8
8:17–25	263	4:1	29
8:18–23	275	4:4–5	34
8:18–21	262	4:7–11	281
8:20–22	233, 243, 264	4:9	256
8:21	248	6:11	33
8:23	247, 275	7:10	4n.6
8:28–30	254	10:4	48
8:28	259, 263	10:13	262
8:29	247, 257, 276	10:31	254
8:35–39	262	11:23–26	88
8:37	5n.8	11:23	4n.6
9:3–5	50	11:26	46, 88
9:4	247, 275	11:31–32	260
9:5	46	12:10	207
9:14–24	237	13:12	232
9:17	4, 255, 260	14:33	217
9:19–21	240n.55	14:37	29, 276
9:22–23	255	15	84, 94
9:32–33	55	15:1–19	98
9:33	49	15:1–5	274
10:4	274	15:1–4	61
10:8–13	274	15:1–2	29
10:9	33	15:3–7	64, 65, 80, 88
10:12–17	281	15:3–4	31n.3, 64
10:13	45, 47	15:3	56
11:8	5n.8		15:4–7, 86
12:2	xiii	15:4	66
12:19	5n.8, 249	15:7	84, 85
14:10	275	15:8	84, 95
14:11	5n.8	15:12–19	xxii, 98
15:3	5n.8	15:14	62
15:9	5n.8	15:17	62
15:21	5n.8	15:20–26	262
		15:20–22	249
		15:21	31n.3
		15:26	245

1 CORINTHIANS

1 Corinthians	64, 81, 91	15:35–54	249
1:2	45	15:41	26
1:3	38	15:47	32
1:30	47, 275	15:50–58	301

(1 Corinthians continued)

15:54	249
16:2	87

2 CORINTHIANS

2 Corinthians	64, 91
1:2	38
1:3–7	260
1:3–5	260
1:3–4	262
1:21	275
3:3	247, 275
4:4	270n.3
4:7–18	260
4:16–18	262
4:16–17	262
5:7	232
5:10	34, 47, 224n.3, 263, 270n.3
5:17	275
5:18–21	33
5:21	32, 245, 273, 274
6:16	5n.7
11:2	48
11:23–33	82
12:1–5	95n.87
12:7–10	262
12:7–9	281
12:7	281

GALATIANS

Galatians	64, 91
1:3	38
1:11–16	29
1:19	84, 85
2:11–14	276
2:11–12	84n.48
2:14	276
2:20	31n.3, 274, 275
3:1–14	275
3:8	4
3:10	5n.8
3:13	5n.8, 68n.18, 273
3:16	4n.6, 54, 57
3:22	255
3:26	247, 275
3:28	185

4:5–7	247, 275
4:6	38
4:22	5n.8
5:17	269
6:2	276
6:15	275

EPHESIANS

Ephesians	64, 91
1:2	38
1:3–6	254
1:4–5	252
1:5–6a	255
1:5	247, 275
1:7	47
1:11–12	255
1:11	237, 252
1:18–23	257
1:20–22	34, 48
2:2	270n.3
2:8–9	xvii, 252, 274, 275, 281
2:10	276, 281
2:19–20	29
2:19	247, 275
3:8–10	256
3:17	275
4:8	55
4:11–16	247
4:19	265
4:25—5:21	253
5:2	31n.3, 276
5:18	207
6:10–18	xiii

PHILIPPIANS

Philippians	50, 64, 65, 91
1:2	38
2:5–11	50, 61, 254
2:5–7	46
2:6–11	64
2:6–8	46n.35, 61
2:6–7	32
2:7	31n.3
2:8	31n.3, 65
2:8–11	257
2:9–11	34, 48, 50, 88

Scripture Index

2:9	45
2:10–11	47
2:12–13	240, 240n.55, 247
2:12	281
2:13	281
3:4–5	83
3:6	84
3:7–11	260
3:21	48
4:12–13	262

COLOSSIANS

Colossians	64, 91
1:2	38
1:13	270n.3
1:15–17	32
1:15	32
1:16	48, 254
1:17	48, 54, 198n.173, 236
1:18	257
1:19	32
1:20	233
1:27	275
2:9	31n.3, 32, 46
2:10	34
2:12	88
2:13–14	273
2:13	48
3:11	185

1 THESSALONIANS

1 Thessalonians	64, 91
2:2–9	4n.6
2:13	4n.6, 276
5:12–22	281
5:23–24	281

2 THESSALONIANS

1:1	38
1:6–10	263
2:9–10	281
2:11	281
2:12	281
2:15	29, 276
3:14	29, 276

1 TIMOTHY

1 Timothy	64
1:7b–8	xiii
1:13	84
2:4	252, 261n.113
2:5–6	273
2:5	31n.3
3:16	31n.3, 256
4:10	47
5:1–2	275
6:18–19	276n.19

2 TIMOTHY

2 Timothy	64, 91
1:10	34
2:22	45
2:26	270n.3
3:16–17	4n.6
3:16	xiii, 281
4:1	47, 54

TITUS

2:13–14	47
2:13	46, 47, 50

PHILEMON

3	38

HEBREWS

Hebrews	10, 64
1:1–2	32, 40n.22
1:2	32, 48
1:3	32, 34, 48, 55, 113, 236
1:4	44
1:5–10	50
1:8–9	47
1:8	46, 48
1:10–12	48
2:1–4	29
2:9–10	254
2:14–15	61
2:14	31n.3
2:17–18	274

(Hebrews continued)

2:18	32n.3
3:1	54
3:2	32
3:7	5n.7
3:12–13	269
4:15	32, 32n.3, 273
4:16	275
5:5–6	54
5:7	32n.3
5:8	31n.3
7:14	54
7:19	275
7:26	32, 47
8:10	276
9:14	32
9:27	224n.3, 270n.3
10:5	31n.3
10:7	5n.8
10:19–20	57
11:22	20
12:1	256
12:2	xvii
12:4–11	260
13:5	262
13:20	48

JAMES

James	10
1:2–4	260, 262
1:2	242
1:3	260
1:12	242
1:13–15	242
1:13	184, 225, 269
1:27	253
3:9–10	271
4:12	54
4:13–15	281
5:11	255

1 PETER

1 Peter	64, 91
1:3–4	62
1:7	260
1:10–12	4n.5
1:19	32, 37
2:4–8	48
2:4	274
2:7	55
2:8	49
2:22	32, 37
2:24	31n.3, 273
2:25	48
3:18	274
3:22	34
4:11	254
4:13	260
5:4	48
5:14	275

2 PETER

2 Peter	10, 64
1:1	46, 47, 50
1:16	17n.80
1:19	20
1:20–21	4n.6, 281
3:3–13	263, 275
3:7	48
3:9	252, 261n.113, 272
3:10	248
3:13	248
3:14–16	4n.6
3:15–16	29
3:16	84n.45

1 JOHN

1 John	64
1:1–3	17n.80, 31n.3
1:8–9	274
2:1	37
2:23	50, 52
2:29	37
3:1	247, 275
3:5	37
3:7	37
3:24	275
4:6	29
4:8	272
4:9–10	32
4:14	32
4:15	52

4:19	276	3:21	38
5:11–13	34	5:1–14	50
5:11–12	275	6:9–11	281
5:19	270n.3	6:10	260
5:20	32, 34, 46	8:1–19	242n.62
		8:20–21	242n.62
		15:3–4	256

2 JOHN

2 John	10
7	31n.3
9	52

15:4	263
17:1–16	281
17:14–17	237
17:14	34, 47
17:17	238, 281
19:1–6	256
19:10	50

3 JOHN

3 John	10

19:11–16	34
19:16	47
19:20	263
20:6	263
20:10–15	224n.3, 248, 270n.3
20:10	263

JUDE

Jude	10

REVELATION

Revelation	10, 40n.22, 64, 242n.62, 281
1:3	20, 29
1:5	34
1:7	48, 49
1:8	32, 40n.22, 47
1:10	87
1:11	276
1:13–14	42
1:17	40n.22, 42, 47, 54
1:18	29, 34, 99
2:8	47, 54
2:18–19	xiv
2:21	261n.113
2:23	48
2:27	38
3:5	29, 38

20:11–15	248, 263
20:14–15	263
21:1–11	275
21:1–4	262
21:1–2	263
21:1	236, 248
21:2	48
21:4	236, 248
21:5–6	47
21:6	40n.22
21:10—22:6	249
21:10	263
21:23	254
22:3	236, 248
22:8–9	50
22:12	34, 263
22:13	40n.22, 47, 54
22:16	54
22:18–19	11, 29